J. ROBERT OPPENHEIMER
A Life

ALSO BY ABRAHAM PAIS

The Genius of Science:
A Portrait Gallery of Twentieth-Century Physicists

A Tale of Two Continents:
A Physicist's Life in a Turbulent World

Einstein Lived Here

Niels Bohr's Times, in Physics, Philosophy, and Polity

Inward Bound:
Of Matter and Forces in the Physical World

Subtle Is the Lord:
The Science and the Life of Albert Einstein

Twentieth Century Physics I–III
(eds. with Laurie K. Brown and Sir Brian Pippard)

ALSO BY ROBERT P. CREASE

The Prism and the Pendulum:
The Ten Most Beautiful Experiments in Science

Making Physics:
A Biography of Brookhaven National Laboratory

Peace and War:
Reminiscences of a Life on the Frontiers of Science
(with Robert Serber)

The Play of Nature:
Experimentation as Performance

The Second Creation:
Makers of the Revolution in Twentieth-Century Science
(with Charles C. Mann)

J. ROBERT OPPENHEIMER
A Life

ABRAHAM PAIS

WITH SUPPLEMENTAL MATERIAL
BY ROBERT P. CREASE

OXFORD
UNIVERSITY PRESS
2006

OXFORD
UNIVERSITY PRESS

Oxford University Press, Inc., publishes works that
further Oxford University's objective of excellence
in research, scholarship, and education.

Oxford   New York
Auckland   Cape Town   Dar es Salaam   Hong Kong   Karachi
Kuala Lumpur   Madrid   Melbourne   Mexico City   Nairobi
New Delhi   Shanghai   Taipei   Toronto

With offices in
Argentina   Austria   Brazil   Chile   Czech Republic   France   Greece
Guatemala   Hungary   Italy   Japan   Poland   Portugal   Singapore
South Korea   Switzerland   Thailand   Turkey   Ukraine   Vietnam

Published by Oxford University Press, Inc.
198 Madison Avenue, New York, N.Y. 10016
www.oup.com

Oxford is a registered trademark of Oxford University Press

Library of Congress Cataloging-in-Publication Data
Pais, Abraham, 1918–
    J. Robert Oppenheimer : a life / Abraham Pais ; with supplemental material
by Robert P. Crease.
    p. cm.   Includes bibliographical references and index.
    ISBN-13: 978-0-19-516673-6   ISBN-10: 0-19-516673-6
1. Oppenheimer, J. Robert, 1904–1967.   2. Atomic bomb—United States—History.
3. Physicists—United States—Biography.   I. Crease, Robert P.   II. Title.
QC16.O62P35   2005   530'.092—dc22   2005002173

Robert P. Crease and Oxford University Press gratefully acknowledge permission granted for the use
of material from the following sources: by Charles Weiner for Alice Kimball Smith and Charles
Weiner, eds. *Robert Oppenheimer: Letters and Recollections*, originally published by Harvard
University Press in 1980. Reissued in paperback with a new foreword by Stanford University
Press in 1995; by Peter Goodchild, BBC books, and Watson, Little Ltd., for material from
Peter Goodchild's *Robert Oppenheimer: Shattterer of Worlds* (BBC Books, 1980); from *Peace and War*,
by Robert Serber with Robert P. Crease (Columbia University Press, 1998) reprinted with
permission of the publisher; by the Florida State University Libraries for material from an
unpublished interview with Paul Dirac, May 14, 1963; by Olke Uhlenbeck for permission to
print material from an unpublished interview with George Uhlenbeck, March 30, 1962; and by
Columbia University Oral History Office for permission to print material from an interview
with I. I. Rabi, "Reminiscences of I. I. Rabi," 11 January 1983.

9 8 7 6 5 4 3 2 1
Printed in the United States of America
on acid-free paper

To my wife, Ida

CONTENTS

CHAPTER **17**

CHAPTER **18**

CHAPTER **19**

CHAPTER **20**

CHAPTER **21**

CHAPTER **22**

FOREWORD

In spring 2000, at our home in Copenhagen, my husband Abraham Pais presented me with the first copy of his new book, *The Genius of Science*, a series of essays on the great scientists of the twentieth century. Typical of Bram, as he was known to friends, there was no time to celebrate. Without further ado, he excused himself to return to his writing. He was already over twenty-chapters deep into his biography of J. Robert Oppenheimer. He completed the draft of one more chapter before he succumbed to a heart attack and subsequent complications on August 2. How he intended to complete the manuscript, we only know from notes.

Bram began his second career, that of writing history of science, quite late in life. He did so as a scientist who for decades had been in the forefront of particle physics, taking part in seminal colloquia and seminars. He was a colleague of such distinguished scientists of the twentieth century as Albert Einstein, Paul Dirac, Niels Bohr, Wolfgang Pauli, Isidor Rabi, Tsung Dao Lee, Chen Ning Yang, Oskar Klein, John Von Neumann, George Uhlenbeck, Eugine Wigner and Mitchell Feigenbaum. His contributions to the history of physics, *Inward Bound* and *Twentieth Century Physics I–III* (as contributor and editor with Laurie Brown and Sir Brian Pippard), and his biographies and essays on the men and women who gave birth to modern science, have been widely acknowledged. The American Physical Society and the American Institute of Physics have co-sponsored The Abraham Pais Prize, "for outstanding scholarly achievements in the history of physics," awarded for the first time in April 2005, the World Year of Physics.

Over the years, Bram worked systematically on the intriguing life of Robert Oppenheimer, his complex personality and scientific contributions, and, not least, the role he played in the history of the United States. Beginning in the early 1970s, Bram conducted interviews and collected material about the man and his work. Apart from keeping lists with abbreviated references to sources, Bram made no preliminary outlines, not even in the form of a table of contents. Having combed through relevant books, articles, scientific papers, newspaper clippings, etc., and underlined excerpts of almost two full shelves of transcripts of the Oppenheimer hearings, Bram started head on by weaving a largely chronological tale to be intercepted with chapters on themes he found particularly important or illustrative of Oppenheimer and his time. One such unfinished chapter, not included in this book, dealt with Oppenheimer's handling of language, which Bram admired. In that respect, he was, in Bram's judgment, "without peer among scientists."

Bram had a distinct, crisp style of writing with clear ideas of how and what he wanted to communicate to his readers. He read excessively—history, biography, novels—not only for subject matter but for the sheer pleasure of good writing. He was deeply interested in language, a passion he shared with Oppenheimer, not only as a simple means of communication but as a way of conveying information at a more profound level, as intimated in his essay on the history of science entitled, *The Power of the Word*, published in *No Truth Except in the Details*, edited by A. J. Knox and D. M. Siegel (1995).

Bram wrote only a few hours a day, but those were concentrated ones. After a brisk walk in the morning, he would sit down with a cup of coffee and his beloved pipe in front of an open window, get his thoughts together and then write on. Any disturbance during that time was painful to Bram, almost physically so. He wrote only in longhand with his favorite Mont Blanc pen (computers were out of the question): Big, roundish letters across ruled yellow pads with paragraphs, footnotes and references meticulously in place as he proceeded. Though Bram claimed that he worked slowly and had to rewrite a good deal, most of his manuscripts, now in the Rockefeller Archive Center, reveal that in reality little was changed once his thoughts were committed to paper. What did consume his time, apart from the normal addition of phrases and paragraphs, was the insertion of new notes. Bram stuck to a system of consecutive numbering in the manuscript, implying that once a new note was added all subsequent ones had to be renumbered—all again in longhand. This system has been maintained in the printed edition for practical reasons.

As the work progressed, Bram would share his analyses with me and give me chapters for comment. He told me of his decision, for instance, not to weave his account around the Los Alamos period because so many writers, including eminent scientists who themselves had taken part in the Manhattan Project, had already dealt with this subject in depth.

When I reread Bram's manuscript, I found it so close to completion that publication seemed possible. A devoted colleague of Bram, Dr. Frederick Seitz, a former president of Rockefeller University, and Jeffrey Robbins, a senior editor at Joseph Henry Press, kindly read the manuscript and supported this conclusion. Oxford University Press, Bram's main publisher, suggested expanding the manuscipt with supplementary chapters to complete the tale of Oppenheimer's life. Dr. Robert Crease willingly accepted to write these and to review the draft manuscript. I wish to express my deep gratitude for the time and care with which he completed this task.

In 1963, Bram joined Rockefeller University where he enjoyed ideal working conditions and outstanding colleagues for almost four decades. The generosity of this great institution has also been extended to me, granting me ample time and space to deal with Bram's papers and manuscripts, for which I am deeply grateful. I am particularly indebted to Dr. Nicholas Khuri and Dr. Mitchell Feigenbaum at the Center for Studies in Physics and Biology for facilitating my work in every possible respect. I also wish to express appreciation to Jan Mair for her competent assistence in typing the manuscript as she did so many others of Bram's over the years.

Since 1986, Bram worked part of the year at the Niels Bohr Archive, Copenhagen University, Denmark. I wish to thank the director, Finn Aaserud, and other staff members for their kind support of Bram's work.

The Alfred P. Sloan Foundation generously lent its support to this project for which Bram, as well as I, have been most grateful.

Good friends have offered invaluable assistence and advice. I am particularly grateful to Torsten Wiesel, the former president of Rockefeller University, and his wife Jean Stein; to the writer Wendy Gimbel; to Paula Deitz, the editor of *The Hudson Review*; and to John Manger, who edited Bram's first book, *Subtle Is the Lord*. Last but not least, I have had unwavering support from my dear stepson, Joshua Pais, in the completion of Bram's last piece of writing.

Ida Nicolaisen
Senior researcher,
Nordic Institute of Asian Studies,
Copenhagen University

PREFACE

When Abraham Pais passed away, his manuscript on Oppenheimer was about three-quarters complete. It cut off on the morning of the first day of Oppenheimer's hearing following the revocation of his security clearance. Pais's widow, Ida Nicolaisen, and Kirk Jensen, an editor at Oxford University Press, asked me to add just enough material to flesh out the story into a complete biography, keeping my own contributions to a minimum and leaving Pais's manuscript intact. I therefore composed short chapters on Oppenheimer's hearing, on reactions to the hearing, on Oppenheimer's life and work after trial, and on the year of his death. Wherever I could, I quoted from the notes Pais made after his conversations. I tried to steer the narrative toward material that Pais thought important, as indicated by markers or notes in the margins of books, and folders with his handwritten thoughts and notes from interviews—many on yellowing pages, some on the backs of pages which Pais, wearing his physicist's hat, had scribbled equations. I tried to identify Pais's citations of secondary sources, which were not always indicated in the draft manuscript. I noted certain places where, in preparing this ambitious and demanding work, he had paraphrased the secondary literature he found most valuable, passages that he would no doubt have rewritten in the final version. I have attempted to locate and provide citations for each of these, though some cases may have escaped notice. I would like to thank historian Barton Bernstein for his inspiration and help in this effort. I would also like to thank Freeman Dyson for allowing me to read and quote from his correspondence; T. D. Lee, Silvan Schweber, and C. N. Yang for conversations about Oppenheimer. I worked on this book during part of my sabbatical from Stony Brook University while at the Dibner Institute for the History of Science and Technology, at MIT, and am indebted to its director, George E. Smith, and to other members of its staff for help of various kinds.

In his autobiography, Pais observes that one of the major differences between writing a research paper and writing a book is the necessity of following, in the latter, the so-called "iceberg principle": "just show the tip of the iceberg, yet convey—and this is a subtle task—that you are aware of much more that lies beneath the surface." Under the circumstances, to best complete Pais's trajectory I take the iceberg approach myself, being as spare as possible—even when this means not addressing topics that Pais himself clearly intended to discuss, such as Oppenheimer's performance as Institute director, his relations with his children, and various topics in postwar physics; and even when it means seeming to slight subjects of which one would anticipate more discussion in a contemporary biography of Oppenheimer, such as his left-wing associations. There is a kind of unfortunate, dismaying aptness that a biography of Oppenheimer should have to change course abruptly and end up in a different place than expected.

Robert P. Crease
New York, February 2005

INTRODUCTION

In 1991, after my biographies of Einstein and Niels Bohr had come out, and I had also published a book on the twentieth-century history of particles and fields, several friends urged me to do Oppenheimer next. That is a worthwhile idea, I would invariably reply.

That thought had in fact already occurred to me 20 years earlier, not long after Oppenheimer's death, and well before I had begun writing the book just mentioned. Already then I had interviewed a number of persons, many long gone since, who had known Robert well: Ruth Cherniss, classmate from the days he was a boy at the Ethical Culture School in New York City, and Harold, her husband, a close friend of his and mine, later a professor at the Institute for Advanced Study in Princeton; Francis Fergusson, a lifelong friend of Robert's; Frank Oppenheimer, his brother; Melba Phillips and Willis Lamb, students from the Berkeley years, later distinguished colleagues; Henry Smyth and Lloyd Garrison, member of the Atomic Energy Commission and leading defense lawyer respectively, both from the days of the Oppenheimer hearings; Philip Stern, author of a fine book on the Oppenheimer case; Kay Russell and Verna Hobson, his secretaries from the Princeton years; and Tsung Dao Lee, Isidor Rabi, Robert Serber, George Uhlenbeck, Frank Yang, physics colleagues and personal friends. I had made copious notes of those encounters. At that time I was still immersed in physics research, however, and was not yet prepared to devote efforts at historical writing. So I put those interview records aside in a safe place.

Back to 1991. Having written my first three books, which were well received, I turned again, more seriously now, to the idea of writing about Oppenheimer. After considerable thought I decided against it, for two main reasons.

First, I had competing projects in my mind, another book on Einstein, an autobiography. Secondly, and more importantly, I felt reluctance to take on Oppenheimer. I should explain why. When writing on Einstein and Bohr, I had not hesitated to mention points of disagreement with them. Yet, basically, personal experiences had left me with memories of two not just great scientists but also simple and good men. I could not then and still cannot say the same of Robert Oppenheimer.

My reactions to him can be compared with the ways people react to New York City. There are those who just hate the city. They do not understand it. There are also those who just love it. They do not understand it either. I am convinced that the right attitude to New York is a love-hate relation. It is likewise with me in relation to Oppenheimer. I know of largely just love or hate responses among many who knew him—again, those may never understand him. Which goes to explain why, in 1991, I was not ready to write on Oppenheimer; previous experience had not yet taught me how to cope with the life story of a man for whom my feelings were ambivalent.

The books I had contemplated in 1991 had come out by 1997, when the Oppenheimer project came to my mind once again, but now in a context I had not thought of before. For meanwhile I had conceived the idea of assembling in a book a series of word portraits of scientists I have known. Why not include Robert in such a collection? That would relieve me of the task of writing a more detailed biography of him. I could bypass topics I would rather not enter into.

In the course of time I had assembled a substantial collection of books on Oppenheimer. I began my portrait project by taking off a month or so to reread those. As I plowed along, I discovered something I could have but never realized earlier: there did not exist a full-fledged Oppenheimer biography! The topics in those books, topics very well treated in some cases, focused mainly on his leadership in the Los Alamos bomb project and/or on the Oppenheimer hearings of 1954. Here and there one also finds entries on his boyhood and his correspondence. Major topics that were either lacking or incompletely treated were his student years, his role in bringing modern physics to America in the 1930s, in my view the most important contribution of his life, his role as director of the Institute for Advanced Study in Princeton, an assessment of his scientific contributions and of his writings to general audiences. And so I found the answer to a question that had long been at the back of my mind. Could I possibly add something to the plethora of what had been written earlier? Yes, I could. I should write a biography, letting it all hang out.

Now a new problem arose, however. Rough estimates showed that the length of such a biography would exceed by much the planned average length of the portraits, and therefore would throw that project off balance. Hence my final decision—do the portraits first and Oppenheimer later, separately. The portraits have come out in the new millennium under the title *The Genius of Science*. My Oppenheimer story now lies before you.

My sources have been plentiful and include many personal experiences. For 17 years we lived in each other's orbit at the Princeton Institute, Oppenheimer as director, I first as a member, later as a professor there. For most of those years the gardens of our homes bordered on each other. Far more importantly, in those times our relations were close. Furthermore, I have had ample opportunity to observe him in action as a leader of physics at the Institute. Regarding that place, I have added below a sketch of its little-known early history, as well as brief accounts of appointments Robert made. I have also been witness to his role as leader of numerous international conferences.

Other sources include almost complete collections of his papers, both on scientific views and on general subjects, including his four books. Extracts given in what follows from his writings for the general public will illustrate his mastery of language, on occasion perhaps exalted but never stooping to the use of sesquipedalian words. Then there are my interviews and my extensive collection of clippings from newspapers and magazines. Finally, I have in my possession a copy of Oppenheimer's FBI files, 7,400 pages in all. (I know that number because I paid the FBI $740 for xeroxing, at 10 cents a page.)

I have also profited, with gratitude, from others' writings. The principal sources so used are acknowledged in a list at the end of this book, as well as in references in the course of what follows. Needless to say that errors are mine only.

In the course of writing this book I have kept wondering whether this reliving of parts of my past would affect my ambivalence about Robert. It has, somewhat. More strongly than before I feel compassion for a man who could never find enough satisfaction with his signal achievements, who forever was compelled to reach for more. That, not the hearings, was his tragedy, and caused him to have a wretched life.

Abraham Pais

"[I]l semblait immédiatement,
infailliblement atteindre le point
le plus sensible des consciences
cultivées, surexciter le centre
même . . . *où réside ce qui ne peut
pas souffrir de ne pas comprendre.*"

Paul Valéry, lettre sur Mallarmé,
La Revue de Paris, 1er avril 1927.

"[H]e seemed immediately,
infallibly, to strike at the most
sensitive of cultivated
consciousness, to overstimulate the
center itself . . . *where resides
that which cannot suffer not to
understand.*"

J. ROBERT OPPENHEIMER

A Life

FIRST ENCOUNTERS

On September 19, 1946, a week after I had arrived in the United States for the first time, a meeting of the American Physical Society began, held in the building of the Engineering Societies in Midtown Manhattan. From the minutes of that meeting: "Many guests from overseas were present . . . over a thousand people attended."[1] I had been asked to give an invited paper[2] at this gathering of physicists, the biggest I had ever seen.

My friend Hans Kramers, Holland's senior physicist at that time, was also there. I was sitting next to him at one of the sessions when I saw him scribble something on a slip of paper that he handed to me. It read (verbatim), "Turn around and pay your respects to Robert Oppenheimer." I turned and there, right behind me, sat the great man who up to that moment had only been known to me from newspaper pictures. He grinned pleasantly and stretched out his hand, which I shook. Most remarkably—or so I thought—he sat there in a short-sleeved open shirt. I felt I had entered a new civilization, where esteemed gentlemen appeared in public wearing neither jacket nor tie.

I saw Oppenheimer again the next week, in Princeton, where both of us attended the meeting on "The Future of Nuclear Science," part of events in celebration of Princeton University's bicentennial year. After that conference I stayed on in Princeton, to start a one-year fellowship at the Institute for Advanced Study (called the Institute hereafter).

On Friday, January 31, 1947, I took a train from Princeton to New York in order to attend a session of an American Physical Society meeting at Columbia

University. That afternoon Oppenheimer was to give an invited paper on mesons, in the McMillin Theatre.[3]

Oppenheimer spoke before a packed house. He was a rhetor rather than a speaker. Then, as on numerous later occasions, I was struck by his priestly style. It was, one might say, as if he were aiming at initiating his audience into Nature's divine mysteries.

After the conclusion of his lectures I went to say hello to him. He greeted me and then said that he urgently needed to talk to me. Would I please give him a few moments until he could disengage himself from the crowd. As I stood waiting, I tried to play back what he had just told, and recall my thought, What the hell have I retained from his talk? I had been intrigued, nay moved, by his words, but now found myself unable to reconstruct anything of substance. I would now say that this was not just a matter of stupidity from my side.

After a few minutes, Oppenheimer came up to me and said, let's walk down Broadway and find a bar; and so we did. After having settled down, he explained why he wanted to see me. He had been offered the directorship of the Institute—which was unexpected news to me. He continued by saying that this news was confidential and urged me to keep open the possibility of remaining longer at the Institute and, in any case, not to make a move until he called me with firm news on whether or not he would accept the Institute position, a decision he expected shortly. Being anyway in an undecided frame of mind, I had nothing to lose by agreeing to his suggestion.

Weeks passed without any word from Oppenheimer. I became restless, my discontent with the Institute grew. (I had applied there hoping to work with Pauli, who, however, had left for Zurich just before I had arrived.) Then, one afternoon in early April, the telephone rang. I picked up. An operator asked if I was Dr. Pais. Yes, I was. She said, Hold the line, Professor Oppenheimer is calling long distance from California.

In order to appreciate my reaction, you should know that, up till that moment, I had never in my young life received any long-distance call whatsoever. And here the great Oppenheimer was calling, all the way from California!

I remember verbatim not only what Oppenheimer said after he came on the line but also the way he said it, priestly, solemn, "This is Robert Oppenheimer. I have just accepted the directorship of the Institute for Advanced Study, and I desperately hope that you will be there next year, so that we can begin building up theoretical physics there."

Desperately, no less. What could I say? I said yes, of course. The man was such a consummate kingmaker. A week later, Oppenheimer called me up again, this time from Los Alamos, confirming his earlier communication and adding further details.

My fate for the next 16 years was sealed.

I knew Oppenheimer from 1946 until 1967, the year of his death. This essay is built around my impressions of him through those years of personal contacts, on interviews I have conducted with others who knew him well at one time or another, on his own writings, and on the voluminous literature about him, which includes a few very good books. These last have been useful to me for a sketch of his younger years, my next topic.

Much has been written about Oppenheimer's role in the War years as well as about his later turbulent life, to which I shall also have something to add hereafter. I do not think that physics research and teaching is the only road to salvation, but do believe that none of his contributions deserves higher praise and will longer endure than what he did for the growth of American physics in the decade before the Second World War. Popular writings about him justly portray Oppenheimer as a world figure because of his directorship of the atomic bomb project and as a tragic hero because of events in his postwar life. Nowhere does one read there of his leadership as a pure scientist, however. It is one of my aims to set that matter straight in this essay. I shall write of his major role as teacher of quantum field theory, which caused this subject to spread all over the United States, as well as of his own scientific contributions, many of them brilliant. I shall not refrain, however, from noting the many errors he made in his calculations.

CHAPTER 2

BACKGROUND: EARLY YEARS

Ben Oppenheimer, Robert's grandfather, was a peasant farmer and grain merchant from Hanau, in the German state Hessen, near Frankfurt. "He was an unsuccessful businessman, born in a hovel, really, in an almost medieval German village, with a taste for scholarship. . . . It was clear that one of the great joys for him in life was reading but he had probably hardly been to school. He knew that I was interested in architecture and so he gave me . . . an encyclopedia of architecture which I still have."[4] That happened when at age seven Robert visited Ben in Germany. "He gave me also a mineral collection . . . a box with maybe two dozen samples."[4] That triggered his hobby for mineralogy, which was to last for years.

In 1888, Robert's father Julius, then a young man of 17, emigrated to New York. At that time he had very little means and barely spoke English, but steadily worked himself up to become a prosperous textile importer with a good command of the language. He was widely read and developed a good taste for the arts. In due course he acquired paintings by Van Gogh (three of these), Renoir, Vuillard, and Derain, which at that time could be bought for relatively little money.

In 1903 Julius married Ella Friedman, like him of European-Jewish descent. Her family had lived for generations in the Baltimore-Philadelphia region. She was an accomplished painter who taught for a while at Hunter College. Her right arm was always covered with a long sleeve and a glove. "She was born without a right hand; the glove contained a primitive prosthetic device, a spring between the artificial thumb and forefinger."[5]

On April 22, 1904, Robert, their first child, was born in their residence on West 94th Street. He had one brother, Frank (1912–1985), who also became a physicist. (Another brother died in infancy.) The household included grandmother Friedman and two servants. Those who knew them at that time speak of a united family, hospitable people, not concerned with making an impression.[5]

Robert was still very young when the family moved to a large, richly furnished apartment on the eleventh floor of 155 Riverside Drive, near 88th Street, facing the Hudson River. He spent his boyhood and youth there in an atmosphere that "was like Ibsen's *Rosmersholm*, that aristocratic estate where voices and passions were always subdued, and where children never cried— and when they grew up never laughed."[6] Oppenheimer himself has remembered: "I think my father was one of the most tolerant and human of men. His idea of what to do for people was to let them find out what they wanted. . . . I think my mother especially was dissatisfied with the limited interest I had in play and in people of my own age, and I don't know over what years but I know she kept trying to get me to be more like other boys, but with indifferent success."[7] On another occasion he said, "[I became] an abnormally repulsive good little boy [with] no normal healthy way to be a bastard."[8] A friend from his youth has "thought his parents had handled their precocious son very well. They knew they had a changeling in Robert, and a sometimes moody one at that. They did not allow this fact to dominate the household but tried instead to create an environment in which independence and talent could flourish."[9]

Robert's parents had rejected orthodox Jewish society. This may in part explain why he never spoke of himself as a Jew. I recall a discussion with Isidor Rabi in which we both concluded that it might have been much better for him if he had been freer in regard to his Jewish descent.

In September 1911, Robert entered the second grade of the Ethical Culture School on Central Park West near 63rd Street, where he would continue until graduating from the high school division in February 1921. "It is characteristic that I do not remember any of my classmates."[10] In those years he did not participate in any sports. He was driven everywhere, attended by servants, and in school would not even use stairs, always preferring to wait for an elevator. "When I was 10 or 12 years old, minerals, writing poems, and building blocks were the three themes I did. . . . I was a member of the Mineralogical Club very early [at age 11, by far the youngest member]."[4] In his youth he was indifferent to music (he was bored by early piano lessons), which, later, he enjoyed intensely, however.

Rabi has written: "My wife, who was in some classes with him, remembers him as brilliant and as being so recognized by the whole school. From conversations with him I have the impression that his own regard for the school was not affectionate. Too great a dose of ethical culture can often sour the budding intellectual who would prefer a more profound approach to human relations and man's place in the universe."[11]

But Oppenheimer benefited much from those school years: a Greek teacher helped him read Homer and Plato in the original, an English teacher introduced him to T. S. Eliot, Chekhov, Katherine Mansfield, establishing his lifelong tastes in literature. But the most important influence was his science teacher:

> I think the most important change came in my junior year in high school. . . . The teacher of physics and chemistry was marvellous; I got so excited that after the first year, which was physics, I arranged to spend the summer working with him setting up equipment for the following year and I would then take chemistry and would do both. We must have spent five days a week together; once in a while we would even go off on a mineral-hunting junket as a reward for this. I got interested then in electrolytes and conduction; I didn't know anything about it but I did fiddle with a few experiments [although] I don't remember what they were. I loved chemistry so deeply that I automatically now respond when people want to know how to interest people in science by saying, 'Teach them elementary chemistry.' Compared to physics, it starts right in the heart of things and very soon you have that connection between what you see and a really very sweeping set of ideas which could exist in physics but is very much less likely to be accessible. I know that I had a great sense of indebtedness to him.[4]

His contemporaries saw a physically awkward boy, bushy hair worn long, who blushed easily and seemed different and absorbed.[5] A school friend has remembered: "He was physically . . . rather undeveloped, not in the way he behaved but the way he went about, the way he walked, the way he sat. There was something strangely childish about him. . . . He was abrupt when he came out of his shyness but with all that a very polite sort of voice."[12] Another has recalled that he "had bouts of melancholy, deep, deep depressions as a youngster. . . . He would seem to be incommunicado emotionally for a day or two at a time."[13] "He hardly ever laughed. . . . These traits so firmly set him apart from his contemporaries that at summer camp when he was fourteen, he was taunted mercilessly. The harassment culminated in his being locked naked in an icehouse over night."[14] These various comments by schoolmates show a blend of compassion and irritation if not anger. Such disparate responses would follow Oppenheimer all his life.

About the time Robert had graduated from high school, with straight A's, his father presented him with a 28-foot sloop that his son baptized Trimethy, after trimethylene dioxide, a colorless liquid that smells like pickled herring. The boat was moored in Bay Shore, Long Island, where the family had a summer house (and a 40-foot yacht), and Oppenheimer and his small brother would sail all over the area. He "developed a taste for danger. He was no nonchalant daredevil—somehow he needed to challenge some suspected weakness within himself."[15]

Robert had been admitted to Harvard, but "I didn't get to go to Harvard immediately." During a trip to Europe the following summer "I went off on a long prospecting trip into the old mines, Joachimsthal [in Bohemia], and I came down with a heavy, almost fatal case of trench dysentery. . . . I was sick abed—in Europe, actually, at the time."[4] His dysentery gave rise to a bout of colitis, leading to ongoing digestive problems. He spent a year recuperating, first at home in New York, then, in the summer of 1922 on a trip to the West.

Time spent in New Mexico's Pecos Valley, in the Sangre de Cristo mountains northeast of Santa Fe, opened a new world for him. He became an enthusiastic, expert, fearless horseman, developing a natural ability with horses. His first ride across the Rio Grande and up to the Los Alamos Ranch school on the Parajito plateau would determine the site of the wartime laboratory that, 20 years later, was to become part of the Oppenheimer legend.

CHAPTER 3

UNIVERSITY STUDIES

In September 1922 Oppenheimer entered Harvard College, majoring in chemistry. In high school he had been called Bob. Now he became Robert. "At Harvard I did a great deal; the maximum number of courses you could take was six but I audited two or three more in my third year . . . the free availability of the whole library . . . got me reading very widely. . . . I almost became alive."[4] His scientific courses were a mix of theory and experiment. He applied himself diligently to his laboratory work, but got more and more drawn to theory. As is not uncommon, his interests began to move toward physics, particularly influenced by courses given by the great experimental physicist Percy Bridgman (1882–1961) and by personal discussions with him on physics and philosophy. "I must have started physics in a major way."[4] He petitioned the physics department to take graduate courses, adding a list of books he had read. (This list is reproduced in ref. 5, p. 29.) "I can quote a story—it may be apocryphal—that, when the faculty met to consider this request, [one member] said: 'Obviously he is a liar, but he should get a Ph.D. for knowing their titles.'"[4]

His reading of current journals revealed to Oppenheimer that in those years, the early twenties, physical theory was in a state of intense ferment. Harvard was not the best place for experiencing those intellectual tensions. "For Harvard in '24 and '25 [it] was not true [that there existed] an awareness of the theoretical picture on a grand scale."[4]

Having completed his undergraduate studies in three years instead of the standard four, Oppenheimer received the A.B. degree *summa cum laude* in chemistry in 1925, at age 21. In those years, Robert diverted himself by writing short stories.

In spite of his growing interest in theory, Oppenheimer was not yet quite prepared to abandon his active interests in experiment, as witness his choice of place for post-graduate studies. "I don't know why I picked Cambridge [England], but I wanted to go to Rutherford's laboratory."[4]

In September 1925 Oppenheimer was admitted to Christ College, Cambridge University, and presented himself to Sir Ernest Rutherford (1871–1937), at that time the world's most renowned experimental physicist. "But Rutherford wouldn't have me. My credentials were peculiar and not impressive."[4] He was sent instead to the laboratory of Sir Joseph John Thomson (1856–1940), another famous physicist, who by then was well past his prime, however. He worked there until September 1926, but in the meantime "I went to the theoretical seminars and then I really began to read the contemporary journals. . . . I was still, in the bad sense of the word, a student."[4] That brought him face to face with Heisenberg's paper announcing the discovery of quantum mechanics, received the preceding July 25 by the German journal *Zeitschrift für Physik*. That article marks the birth of a new era in theoretical physics, the end of the quantum paradoxes that had plagued the century's first quarter. "I didn't learn about quantum mechanics until I got to Europe. . . . I remember not liking it. . . . I think I was interested in what the hell the electrons were doing. . . . I didn't like the looseness of the relation between the waves and events."[4] Nevertheless, Heisenberg's paper greatly aroused Oppenheimer's interest.

Of great importance to Robert were his meetings in Cambridge with leading theorists. His recollection about his first encounter with Niels Bohr is characteristic for both men. "When Rutherford introduced me to Bohr, he asked me what I was working on. I told him and he said, 'How is it going?' I said 'I'm in difficulties.' He said 'Are the difficulties mathematical or physical?' I said 'I don't know.' He said 'That's bad.'"[4] Other first encounters: with another Cambridge student, the not-quite-two-years-older Paul Dirac (1902–1984), who had just completed a seminal paper on the principles of quantum mechanics ("He was not easily understood, not concerned with being understood. I thought he was absolutely grand")[4]; with James Chadwick (1891–1974); with Ralph Fowler (1889–1944); with Paul Ehrenfest (1880–1933), ("who had been extraordinarily warm and friendly")[4]; with George Uhlenbeck (1900–1988); with Max Born (1882–1970), the leader of the theory group in Goettingen; all of them actively engaged in the analysis of the new mechanics.

The result of all this was Oppenheimer's first two research papers[18] ever, written in Cambridge, submitted in May and July 1926 respectively, and dealing with issues in quantum mechanics—what else? "That was a mess, that first paper [on molecular spectra]," he has said.[4] The second paper dealt with transitions to continuum states in hydrogenic atoms. With these papers, Oppenheimer ranks among the first to use quantum mechanics for solving problems that had been unmanageable before. These papers "made Born ask me to come to Goettingen. . . . [At that time] I had very great misgivings about myself on all fronts, but I clearly was going to do theoretical physics if I could. I did."[4]

In September 1926, Oppenheimer settled in Goettingen for a stay that was to last until the summer of 1927. This period was to be quite important for his personal and professional growth, and proved to be quite productive; he published five papers. One of these, jointly with Born,[20] dealing with the quantum theory of molecules, contains the "Born–Oppenheimer method," a famous paper, still the basis of any treatment of molecules, in which they handle the problem with the help of an expansion in terms of the fourth root of the electron–nucleus mass ratio. Also quite important was his work, by himself, on the theory of continuous spectra, *unexplored territory at that time.*[21] He developed a method for normalizing eigenfunctions in the continuous spectrum, calculated various transition probabilities, the photoelectric effect for hydrogen and for X-rays. Nowadays the opacity of hydrogen in the sun, calculated with the help of his theory, is a main ingredient for understanding stellar interiors. For this work he received the Ph.D. in the spring of 1927, "with distinction," in an uncommonly short time of preparation, two years.

In Goettingen "I got to be quite a friend with [John] von Neumann. . . . He had a mind which was in some ways not like any I have ever known. . . . The most exciting time I had in Goettingen and perhaps the most exciting time in my life was when Dirac arrived and gave me the proofs of his paper on the quantum theory of radiation,"[22] the first paper ever on quantum electrodynamics. When during an interview, Dirac once was asked, "Oppenheimer indicates that, when he was in Goettingen, he thinks you saw as much or more of him than anyone else there," he replied, "That is so. We sometimes went for long walks together, although I had many walks alone."[24]

Also in Goettingen, Oppenheimer made the first personal acquaintance with Heisenberg and Pauli. He has characterized his stay there like this: "I find the work hard, thank God, and almost pleasant. . . ."[23] Much later, he recalled, "I was part of a little community of people,"[22] unlike his earlier Harvard and Cambridge days.

From the Goettingen days dates the first documented evidence (I know of) of a character trait of Oppenheimer that was to cause him much trouble, especially in his later life: his extreme arrogance. Born has remembered: "He was a man of great talent, and he was conscious of his superiority in a way which was embarrassing and led to trouble. In my ordinary seminar on quantum mechanics, he used to interrupt the speaker, whoever it was, not excluding myself, and to step to the blackboard, taking the chalk and declaring: 'This can be done much better in the following manner. . . .' I felt that the other members did not like these perpetual interruptions and corrections."[25] Born has also recalled how, after having finished a paper of his own, "I gave it to Oppenheimer in order for him to check the involved calculations. He brought it back and said: 'I couldn't find any mistake—did you really do this all alone?'"[26] Edward Condon (1902–1974), another young American then in Goettingen, has said, "Trouble is that Oppie is so quick on the trigger intellectually, he puts the other guy at a disadvantage. And, dammit, he is always right, or right enough."[25]

During his short stay at the Cavendish, Oppenheimer had been disturbed and miserable. I have no firsthand knowledge of what caused this, nor do I know whether these moods had already manifested themselves at earlier times. There are sufficient indications, however, utterances by acquaintances who knew him then, to indicate that these emotional problems were serious.

I do not know either what had caused these difficulties, but find significant a comment by a friend who had "sensed [O.'s] disappointment that he was not two or three years older and ready to participate [in physics] on an advanced level."[26] At that time, when physics was roaring forward, an age difference of just a few years meant a difference of a generation. Heisenberg, Dirac, and Pauli, founders of the new mechanics, were only two to four years older than Oppenheimer when they had ushered in the new era of quantum mechanics. It is no criticism of those who started next that they did not contribute in equal measure. I should stress at this point that in my opinion Oppenheimer's scientific contributions between 1925 and 1940 were very substantial indeed, nothing to be ashamed of, quite the contrary. All that said, I can well understand that a brilliant and ambitious young man would feel that by just a few years he had missed his chance for immortality.

To come back to Robert's problems, already in his Cambridge years his American friend Francis Fergusson (1904–1986), himself an Oxford student, had "realized how emotionally upset Robert had become."[27] In a letter to him (F.) we find these lines: "Your [F.'s] . . . social adaptivity [is] likely to make him [O.] despair. . . . I'm afraid he'd merely cease to think his own life worth living."[27] Fergusson became

> alerted to Robert's abnormal emotional condition by a bizarre incident during their holiday reunion in Paris. In the course of one of their customary exchanges about intellectual and personal matters, Robert suddenly leapt upon Fergusson with the clear intention of strangling him. As tall as Robert and more solidly built, Francis had easily warded off the attack, but this uncharacteristic display of violence, combined with Robert's despair over his inept performance in the laboratory and confidences about unsatisfactory sexual ventures, convinced Francis that his friend was seriously troubled. Robert was immediately contrite.[28]

Some years after Oppenheimer's death I asked Fergusson (whom I knew rather well) about this incident. He confirmed it but was not inclined to elaborate. (He did tell me that Oppenheimer visited prostitutes in London.) In those later years I once asked Dirac whether he had noted any unusual behavior in the Cambridge period. All he replied was that in 1925 or 1926 Rutherford had once asked him that very same question. Another instance of erratic behavior: once, while sitting in a cafe in Goettingen, with some young couples, Oppenheimer suddenly crept under the tables and started barking like a dog. (Told by Walter Heitler [1904–1981], another Goettingen postdoc, to my late friend Res Jost [1918–1990], who in turn told it to me.) That behavior brings to mind the lines by the poet John Dryden (1631–1670):

> Great wits are sure to madness near allied,
> And thin partitions do their bounds divide.

While in Europe, Oppenheimer sought help of at least two psychiatrists:

> In June of 1926 [he told an acquaintance] that he had dementia praecox [now called schizophrenia] and that his psychiatrist had dismissed him because in a case like this further analysis would do more harm than good. . . . In the late spring or early summer of 1926 . . . [Fergusson met Robert] outside the office of a Harley Street psychiatrist. The occasion made a lasting impression on Fergusson. "I [saw him] standing on the corner, waiting for me, with his hat on one side of his head, looking absolutely weird. I joined him . . . and he walked with terrific speed; when he walked his feet turned out . . . and he sort of leaned forward, traveled at a terrific clip. I asked him how it had been. He said . . . that the guy was too stupid to follow him and that he knew more about his troubles than the [doctor] did, which was probably true."[29]

In the years I knew Oppenheimer I had plenty of opportunity to note that he could act in unusual ways, but have never observed anything like the behavior related above, nor to my knowledge has anyone else in later times.

In the summer of 1926, following his psychiatric interlude, Oppenheimer and two friends went hiking in Corsica—just the break he needed. On that holiday he met a girl who became his first serious love.

"On their last night in Corsica, Oppenheimer became quite agitated, saying he must return to Cambridge at once. The reason which he gave later in the evening, when he had relaxed somewhat, was that he had left a poisoned apple on Patrick Blackett's desk and must return to make sure that Blackett was all right. Was this some elaborate metaphor that Oppenheimer had constructed or was it hallucination? Neither [friend] could ever be sure."[30] [Some historians think that this may simply refer to a dubious paper that Oppenheimer had left on Blackett's desk.—RPC]

Following his Corsica trip, Oppenheimer started his Goettingen period, just described.

CHAPTER 4

POSTDOCTORAL STUDIES

Harvard

In mid-July 1927, Oppenheimer sailed again for the United States, where a National Research Council Fellowship was awaiting him. That autumn he went back to Harvard. A graduate student, who attended his colloquium there on the Born-Oppenheimer paper, has recalled: "I never could figure out whether his sibylline declarations were just a form of one-upmanship or whether he really did see a lot more in the theory than I did. Some of both, I finally decided."[31] While at Harvard he produced three interesting papers, one[32] on the polarization of light excited by electronic impact on atoms, another[33] on a further elaboration of his work on continuous spectra, and a third[34] on the quantum mechanics of electron capture.

Caltech

In the beginning of 1928, Robert moved on to the California Institute of Technology in Pasadena. There he made his perhaps most original contribution, his theory of field emission, *the first example of a quantum effect due to barrier penetration*, antedating by several months the explanation of radioactive alpha decay. "Any external electric field, no matter how weak, will in time dissociate an atom."[35] In Pasadena we see the first evidence of a feature later to be so prominent in his work, close collaboration with experimentalists.

While in California he began receiving more job offers, and among those he declined was one from Harvard, being more tempted by two other proposals. "I visited Berkeley and I thought I'd like to go to Berkeley because it was a desert. There was no theoretical physics and I thought it would be nice to try to start something. I also thought it would be dangerous because I'd be too far out of touch so I kept the connection with Caltech. . . . I liked it enough to want to come back and enough to feel that it was a place where I would be checked if I got too far off base and where I would learn of things that might not be adequately reflected in the published literature."[22] He convinced Berkeley to release him in time to teach in the spring semester at Caltech. So it came about that Oppenheimer was soon to hold concurrent assistant professorships on the West Coast. In 1931 he was promoted to associate professor, in 1936 to full professor, at both places.

Robert's experience at Caltech in 1928 revealed to him his deficiencies in mathematics, and he secured a Fellowship of the International Education Board to return to Europe for another year, delaying assumption of his California posts. By that summer he was diagnosed with tuberculosis, however, and for relief he went to the New Mexico mountains.

On that trip he also visited friends with whom, one day, he went on a horseback ride to the high country. There he fell in love with a property, a cabin built of trunks and adobe, surrounded by 160 acres of pasture. It was for rent. "Hot dog," Robert exclaimed, leased the place, later bought it, and acquired several saddle horses. He called his own horse Crisis (!) and the property Perro Caliente, which is Spanish for hot dog. The cabin—Robert called it the ranch—had a large porch, two rooms downstairs, two bedrooms upstairs, and initially lacked sanitary facilities. It became the base for expeditions over the whole area, and a vacation spot for his family for the rest of his life. It was at the end of a sloping meadow of wild grass and flowers and offered a spectacular view of the Sangre de Cristo mountains.

At the end of the long summer Oppenheimer's tuberculosis was under control. He was now ready to take off again for Europe.

Leiden

Robert went first to Leiden, to work with Ehrenfest, "because he had asked me to [they had met earlier in Cambridge, as mentioned] and I was a great admirer of his. . . . I thought I would learn something from him and I certainly did. . . . There was not a great deal of life in physics in Leiden at that time. I think Ehrenfest was depressed. . . . I gave a seminar or two in Dutch. I don't think it was very good Dutch but it was appreciated. . . .

there were some younger students whom I worked with. . . . Then I went for a month to Utrecht where Kramers was."[22]

From Uhlenbeck's recollections: "I stayed in Leiden for about a month with Oppenheimer. . . . Robert was one of the leaders there among the younger students. . . . He was very difficult to understand but very quick, and with a whole group of admirers. . . . He was really a kind of oracle. He knew very much. . . . Oppenheimer and Ehrenfest got along very well. They liked each other very much. Ehrenfest didn't understand Oppenheimer at all well but he at least was willing to try. He was very patient."[36]

In Leiden Oppenheimer received the nickname Oppie, sometimes written Opje, the Dutch diminutive of his name. "Oppie" is the slightly more vulgar version of Opje, also Dutch. Some kept calling him that all his life. I always called him Robert.

While in Leiden, Robert had an affair with a woman called Suus (Dutch for Susan). In 1946 Hendrick Casimir wrote to him that she was in financial trouble. From Robert's reply to him: "I am sending you a check for $300 and I wish that you would give it to Suus [with] warm greetings. . . . I do not think that I should send money again in the future. It would be an arrangement that in the end would surely prove to be disturbing and unhealthy for all of us."[36a]

Robert's plan to go from Leiden to Copenhagen did not materialize because of "Ehrenfest's certainty that Bohr with his largeness and vagueness was not the medium I needed but that I needed someone who was a professional calculating physicist and that Pauli would be right for me,"[22] a wise judgment with far-reaching consequences for Robert's career. Accordingly, Ehrenfest sent one of his marvelous epistles[37] to Pauli:

> [I write] about a physicist (a good one though), namely Oppenheimer. The poor devil is with us in Leiden . . . under the pressure of my schoolmasterly character. He has always very witty ideas. . . . But then the great misery starts that I cannot grasp anything that cannot be "visualized." And, although he then with imperturbable calm and kindness tries to meet my wishes, the result is that I bother more than help him. He does not think of complaining. . . . I am really convinced that, for the full development of his (great) scientific talent, Oppenheimer still needs "RECHTZEITIG a bisserl (!) LIEBEVOLL zurechtgeprügelt werden sollte" [timely and a bit lovingly to be beaten in shape (Ehrenfest's capitals)]. He thoroughly deserves this kindness since he is a quite rare and decent fellow. . . . Therefore I would like it very much if he can come to you after Leiden. This idea appeals very much to him.

And so Oppenheimer spent his concluding time of postdoctoral studies in Zurich, from June to July 1929. What he learned there was to be decisive for his further research.

A postscript to the Ehrenfest period. "Ehrenfest was in Ann Arbor [summer 1930] and there was this question: how to prove that if you have composite particles of which each component has the Fermi statistics, then the compound particle could have Bose statistics if composed of an even number—how do you prove that? . . . Then Ehrenfest went to the West Coast. There he was again very much together with Oppenheimer. And then they wrote this paper[38] which is an always quoted paper, because it is the 'proof' of the theory. . . . It was completely written by Oppenheimer."[36]

Zurich

Pauli to Ehrenfest:

> I believe that Oppenheimer is quite comfortable in Zurich, that he can work well here, and that scientifically it will still be possible to pull many good things out of him. His strength is that he has many and good ideas, and has much imagination. His weakness is that he is much too quickly satisfied with poorly based statements, that he does not answer his own often quite interesting questions for lack of perseverance and thoroughness, and that he leaves his problems in a half-digested stage of conjecture, belief or disbelief. I definitely believe, however, that all this may much improve by energetic persuasion, he is of good will and not stubborn. Unfortunately, he has a very bad trait: he confronts me with a rather unconditional belief in authority and considers all I say as final and definitive truth. I do know the origins of this need for others' authority. They should solve his problems and answer his questions, so that he need not do so himself. I do not know how to make him give that up.[39]

Pauli's attitude toward Oppenheimer may be described as one of respect for his brilliance tempered with criticism for his technical abilities. He said in those days that Robert's ideas were always very interesting but his calculations were always wrong. Then and occasionally later Pauli would refer to him as the "nim-nim-nim man," imitating with glee Oppenheimer's mumbling interspersions of his otherwise eloquent diction, a habit of his familiar to all who knew him for some time.

From Rabi's recollections:

> My longest period of close personal interaction with Oppenheimer came in the spring of 1929 when he and I were both in Zurich at Pauli's Institute. Oppenheimer worked very hard that spring but had a gift of concealing his assiduous application with an air of easy nonchalance. Actually, he was engaged in a very difficult calculation of the opacity of surfaces of stars to their internal radiation, an important constant in the theoretical construction of stellar models. He spoke little of these problems and seemed to be much more interested in literature, especially the Hindu classics and the more esoteric Western writers. Pauli once remarked to me that Oppenheimer seemed to treat physics as an avocation and

psychoanalysis as a vocation. As I shared many of his interests, I found him a delightful and fascinating companion. Even at that time his presence conveyed a sense of excitement and heightened awareness.[11]

Pauli's hope that it might be possible "to pull good things" out of Oppenheimer proved to be quite justified. Robert soon completed a paper on the radiation of electrons in a Coulomb field,[40] about which Pauli wrote approvingly to Sommerfeld: "Using flawless methods he has calculated everything one can desire."[41] Then "Pauli told me a little of his work with Heisenberg, and I showed, I guess, more than a little interest in it."[22] Out of this interest grew Oppenheimer's involvement with quantum field theory, the main focus of his later scientific career.

For that purpose the timing of Robert's arrival in Zurich was perfect. In March 1929, Heisenberg and Pauli had completed part one of their joint work on quantum electrodynamics (QED),[42] after which they went right away to work on part two.[43] Thus Oppenheimer had the great good fortune to enter practical QED on the ground floor. (His later reference to the Heisenberg Pauli papers as "a monstrous boo-boo"[22] is rather excessive, even with the hindsight of the advances due to renormalization.) Using this young new theory he went to work on the self-energy problem, to this day one of the most intractable issues in fundamental physics, making an important discovery: a new source of self-energy, a typical quantum effect without classical counterpart. He further observed that self-energy effects cause infinite displacements of atomic energy levels. The hope was that light frequencies (that is, energy-level differences) would remain finite, even though the energies had infinite shifts, but this did not turn out to be the case. The way in which the shifts differ for states of different energy was not understood until nearly 20 years later. Oppenheimer did observe that the leading divergent terms were equal for states of the same energy and pointed out that the applicability of the theory to the fine-structure splitting could be ascribed to this circumstance.

Pauli thought well of this effort, which was "a continuation of the work of Heisenberg and myself on QED."[44] Heisenberg suggested a three-man publication.[45] Oppenheimer has remembered, "The part of it I got into was something it was at first thought the three of us should publish together; then Pauli thought he might publish it together with me, and then it seemed better . . . to let this be a separate publication."[22] A separate paper it became,[46] published after he had returned to the United States in July 1929, at age 25.

Robert's postdoc years were now for good behind him. It had been a richly productive period for him, rich also in new experiences. "I would think that the [subsequent] transition was rather from that of a person who had been learning and also explaining in European centers and in Harvard and Caltech to someone who couldn't much any longer learn from masters but could learn from the literature and from what he did himself; one who had a lot of explaining to do because there was no one else. . . . I would think that the big change was that I wasn't an apprentice any longer and I had decided where to make my bed. . . . I hardly left California until the war . . . I had really made a bed that I was content to be in."[22] He would not return to Europe until 19 years later.

CHAPTER **5**

THE CALIFORNIA PROFESSOR
AS TEACHER

If ever there was a period during which Robert was happy, those were his California years of the 1930s, I would think. It was the time in which he single-handedly created, in Bethe's words, "the greatest school of theoretical physics that the United States has ever known. . . . More than any other man he was responsible for raising American theoretical physics from a provincial adjunct of Europe to world leadership. . . . The majority of the best American theoretical physicists who grew up in those years [the 1930s] were trained by Oppenheimer at one stage of their lives."[10] It was also the time in which he made important research contributions, to quantum electrodynamics, nuclear physics, and astrophysics. I shall first sketch his role as teacher, thereafter his further research.

I found myself entirely in Berkeley and almost entirely at Caltech as the only one who understood what this [the recent developments in physics] was all about, and the gift which my high school teacher of English had noted for explaining technical things came into action. I didn't start to make a school; I didn't start to look for students. I started really as a propagator of the theory which I loved, about which I continued to learn more, and which was not well understood but which was very rich. The pattern was not that of someone who takes on a course and teaches students preparing for a variety of careers but of explaining first to faculty, staff, and colleagues and then to anyone who would listen, what this was about, what had been learned, what the unsolved problems were.

I think from all I hear [that] I was a very difficult lecturer, I started as a lecturer who made things very difficult. I had some help; I remember Pauling's advice, almost certainly in '28. He said, "When you want to give a seminar or lecture, decide what it is you want to talk about and then find some agreeable subject of contemplation not remotely related to your lecture and then interrupt that from time to time to say a few words." So you can see how bad it must have been. In Pasadena I taught all right, but it was never an important part of the Caltech curriculum except conceivably that first year in the spring of '30 when I was there a long time and where I probably gave a pretty good "course of sprouts" in quantum theory.

In Berkeley I gave what was normally a graduate course and in practice usually a second year graduate course which had not been given before on quantum theory and quantum mechanics and which varied in content but was always all right for someone who had some background in classical physics and preferably at least a qualitative introduction to atomic theory, though it didn't too much matter. I usually gave a seminar on one other aspect of theoretical physics, typically statistical mechanics and relativity, both things that I loved very much. But these were all with people who didn't have to learn these things [but] wanted to. . . . [It] was very rarely and only in quite different contexts that I ever worked with undergraduates. I think they didn't think I'd be any good for them and it didn't occur to me to ask to teach freshman physics or anything like that.

You live in the department and if it's a growing and active department as Berkeley got to be and as Caltech was, there are problems that arise because people are doing experiments. I found this a very great source of stimulation and pleasure and I think actually the beginnings of collaboration with graduate students came very early, but the students weren't very good and I picked rather exotic problems. It wasn't really until the positron [in 1932] and more or less the full shape of the relativistic débacle, [when] the clues of cosmic rays came into the picture, that the collaboration with students began to take a more effective turn.[22]

In 1928 Ernest Lawrence (1901–1958) had been appointed associate professor in Berkeley. In 1930 he constructed the first two models of what became known as cyclotrons. Under his direction these accelerators were improved, their energies increased, and their results became ever more important for Oppenheimer's work. In the early years the relations between the two men were quite cordial.

In 1934, Robert Serber arrived in Berkeley as postdoctoral research assistant to Oppenheimer. He became Oppenheimer's closest confidant in the Berkeley years. He has left us an eloquent account of Oppenheimer the teacher.

By the time of my arrival in Berkeley, Oppie's course in quantum mechanics was well established. Oppie was quick, impatient, and had a sharp tongue. In the earliest days of his teaching he was reputed to have terrorized the students. Now, after five years of experience, he had mellowed—if his earlier students were to be believed. His course was an inspirational as well as an educational achievement. He transmitted to his students a feeling of the beauty of the logical structure of physics and an excitement in the development of science. Almost everyone listened to the course more than once, and Oppie occasionally had difficulty in preventing students from coming a third time. One Russian woman attempted to come a fourth time, and defeated Oppie's efforts to dissuade her by going on a hunger strike. [His students] carried [the course], each in his own version, to many campuses.

Oppie's way of working with his research students was also original. His group would consist of eight or ten graduate students and about a half dozen postdoctoral fellows. He would meet the group once a day in his office. A little before the appointed time its members would straggle in and dispose themselves on the tables and about the walls. Oppie would come in and discuss with one after another the status of the student's research problem, while the others listened and offered comments. All were exposed to a broad range of topics. Oppenheimer was interested in everything, and one subject after another was introduced and coexisted with all the others. In an afternoon we might discuss electrodynamics, cosmic rays, astrophysics, and nuclear physics.[48]

Elsewhere, Serber recalled:

Oppie's relations with his students were not confined to office and classroom. He was a bachelor then, and a part of his social life was intertwined with ours. Often we worked late and continued the discussion through dinner and then later at his apartment on Shasta Road. When we tired of our problems, or cleaned up the point at issue, the talk would turn to art, music, literature, and politics. If the work was going badly we might give up and go to a movie. Sometimes we took a night off and had a Mexican dinner in Oakland or went to a good restaurant in San Francisco. In the early days this meant taking the Berkeley ferry and a ride across the bay. The ferries back to Berkeley didn't run very often late at night, and this required passing the time waiting for them at the bars and nightclubs near the ferry dock. Frequently we missed several ferries. Ed McMillan [1907–1991, a later Nobel laureate] was often our companion in these adventures.

We held regular joint seminars with Felix Bloch [1905–1983, another future Nobel laureate] and his students from Stanford. Afterward, Oppie would frequently treat the whole entourage to dinner at Jack's in San Francisco. These were postdepression days, and students were poor. The world of good food and good wines and gracious living was far from the experience of many of them, and Oppie was introducing them to an unfamiliar way of life. We acquired something of his tastes. We went to concerts together and listened to chamber music, Oppie and Arnold Nordsieck [1911–1971, a postdoc] read Plato in the original Greek. There were many evening parties where we drank and talked and danced until late, and where, when Oppie was supplying the food, the novices suffered from the hot chili that social example required them to eat.

During this time Oppie was a professor at both Berkeley and Caltech (where his name metamorphized into Robert). The arrangement was made possible because the Berkeley spring semester ended early in April, and Robert could then teach the spring quarter in Pasadena. Many of his students made the annual trek with him. Some things were easier in those days. We thought nothing of giving up our houses or apartments in Berkeley, confident that we could find a garden apartment in Pasadena for twenty-five dollars a month. We didn't own more than could be packed in the back of a car. In Pasadena, in addition to being exposed to new information on physics, we led an active social life. The Tolmans [Richard, 1906–1948, and his wife Ruth] were good friends, and we had very warm relations with Charlie Lauritsen and his group. Willy Fowler [1911–1995, yet another future Nobel laureate] was a graduate student then, and Tommy Lauritsen was still in high school. We spent many evenings at the Mexican restaurants on Olvera Street and many nights partying in Charlie Lauritsen's garden. . . .

One feature of the times which contrasts with present customs was the relatively little personal contact we had with the outer world of physics. The meetings we went to were the West Coast meetings of the American Physical Society. The first conference I can recall was a Cosmic Ray Symposium in Chicago to which Oppie and I drove from his New Mexico ranch in the early summer of 1939. We had a few visitors, however. Niels Bohr, Dirac, and Pauli made short visits to Berkeley or Pasadena, and I met Victor Weisskopf [1908–2002], Hans Bethe [1906–2005], George Placzek [1905–1955], George Gamow [1904–1968] and Walter Elsasser [1904–1991] at the ranch.

Many facets of Oppenheimer's character contributed to his greatness as a teacher: his great capacity as a physicist, his wide intellectual interests, his astonishing quickness of mind, his great gift for expression, his sensitive perception, his social presence, which made him the center of every gathering. His students emulated him as best they could. They copied his gestures, his mannerisms, his intonations. He truly influenced their lives.[47]

Serber's account[47] also includes a list of Oppenheimer's prewar students, among whom we find still another future Nobel laureate: Willis Lamb (1913–), who has recalled: "Oppenheimer's Berkeley office was room 219, LeConte Hall. As were many of his students, I was given a small table in the room. Oppenheimer had no desk, but only a table in the middle of the room, heavily strewn with papers. One wall was entirely covered by a blackboard and hardly ever erased. One set of open shelves had reprints of Oppenheimer's publications."[49]

CHAPTER 6

THE CALIFORNIA PROFESSOR AS RESEARCHER

A list of Oppenheimer's physics publications[10] shows 73 entries in all, of which 51 stem from his California years, 1929–1942. His oeuvre in that period ranges over topics in quantum field theory, particle physics, theory of cosmic radiations, nuclear physics, and cosmology. In preparing a survey of that work I have been greatly helped by the writings of Robert Serber,[47,50] who, as said, himself came to Berkeley in 1934 as research associate.[51]

More on QED

We have already met one of Oppenheimer's California papers, the one begun in Zurich, in which he had shown that QED leads to infinite linear shifts in atomic spectra.[46] From the conclusion of that paper:

> We have treated these difficulties in some detail, because they show that the present theory will not be applicable to any problem where relativistic effects are important, where, that is, we cannot be guided throughout by the limiting case $c \to \infty$. The theory can thus not be applied to a discussion of the structure of the nuclei. It appears improbable that the difficulties discussed in this work will be soluble without an adequate theory of the masses of the electron and the proton; nor is it certain that such a theory will be possible on the basis of the special theory of relativity.[46]

Here we meet for the first but not the last time Robert's conviction— which in fact never changed during the 1930s—that QED was wrong, not only in its infinities but also in its finite predictions. As Serber has commented, "This view colored our work. . . . He could hardly write a paper without a lament. . . . A naive faith might have made us more resolute in trying to understand the real problems of QED."[50]

In the same issue of the *Physical Review*—which dates from 1930—Oppenheimer noted a difficulty with Dirac's theory of the electrons. It was a time of great confusion: this theory dictates that electrons can be in states of negative energy—inadmissible. Dirac had suggested (1929) that these states should all be occupied, and that a hole in that distribution should be a proton. Oppenheimer was the first to point out that that cannot be, since it would allow for the process

$$\text{proton} + \text{electron} \rightarrow \text{two photons}$$

so that a hydrogen atom would spontaneously and rapidly annihilate into radiation.

The identification of holes with particles is fine, but why protons? Dirac later remarked, "At that time everyone felt pretty sure that the electrons and the protons were the only elementary particles in Nature."[53]

Now hear this. In his paper on Dirac's hole theory,[52] Oppenheimer remarked that the difficulties disappear if one makes "the assumption of two independent elementary particles of opposite charge and dissimilar mass [electrons and protons] and retains the hypothesis that the reason why no transitions to states of negative energy occur either for electron or for proton is that all such states are occupied." Here Oppenheimer was the first to predict implicitly the existence of the positron (explicitly predicted by Dirac in 1931 (discovered in 1932), and of the antiproton (discovered in 1955)!

In a sequel to his paper[54] Oppenheimer gave a detailed calculation of the (alleged) hydrogen-atom disintegration. His result was correct, apart from a missing factor $(2\pi)^4$.

Oppenheimer's carelessness was more serious in his next paper, the relativistic theory of the photoelectric effect.[55] With this work Robert began publishing together with his young co-workers. The theoretical prediction appeared to be 25 times larger than the experimental result. "We see here another breakdown with present electromagnetic theory." Robert now believed that the theory was already wrong at energies of order mc^2, m = electron mass. The error was his, however; the theoretical answer was off by a factor of 44/3. In Serber's words: "[Oppenheimer's] physics was good, but his arithmetic awful."[50]

In 1931 Robert attempted to get a first-order differential equation for light, in some ways similar to the Dirac equation for the electron.[56] He failed, but in the process recognized the fundamental difference between particles of spin one-half and of integral spin, an insight that was to lead to the theory of the relations between spin and statistics.

Cosmic Rays

Oppenheimer's active interest in cosmic ray physics also began in 1931, as the result of his association with the Caltech experimenters. In an effort to understand the great penetrating powers of these rays he, together with his student Frank Carlson (1899–1954), wrote two papers on the properties of fast electrons and "magnetic neutrons," the first[57] presented in December 1931, the second[58] in July 1932.

That work was done at a time when nuclear physics was in a state of maximal confusion. Nuclear spins and statistics exhibited paradoxical properties.[59] So did β-spectra that, in December 1930, had led Pauli to propose[60] a new particle that he then called a neutron and that we now call a neutrino. Initially Pauli erroneously believed that nuclei are built up of protons, electrons, and "his" neutrons. The "magnetic neutron" in the Oppenheimer-Carlson paper refers to the Pauli neutron, which Oppenheimer had heard Pauli report on at the 1931 Ann Arbor summer school.

Our "neutron" was announced in a paper submitted[61] in February 1932—after the first and before the second of the Oppenheimer-Carlson publications. Their work needs to be seen against the background of this confused situation. This is what they wrote on these matters. They first refer to the "third element in the building of nuclei"—Pauli's neutrons—which, Pauli thought, could solve *both* "the anomalous spin and statistics paradoxes *and* the apparent failure of the conservation of energy in beta-particle disintegration." Then they go on: "One may, however, assume that the neutron has a mass very close to that of the proton. . . . Such neutrons would help explain the anomalous spin and statistics of nuclei, although they would throw no light on beta-ray disintegrations. The experimental evidence on the penetrating beryllium radiation suggests that neutrons of nearly protonic mass do exist [the data that led to 'our' neutron]." . . . To my knowledge this is the first time that it is stated in the literature that the neutron saves spin and statistics *and* that energy conservation in β-decay is a separate issue.

Now to the cosmic rays. Carlson and Oppenheimer calculated the ionization loss of electrons in close collisions and also the loss of the "magnetic neutrons," supposed to have a magnetic moment comparable to the proton's.

They found that the latter was in better agreement with cosmic-ray data at high energies and therefore suggested that "magnetic neutrons" were the primary component of cosmic rays. "No latitude effect shows that primary cosmic rays are neutral."[58] A latitude effect *had* been reported already in 1927 but was not believed in California in 1931. In 1932 Carlson and Oppenheimer wrote a follow-up paper,[62] in which they gave up on "magnetic neutrons" that, they now said, would not produce the observed cloud-chamber tracks.

Meanwhile, Carl Anderson (1905–1991) from Caltech had announced his discovery of the positron.[63] In 1933 Oppenheimer and Milton Spinoza Plessett (1908–1991) were the first to calculate the production of electron-positron pairs near threshold and at high energies. "If we allow gamma rays of [sufficient] energy to fall upon a nucleus, we should expect pairs to appear."[64] This effect, they note, can be seen as a photoelectric absorption of the γ by an electron in the filled negative energy states, the nucleus picking up some recoil momentum. Their final formula was wrong, as usual, as others rapidly noted.[65]

Oppenheimer and Plessett correctly remarked that their results indicated serious disagreements with the mass absorption law of cosmic rays. "One is tempted to see in this discrepancy a failure of the theory when applied to radiation whose wave-length is of the order of e^2/mc^2 which marks the limit of applicability of classical electron theory."[64] Thus doubts moved from $2mc^2$ to $137mc^2$.

There is another major new idea in this paper, the shower mechanism:

High energy electrons passing through matter → photons →
pairs → more photons → more pairs . . .

that, they say, "demands detailed study." The remark on showers was no more than a throw-away at the end of their paper—but was all the same a fundamental observation.

This work was followed by a paper by Leo Nedelsky (1903–), and Oppenheimer on the internal absorption of nuclear gamma rays that convert into electron-positron pairs.[66] An erratum[67] records that a factor 1/3 in their final formula is missing—the only occasion I have seen in which Oppenheimer himself published one of his errors.

On December 28, 1933, the first symposium on the positron was held at an American Physical Society meeting. Uhlenbeck, Anderson, and Oppenheimer were the speakers. "This proved to be a session of great interest and importance and the attendance was about five hundred."[68]

Electron-Positron Theory

The quantization of the electron wave field goes back to 1927, but the practice of using this technique for describing electron-positron systems began in 1934, where it is used to this day. Among the pioneers of this method we find Oppenheimer and his research associate Wendell Furry (1907–1984).[69] They showed that the theory was symmetrical in electrons and positrons and could be formulated without reference to a filled negative sea. According to this theory an electromagnetic field can momentarily produce an electron-positron pair out of the vacuum. Since the field pushes electrons and positrons in opposite directions, this produces a polarization of the vacuum just like the polarization of a dielectric medium, and as a consequence the Maxwell field equations needed to be modified. A point charge, for instance, no longer produces a pure Coulomb field that falls off with the inverse square of the distance. At distances less than the Compton wavelength of the electron, 2.4×10^{10} centimeters, there would be appreciable corrections to this law. They said (incorrectly) that the remaining finite vacuum polarization effects would not be observable in atoms because they are not larger than the shifts "which arise from our ignorance of the reaction of the electron to its own radiation field"; however, it should be possible to see them in proton-proton scattering. The paper gave the correct formula for the modification of the Coulomb field at short distances. They also said that Lawrence had just returned from Brussels and had shown them Dirac's report to the Solvay congress on vacuum polarization and charge renormalization (which was published in 1934).[70] This work led to two important papers by Oppenheimer's research associates: one by Serber, who generalized the Oppenheimer-Furry results to time-dependent external sources,[71] and one by Edwin Uehling (1901–1985), who gave the explicit results for vacuum polarization effects in a hydrogen atom.[72]

The Furry-Oppenheimer paper contains another of Robert's laments, this one concerning the new infinities diagnosed to occur due to vacuum polarization: "The difficulties are of such a character that they are apparently not to be overcome merely by modifying the electromagnetic field of an electron within small distances but require here a more profound change in our notions of space and time." It needs also to be noted that their discussion of particle position, momentum and spin in terms of quantum field theory is incorrect, as was noted years later.[73]

Electron-positron theory remained Oppenheimer's main research interest during 1934–35. He treated annihilation radiation of positrons absorbed in matter,[74] field fluctuations due to pair creation,[75] and internal conversion by pair production of the radiation emitted in the impact of charged particles on matter.[76] In a paper on the absorption of cosmic-ray electrons[77] he again pointed out the shower mechanism, which would lead to rapid degradation of high-energy particles. He concluded that either the formulae were wrong or that there was some other and less absorbable component. This could not be the proton: equal numbers of positives and negatives were seen, few slow protons and no corresponding antiprotons were seen, and the distribution of recoil electrons was wrong for protons. But, having argued himself into a correct conclusion (i.e., "some other and less absorbable component"), Oppenheimer did not stick with it; he made a tortured argument that if the correct theory were nonlinear, the presence of high-frequency components could damp low-frequency effects.

Nuclear Physics

Oppenheimer's first paper on nuclear physics dates from 1933, when he had calculated the energy dependence of the nuclear reaction produced by bombarding lithium with protons.[78] His most important contribution in this area (1935) is the "Oppenheimer-Phillips process," in which a deuteron, entering a heavy nucleus, is split into proton plus neutron, one of these particles being retained by the nucleus while the other is re-emitted.[79] "After the War, this process became an important tool in the study of nuclear energy levels and their properties."[10]

Further contributions to nuclear physics: with Serber, on nuclear level-densities on the basis of Bohr's liquid drop model;[80] a paper with the intriguing title "The disintegration of high-energy protons"[81] in which it is noted that in collisions protons may transfer a considerable fraction of their energy to positrons + neutrinos; a discussion of the nuclear photoeffect at high energies;[82] sharp resonance effects in transmutations of light nuclei;[83] an analysis of boron plus proton reactions, in which the first example of an isotopic spin selection rule is given.[84,48]

Shower Theory

Meanwhile Oppenheimer had turned to electron-positron showers, a subject he had broached earlier in passing. In June 1936 he announced the first results at an American Physical Society meeting.[85] More details of this important problem were given shortly afterward in an elegant paper with

Carlson.[86] Their theory of cascades, a wonderful problem in fundamental interactions combined with statistical considerations, clarified satisfactorily the nature of what became known as the soft component of cosmic rays. Here we encounter Robert in an assertive mood, no more wailing about the breakdown of theory. The formalism was improved by Oppenheimer's student Hartland Snyder[87] (1913–1962), and the analysis of experiments by Serber.[88]

There was another, "hard" component, for which Dirac's electron-positron appeared to fail. Here Carlson and Oppenheimer came with a daring and, in the event, correct proposal, the need for an as-yet-unknown kind of particle: "One can conclude, either that the theoretical estimates of the probability of these processes are inapplicable in the domain of cosmic-ray energies, or that the actual penetration of these rays has to be ascribed to the presence of a component other than electrons and photons. The second alternative is necessarily radical; for cloud chamber and counter experiments show that particles with the same charge as the negative electron belong to the penetrating component of radiation; and if these are not electrons, they are particles not previously known to physics."[86]

At about that same time, Heisenberg had come forth with a quite different proposal: shower particles are generated in a single act of plural production.[89] When he heard of the cascade theory he at once conceded[90] that its authors had a point, but noted that rarer showers might still leave room for his explosions, an idea that continued to intrigue him several more years. I well recall discussions at early postwar conferences on the issue "plural versus multiple production."

Mesons

In May 1937 the first announcements were made of observations of mesons in cosmic rays.[91] One month later, Oppenheimer and Serber suggested[92] that these particles were those suggested[93] by Hideki Yukawa (1907–1981) to explain nuclear forces. Serber has recalled, "Although Yukawa's paper appeared in 1935, we had never seen a reference to it and knew of it only because Yukawa had sent Oppenheimer a reprint. One purpose of our letter was to bring it to attention."[94] Their letter was in fact the first instance in which Yukawa's idea is mentioned in a Western publication. In this letter they noted that the new particles are not primary cosmic rays but are produced by γ rays in nuclear collisions (and by pair production) in the upper atmosphere and are the "hard," penetrating component. Also, the production of showers at sea level and below is due to knock-on electrons from the penetrating component. They calculated the production rate, which was about right. They were not unmindful of the paradox between nuclear interaction and penetrating component. I take this last comment to mean that they had an inkling that the meson experimentally discovered in 1937, now called the muon, was in fact *not* Yukawa's meson, now known as the pion, which was experimentally discovered in 1947.[95]

In 1939, Oppenheimer, Snyder, and Serber returned to the question of showers produced by the hard component. At that time the cosmic-ray mesons were believed to have spin 1 but if so, the authors noted, mesons radiate too rapidly.[96] More detailed studies by Robert Christy (1916-) and Shuichi Kusaka (1916-1947), Oppenheimer students, confirmed this conclusion.[97] Whereupon Oppenheimer concluded in 1941 that the mesons had to be pseudoscalar[98]—correct for *pions* as it happened. In another remarkable paper of that year, Oppenheimer and Christy suggested[99] that the soft component at high altitude could be explained by assuming that, in addition to the penetrating mesons, there were roughly equal numbers of neutral mesons that decay rapidly into electrons and positrons. Oppenheimer's paper[100] of 1948 on the role of the π° (well before the discovery of that particle) in the generation of the soft component was a natural sequel to this earlier work. Back to 1941, in that year he published a speculative paper on a possible small neutrino rest mass.[101]

Finally, I note that the intensive work in meson theory by the Berkeley group in 1940–41 also included the work of Oppenheimer and Julian Schwinger[102] (with whom he had earlier published a paper on electron-positron production[103]) on the strong coupling theory for charged scalar and neutral pseudoscalar mesons, in which they calculated scattering cross-sections and predicted nucleon isobars. These efforts continued until interrupted by World War II.

Astrophysics and Cosmology

Oppenheimer's connections at Pasadena with the staff of the Mt. Wilson Observatory and with Richard Tolman led to his interest in astrophysics and general relativity. Principally as an exercise in nuclear physics, he and Serber decided the study the relative influence on nuclear and gravitational forces in neutron stars.[104] One of their aims was to improve the estimate made by Lev Davidovich Landau (1908–1968) for the limiting mass above which an ordinary star becomes a neutron star. (Landau discussed a model in which this mass is ≈ 0.001 ☉ [the symbol means one solar mass]. He also suggested that every star has an interior neutron core.[105] Their work attracted the attention of Richard Chase Tolman. As a result of discussions between Tolman and Oppenheimer and his co-workers, there appeared in 1939 a pair of papers, one by Tolman on static solutions of Einstein's field equations for fluid spheres,[106] and one, directly following it, by Oppenheimer and George Volkoff (1914–2000), entitled "On massive neutron cores."[107] In this paper, the foundations are laid for a general relativistic theory of stellar structure. The model discussed is a static spherical star consisting of an ideal Fermi gas of neutrons. The authors found that the star is stable as long as its mass $\leq 1/2$ ☉. (The present best value for a free-neutron gas is ≈ 0.7 ☉ and is called the Oppenheimer-Volkoff limit.)[108] Half a year later, the paper "On continued gravitational attraction" by Oppenheimer and Hartland Snyder came out.[109] The first line of its abstract reads, "When all thermonuclear sources of energy are exhausted, a sufficiently heavy star will collapse; [a contraction follows which] will continue indefinitely." Thus began the physics of black holes, the name for the ultimate collapsed state proposed by John Archibald Wheeler at a conference held in the fall of 1967 at the Goddard Institute of Space Studies in New York.[110] At that time, pulsars had just been discovered and neutron stars and black holes were no longer considered "exotic objects [that] remained a textbook curiosity. . . . Cooperative efforts of radio and optical astronomers [had begun] to reveal a great many strange new things in the sky."[111]

CHAPTER 7

OPPENHEIMER'S OPINION OF HIS OWN TEACHING AND RESEARCH IN CALIFORNIA

When in 1963 Oppenheimer, then director of the Princeton Institute, was asked whether he missed his earlier successful teaching activities, he replied, "I think that the charm went out of teaching after the great change of the war because I did teach at Caltech and Berkeley and for one thing I was always called away and distracted because I was thinking about other things, but actually I don't think I ever taught well after the war. I have a feeling that what my job was was to get a part of the next generation brought up and that job was done when I came here."[22]

Also in the early 1960s, I once asked Robert which he considered to be his most creative physics papers. I remember two aspects of his reply. First, that he found his work on electron-positron theory to be his principal contribution. Secondly, that he did not mention at all his highly important work on cosmology.

In my opinion, Robert would have been entitled to look back with much satisfaction on his contributions to physical theory, covering papers, quite a few seminal, on QED, cosmic rays, particularly shower theory, electron-positron theory, meson theory, and cosmology—never mind that he had made mistakes, as I have mentioned. Satisfaction with self was not given him, however.

CHAPTER 8

PERSONAL LIFE IN THE 1930s

I turn to the great changes in Robert's life in the 1930s other than those in science.

Visits to California by Robert's parents came to an end when his mother became gravely ill with leukemia. Now it was his turn to visit them in New York. To a friend he wrote, "I found my mother terribly low, almost beyond hope. . . . She is unbelievably sweet."[112] She died in October 1931. Toward her end, Robert had said to another friend, "I am the loneliest man in the world."[113] Yet, years later, his brother Frank "was surprised to hear Robert confess that he had had difficulty in finding things to talk about with his mother and that his attentions were what he supposed were expected from an affectionate son rather than a sign of deep understanding between them."[114] His father continued to visit him often in California. He was very popular with Robert's friends. In September 1937 he died of a heart attack. "We had an intimate and close relationship until his death. . . . A little later, when I came into an inheritance, I made a will leaving this to the University of California for fellowships to graduate students."[115] All through the thirties "I spent some weeks each summer with my brother Frank at our ranch in New Mexico. There was a strong bond of affection between us,"[115] as is also seen from the voluminous correspondence between the two.[5] The brothers would also often receive friends at their ranch.

My friends, both in Pasadena and in Berkeley, were mostly faculty people, scientists, classicists, and artists. I studied and read Sanskrit with Arthur Rider. I read very widely, mostly classics, novels, plays, and poetry; and I read something of other parts of science. I was not interested in and did not read about economics or politics. I was almost wholly divorced from the contemporary scene in this country. I never read a newspaper or a current magazine like *Time* or *Harper's*; I had no radio, no telephone; I learned of the stock market crash in the fall of 1929 only long after the event; the first time I ever voted was in the presidential election of 1936. To many of my friends, my indifference to contemporary affairs seemed bizarre, and they often chided me with being too much of a highbrow. I was interested in man and his experience; I was deeply interested in my science; but I had no understanding of the relations of man to his society.[115]

There are many Oppenheimer stories of those years, one that achieved wide notoriety. It involved him and Melba Phillips (1907–2004), his first doctoral student.

According to the story, the Berkeley police found Melba sound asleep in a car in the Berkeley hills. When they awakened her, she said Oppie had driven her up there, and she had no idea what had become of him. After a search, they found him asleep in his room at the Faculty Club, having apparently walked home and—forgetting all about his girl and his car—gone to bed. The story was picked up by the world press as a classic in the genre of absent-minded-professor tales; Oppie's brother, Frank, saw it in the Cambridge, England, papers. Oppie was still a little defensive about it. His version was that he had told Melba that he was going to walk home and that she should drive the car back, but that she dozed off and hadn't heard him.[116]

Other stories: There were those about Robert's eating habits—apparently his Spartan indifference to what and how much he ate sometimes left his guests hungry, that were punctuated by a gourmet's delight in special dishes, focusing on excessively hot dishes. His fast driving was legendary. His car at that time was a Packard roadster named Geryda, after the Sanskrit messenger of the gods: "On one occasion in the early 1930s he crashed the car while racing the coast train near Los Angeles. His passenger . . . though not seriously injured . . . was knocked unconscious, and Oppenheimer thought at first that she was dead. [His father] gave her a Cezanne drawing and a small Vlaminck painting by way of apology."[117]

"When Oppenheimer went to Pasadena during the Berkeley term, at the last moment he sometimes asked Nedelsky to lecture for him. 'It won't be any trouble,' said Oppenheimer on one such occasion, 'it's all in a book.' Finding that the book was in Dutch, which he could not read, Nedelsky demurred. 'But it's such easy Dutch,' said Oppenheimer."[118]

My favorite story of that time is one told by Uhlenbeck's wife, who has recalled "what fun it was to be with Robert at this period of his life and what crazy situations he could get into. 'How do you manage to make things so complicated?' she once asked. 'It's a gift,' Robert replied."[119]

In the 1930s there arose in Robert a new awareness of the world around him. In his own words:

> Beginning in late 1936, my interests began to change. These changes did not alter my earlier friendships, my relations to my students, or my devotion to physics; but they added something new. I can discern in retrospect more than one reason for these changes. I had had a continuing, smoldering fury about the treatment of Jews in Germany. I had relatives there, and was later to help in extricating them and bringing them to this country. I saw what the Depression was doing to my students. Often they could get no jobs, or jobs which were wholly inadequate. And through them, I began to understand how deeply political and economic events could affect men's lives. I began to feel the need to participate more fully in the life of the community. But I had no framework of political conviction or experience to give me perspective in these matters.[115]

In the spring of 1936 Oppenheimer met Jean Tatlock, who was then in her midtwenties, working for her doctorate in psychiatry at Stanford. Her father was a professor of medieval literature at Berkeley and well known locally for his right-wing views. His daughter had become increasingly involved in left-wing activities, and, by the time she met Robert, was an active member of the Communist Party, and introduced him to her left-wing friends. She was dark haired, tall and slender, with green eyes, a combination of beauty and intelligence that Oppenheimer found irresistible. "We were at least twice close enough to marriage to consider ourselves engaged," Robert has recalled,[115] but each time marriage was imminent it was Jean who shied away. Much of the problem stemmed from her severe bouts of depression. "At times of crisis in her relationship with Oppenheimer," Robert Serber recalls, "she disappeared for weeks, months sometimes, and then would taunt Robert mercilessly. She would taunt him about who she had been with and what they had been doing. She seemed determined to hurt him, perhaps because she knew Robert loved her so much."[120] In January 1944, she committed suicide.

A few days later, Serber's wife came into her husband's office in Los Alamos with a telegram from a Berkeley friend, saying that Jean had committed suicide. She asked him to break the news to Robert. "When I got to his office I saw by his face that he had already heard. He was deeply grieved."[120a]

Robert has written:

> I should not give the impression that it was wholly because of Jean Tatlock that I made left-wing friends, or felt sympathy for causes which hitherto would have seemed so remote from me, like the Loyalist cause in Spain, and the organiza-

tion of migratory workers. I have mentioned some of the other contributing causes. I liked the new sense of companionship, and at the time felt that I was coming to be a part of the life of my time and country. . . .

This was the era of what the Communists then called the United Front, in which they joined with many non-Communist groups in support of humanitarian objectives. Many of these objectives engaged my interest. I contributed to the strike fund of one of the major strikes of Bridges' union; I subscribed to the *People's World*; I contributed to the various committees and organizations which were intended to help the Spanish Loyalist cause. I was invited to help establish the teacher's union, which included faculty and teaching assistants at the university, and school teachers of the East Bay. I was elected recording secretary. My connection with the teacher's union continued until some time in 1941, when we disbanded our chapters. . . .

The matter which most engaged my sympathies and interests was the war in Spain. This was not a matter of understanding and informed convictions. I had never been to Spain; I knew a little of its literature; I knew nothing of its history or politics or contemporary problems. But like a great many other Americans I was emotionally committed to the Loyalist cause. I contributed to various organizations for Spanish relief. I went to, and helped with, many parties, bazaars, and the like. Even when the war in Spain was manifestly lost, these activities continued. The end of the war and the defeat of the Loyalists caused me great sorrow. . . .

I went to a big Spanish relief party the night before Pearl Harbor; and the next day, as we heard the news of the outbreak of war, I decided that I had had about enough of the Spanish cause, and that there were other and more pressing crises in the world. . . .

I never was a member of the Communist Party. I never accepted Communist dogma or theory; in fact it never made sense to me.[121]

Oppenheimer had several short affairs after parting with Tatlock. Then, in August 1939 he met Katherine ("Kitty") Puening (1910–1972) at a colleague's garden party in Pasadena. Serber, who was also at that party, has told me of that encounter. When Robert came in, Kitty took one look at him, then determinedly steered toward him, never to let go thereafter.

Kitty was born in Germany. She has said that she was a niece of Field Marshall Wilhelm Keitel (1882–1946). At age two she and her parents moved to Pittsburgh. At the time she first met Robert she was married to Stuart Harrison, who was studying for an M.D. degree. A previous husband had been an active Communist. This had caused her to join the Party, which she left for good in 1936.

According to those who knew her, Kitty engineered a visit to Robert's ranch. From the ranch, the two went on an overnight visit to nearby friends of Robert. "The next day, after they returned, [their hostess] came trotting up to the ranch house and presented Kitty with her nightgown, which had been found under Robert's pillow."[124]

In the fall of 1940 Kitty established residence in Reno, Nevada, where on November 1 she obtained a divorce and married Robert, husband number four.

Jackie Oppenheimer, wife of Frank (they had married in 1936) has said: "Kitty was a schemer. If Kitty wanted anything she would always get it. I remember one time when she got it into her head to do a Ph.D. and the way she cosied up to this poor little Dean of the biological sciences was shameful. She never did the Ph.D. It was just another of her whims. She was a phoney. All her political convictions were phoney, all her ideas were borrowed. Honestly, she's one of the few really evil people I've known in my life."[125] Later I was to agree with that opinion.

In May 1941 Kitty gave birth to their first child, Peter, who was nicknamed Pronto, from the speed of his arrival after the marriage. Robert has recalled what happened next:

> In August 1941, I bought [a house at number 1] Eagle Hill at Berkeley for my wife, which was the first home we had of our own. We settled down to live in it with our new baby. We had a good many friends, but little leisure. My wife was working in biology at the university. Many of the men I had known went off to work on radar and other aspects of military research. I was not without envy of them; but it was not until my first connection with the rudimentary atomic-energy enterprise that I began to see any way in which I could be of direct use.[126]

CHAPTER 9

"THE SHATTERER OF WORLDS"

On January 6, 1939, it was announced[127] by Otto Hahn (1879–1968) and Fritz Strassmann (1902–1980) that they had made a discovery that must be called staggering. Among the byproducts of neutron-uranium collisions they had identified three isotopes of barium, which have nuclear charge roughly half that of uranium! Up till that time nuclear reactions never had produced changes in nuclear charge larger than two units. It was the first observation of nuclear fission. (The first explanation, and the name "fission," came from Lise Meitner and Otto Frisch.)

Glenn Seaborg (1912–1999) has remembered "a seminar [in Berkeley] in January 1939 when [fission was] excitedly discussed. I do not recall ever seeing Oppie so stimulated and so full of ideas. . . . [It was] his first encounter with the phenomena that was to play such an important role in shaping the future course of events in his life."[128] A letter by Robert to a colleague, starting with "The U business is unbelievable,"[129] is also bubbling with ideas about this novel branch of nuclear physics. Later he has written, "Ever since the discovery of nuclear fission, the possibility of powerful explosives based on it had been very much on my mind, as it had on that of many other physicists."[130]

When in 1941 Lawrence began work in Berkeley on separating the uranium isotope 235, Oppenheimer and a group of his students worked directly with him. In June of that year the United States Office of Scientific Research and Development (OSRD) was established for the purpose of coordinating scientific-military projects. In December came Pearl Harbor and the United States' entry into World War II. In January 1942 Oppenheimer was made responsible for fast-neutron research in Berkeley, part of OSRD's Section S-1 on uranium work. Soon thereafter Robert acquired regular secretarial help and began keeping files of official correspondence. In May he was appointed director of S-1. In the summer of 1942 he organized a session in Berkeley to explore theoretical aspects of nuclear explosions, for which he was now directly responsible. "After these studies there was little doubt that a potentially world-shattering undertaking lay ahead."[130] So got underway what was then assumed to be a race with Germany to develop a fission weapon.

Enter Leslie Richard Groves (1896–1970).

Early in 1942 Colonel Groves was in charge of all Army construction, including that of the Pentagon. On September 17, 1942, he was ordered to drop everything else and devote himself to Project Y, the code name for the atomic bomb work. Feeling that physicists could best be awed by military rank, he put off meeting them for a few days until a promised promotion to brigadier general came through.

Right away a difficult question arose: who should be the scientific head of the project? Consulting physicists, Robert's name continued to be mentioned. However, according to Groves, "Oppenheimer had two major disadvantages—he had almost no administrative experience of any kind, and he was not a Nobel Prize winner."[132] The first reservation was true, the second was irrelevant, as Groves himself admitted later.

The two men met for the first time in Berkeley in October 1942. Groves started to fire questions at Robert which he answered to his [G.'s] satisfaction. When Groves congratulated him on being intelligible about the bomb, Oppenheimer made the reply that he made to everybody in those days. "There are no experts," he said absently. "The field is too new."[133] Groves liked that and so, from the very beginning, the two of them got along, though there would be occasional moments of friction later on.

Groves has written:

> In a few weeks it became apparent that we were not going to find a better man; so Oppenheimer was asked to undertake the task.
> But there was still a snag. His background included much that was not to our liking by any means. The security organization, which was not yet under my complete control, was unwilling to clear him because of certain of his associations, particularly in the past. I was thoroughly familiar with everything that had been reported about Oppenheimer. As always in security matters of such importance, I had read all the available original evidence; I did not depend upon the conclusions of the security officers.

Finally, because I felt that his potential value outweighed any security risk, and to remove the matter from further discussion, I personally wrote and signed the following instructions to the District Engineer on July 20, 1943:

> In accordance with my verbal directions of July 15, it is desired that clearance be issued for the employment of Julius Robert Oppenheimer without delay, irrespective of the information which you have concerning Mr. Oppenheimer. He is absolutely essential to the project.

I have never felt that it was a mistake to have selected and cleared Oppenheimer for his wartime post. He accomplished his assigned mission and he did it well.[134]

Meanwhile Oppenheimer had discussed with Groves the need for an atomic bomb laboratory.

> There had been some thought of making this laboratory a part of Oak Ridge. For a time there was support for making it a Military Establishment in which key personnel would be commissioned as officers; and in preparation for this course I once went to the Presidio to take the initial steps toward obtaining a commission. After a good deal of discussion with the personnel who would be needed at Los Alamos and with General Groves and his advisors, it was decided that the laboratory should, at least initially, be a civilian establishment in a military post. While this consideration was going on, I had showed General Groves Los Alamos; and he almost immediately took steps to acquire the site. . . .
>
> The last months of 1942 and early 1943 had hardly hours enough to get Los Alamos established. The real problem had to do with getting to Los Alamos the men who would make a success of the undertaking. For this we needed to understand as clearly as we then could what our technical program would be, what men we would need, what facilities, what organization, what plan. . . . We had to recruit at a time when the country was fully engaged in war and almost every competent scientist was already involved in the military effort.
>
> The primary burden of this fell on me. To recruit staff I travelled all over the country talking with people who had been working on one or another aspect of the atomic-energy enterprise, and people in radar work, for example, and underwater sound, telling them about the job, the place that we were going to, and enlisting their enthusiasm.[135]

On March 15, 1943, Oppenheimer and a few of his staff arrived in Los Alamos. In the official history of the laboratory it has been recorded:

> The Los Alamos site, together with a large surrounding area, was established as a military reservation. The community, fenced and guarded, was made an army post. The laboratory, in turn, was built within an inner fenced and guarded area, called "Technical Area." Both the military and technical administrations were responsible to Major General L. R. Groves, who had overall executive responsibility for the work. . . . Oppenheimer, as Scientific Director, was also responsible to General Groves . . . [He] was responsible for security policy and administration."[136]

Los Alamos participants included a group of British physicists. An anecdote: Groves once remarked about them, "These Britishers are odd. At four o'clock in the afternoon they don't drink Coca Cola. They drink *tea*!

Quite understandably, a few months after starting this colossal enterprise, Oppenheimer

> was undergoing a real crisis in self-confidence. The heady experience of creating a new laboratory and pulling together the disparate parts of the scientific work had been stimulating and euphoric. Then came a reaction. On several occasions in the early summer of 1943 [a friend] found Oppenheimer depressed by the magnitude and complexity of the director's task. He told [the friend] he could not go through with it, but [his friend's] advice was simple: Oppenheimer had no alternative, for no one else could do the job.[137]

In 1944 Robert's second child was born in Los Alamos, Katherine, called Toni by everyone.

Without exception, all those who participated in the work at Los Alamos speak with great admiration and high praise of Oppenheimer's leadership of the atomic bomb project. I myself was not there, having lived in Holland until well after the two bombs on Japan were dropped. I shall give two samples of opinions of friends of mine who themselves have played leading roles in the enterprise.

By Weisskopf:

> [Oppenheimer] did not direct from the head office. He was intellectually and even physically present at each significant step; he was present in the laboratory or in the seminar rooms when a new effect was measured, when a new idea was conceived. It was not that he contributed so many ideas or suggestions; he did so sometimes, but his main influence came from his continuous and intense presence, which produced a sense of direct participation in all of us. It created that unique atmosphere of enthusiasm and challenge that pervaded the place throughout its time. I remember vividly the sessions of the co-ordinating council, a regular meeting of all group leaders where progress and failures were reviewed and future plans were discussed. The discussions covered everything: physics, technology, organization, administration, secrecy regulations and our relations to the Army.
>
> It was most impressive to see Oppie handle that mixture of international scientific prima donnas, engineers, and army officers, forging them into an enthusiastically productive crowd. The project was not without tensions and clashes between personalities, but he dealt with these problems with a light hand, and he knew how to exploit conflicts in a productive way. I remember the weekly colloquium. . . . Oppenheimer insisted on having these regular colloquia against the opposition of the security-minded people, who wanted each man only to know his part of the work. He knew that each one must know the whole thing if he was to be creative.[138]

By Bethe:

> Los Alamos might have succeeded without him, but certainly only with much greater strain, less enthusiasm, and less speed. As it was, it was an unforgettable

experience for all the members of the laboratory. There were other wartime laboratories of high achievement. . . . But I have never observed in any one of these other groups quite the spirit of belonging together, quite the urge to reminisce about the days of the laboratory, quite the feeling that this was really the great time of their lives.

That this was true of Los Alamos was mainly due to Oppenheimer. He was a leader. It was clear to all of us, whenever he spoke, that he knew everything that was important to know about the technical problems of the laboratory, and he somehow had it well organized in his head. But he was not domineering, he never dictated what should be done. He brought out the best in all of us, like a good host with his guests. And because he clearly did his job very well, in a manner all could see, we all strove to do our job as best we could.

One of the factors contributing to the success of the laboratory was its democratic organization. . . . Everybody in the laboratory felt a part of the whole and felt that he should contribute to the success of the program. Very often a problem discussed would intrigue a scientist in a completely different branch of the laboratory, and he would come up with an unexpected solution.

This free interchange of ideas was entirely contrary to the organization of the Manhattan District as a whole. . . . Oppenheimer had to fight hard for free discussion among all qualified members of the laboratory. But the free flow of information and discussion, together with Oppenheimer's personality, kept morale at its highest throughout the war.[139]

The first atomic bomb explosion occurred in 1945. The place: a corner of Alamogordo Air Force Base, baptized Trinity by Oppenheimer, situated in the desolate area aptly called Jornado del Muerto, some 300 miles south of Los Alamos. The time: July 16, at 5:30 AM. The purpose: to test if such gadgets would work and if so what their yield would be. The test object: Fat Man, a five-kilogram plutonium bomb and its very bulky detonating mechanism, an implosion device, the whole encased in a five-foot-wide, nine-and-a-half-foot-long container, sprouting incongruous tail fins at the narrow end. (A model can be viewed at the Los Alamos Museum.)

I shall not try to describe the intense labors by many at Los Alamos, with its downs and ups, which climaxed at Trinity since, as said, I was far away from that scene, and also because a quite detailed official account[136] and a superb history[140] of these efforts have meanwhile been published. Instead I shall confine myself to a few comments on Robert while he was present at the test. "Physicists gathered around Oppenheimer to bandy a dreary new word of the twentieth century—*fallout*. . . . [He] was the only one wearing a coat. Too emaciated to sweat, he had kept on his familiar sloppy tweed suit, which now fitted him like a tent. . . . [According to a colleague] Oppenheimer . . . struck me as keyed up to the last degree of strain and tension. . . . Oppenheimer's face was tense and dreamy—

withdrawn—until the moment that it was lit by reflections from the sand. Then it relaxed visibly."[141]

What he and his colleagues saw at that moment must count among the most spectacular events in the history of the world. "Without a sound, the sun was shining; or so it looked."[142] For a few seconds there was silence then a thunderous roar.

"A few people laughed, a few people cried, most people were silent," Oppenheimer recalled. "There floated through my mind a line from the Bhagavad-Gita in which Krishna is trying to persuade the Prince that he should do his duty: 'I am become death, the shatterer of worlds.'"[143] Typical Robert, too exalted for my taste. I like ever so much better what Ken Bainbridge (1904–1996), the official test leader, said to Oppenheimer when, flushed with the success of the test, he came over to Robert, "Now we're all sons of bitches!" Also typical was the immediate reaction by Groves, "This is the end of traditional warfare!"[144]

Some ten years later, Robert reflected like this about Trinity:

It was a success. I believe that in the eyes of the War Department, and other knowledgeable people, it was as early a success as they had thought possible, given all the circumstances, and rather a greater one. There were many indications from the secretary of war and General Groves, and many others, that official opinion was one of satisfaction with what had been accomplished. At the time, it was hard for us in Los Alamos not to share that satisfaction, and hard for me not to accept the conclusion that I had managed the enterprise well and played a key part in its success. But it needs to be stated that many others contributed the decisive ideas and carried out the work which led to this success and that my role was that of understanding, encouraging, suggesting and deciding. It was the very opposite of a one-man show.[145]

I conclude this account of Trinity with a recollection of Rabi, who was also there, retold by Davis, which sets the tone of what is to follow.

"The experience was hard to describe," he says, "I haven't got over it yet. It was awful, ominous, personally threatening. I couldn't tell why." Dawn found him still in reverie as he watched the blockhouse party approaching from a long way off across the sand. Oppenheimer parked too far away for Rabi to see his face, but something in his bearing brought Rabi's gooseflesh back again. He moved like a confident stranger, darkly glittering, at ease, in tune with the thing. "I'll never forget his walk," says Rabi. "I'll never forget the way he stepped out of the car."[146]

CHAPTER 10

IN WHICH OPPENHEIMER ENTERS THE WORLD STAGE

On April 12, 1945, President Roosevelt died. Three days later Oppenheimer scheduled a Sunday morning memorial service in Los Alamos, where "Oppie spoke very quietly for two or three minutes out of his heart and ours. It was Robert Oppenheimer at his best: 'When, three days ago, the world had word . . . many wept who are unaccustomed to tears, many men and women, little enough accustomed to prayer, prayed to God.'"[147]

In the early hours of May 7, 1945, General Eisenhower dictated the following telegram to the combined chiefs of staff of United States military forces: "The mission of this Allied force was fulfilled at 0241, local time." The war in Europe was over.

It was therefore obvious that atomic weapons, not yet even tested that day, would be deployed against Japan, if used at all. On May 9, a committee appointed by President Truman to study this issue, known as the Interim Committee on Atomic Energy, held its first meeting. On May 31, Oppenheimer was in Washington to start a new phase of his career: statesman of science.

"I welcomed the opportunity . . . to serve, along with [Arthur] Compton, Lawrence, and Fermi, on an advisory Scientific Panel to [the] Interim Committee."[145] On that May 31, the Committee met in full dress together with the Scientific Panel. From the notes of that meeting we learn that it was decided not to give the Japanese advance warnings if atomic weapons were to be dropped.[148] On June 16 the Panel made recommendations on the immediate use of atomic weapons.[149] Writing for the Panel, Oppenheimer said:

The opinions of our scientific colleagues on the initial use of these weapons are not unanimous: they range from the proposal of a purely technical demonstration to that of the military application best designed to induce surrender. Those who advocate a purely technical demonstration would wish to outlaw the use of atomic weapons, and have feared that if we use the weapons now our position in future negotiation will be prejudiced. Others emphasize the opportunity of saving American lives by immediate military use, and we believe that such use will improve the international prospects, in that they are more concerned with the prevention of war than with the elimination of this specific weapon. We find ourselves closer to these latter views; we can propose no technical demonstration likely to bring an end to the war; we see no acceptable alternates to direct military use.[149]

As he was later to recall, "We didn't know beans about the military situation in Japan. We didn't know whether they could be caused to surrender by other means or whether the invasion was really inevitable. But in the backs of our minds was the notion that the invasion was inevitable because we had been told that."[149a]

On August 6, 1945, at 8:16:02 local time, an atomic bomb exploded over Hiroshima at a height of about 1,800 feet, with a yield of 12,500 tons TNT. It was a uranium bomb, nicknamed Little Boy.

"Back at Los Alamos, Oppenheimer read the message flashed [to him] fifteen minutes after the drop, and called the whole staff of the laboratory together in one of the camp auditoria. 'He entered that meeting like a prize fighter [recalls one scientist]. As he walked through the hall there were cheers and shouts and applause all round and he acknowledged them with the fighters' salute—clasping his hands together above his head as he came to the podium.'"[150]

On August 9 at 11:02 AM a Fat Man exploded over Nagasaki with a force estimated at 22,000 tons TNT. Two days earlier, 6 million leaflets had been dropped over 47 Japanese cities with populations exceeding 100,000 in which the Japanese were urged to petition the emperor to end the war. On August 10, the Japanese conditional surrender offer reached Washington.

I recall a discussion with Rabi, many years after these events, in which I said that I could understand the dropping of the first bomb but that the second one seemed criminal to me. Rabi replied that I clearly did not understand the military mind. After having produced two distinct kinds of weapons at enormous cost, he said, it was inconceivable that the military would not try out both with at least one shot. Whereupon I said that his point was well taken but did not change my mind.

The work of the Scientific Panel was by no means done after war's end. Their next assignment was to consider further planning regarding atomic weapons. Already on August 16 we find Oppenheimer back in Washington, carrying a report on these matters to Secretary of War Harry Stimson (1867–1950). It is a wise and far-seeing document. I quote from its covering letter.[151]

TO THE SECRETARY OF WAR
                                                    August 17, 1945
Dear Mr. Secretary:

The Interim Committee has asked us to report in some detail on the scope and program of future work in the field of atomic energy. One important phase of this work is the development of weapons; and since this is the problem which has dominated our war time activities, it is natural that in this field our ideas should be most definite and clear, and that we should be most confident of answering adequately the questions put to us by the committee. In examining these questions we have, however, come on certain quite general conclusions, whose implications for national policy would seem to be both more immediate and more profound than those of the detailed technical recommendations to be submitted. . . .

1. We are convinced that weapons quantitatively and qualitatively far more effective than now available will result from further work on these problems. . . .
2. We have been unable to devise or propose effective military countermeasures for atomic weapons. . . . It is our firm opinion that no military countermeasures will be found which will be adequately effective in preventing the delivery of atomic weapons. . . .
3. We are not only unable to outline a program that would assure to this nation for the next decades hegemony in the field of atomic weapons; we are equally unable to insure that such hegemony, if achieved, could protect us from the most terrible destruction.
4. The development, in the years to come, of more effective atomic weapons, would appear to be a most natural element in any national policy of maintaining our military forces at great strength; nevertheless we have grave doubts that this further development can contribute essentially or permanently to the prevention of war. We believe that the safety of this nation—as opposed to its ability to inflict damage on an enemy power—cannot lie wholly or even primarily in its scientific or technical prowess. It can be based only on making future wars impossible. It is our unanimous and urgent recommendation to you that . . . all steps be taken, all necessary international arrangements be made, to this one end.

                                                    Very sincerely,
                                                    J. R. Oppenheimer
                                                    For the Panel

Some time later, Oppenheimer sat in a barber shop with Stimson shortly before the latter left office. The two talked about the bomb: "At the end the old man rose from the chair and turned to Oppenheimer, 'Now it is in your hands,' he said."[152]

These few words summarize succinctly yet eloquently Robert's meteoric rise to influence in the corridors of power. His fame had spread far and wide. Rabi has said, "After the war Oppenheimer was hailed in print and talk as the great humanist, sage and wizard of the scientific world. His name carried magic. When he showed up in San Francisco, crowds gathered on the pavement around him."[153] Already on August 7, the day after Hiroshima, we find in the *New York Times* the first mention of Oppenheimer as the director of the scientific aspects of the atomic bomb project. The article is accompanied by the first picture ever of Robert in the world press, in which he looks quite haggard. On August 8 the *Times* quoted an associate of Robert, "Oppie is smart . . . he's the smartest of the lot in everything."

In March 1946, Robert Patterson, Stimson's successor, presented Oppenheimer with the United States Medal for Merit. The accompanying citation praised him for "his great scientific experience and ability, his inexhaustible energy, his rare capacity as an organizer and executive, his initiative and resourcefulness, and his unswerving devotion to duty."

On October 16, 1945, General Groves presented the Los Alamos Laboratory with a certificate of appreciation from the secretary of war. Robert's brief acceptance speech is a masterpiece of his elegant use of the English language:

> It is with appreciation and gratitude that I accept from you this scroll for the Los Alamos Laboratory, for the men and women whose work and whose hearts have made it. It is our hope that in the years to come we may look at this scroll, and all that it signifies, with pride.
> Today that pride must be tempered with profound concern. If atomic bombs are to be added as new weapons to the arsenals of the warring world, or to the arsenals of nations preparing for war, then the time will come when mankind will curse the names of Los Alamos and Hiroshima.
> The peoples of this world must unite or they will perish. This war that has ravaged so much of the earth has written these words. The atomic bomb has spelled them out for all men to understand. Other men have spoken them, in other times, of other wars, of other weapons. They have not prevailed. There are some, misled by a false sense of human history, who hold that they will not prevail today. It is not for us to believe that. By our works we are committed, committed to a world united, before this common peril, in law, and in humanity.[153a]

The next day Oppenheimer's successor as director took over.

CHAPTER 11

AN ATOMIC SCIENTIST'S CREDO

On November 2, 1945, Robert gave his farewell speech to Los Alamos, long remembered by the packed audience of some 500 members of the Association of Los Alamos Scientists. That address might well have been entitled "An Atomic Scientist's Credo." It shows how, only three months after the fateful atomic bombing of Japan, Oppenheimer, the man who, one may assume, knew more about both the technological and the political consequences of the new weapons than anyone else, had already a clear view of what he called "the fix we are in," to wit, the insuperable difficulties attendant on atomic arms control, the central issue of what soon would become known as the Cold War, which was to last for the next 40 years. I find this address so important that I reproduce it here in full:

> I am grateful to the Executive Committee for this chance to talk to you. I should like to talk tonight—if some of you have long memories perhaps you will regard it as justified—as a fellow scientist, and at least as a fellow worrier about the fix we are in. I do not have anything very radical to say, or anything that will strike most of you with a great flash of enlightenment. I don't have anything to say that will be of an immense encouragement. In some ways I would have liked to talk to you at an earlier date—but I couldn't talk to you as a Director. I could not talk, and will not tonight talk, too much about the practical political problems which are involved. There is one good reason for that—I don't know very much about practical politics. And there is another reason, which has to some extent restrained me in the past. As you know, some of us have been asked to be technical advisors to the Secretary of War, and through him to the President. In the course of this we have naturally discussed things that were on our minds and have been made, often very willingly, the recipient of confidences; it is not possible to speak in detail about what Mr. A thinks and Mr. B doesn't think, or

what is going to happen next week, without violating these confidences. I don't think that's important. I think there are issues which are quite simple and quite deep, and which involve us as a group of scientists—involve us more, perhaps than any other group in the world. I think that it can only help to look a little at what our situation is—at what has happened to us—and that this must give us some honesty, some insight, which will be a source of strength in what may be the not-too-easy days ahead. I would like to take it as deep and serious as I know how, and then perhaps we come to more immediate questions in the course of the discussion later. I want anyone who feels like it to ask me a question and if I can't answer it, as will often be the case, I will just have to say so.

What has happened to us—it is really rather major, it is so major that I think in some ways one returns to the greatest developments of the twentieth century, to the discovery of relativity, and to the whole development of atomic theory and its interpretation in terms of complementarity, for analogy. These things, as you know, forced us to reconsider the relations between science and common sense. They forced on us the recognition that the fact that we were in the habit of talking a certain language and using certain concepts did not necessarily imply that there was anything in the real world to correspond to these. They forced us to be prepared for the inadequacy of the ways in which human beings attempted to deal with reality, for that reality. In some ways I think these virtues, which scientists quite reluctantly were forced to learn by the nature of the world they were studying, may be useful even today in preparing us for somewhat more radical views of what the issues are than would be natural or easy for people who had not been through this experience.

But the real impact of the creation of the atomic bomb and atomic weapons— to understand that one has to look further back, look, I think, to the times when physical science was growing in the days of the Renaissance, and when the threat that science offered was felt so deeply throughout the Christian world. The analogy is, of course, not perfect. You may even wish to think of the days in the last century when the theories of evolution seemed a threat to the values by which men lived. The analogy is not perfect because there is nothing in atomic weapons—there is certainly nothing that we have done here or in the physics or chemistry that immediately preceded our work here—in which any revolutionary ideas were involved. I don't think that the conceptions of nuclear fission have strained any man's attempts to understand them, and I don't feel that any of us have really learned in a deep sense very much from following this up. It is in a quite different way. It is not an idea—it is a development and a reality—but it has in common with the early days of physical science the fact that the very existence of science is threatened, and its value is threatened. This is the point that I would like to speak a little about.

I think that it hardly needs to be said why the impact is so strong. There are three reasons: one is the extraordinary speed with which things which were right on the frontier of science were translated into terms where they affected many living people, and potentially all people. Another is the fact, quite accidental in many ways, and connected with that speed, that scientists themselves played such a large part, not merely in providing the foundation for atomic weapons, but in actually making them. In this we are certainly closer to it than any other group. The third is that the thing we made—partly because of the technical nature of the problem, partly because we worked hard, partly because we had good breaks—really arrived in the world with such a shattering reality and suddenness that there was no opportunity for the edges to be worn off.

In considering what the situation of science is, it may be helpful to think a little of what people said and felt of their motives in coming into this job. One always has to worry that what people say of their motives is not adequate. Many people said different things, and most of them, I think, had some validity. There was in the first place the great concern that our enemy might develop these weapons before we did, and the feeling—at least, in the early days, the very strong feeling—that without atomic weapons it might be very difficult, it might be an impossible, it might be an incredibly long thing to win the war. These things wore off a little as it became clear that the war would be won in any case. Some people, I think, were motivated by curiosity, and rightly so; and some by a sense of adventure, and rightly so. Others had more political arguments and said, "Well, we know that atomic weapons are in principle possible, and it is not right that the threat of their unrealized possibility should hang over the world. It is right that the world should know what can be done in their field and deal with it." And the people added to that that it was a time when all over the world men would be particularly ripe and open for dealing with this problem because of the immediacy of the evils of war, because of the universal cry from everyone that one could not go through this thing again, even a war without atomic bombs. And there was finally, and I think rightly, the feeling that there was probably no place in the world where the development of atomic weapons would have a better chance of leading to a reasonable solution, and a smaller chance of leading to disaster, than within the United States. I believe all these things that people said are true, and I think I said them all myself at one time or another.

But when you come right down to it the reason that we did this job is because it was an organic necessity. If you are a scientist you cannot stop such a thing. If you are a scientist you believe that it is good to find out how the world works; that it is good to find out what the realities are; that it is good to turn over to mankind at large the greatest possible power to control the world and to deal with it according to its lights and its values.

There has been a lot of talk about the evil of secrecy, of concealment, of control, of security. Some of that talk has been on a rather low plane, limited really to saying that it is difficult or inconvenient to work in a world where you are not free to do what you want. I think that the talk has been justified, and that the almost unanimous resistance of scientists to the imposition of control and secrecy is a justified position, but I think that the reason for it may lie a little deeper. I think that it comes from the fact that secrecy strikes at the very root of what science is, and what it is for. It is not possible to be a scientist unless you believe that it is good to learn. It is not good to be a scientist, and it is not possible, unless you think that it is of the highest value to share your knowledge, to share it with anyone who is interested. It is not possible to be a scientist unless you believe that the knowledge of the world, and the power which this gives, is a thing which is of intrinsic value to humanity, and that you are using it to help in the spread of knowledge, and are willing to take the consequences. And, therefore, I think that this resistance which we feel and see all around us to anything which is an attempt to treat science of the future as though it were rather a dangerous thing, a thing that must be watched and managed, is resisted not because of its inconvenience—I think we are in a position where we must be willing to take any inconvenience—but resisted because it is based on a philosophy incompatible with that by which we live, and have learned to live in the past.

There are many people who try to wiggle out of this. They say the real importance of atomic energy does not lie in the weapons that have been made; the real importance lies in all the great benefits which atomic energy, which the various radiations, will bring to mankind. There may be some truth in this. I am sure that there is truth in it, because there has never in the past been a new field opened up where the real fruits of it have not been invisible at the beginning. I have a very high confidence that the fruits—the so-called peacetime applications—of atomic energy will have in them all that we think, and more. There are others who try to escape the immediacy of this situation by saying that, after all, war has always been very terrible; after all, weapons have always gotten worse and worse; that this is just another weapon and it doesn't create a great change; that they are not so bad; bombings have been bad in this war and this is not a change in that—it just adds a little to the effectiveness of bombing; that some sort of protection will be found. I think that these efforts to diffuse and weaken the nature of the crisis make it only more dangerous. I think it is for us to accept it as a very grave crisis, to realize that these atomic weapons which we have started to make are very terrible, that they involve a change, that they are not just a slight modification: to accept this, and to accept with it the necessity for those transformations in the world which will make it possible to integrate these developments into human life.

As scientists I think we have perhaps a little greater ability to accept change, and accept radical change, because of our experiences in the pursuit of science. And that may help us—that, and the fact that we have lived with it—to be of some use in understanding these problems.

It is clear to me that wars have changed. It is clear to me that if these first bombs—the bomb that was dropped on Nagasaki—that if these can destroy ten square miles, then that is really quite something. It is clear to me that they are going to be very cheap if anyone wants to make them; it is clear to me that this is a situation where a quantitative change, and a change in which the advantage of aggression compared to defense—of attack compared to defense—is shifted, where this quantitative change has all the character of a change in quality, of a change in the nature of the world. I know that whereas wars have become intolerable, and the question would have been raised and would have been pursued after this war, more ardently than after the last, of whether there was not some method by which they could be averted. But I think the advent of the atomic bomb and the facts which will get around that they are not too hard to make—that they will be universal if people wish to make them universal, that they will not constitute a real drain on the economy of any strong nation, and that their power of destruction will grow and is already incomparably greater than that of any other weapon—I think these things create a new situation, so new that there is some danger, even some danger in believing, that what we have is a new argument for arrangements, for hopes, that existed before this development took place. By that I mean that much as I like to hear advocates of a world federation, or advocates of a United Nations organization, who have been talking of these things for years—much as I like to hear them say that here is a new argument, I think that they are in part missing the point, because the point is not that atomic weapons constitute a new argument. There have always been good arguments.

The point is that atomic weapons constitute also a field, a new field, and a new opportunity for realizing pre-conditions. I think that when people talk of the fact that this is not only a great peril, but a great hope, this is what they should mean. I do not think they should mean the unknown, though sure, value of industrial and scientific virtues of atomic energy, but rather the simple fact that in this field, because it is a threat, because it is a peril, and because it has certain special characteristics, to which I will return, there exists a possibility of realizing, of beginning to realize, those changes which are needed if there is to be any peace.

Those are very far-reaching changes. They are changes in the relations between nations, not only in spirit, not only in law, but also in conception and feeling. I don't know which of these is prior; they must all work together, and only the gradual interaction of one on the other can make a reality. I don't agree with those who say the first step is to have a structure of international law. I don't agree with those who say the only thing is to have friendly feelings. All of these things will be involved. I think it is true to say that atomic weapons are a peril which affect everyone in the world, and in that sense a completely common problem, as common a problem as it was for the Allies to defeat the Nazis. I think that in order to handle this common problem there must be a complete sense of community responsibility. I do not think that one may expect that people will contribute to the solution of the problem until they are aware of their ability to take part in the solution. I think that it is a field in which the implementation of such a common responsibility has certain decisive advantages. It is a new field, in which the position of vested interests in various parts of the world is very much less serious than in others. It is serious in this country, and that is one of our problems. It is a new field, in which the role of science has been so great that it is to my mind hardly thinkable that the international traditions of science, and the fraternity of scientists, should not play a constructive part. It is a new field, in which just the novelty and the special characteristics of the technical operations should enable one to establish a community of interest which might almost be regarded as a pilot plant for a new type of international collaboration. I speak of it as a pilot plant because it is quite clear that the control of atomic weapons cannot be in itself the unique end of such operation. The only unique end can be a world that is united, and a world in which war will not occur. But those things don't happen overnight, and in this field it would seem that one could get started, and get started without meeting those insuperable obstacles which history has so often placed in the way of any effort of cooperation. Now, this is not an easy thing, and the point I want to make, the one point I want to hammer home, is what an enormous change in spirit is involved. There are things which we hold very dear, and I think rightly hold very dear; I would say that the word democracy perhaps stood for some of them as well as any other word. There are many parts of the world in which there is no democracy. There are other things which we hold dear, and which we rightly should. And when I speak of a new spirit in international affairs I mean that even to these deepest of things which we cherish, and for which Americans have been willing to die—and certainly most of us would be willing to die—even in these deepest things, we realize that there is something more profound than that; namely, the common bond with other men everywhere. It is only if you do that that this makes sense; because if you approach the problem and say, "We know what is right and we would like to use the atomic bomb to persuade you

to agree with us," then you are in a very weak position and you will not succeed, because under those conditions you will not succeed in delegating responsibility for the survival of men. It is a purely unilateral statement; you will find
yourselves attempting by force of arms to prevent a disaster.

I want to express the utmost sympathy with the people who have to grapple
with this problem and in the strongest terms to urge you not to underestimate
its difficulty. I can think of an analogy, and I hope it is not a completely good
analogy: in the days in the first half of the nineteenth century there were many
people, mostly in the North, but some in the South, who thought that there
was no evil on earth more degrading than human slavery, and nothing that they
would more willingly devote their lives to than its eradication. Always when I
was young I wondered why it was that when Lincoln was President he did not
declare that the war against the South, when it broke out, was a war that slavery
should be abolished, that this was the central point, the rallying point, of that
war. Lincoln was severely criticized by many of the Abolitionists as you know,
by many then called radicals, because he seemed to be waging a war which did
not hit the thing that was most important. But Lincoln realized, and I have only
in the last months come to appreciate the depth and wisdom of it, that beyond
the issue of slavery was the issue of the community of the people of the country,
and the issue of the Union. I hope that today this will not be an issue calling for
war; but I wanted to remind you that in order to preserve the Union Lincoln
had to subordinate the immediate problem of the eradication of slavery, and
trust—and I think if he had had his way it would have gone so—to the conflict of
these ideas in a united people to eradicate it.

These are somewhat general remarks and it may be appropriate to say one or
two things that are a little more programmatic, that are not quite so hard to get
one's hands on. That is, what sort of agreement between nations would be a
reasonable start. I don't know the answer to this, and I am very sure that no a
priori answer should be given, that it is something that is going to take constant
working out. But I think it is a thing where it will not hurt to have some reasonably concrete proposal. And I would go a step further and say of even such
questions as the great question of secrecy—which perplexes scientists and other
people—that even this was not a suitable subject for unilateral action. If atomic
energy is to be treated as an international problem, as I think it must be, if it is to
be treated on the basis of an international responsibility and an international common concern, the problems of secrecy are also international problems. I don't
mean by that that our present classifications and our present, in many cases inevitably ridiculous, procedures should be maintained. I mean that the fundamental
problem of how to treat this peril ought not to be treated unilaterally by the
United States, or by the United States in conjunction with Great Britain.

The first thing I would say about any proposals is that they ought to be
regarded as interim proposals, and that whenever they are made it be understood and agreed that within a year or two years—whatever seems a reasonable
time—they will be reconsidered and the problems which have arisen, and the
new developments which have occurred, will cause a rewriting. I think the only
point is that there should be a few things in these proposals which will work in
the right direction, and that the things should be accepted without forcing all of
the changes, which we know must ultimately occur, upon people who will not
be ready for them. This is anyone's guess, but it would seem to me that if you

took these four points, it might work: first, that we are dealing with an interim solution, so recognized. Second, that the nations participating in the arrangement would have a joint atomic energy commission, operating under the most broad directives from the different states, but with a power which only they had, and which was not subject to review by the heads of State, to go ahead with those constructive applications of atomic energy which we would all like to see developed—energy sources, and the innumerable research tools which are immediate possibilities. Third, that there would be not merely the possibility of exchange of scientists and students; that very, very concrete machinery more or less forcing such exchange should be established, so that we would be quite sure that the fraternity of scientists would be strengthened and that the bonds on which so much of the future depends would have some reinforcement and some scope. And fourth, I would say that no bombs be made. I don't know whether these proposals are good ones, and I think that anyone in this group would have his own proposals. But I mention them as very simple things, which I don't believe solve the problem, and which I want to make clear are not the ultimate or even a touch of the ultimate, but which I think ought to be started right away; which I believe—though I know very little of this—may very well be acceptable to any of the nations that wish to become partners with us in this great undertaking.

One of the questions which you will want to hear more about, and which I can only partly hope to succeed in answering, is to what extent such views— essentially the view that the life of science is threatened, the life of the world is threatened, and that only [by] a profound revision of what it is that constitutes a thing worth fighting for and a thing worth living for can this crisis be met—to what extent these views are held by other men. They are certainly not held universally by scientists; but I think they are in agreement with all of the expressed opinions of this group, and I know that many of my friends here see pretty much eye to eye. I would speak especially of Bohr, who was here so much during the difficult days, who had many discussions with us, and who helped us reach the conclusion that [it was] not only a desirable solution, but that it was the unique solution, that there were no other alternatives.

I would say that among scientists there are certain centrifugal tendencies which seem to me a little dangerous, but not very. One of them is the attempt to try, in this imperiled world, in which the very function of science is threatened, to make convenient arrangements for the continuance of science, and to pay very little attention to the preconditions which give sense to it. Another is the tendency to say we must have a free science and a strong science, because this will make us a strong nation and enable us to fight better wars. It seems to me that this is a profound mistake, and I don't like to hear it. The third is even odder, and it is to say, "Oh give the bombs to the United Nations for police purposes, and let us get back to physics and chemistry." I think none of these are really held very widely, but they show that there are people who are desperately trying to avoid what I think is the most difficult problem. One must expect these false solutions, and overeasy solutions, and these are three which pop up from time to time.

As far as I can tell in the world outside there are many people just as quick to see the gravity of the situation, and to understand it in terms not so different from those I have tried to outline. It is not only among scientists that there are wise people and foolish people. I have had occasion in the last few months to meet people who have to do with the Government—the legislative branches, the administrative branches, and even the judicial branches, and I have found many in whom an understanding of what this problem is, and of the general lines along which it can be solved, is very clear. I would especially mention the former Secretary of War, Mr. Stimson, who, perhaps as much as any man, seemed to appreciate how hopeless and how impractical it was to attack this problem on a superficial level, and whose devotion to the development of atomic weapons was in large measure governed by his understanding of the hope that lay in it that there would be a new world. I know this is a surprise, because most people think that the War Department has as its unique function the making of war. The Secretary of War has other functions.

I think this is another question of importance: that is, what views will be held on these matters in other countries. I think it is important to realize that even those who are well informed in this country have been slow to understand, slow to believe that the bombs would work, and then slow to understand that their working would present such profound problems. We have certain interests in playing up the bomb, not only we here locally, but all over the country, because we made them, and our pride is involved. I think that in other lands it may be even more difficult for an appreciation of the magnitude of the thing to take hold. For this reason, I'm not sure that the greatest opportunities for progress do not lie somewhat further in the future than I had for a long time thought.

There have been two or three official statements by the President which defined, as nearly as their in some measure inevitable contradictions made possible, the official policy of the Government. And I think that one must not be entirely discouraged by the fact that there are contradictions, because the contradictions show that the problem is being understood as a difficult one, is temporarily being regarded as an insoluble one. Certainly you will notice, especially in the message to Congress, many indications of a sympathy with, and an understanding of, the views which this group holds, and which I have discussed briefly tonight. I think all of us were encouraged at the phrase "too revolutionary to consider in the framework of old ideas." That's about what we all think. I think all of us were encouraged by the sense of urgency that was frequently and emphatically stressed. I think all of us must be encouraged by the recognition, the official recognition by the Government of the importance—of the overriding importance—of the free exchange of scientific ideas and scientific information between all countries of the world. It would certainly be ridiculous to regard this as a final end, but I think that it would also be a very dangerous thing not to realize that it is a precondition. I am myself somewhat discouraged by the limitation of the objective to the elimination of atomic weapons, and I have seen many articles—probably you have, too—in which this is interpreted as follows: "Let us get international agreement to outlaw atomic weapons and then let us go back to having a good, clean war." This is certainly not a very good way of looking at it. I think, to say it again, that if one solves the problems presented by the atomic bomb, one will have made a pilot plant for solution of the problem of ending war.

But what is surely the thing which must have troubled you, and which troubled me, in the official statements was the insistent note of unilateral responsibility for the handling of atomic weapons. However good the motives of this country are—I am not going to argue with the President's description of what the motives and the aims are—we are 140 million people, and there are two billion people living on earth. We must understand that whatever our commitments to our own views and ideas, and however confident we are that in the course of time they will tend to prevail, our absolute—our completely absolute—commitment to them, in denial of the views and ideas of other people, cannot be the basis of any kind of agreement.

As I have said, I had for a long time the feeling of the most extreme urgency, and I think maybe there was something right about that. There was a period immediately after the first use of the bomb when it seemed most natural that a clear statement of policy, and the initial steps of implementing it, should have been made; and it would be wrong for me not to admit that something may have been lost, and that there may be tragedy in that loss. But I think the plain fact is that in the actual world, and with the actual people in it, it has taken time, and it may take longer, to understand what this is all about. And I am not sure, as I have said before, that in other lands it won't take longer than it does in this country. As it is now, our only course is to see what we can do to bring about an understanding on a level deep enough to make a solution practicable, and to do that without undue delay.

One may think that the views suggested in the President's Navy Day speech are not entirely encouraging, that many men who are more versed than we in the practical art of statesmanship have seen more hope in a radical view, which may at first sight seem visionary, than in an approach on a more conventional level.

I don't have very much more to say. There are a few things which scientists perhaps should remember, that I don't think I need to remind us of; but I will, anyway. One is that they are very often called upon to give technical information in one way or another, and I think one cannot be too careful to be honest. And it is very difficult, not because one tells lies, but because so often questions are put in a form which makes it very hard to give an answer which is not misleading. I think we will be in a very weak position unless we maintain at its highest the scrupulousness which is traditional for us in sticking to the truth, and in distinguishing between what we know to be true from what we hope may be true.

The second thing I think it right to speak of is this: it is everywhere felt that the fraternity between us and scientists in other countries may be one of the most helpful things for the future; yet it is apparent that even in this country not all of us who are scientists are in agreement. There is no harm in that; such disagreement is healthy. But we must not lose the sense of fraternity because of it; we must not lose our fundamental confidence in our fellow scientists.

I think that we have no hope at all if we yield in our belief in the value of science, in the good that it can be to the world to know about reality, about nature, to attain a gradually greater and greater control of nature, to learn, to teach, to understand. I think that if we lose our faith in this we stop being scientists, we sell out our heritage, we lose what we have most of value for this time of crisis.

But there is another thing: we are not only scientists; we are men, too. We cannot forget our dependence on our fellow men. I mean not only our material dependence, without which no science would be possible, and without which we could not work; I mean also our deep moral dependence, in that the value of science must lie in the world of men, that all our roots lie there. These are the strongest bonds in the world, stronger than those even that bind us to one another, these are the deepest bonds—that bind us to our fellow men.[153b]

Some days after his farewell speech, the Oppenheimers left for Pasadena. "In November 1945, I resumed my teaching at the California Institute of Technology, with an intention and hope, never realized, that this should be a full-time undertaking. The consultation about postwar matters which had already begun continued, and I was asked over and over both by the Executive and the Congress for advice on atomic energy. I had a feeling of deep responsibility, interest, and concern for many of the problems with which the development of atomic energy confronted our country."[154]

I shall have much more to say about Robert's advisory activities regarding atomic energy but shall turn first to what happened next in his academic life.

CHAPTER 12

THE INSTITUTE PRIOR TO OPPENHEIMER'S ARRIVAL

In the early 1950s, Oppenheimer, then director of the Institute, commissioned Mrs. Beatrice Stern (1895–1987) to write the Institute's early history. During 1955–1957 she interviewed a number of people, including me. In 1964 she had completed a 700-page typed manuscript, "A History of the Institute for Advanced Study, 1930–1950," which has never appeared in print because Robert felt that some of the material was too personal to be made public. I understand why he thought so but have never considered it a reasonable position, particularly because that document is well written and contains quite valuable information on the origins and early years of one of the most important American institutions of higher learning. Since I find this material so interesting—I own a copy of the manuscript—I thought it would be fitting to use it for giving at this point a few glimpses of the Institute's history up to the time that Oppenheimer took over as director. I shall go easy on personal matters, which would cause no raised eyebrows anyway, since the persons involved are all deceased by now. I may also note that in 1980 the Institute has published a book, *A Community of Scholars*, published by Princeton University Press.

I now turn to explaining how the Institute came to owe its origins and immediate renown to a bizarre confluence of factors: generous philanthropy, the Wall Street crash of 1929, and the rise of Nazism in the early 1930s.

In the autumn of 1929, two elderly residents of South Orange, New Jersey, near Newark, were quietly searching for a philanthropy worthy to be endowed with their ample fortune. One was Louis Bamberger (1855–1944), a lifelong bachelor, the other his sister Julie Carrie Fuld (1864–1944), the childless widow of Felix Fuld (1868–1929). Both were natives of Baltimore; their parents were German Jews of Bavarian origin. In 1929 they were living on the 30-acre Fuld Estate in South Orange.

Louis was a modest and quiet man. Almost shy in manner, he gave an impression that was belied by his shrewd, quick mind and the firmness of his decisions. He attended Baltimore public schools until age 14, when he went to work as a clerk and errand boy in a dry goods store, working himself up steadily. In 1892 he was ready to start his own business, in Newark. The firm, run in partnership with Felix Fuld, a personal friend, and a native of Frankfurt-am-Main who had come to America at age 14, was named L. Bamberger and Company. It grew into New Jersey's largest retail business and one of the nation's largest department stores. Under Bamberger's direction the store pioneered in modern retailing techniques and was among the first to provide such conveniences as a restaurant and customer parking. Always interested in the welfare of his employees, Louis provided a fully staffed educational department for their benefit.

In 1927 the firm issued $10 million worth of 6.5 per cent preferred stock, of which the original partners held $2 million, allowing senior employees to purchase shares on the installment plan. The borrowing financed an expansion of the store to afford more than one million square feet of floor space. With the growth of L. Bamberger and Company the area around it became one of the most prosperous in the city.

Mr. Bamberger and the Fulds came to be known as wise and generous contributors to civic programs for the health and welfare of their fellow citizens, as well as for their cultural development. Aside from regular support of community charities, they gave the city a delightful Art Museum and many *objets d'art*.[155] Mr. Bamberger was a trustee of the New Jersey Historical Association, to which he gave a building. Mrs. Fuld, a shy woman, avoiding publicity, frequently seeking anonymity in making her donations, is credited with bringing to Newark its first chamber music ensemble. The two were also patrons of Jewish organizations.

On January 20, 1929, Felix Fuld died. The next day the flags on Newark's public buildings were flown at half staff, the first time such a tribute was paid there to a private citizen. On January 22, he was memorialized in a *New York Times* editorial, where it was estimated that his contributions to public charity had totaled more than 2.5 million.

Mr. Bamberger and Mrs. Fuld realized that they could now no longer carry the burdens of the business. The following summer they decided to sell the store to R. H. Macy & Co. and to devote their time and fortune to philanthropy. The sale was consummated in early September. They received $11 million in cash plus 69,210 shares of Macy's stock, which on September 4 reached a high of $255.50 a share on the New York Stock Exchange.

Six weeks later, on October 29, the stock market crashed. On November 13 the Macy shares had fallen to $110; by June 1932 they had sunk to $17. Whatever the Bambergers did with their shares, they still had $11 million in the bank.

These events marked the beginning of a tragic period in world history, yet in those very same years they led to the founding of an institution that would leave its glorious mark on the world of thought and learning.

From the outset Louis and Carrie wanted to direct their philanthropy toward the support for higher learning. Their initial inclination was to establish and endow a medical school either in Newark or on the Fuld Estate. Because they knew that men and women of Jewish extraction were discriminated against by existing medical schools in the selection of staff and students, they preferred preferential treatment of Jews in both groups.

However, they needed assurances that such a project was feasible and could be realized with the means they intended to devote to it. Upon confidential consultations they learned that one individual was recurrently mentioned as the outstanding authority in medical education: Dr. Abraham Flexner (1866–1959).

Flexner has been characterized as brilliant, imaginative, intense, and indefatigable, a man of great energy and strong convictions, animated by high ideals. He began his career by teaching Greek at a high school in his native Louisville. In 1905 he left that city, intending with the zeal of a true reformer to work in national education administration.[156] In 1908 he published a small, bold book[157] decidedly critical of the American college system, whereupon he was commissioned by the Carnegie Foundation for the Advancement of Teaching to survey the quality of medical colleges in the United States and Canada. In 1910 the Foundation published their *Bulletin No. 4*, which became known as the *Flexner Report*.[158] It exposed American medicine as a shallow enterprise and made its author internationally renowned. Eighteen years later, the *New York Times* editorialized as follows about this report:

It dealt fearlessly, trenchantly and discerningly with the standards, methods and personnel of the existing American medical schools, mercilessly castigating all that was sordid and unwholesome, and holding up to view the ideals toward which they should aspire. This knight errant, whose lance was at the command of those ideals, was anathematized by some who suffered from his criticisms, [but according to others] it is now generally recognized that the thorough ventilation of the subject by the report was most timely, and that Mr. Flexner's investigations and recommendations were weighty contributions to the progress of educational reform. . . .

. . . His knight-errantry has not been confined to the field of medical education. He has tilted not only against diploma mills but also against the opium traffic. He has dared to say what he thinks about the movies, motors and jazz. He has spoken out plainly about education in high places—attacking certain traditional methods and disciplines, but condemning also the introduction of new courses wholly devoid of educational values just for the sake of adding to numbers or gratifying a vulgar demand. He has had the temerity even to raise the question whether we Americans really value education in spite of the amount we spend for it. He has a bright record of achievement to his credit, and though he has approached the time of official retirement, it is to be hoped that there will be an epilogue, for he is a wholesome challenging force in the world.[159]

That epilogue became his central role in the founding of the Institute for Advanced Study.

The first contact between Flexner and representatives of Bamberger took place in December 1929. It became immediately evident that Flexner disapproved of the proposed medical school. Such a school, he said, should be a graduate school in a strong university, administered by the trustees of the whole institution. It must offer opportunities for training in the medical sciences. It must moreover own or control and operate a good hospital where its clinical staff could devote their full time to teaching at the bedside, to the care of patients, and to research. Newark was too close to New York with its several great medical schools to offer effective competition for staff or students. It possessed neither a university nor an available hospital. If these failings were not enough to dispose of the idea, Flexner said his experience had convinced him that men and women of the Jewish faith or origin were not being discriminated against, and that none but the highest professional standards should ever be applied in selecting the staff and students in any institution of learning. There was no ground for discrimination by other criteria, he maintained.

At the time of that meeting, Flexner was finishing a book that came out in 1930.[160] In its first chapter, entitled: "The Idea of a Modern University," already at hand, he revealed his plan for a "society of scholars," and pleaded for "creative activity, productive and critical inquiry . . . minds which can both specialize and generalize." He suggested to the Bambergers that no better use of the money could be made in the public interest than through the endowment of such an institution as it described. His visitors, deeply impressed with his vision and his fervor, departed with a copy in hand, promising to read it and to refer it to their principals.

Mr. Bamberger and Mrs. Fuld were interested. Promptly they invited their advisors and Dr. Flexner to dine with them. They recognized in Flexner an authority in medical education that caused them quickly to relinquish their own idea, for it seems that most of the discussion thereafter was devoted to consideration of various applications of Flexner's *Idea*. He had much in his favor; he was an able advocate, well informed, and convincing. To them he must have been even more than that, with the prestige derived from his connection with the General Education Board, and his well-publicized management of the Rockefeller money for medical education. Indeed, there seemed to be little difficulty in persuading them to abandon their intention to benefit preferentially the people of any particular race or religion. When they separated, it was with plans to continue their discussions at lunch on Saturdays at the Biltmore Hotel.

Thus the origins of the Institute can be traced to an extraordinary set of circumstances: philanthropists wishing to establish a medical school contact America's leading expert on the subject, who dissuades them from their plans and guides them to his own concept of a society of scholars.

Flexner has left in the files of the Institute for Advanced Study copies of three separate plans, each differing in important respects from the others, and all sequestered in an envelope bearing in his handwriting the legend "Legal Papers. Working Papers, Formation of the Institute." I select from these documents those items that have become central to the Institute's style of operation.

Its teachers were to be men and women of the "highest calibre;" they were to specialize as teachers "in the subjects in which they have achieved unusual proficiency." They would have "unlimited opportunity to continue study and enlarge their knowledge," and would teach only students selected because of "their qualifications and adeptness." The entire atmosphere would be such as to develop "great specialists in particular fields of the arts and sciences." No regard was to be given to race or creed in operating the institution. It should be established in the vicinity of Newark, "upon lands which one may convey or devise to it for the purpose or failing which, upon such lands as it may acquire. . . . As conditions in the realm of advanced instruction and research improve, it is our desire that the trustees of this institution advance the ideals of the institution so that it may at all times be distinguished for quality and at no time by consideration of numbers." These plans appear to have been almost wholly acceptable to Mr. Bamberger and his sister, as is seen by their memorandum dated January 20, 1930, also found in the "Legal Papers" envelope.

Early in 1930 the plan began to take shape. Flexner to the Bambergers:

> The Institute will be neither a current university nor a research institution. . . . It may be pictured as a wedge between the two—a small university in which a limited amount of teaching and a liberal amount of research are both to be found. It should be small, its staff and students should be few, the administration should be inconspicuous. . . . I should, one by one . . . create a series of schools—in mathematics, in economy, in history, etc. . . . [The faculty will] know their own minds. . . . No organizer can do more than furnish conditions favorable to the restless prowling of an enlightened and informed human spirit.

A draft by the Bambergers, dated April 23, 1930 (again in the "Legal Papers"), starts out as follows: "To (naming proposed Trustees): We are asking you to serve with us as Trustees of an Institute of Higher Learning or Advanced Studies to the endowment of which we propose ultimately to devote our residual estate—the proposed Institute to be situated in the State of New Jersey in grateful recognition of the opportunities which we have enjoyed in this community."

I name here only one of the founding Trustees since, as we shall see, his path will cross on a variety of occasions with Oppenheimer. Lewis Lichtenstein Strauss (1869–1974)(he pronounced his name "Straws," as they did back in Virginia, from where he hailed), who at that time was the president of the Bamberger Corporation, also trustee of New York University and the New York Public Library.

On May 20, 1930, the certificate of incorporation of the Institute was signed. Its complete text is found in *Bulletin No. 1*, published in December 1930 by the Institute, the address for which was given as 100 East 42nd Street, New York. An initial donation of $5 million was made. Louis Bamberger became the first president of the Board of Trustees, Mrs. Fuld the first vice president, Flexner the first director. On June 6, the founders addressed a letter to the Trustees that said in part:

> It is fundamental in our purpose, and our express desire, that in the appointments to the staff and faculty, as well as in the admission of workers and students, no account shall be taken, directly or indirectly, of race, religion, or sex. We feel strongly that the spirit characteristic of America at its noblest, above all, the pursuit of higher learning, cannot admit of any conditions as to person-

nel other than those designed to promote the objects for which this institution is established, and particularly with no regard whatever to accidents of race, creed or sex.

The *New York Times* generously reported these events, quoting the entire Letter of the Founders to the Trustees, and giving additional details. The founders and the director were commended for the deliberateness with which this unique institution was to be developed. It would be the first and only one of its kind in the country. When Dr. Flexner returned from Europe he "would undertake to enlist outstanding teachers in their respective fields as members of the faculty." The Institute would be coeducational, accepting on an equal footing people of all races and creeds meeting its high standards. The laudable purpose to establish an institution exclusively post-graduate in its activities was warmly approved.

The story continued: "At the Bamberger offices it was said that temporary quarters . . . could be obtained without using any of the $5 million endowment. It was also explained that the initial endowment would be augmented from time to time to provide for such expansion as might become necessary. For the present no medical department will be operated, but it is expected that such a department may be added eventually."[161]

Four months later another *Times* item appeared with the headlines: "Dr. Flexner says Bamberger new Institute bans collegiate ideas/University will be without rules/Athletics also banned," and reported that it will be "somewhere in or near New Jersey."[162]

During the first half of 1931, Flexner elicited advice from leading scholars in America and Europe. This resulted in a confidential memorandum to the trustees, dated September 26, 1931. It is an excellent document, in which one finds the main outline of what the Institute was to become all about. I quote from this long memorandum:

> I have in mind the evolution that in the process of centuries has taken place at All Souls College, Oxford, where, as in the proposed Institute, there are no undergraduate students, and where advanced students and the older Fellows live under ideal conditions, whether for their individual work or for collaboration and cooperation. No one planned all this. It grew up because scholars were left free to work out their own salvation. . . .
>
> The decision not to begin with the physical or biological sciences has become stronger; they are already better done than other subjects; moreover, they are creating problems with which universities are not now dealing competently . . . they are not at the very foundation of modern science. That foundation is mathematics; and it happens that mathematics is not a subject in which at present many American universities are eminent. Mathematics is the severest of all disciplines, antecedent, on the one hand, to science, on the other, to philosophy

and economics and thus to other social disciplines. With all its abstractness and indifference both pure and applied scientific and philosophic progress of recent years has been closely bound up with new types and methods of sheer mathematical thinking. . . .

Beyond these two schools [mathematics and economics], I do not now look, though it is obvious how readily history and other schools—literature, music, or science—can be added when money, men, and ideas are available.

A contributory pension scheme should be open to all connected with the Institute. It does not help the clarity or concentration of a man's thinking, if he is oppressed by the fear of a needy or precarious old age, if on retirement his scale of living, already none too lavish, has to be suddenly reduced, if his wife is compelled to forego domestic help, if his children are deprived of liberal educational opportunities. . . . Surely the nation which has built palaces for libraries, laboratories, and students will not permanently ignore the professor who is in truth the University itself. . . .

The Institute for Advanced Study needs no press. . . . I favor a strict policy in respect to publication . . . Publicity need not be sought: if the Institute succeeds, the real problem will be how to avoid or restrict it. . . .

We shall find ourselves dealing with men and women, not with angels or super-men. Difficulties will arise; disappointments will occur. But we shall be helped, not harmed, by the high level at which we have pledged ourselves to act. In any case, unless we attempted something much higher than is now attained, there would be little reason to attempt anything at all.

Next Flexner turned to the recruitment of faculty. For that purpose he went in January 1932 on a visit to the California Institute of Technology, invited by Robert Millikan. That institution was of particular interest to him for his present purposes. It had started out in 1891 as Throop College, and had only recently been modernized under its new name with a much-expanded prominent faculty—just what Flexner was after.

By Flexner's own account, it was serendipitous that there in Pasadena he met, for the first time, Albert Einstein, who was a guest professor that winter term. Flexner of course used the opportunity to consult with the great man on his projects. When they met again, in Oxford in the spring of 1932, he asked Einstein if he might be interested in joining the Institute himself. During a third encounter the next June, this time in Einstein's summer house in Caputh, near Berlin, Einstein expressed enthusiasm about coming and requested an annual salary of $3,000. "He asked . . . could I live on less?"[163] Formal negotiations began at once. In October 1932 the appointment was approved, with an annual salary of $15,000.[164] Einstein regarded Flexner's offer as a "sign from heaven" that he should prepare to migrate to America.[165] He made his definitive move in October 1933. Also that autumn the appointment was made of the mathematician Oswald Veblen

(1880–1960)—the nephew of the social scientist Thorstein Veblen (1857–1929)—who had been on Princeton University's faculty since 1905.

There was no ceremony as the Institute opened at the beginning of October 1933, days before Einstein's arrival. From that time on through 1938 its official address was 20 Nassau Street, Princeton. The Institute was open year-round but term times were short—from mid-September to mid-December, and from late January to late April. And so it has remained.

It may be noted that in 1931 the New Jersey State Board of Education had granted the Institute the authority to issue the Ph.D. degree—an authority that the Institute never has made use of.

Meanwhile a committee with the directive to choose a site for Institute buildings had been constituted. It had already begun its deliberations in December 1931. The founders had expressed the desire to house the Institute in Newark, preferably on the Fuld Estate. This idea was abandoned after outside advisers had opposed the idea. In 1935 a consensus developed to buy the Olden Farm in Princeton—265 acres of field, woodland, and meadows. Olden Manor, the old colonial house on the farm, would eventually become the director's home. In 1938 construction was put in the hands of the Hegemann-Harris firm of New York at an estimated cost of $312,000. By the time Fuld Hall, the main building ("named to commemorate both Mrs. Fuld and her late husband"[166]), was completed, the total cost (including furnishings) had come to $520,000. The top floor of the Hall housed a cafeteria and a board room. The Bambergers provided additional funds, and by 1952 their total gifts had risen to $16 million, including the $9 million Bamberger had left as a residual estate upon his death in 1944.

Twelve more professorial appointments were made in the 1930s. They were, in mathematics (year of appointment and country of birth in parentheses): James Alexander (1933, U.S.) (1888–1971); Marston Morse (1935, U.S.) (1892–1977); John von Neumann (1933, Hungary) (1903–1957); and Herman Weyl (1933, Germany) (1885–1955). In economics: David Mitrany (1933, Romania) (1888–1975); Winfried Riefler (1935, U.S.) (1897–1974); Walter Stewart (1938, U.S.) (1885–1958); and Robert Warren (1939, U.S.) (1891–1956). Also Edward Earle (1934, U.S.) (1894–1954) in political history; Erwin Panofsky (1935, Germany) (1892–1968) in history of art; Hetty Goldman (1935, U.S.) (1881–1972) in archeology; and Elias Lowe (1936, U.S.) (1879–1969) in paleography. Hitler's contributions to this elite group will be obvious. Thus came into being the Institute's initial three schools: of mathematics, including physics; of economics and politics; and of humanistic studies.

Additional temporary appointments of junior people were made from the start. Through 1935 Institute *Bulletins* listed them as "workers," initially all in the school of mathematics. The *Bulletin* for 1934 lists 23: 6 from Europe, 17 from the United States. Beginning in 1936 they were called "members." Academic year 1935–1936 saw the arrival of the first nonmathematics members. By 1938, members from 18 foreign countries had been in attendance. Furthermore, scientists of high distinction were invited to come; in physics: Dirac (in academic year 1934–1935), Pauli (1935–1936; he also spent the war years in Princeton, from 1940–1946), Niels Bohr, and I. I. Rabi (both for part of 1938–1939). Where did all these people find working space?

Arrangements were made with the University to rent space for the mathematicians and physicists in Fine Hall, the gracious old mathematics building (now Jones Hall). Humanists found their quarters in McCormick Hall. The Institute bought a large old residence at 69 Alexander Street and remodeled it for use as offices, where they installed the economists. (The house was sold during the war.)

Until late 1939 there were almost no meetings of the faculty as a whole— Flexner did not approve of them. Beginning on October 8, 1935, the School of Mathematics faculty did meet on its own, however, and Veblen became the powerful though unofficial leader of that group. It may be noted that he led opposition to Einstein, for example refusing to lend funds for an assistant. The reason was presumably the mathematicians' insistence on keeping mathematics "pure" (more about that later). Einstein's lack of success in formulating a unified field theory and his critical position toward quantum theory may also have been contributing factors.

Aided by his appointment to the Board of Trustees, Veblen became the power broker of the faculty, often at odds with the director. He made himself responsible for many business affairs and played a role in the selection of new faculty members. His colleagues were complaisant with his control as long as they got what they needed—which was not always the case. And so, since its early years, the Institute has served as an apt example of the dictum that academic politics is such a big thing because its problems are so small.

One last item concludes my brief account of the Institute's beginnings: the acquisition of the Gest Oriental Library. In 1937 the Institute purchased the Gest collection, assisted by a grant of $62,500 from the Rockefeller Foundation,[167] with the understanding that it was to be administered as part of the Princeton University Library. The collection was initially installed at 20 Nassau Street, but in 1948 it was moved into the Firestone Library. It is now on permanent loan in the library of the Gest Institute in the top floor of Palmer Hall.

The Gest collection is matchless among all Chinese collections outside of China and Japan. It contains books printed well before the appearance of the Gutenberg Bible (book shops have been recorded in China as early as the first century AD), and a large collection of manuscript volumes, the oldest of which dates from the sixth century and is a copy of chapters from a Buddhist *sutra*. The library contains some 700 books from the Sung (960–1279), 1,700 from the Yüan (1279–1368), and 24,000 from the Ming (1368–1644) dynasties. By 1965 the Gest collection comprised 190,000 books, of which over 100,000 are stitched volumes (ts'ê).[168]

In 1939, the year of completion of Fuld Hall, Flexner resigned as director, no doubt worn out by quarrels with his faculty. He was succeeded by Frank Aydelotte (1880–1956), president of Swarthmore College, who, on November 24, 1939, called the first full faculty meeting held in Fuld Hall. It was fitting that the first order of business would deal with a resolution of thanks from faculty and trustees to Dr. Flexner.

The main contribution of Aydelotte was the introduction in 1944 of Institute fellows, mainly recent postdocs appointed for one or two years. No further professorial appointments were made during his tenure. That was the situation when Robert Oppenheimer arrived on the scene.

As I reflect on Oppenheimer's appointment to Institute director, I wonder again, as I have done before, whether he would have accepted that position had he known what a hornet's nest he would get into. A few glances back may explain that state of affairs.

The Flexner Years

On February 10, 1936, Flexner had called the whole faculty together—a rare event at that time—to discuss his proposal to appoint an associate director. The background for this idea lay in his choice of Frank Aydelotte (1880–1956), president of Swarthmore College, Institute trustee since 1930, as his successor. Already in 1933 he had written to Bamberger: "I feel that I have in him [A.] an 'understudy' whom you and Mrs. Fuld were rightly anxious that I procure."[169] Shortly before talking to the faculty, Flexner had already informed the Board of Trustees of this idea, whereupon that body adopted a resolution that stated in part: "The Director is hereby authorized to submit to the annual meeting of the Board a nomination for the post of Associate Director."[170]

At the February meeting with the faculty, Flexner explained the resolutions recently passed by the trustees. The faculty insisted, however, that in its opinion the idea of an associate director was not feasible.[171]

As far as I know, that point in question marked the beginning of ever-growing discord between Flexner and the faculty, with Veblen as the self-anointed spokesman for the opposition. At the roots of dissension lay the power play between the founders, the trustees, the director and the faculty. Specific issues included new faculty appointments, allocations of space and of funds, financing of homes and of pensions for professors, and the relations between the Institute and Princeton University. I shall pass by a description, given by Mrs. Stern, of what transpired the next few years—not a pleasant story—and move onto 1939. In that year Flexner published a much-quoted article: "The usefulness of useless knowledge,"[172] in which he pointed out that American universities were, it is true, developing, so that seekers after a Ph.D. degree could obtain admirable opportunities; but nowhere, except for the Institute, did there exist the untrammeled facilities for easy-going and informal work between men who had passed the Ph.D. degree stage, had given promise of unusual ability, and who needed now the informal contact with the masters.

Early that same year, Veblen had decided that the director must go; and any way to get him to discredit himself was useful to that purpose. To strike him where he was vulnerable was good tactics even if it was also bad taste and poor ethics. Flexner was well aware of Veblen's overwhelming interest in managing the disposal of rooms within Fuld Hall, the Institute's new home, and determined that the other schools should receive justice in the apportionment of space for their professors and members.

Veblen now started a campaign in the faculty for Flexner's retirement. That he was was able to put Professor Einstein in the forefront of the campaign in the faculty was a masterful achievement. For Einstein was known as one who had been indifferent throughout his academic career to academic politics and administrative matters. His position among all the faculty members was very high; his probity, his independence of thought and judgment, his signal achievements, and his prestige made Veblen's triumph indeed a great one. But Einstein did not engage in intrigue. He felt, however, as did others in the faculty, that great as had been the director's contribution to education and the advancement of knowledge, he was now tired and spent, incapable of further leadership in Institute affairs.

When the trustees were informed of the prevailing mood, its chairman wrote to Flexner: "I confess that I look forward with dismay to your separating yourself from the Institute. You have, in fact, been the Institute. It owes everything except financial support to your vision and your wisdom and your executive direction."[173] Whatever were Flexner's intentions in 1939, he wanted to receive appointment for the next year.[174] The Board did reappoint the director. There appears to have been no discussion.[175]

The ceremonious laying of Fuld Hall's cornerstone took place on May 22, 1939. The founders did not attend. It is not clear whether that was due to Mrs. Fuld's earlier accident that had caused her to be briefly hospitalized. The president of Princeton University gave a brief speech. Thereafter, Miss Lavinia Bamberger, a sprightly sister of the founders, wielding a silver trowel, sealed the cornerstone, speaking the conventional words: "I declare this stone to be well and truly laid."

Dr. Flexner did not speak. Available photographs indicate that there was nothing in the way of a rostrum or speakers' platform outside the bleak and untidy early stages of construction. They also show the director standing alone within the scaffolding amid the bricks and mortar and other paraphernalia of construction, looking bitterly unhappy and discouraged, as though he doubted the reality of the spiritual and intellectual edifice of which the building was to be the outward symbol.

Meanwhile, Professors Earle and Einstein had told some of the trustees that the welfare of the Institute made it necessary that Flexner now retire. Whereupon in late May these trustees told the director that they felt he must do so. Flexner decided, however, to do nothing for the present.[176] This impasse precipitated conflict and intrigue that endured throughout the summer. Veblen accused Flexner of having imperiled the solvency of the Institute. In a letter sent in June, Earle "expressed [to Flexner] my alarm . . . for your openly expressed contempt for fellow-members of the Faculty, sometimes taking the form of personal abuse. . . . It has not been pleasant for me to tell you these things, and it has not been pleasant for you to hear them. . . . All of this proceeds from one who still would make every decision primarily from the point of view of what is best for you and for the great reputation which you have built up over the years. Always affectionately. . . ."[177] Earle also wrote to Aydelotte that 11, perhaps 12, of the 16 professors would likely vote their lack of confidence in the director.[178]

Finally, at a trustee meeting in October, Flexner did announce his retirement. He said that he had not changed his mind as to the impracticability of faculty government but added that "insofar as experience has proved me wrong, my successor should do differently."[179] The trustees accepted the resignation, whereupon Flexner and Aydelotte left the room. After the Board approved Aydelotte, the two men returned, and Aydelotte accepted the position. Flexner had prepared the minutes up to the moment the two men had stepped out. The new director did so for the rest of the meeting.

By then the two men had known each other for 35 years, beginning in Louisville, where young Aydelotte taught English at the school where Flexner taught Greek. At that time Aydelotte was the disciple, Flexner the respected master. As time went by their relation grew into a warm friendship, as witness for example the telegram Aydelotte sent to Flexner after his appointment to Institute director: "Look forward with humility and enthusiasm to the task of carrying out the great dream of foundations [you have] laid."[180]

At that time Flexner wrote to Aydelotte: "I had a long talk with Veblen. . . . He said things not one of which was true. . . . I do not believe that he is wilfully dishonest but he is a queer duck with what [one professor calls] a twisted mind."[181]

In January 1940 a Joint Trustee and Faculty Resolution was offered which starts as follows: "The Trustees and Faculty of the Institute for Advanced Study take the occasion of Dr. Flexner's retirement to record in this joint resolution their sense of permanent indebtedness to him. The character of the Institute has been determined by his faith in the role of the creative scholar in society."[182]

After having garnered from archives my account of Flexner's last years at the Institute, I turned to his autobiography in order to see what retrospective comments he himself might have made on that period that must have been difficult for him. All I found were two phrases on the last page of that book, heavy with meaning:

> The Institute was conceived as a paradise
> for scholars, and such it really is. But not
> all men—not all gifted men—know how to
> live in paradise.[183]

He may have been difficult to get along with at times—I never knew him—but he should be remembered with gratitude as a man of high ideals, without whom there might never have been an Institute.

I did know Veblen, Flexner's main protagonist, with whom I got along very well. I remember the time he took me to lunch in the Nassau Club, when he told me how, after his retirement (in 1950) he planned to read all the books for which he had not found the time in earlier years.

On March 11, 1944, Louis Bamberger died in his sleep just before his ninetieth birthday. From a commemorative editorial: "He wielded his great power with a delicacy and restraint which marked all his actions, and his humility and self-effacing spirit made him appear to be unconscious of his eminence."[184]

Speaking for the Institute, Dr. Aydelotte told the press:

> A native shrewdness and knowledge of human nature . . . enabled him to form sound opinions of men connected with higher scholarship as well as of men of business. He and his sister, Mrs. Fuld, saw instantly the merit of Dr. Abraham Flexner's proposal for an institute devoted to advanced research beyond the doctor's degree. . . . Without pretending to any broad knowledge of education and scholarship Mr. Bamberger sensed the fact that emphasis upon excellence rather than upon size was the greatest need of higher studies in the United States. He made himself one of the great benefactors of American scholarship not merely by the amount of money he gave but still more, I should say, by his selection of the purposes to which his generosity was devoted.[185]

Four months later, on July 18, Carrie Fuld followed her brother in death. She left her residual estate, estimated at $2 million, to the Institute.[186] Aydelotte has written about the founders:

> Mr. Bamberger and Mrs. Fuld sought no recognition for themselves. They left to the Trustees and the Faculty the task of determining the fields of work and the educational policies of the institution which they founded. They wished only to make it as useful as possible to higher learning in America. Their self-lessness, their public spirit, their complete absence of vanity and prejudice are a lesson to every Trustee and to every individual who may benefit by their generosity. They made no speeches to Trustees, Faculty or Members, but by their acts they have laid upon everyone connected with the Institute the injunction "Establish thou the work of our hands."[187]

The Aydelotte Years

Aydelotte's main contribution was the introduction in 1944 of Institute fellows, mainly recent postdocs appointed for one or two years. No further professorial appointments were made during his tenure.

The new director was known among his associates as generous and understanding, warm and kind. These qualities were deeply appreciated by the faculty. Einstein once remarked to Aydelotte's son that it was rare "to find someone who is devoted and independent without vanity—rare to find a man of capacity without vanity."[188]

Veblen's relations with Aydelotte were cordial and warm, as they had never been with Flexner, who inclined to lecture him, while Aydelotte sought his advice. Already, in preparing for his first Board meeting, the new director asked Veblen for comments on his plans.[189]

The next few years were peaceful at the Institute. One reason for this was, oddly, the Second World War:

> For some time before [Pearl Harbor], various members of the Faculty had already been called upon for national service—defense work as it was then called. With the coming of the war the members of our staff began to be greatly in demand for such service and the Trustees adopted a generous policy of releasing members of the Faculty for important war work for which they possessed special qualifications. The requirements of military secrecy make it impossible as yet to tell in detail the story of the war work of the members of our Faculty, but when that story can be told, it will be an extremely interesting and creditable one.
>
> The war has made heavy demands likewise upon our temporary members. Mathematicians and physicists have been needed for teaching and for war research. Economists have been called upon for various types of government service and the members of the School of Humanistic Studies have been able to make interesting and important contributions to the war effort in connection with the invasion of North Africa, Sicily, Italy and Greece, and in the preservation of cultural monuments.
>
> Nevertheless, in the intervals of war work, scholarly research has progressed steadily.[187]

In late 1944 the calm came to an end, however, when tensions arose between Flexner and his successor, who had bitterly disappointed him by not following some of his policies. Flexner was particularly aggrieved by the power Veblen had assumed in the first three and a half years of Aydelotte's administration. Matters came to a head when Flexner heard of Aydelotte's intention to retire at age 65. That focused his rage against the director for what he regarded as a dereliction of duty.

The effect was tragic. Aydelotte, as had Flexner earlier, suddenly found himself not in the position of one who folds his tent and departs with dignity and honor, but on trial, forced to defend his reputation and his administration. The sunny extrovert disappeared; a brooding, bitter introspective man took his place. His many penciled notes show that he suffered torments, listing possible causes for Flexner's disaffection, and concluding that his old friend had connived to cause his downfall. He was entirely unwilling to accept that. With the "permission of the Committee on Policy," he decided to tell the faculty of his intention to retire, feeling that in the new circumstances the faculty would support him.

And so at a social luncheon of the faculty on November 6, Aydelotte mentioned casually that he had told the Committee on Policy that he intended to retire on June 30, 1946, in accord with the retirement policy for professors. He lingered at the meeting long enough to know that his news created consternation and confusion.

The faculty did not like the idea of Aydelotte's retirement either, as is seen by a letter from Veblen to the Policy Committee sent off a few days later:

> I was requested by the Professors to report the consensus of opinion to the Trustees. The consensus was that it is not in the interest of the Institute that Dr. Aydelotte should retire when he reaches the age of sixty-five. The discussion began with expressions of personal regard which must have been most gratifying to Dr. Aydelotte. The essential point brought out by the further discussion was, however, the strong feeling that the present Director knows how to work with scholars. As a result there exists in the Institute a spirit of harmony and effective cooperation which has been reflected in substantial achievements in the past five years. . . . The general opinion was that the Faculty did not wish him to retire at the age of sixty-five.[190]

Aydelotte's reaction: "Endorsement of the Faculty meant more to me than Trustees'. Would like to retire but would not let Faculty down."[191] The upshot of the commotion was the trustees' decision that Aydelotte should retire at age 67. In January 1945 a committee was appointed to nominate the next director.[192]

From the *Institute Bulletin* for 1945–1956:

> The housing shortage in Princeton is even more acute than in most university towns and has been for many years. It has been created partly by the recent advent of research groups connected with the Institute for Advanced Study and the laboratories of the Radio Corporation of America. The difficulty of housing our members has now become so great that the Trustees were faced this summer with the necessity of doing something to meet it or, as an alternative, curtailing the activities of the Institute. We have been so fortunate as to be able to purchase from the Federal Public Housing Authority eleven buildings containing roomy and comfortable apartments for thirty-eight families. During the summer these buildings are being transported from their present location in Mineville, New York, and are being erected in the square bounded by Cook and Goodman Roads between Springdale Avenue and Olden Lane.[193]

They were cut into panels, shipped from Mineville, New York, to Princeton, reassembled and erected where the present housing project stands, and were occupied during the spring semester in 1947. Intrinsically and aesthetically they were no bargain. Yet they had plumbing fixtures and other things which did not become available in the consumers' market for some time. Even with the 38 units, the Institute continued to rent rooms and apartments in the Borough and Township where it was possible to do so, until new housing was provided and became available in 1958. The neighbors on

Newlin Road vocally opposed the new rustic cottages, and the Institute miti-
gated the effect by careful placing and screening shrubs. This housing was
largely replaced to make way for a new modern project in 1958.

> As a logical sequence to the theoretical work which he has been doing for
> some years on the mathematical and logical problems involved in very high-
> speed electronic computing, John von Neumann has begun this year the con-
> struction of an all-purpose computer. This project is supported partly by the
> Institute and partly by the Army Bureau of Ordnance, the Radio Corporation
> of America and Princeton University. A building to house the computer is now
> under construction. When finished the computer will be devoted to theoretical
> work in mathematics such as the solution of non-linear differential equations
> and the theory of meteorology rather than to practical problems.[193]

The formal dedication of the computer did not occur until June 10, 1952.[194]

The Aydelotte episode was Flexner's last involvement with Institute affairs. Upon his retirement as Institute director he devoted his final years to
reading and writing. In 1940 he published his autobiography.[183] In 1942 his
book *Funds and Foundations* came out, a subject on which he was expert. In
1943, partly in fond recollection of his association, first as a student and
later as a close friend of the first president of Johns Hopkins University, he
published *The Biography of President Daniel G. Gilman*. On September 21, 1959,
he died at age 92 in his retirement home in Falls Church, Virginia. Funeral
services and burial were held in his native Louisville.

Flexner was one of the twentieth century's most influential personalities
in the promotion of America's higher education, not only because of his
role in the founding of the Institute but also because of his critique, mentioned earlier,[158] of medical education in the United States, an exposé so
damning that nearly half of its medical schools had to shut down. His later
remark on that activity may serve as a fitting epitaph: "I struck from the
shoulder, naming names and places."[195]

CHAPTER 13

IN WHICH OPPENHEIMER IS ELECTED DIRECTOR OF THE INSTITUTE AND CHAIRMAN OF THE GENERAL ADVISORY COMMITTEE

In October 1945, the chairman of the Trustee Committee on selection wrote his first letter to the members of the faculty, reading in part:

> At the first meeting of the Committee I was instructed to ask members of the Institute's Faculty to suggest persons who should be considered for the directorship. We desire that all members of the Faculty shall be heard on the subject. It is left to the Faculty to decide in what way these suggestions shall be arrived at: the Committee is equally ready to consider one letter from the Faculty as a whole, or individual letters from each member . . . or communications based on any procedures between those two extremes. . . .
>
> During the period of its deliberations the Committee will be glad to confer with individual members of the Faculty, or with a committee representing the Faculty as a whole. . . .[196]

In November 1945, Aydelotte appointed a Faculty Committee on Succession consisting of Professors Alexander, Earle, and Panofsky. In February 1946 these three addressed a letter[197] to the faculty listing seven candidates who had been suggested to it, to which they added two more names shortly afterward. Two on this list are of particular interest: Robert Oppenheimer and Lewis Strauss. It may be noted that Oppenheimer had earlier been considered for a chair in the School of Mathematics, but no action had been taken.[198]

As mentioned before, Strauss had been one of the early Institute trustees. He was reelected to the Board in 1945 and to its chairmanship in 1946. He had been called from his partnership at Kuhn Loeb & Company to active service in the Navy Department in 1941 with the rank of lieutenant commander. He was then 45 years of age. Assigned to the Bureau of Ordnance, where his business experience made him useful, he was soon selected by James Forrestal (1892–1949), then undersecretary, to be one of his several personal assistants. He accompanied his chief to the office of the secretary when Mr. Forrestal was promoted in 1944. He left the Navy early in 1946 with the honorary rank of rear admiral and returned to New York, with a desire to enter public service. He had ample means, and did not need to return to the financial district.

We have now reached the point where Oppenheimer's and Strauss's paths cross—with, eventually, disastrous consequences for both men, as we shall see. This part of the narrative does not start in Princeton, however, but in Washington.

On October 3, 1945, President Truman sent a message to Congress, requesting the establishment of a commission to control the production and use of atomic power in the United States. This led Edwin Johnson (1884–1970), senator from Colorado, and Andrew May (1875–1959), congressman from Kentucky, to introduce a bill that month that did not bar military officers from serving either as administrators or as members of a supervising committee on atomic energy. That feature led many atomic scientists to oppose this bill.

Oppenheimer later recalled that on October 18, "at the request of Secretary Patterson, I testified before the House Committee on Military Affairs in support of the May-Johnson Bill, which I endorsed as an interim means of bringing about without delay the much-needed transition from the wartime administration of the Manhattan Project to postwar management of the atomic energy enterprise."[199] At that time he also urged a worldwide curb on atomic weapons. "Asked if it was a fair estimate that an atomic raid on the U.S. would kill 40 million people, he replied 'I am afraid it is.'"[200]

Already a few days earlier, 400 scientists had protested against the May-Johnson Bill that Oppenheimer had endorsed.[201] "[I]n so many ways Oppenheimer was behaving true to character. He had expected total loyalty and trust when he was teaching and the same when running Los Alamos. Yet again he wanted to do things his way and he was expecting the same level of trust, but now he was operating inside the hard world of American politics and such an approach was certain to be a difficult one."[202]

In November, Robert was in Pasadena to participate in a meeting of a declassification committee set up by Groves.[203] (At this writing [1999] all nontechnical material about Los Alamos 1943–1945 has been declassified, but the Los Alamos Technical Series is still largely secret.[204]) Then, on December 20, Brien McMahon (1903–1953), senator from Connecticut, introduced a bill alternative to May-Johnson, this one excluding the military from any real voice in developing atomic energy.[205] "In December 1945, and later, I appeared at Senator McMahon's request in sessions of his Special Committee on Atomic Energy."[199] The upshot was that May-Johnson was shelved and that, on August 1, 1946, Truman signed the McMahon Bill into law as the Atomic Energy Act of 1946.[206]

In October 1946, President Truman announced the appointment of Strauss to the newly established United States Atomic Energy Commission (AEC).[207] In December the president appointed Oppenheimer to a six-year term as member of the General Advisory Committee (GAC) of the AEC.[208] His colleagues on the GAC elected him as their chairman. Obviously these were positions that would put great demands on these men's time. At any rate, by the end of 1946 no decision on the succession at the Institute had yet been made, even though by then it had been publicly announced that effective October 16, 1947, Aydelotte would retire as Institute director.[209]

Now back to the Institute.

When in September 1946 I began my first day at the Institute with a call on the director, it was Aydelotte whom I met. He turned out to be an amiable man in his midsixties. I remember practically nothing about him, except that he had unusually large ears. It was also Aydelotte who offered me a year's extension of my fellowship at the Institute.[210]

After February 1946, when the faculty had been informed of the list of candidates for the directorship,[197] there followed a period of consultation. Sample, Veblen to Strauss: "Oppenheimer seems to me to have so many of the qualifications that I would have very little misgiving about the future of the Institute if he were chosen. Von Neumann is not as favorable to Oppenheimer as I am, though he has great admiration for him as a scientist. The general opinion among the Faculty is that Oppenheimer would be very welcome as a colleague."[211] This letter is also of interest because it contains a suggestion that had been bandied about among the faculty for some time since: to consider the advantages that might accrue to the Institute should it be administered by the trustees and the faculty with no director at all. "It might be wise to experiment with the continuation of the type of administration which has been in effect during Aydelotte's absence; namely, to vest the functions of the Director in the hands of a 'standing committee.' This method of administration seems to us to have been very satisfactory."[211] Nothing came of that.

In November 1946 Strauss was elected chairman of the Search Committee.[212] In early 1947 the Committee finally took action.

Before calling a meeting of the Trustees' Committee, Admiral Strauss communicated with Professor Edward Mead Earle, Chairman of the Faculty Committee on the directorship, and received from him a list of suggestions of possible candidates. This list was then supplemented by additional names suggested by members of the Board and from outside sources. At a meeting on January 24, 1947, the Committee on the Directorship approved a slate of five names, all of whom were known to be acceptable to the Faculty of the Institute.

By unanimous vote, the . . . Committee authorized Admiral Strauss to approach first Dr. J. Robert Oppenheimer of the University of California. Admiral Strauss took the matter up informally with Dr. Oppenheimer,[213] and is now happy to report to the Trustees that Dr. Oppenheimer has expressed his willingness to accept the position of Director of the Institute for Advanced Study should the Trustees decide to offer it to him. In that event, Admiral Strauss reported that Dr. Oppenheimer has requested that in addition to administrative duties, he be permitted to devote some of his time to teaching in order that he may remain in direct contact with young scholars.

After the circulation of a short biographical sketch of Dr. Oppenheimer, the meeting was thrown open to questions and discussion. Supplementing the biographical material presented to the Trustees, Admiral Strauss stated that Dr. Oppenheimer had been named to the Joint Research and Development Board of the Army and Navy and had also been elected Chairman of the General Advisory Committee of the Atomic Energy Commission. It is understood that Dr. Oppenheimer will continue these duties should he be elected Director of the Institute. Although Dr. Oppenheimer is primarily a theoretical physicist, he has had sound training as a classicist and is known to be deeply interested in humanistic studies.

There was some discussion of Dr. Oppenheimer's request that he be permitted to devote some of his time to teaching and it was pointed out that the Institute's present policy of opening all lectures and seminars to graduate students at Princeton University would probably give Dr. Oppenheimer the contact with young scholars which he desired. In this connection, Admiral Strauss told the Board that he had given the names of the five candidates to President Dodds of Princeton University and that Dodds had expressed the opinion that any one of these individuals would be an ornament to the Princeton community.

Since there were no further questions, it was moved by Admiral Strauss, seconded and unanimously carried that Professor J. Robert Oppenheimer be appointed Director of the Institute for Advanced Study to succeed Dr. Aydelotte on his retirement, with the understanding that his duties and responsibilities will be the same as those of the present Director, and that he shall receive the same emoluments. It is expected that Dr. Oppenheimer will come into residence before the retirement of Dr. Aydelotte and during that period his status will be that of Director-Elect.

The Chairman then presented for discussion the question of ways and means of publicly announcing this decision. . . . It was finally agreed that Admiral Strauss as Chairman of the Committee should extend a formal invitation to Dr. Oppenheimer, get his formal acceptance and then consult him about his wishes concerning the form and timing of the announcement. Admiral Strauss and the Chairman of the Board will then prepare an announcement on behalf of the Institute to be released to the press.[214]

The School of Mathematics was very pleased with the choice for the new director, as can be seen from a memorandum[215] prepared in 1945 by men no less than Einstein and Weyl, when Oppenheimer was under consideration for a professorship:

The School of Mathematics is of the unanimous opinion that theoretical physics not only should continue to form a part of its scientific activities, but should even be reinforced . . .

Since about 1930 the center of gravity of Oppenheimer's work has shifted to nuclear physics. He has studied the genetic relationship between the several elementary particles and radiation, for instance the perturbation of the process of radiation by generation of electron-positron pairs. Perhaps his most original ideas are contained in his papers on the decomposition of deuterons by impact, and on the multiplicative showers of particles which are such a surprising feature in cosmic radiation.

Everywhere, and in particular in his latter work, he shows considerable strength in pursuing a theory into its last consequences, those consequences which are decisive for the whole theoretical foundation. It is characteristic of Oppenheimer that so many of his papers are written in collaboration with other physicists.

During the war he has done excellent administrative work under formidable political and objective difficulties, and without losing any part of his scientific insight and integrity.

Oppenheimer has been a very great influence in the United States in spreading the knowledge of quantum mechanics. He has an enormous capacity for influencing young people, and has founded the largest school of theoretical physics in this country. His interests are broad; he surrounds himself with a brilliant social circle, and his students are very enthusiastic about him. It may be that he is somewhat too dominant, and his students tend to be smaller editions of Oppenheimer.[215]

Oppenheimer himself has recalled his reactions to the Princeton offer:

I came [to the Institute at Princeton] in the late summer, I think, of 1947. I had been a professor at California Institute of Technology and at the University of California at Berkeley. In late 1946, perhaps, or early 1947, the present Chairman of the Atomic Energy Commission [Mr. Strauss] was chairman of the nominating committee to seek a new director to succeed Dr. Aydelotte at the Institute, and he offered me the job, stating that the Trustees and the Faculty desired this.

I did not accept at once. I like California very much, and my job there, but I had . . . not spent very much time in California. Also, the opportunity to be in a small center of scholarship across the board was very attractive to me. Before I accepted the job, and a number of conversations took place, I told Mr. Strauss there was derogatory information about me. In the course of the confirmation hearings, on Mr. Lilienthal especially, and the rest of the Commissioners, I believe Mr. [J. Edgar] Hoover (1895–1972) sent my file to the Commission, and

Mr. Strauss told me that he had examined it rather carefully. I asked him whether this seemed in any way an argument against my accepting this job, and he said no, on the contrary—anyway no.[216]

Oppenheimer must have accepted around April 1, for a few days later Aydelotte wrote to him that he "was delighted to get the good news by telephone from Admiral Strauss."[217] On April 17 the news appeared in leading New York and Philadelphia papers.

Driving across the bridge from San Francisco to Oakland one night in April, Oppenheimer first heard on his car radio that he had been appointed the Institute's new director. "Well," he said to his wife, "I guess that settles it."

A month earlier, an Institute trustee had visited the Oppenheimers in Berkeley. From his diary:

The Oppenheimers have a beautiful house up in the Berkeley hills overlooking the Bay. Mrs. Oppenheimer is an energetic woman of about thirty who is passionately fond of gardening, and their two and one-half acres are planted in profusion with every conceivable shrub and flower, most of which she tends herself. They returned from Los Alamos to Berkeley a year ago expecting to settle down to a quiet existence teaching theoretical physics. But the demands of the State Department and the Atomic Energy Commission on Oppenheimer's time have been incessant. Last week he was in Washington helping Mr. Truman with his speech on Greece. He has been deeply involved in the Lilienthal confirmation controversy, and his advice on using atomic energy for commercial power is being constantly sought. In physical appearance, he is slender with rather slight features, but he has a piercing and imperturbable eye, and a quickness in repartee that gives him great force, and he would immediately command respect in any company. He is only forty-three years of age, and despite his preoccupation with atomic physics, he has kept up his Latin and Greek, is widely read in general history, and he collects pictures. He is altogether a most extraordinary combination of science and the humanities.[218]

Some years later a faculty member was asked what his and his colleagues' impressions were on hearing the news. He replied: "Hell, this is a mecca for intellectuals and we were reading in the *New York Times* every day that Oppenheimer was the greatest intellectual in the world. Of course we wanted him—then."[6]

From the Institute's records: In the faculty meeting of April 21, Aydelotte announced that Oppenheimer would take up provisional residence in Princeton in July. Von Neumann proposed, and the faculty accepted, that Pais be given a five-year membership with annual salary of $6,000—tripling my earlier stipend.

On May 5, Aydelotte and Oppenheimer are both present at the faculty meeting, the latter as director-elect. It is announced that the trustees have approved Pais's five-year appointment.

From my diary, May 27: Lunch with the Oppenheimers and Trustee Herbert Maass (1878–1957) and his wife, at the Aydelottes. It was my first meeting with Oppenheimer's wife, Kitty, a vivacious, petite brunette. Maass tells a story. When Einstein arrived in Princeton, Maass took care of his luggage. A bit later he received an upset telephone call from Mrs. Einstein: something valuable got lost—five pounds of green peas for Einstein's favorite soup.

In mid-July of an unusually hot and humid summer, Oppenheimer, his wife, his son Peter, and his daughter Toni arrived in Princeton to settle.

Among my personal papers I found a printed announcement which reads: "The Trustees and Faculty of the Institute for Advanced Study cordially invite you to meet Dr. and Mrs. Robert Oppenheimer in the common room of Fuld Hall on Thursday, October ninth from four-thirty to six-thirty."

On December 8, Oppenheimer, now director, presided for the first time over a faculty meeting.

Why would the Oppenheimers leave their beautiful Berkeley home, situated in one of America's best climates? I think they came to Princeton not just because of the intellectual appeal of the Institute, but also because of the nearness to Washington, the center of world power to which Oppenheimer felt so strongly drawn. It was to prove unfortunate but true that he relished belonging to America's center of temporal power. If he knew that politics is a saprogenic profession, he did not behave accordingly.

It was Robert's hunger for dominance that made him accept, as we have now seen, not one but two positions in which he could exercise power. First, he was elected chairman of the GAC; next, to director of the Institute. I believe that his life would have been easier if he had declined the Institute position because of the demands as GAC Chairman—or if he had resigned from the GAC because his Institute directorship would have given him enough to fill his needs. That second option would have avoided his placing himself at loggerheads with extremely powerful and vindictive men who would silence his voice.

I shall come back later to that ugly treatment of his, which, however, Robert could have avoided had he not been so extremely arrogant.

At the root of that tragic story lies the "derogatory information" to which Oppenheimer had alluded to Strauss,[216] as mentioned earlier. To conclude this chapter I mention how that information was handled in 1947.

Under the provisions of the Atomic Energy Act of 1946, Oppenheimer had to undergo an examination of his security status by the Atomic Energy

Commission before becoming chairman of the General Advisory Committee. In February of 1947, the Commission cleared him because they knew a great deal about him, he had been appointed by President Truman, and they "had no occasion to raise any question."[219] However, on Saturday, March 8, 1947, a special messenger from the FBI appeared at the Washington offices of the AEC carrying a letter and a document for the Commission's chairman, David Lilienthal. The document was from the FBI's director, J. Edgar Hoover, and was a summary of the files "relative to Julius Robert Oppenheimer . . . and his brother Frank Friedman Oppenheimer." In the accompanying letter, Hoover pressed for a further inquiry into Oppenheimer's associations and background. Thus, the entire question of security clearance was opened again. On March 11, the general manager of the AEC reported that a detailed analysis of the FBI summary was being prepared by the Commission's security staff, and that written views on Oppenheimer's reliability were to be sought from Dr. Vannevar Bush (1890–1974), chairman of the Joint Research and Development Board, General Leslie R. Groves, commander of the Manhattan District, and Dr. James B. Conant (1893–1978), president of Harvard University.[219]

Secretary of War Patterson, concurring with Dr. Bush's endorsement, wrote to the commission that he had "received a most favorable impression" of Oppenheimer's "ability, judgment, character, and devotion to duty," and that he had "confidence in his character and loyalty to the United States."[220] General Groves wrote that he had "reviewed Dr. Oppenheimer's complete record personally," and after "careful study" had decided that Oppenheimer "was fundamentally a loyal American citizen. . . ." Groves felt that due to his overall value to the Manhattan Project, "I ordered accordingly that he be cleared. . . . Since then, I have learned many things amplifying that record but nothing which, if known at that time, would have changed my decision."[221] Finally, Dr. Conant wrote to the Commission:

> I can say without hesitation that there can be absolutely no question of Dr. Oppenheimer's loyalty. Furthermore, I can state categorically that, in my opinion, his attitude about the future course of the United States Government in matters of high policy is in accordance with the soundest American tradition. . . . I base this statement on what I consider intimate knowledge of the workings of his mind. . . . a more loyal and sound American citizen can not be found in the whole United States.[222]

Commission chairman David Lilienthal went to see J. Edgar Hoover on March 25, with representatives of both the AEC and FBI, to discuss the case. All agreed that Oppenheimer had moved away from his left-wing associations of the 1936 to 1942 period, whereupon, with no objections from the White House, and after examining the FBI materials, the AEC commissioners unanimously reaffirmed their clearance of Oppenheimer, since the new FBI reports "contained no information which would warrant reconsideration of the commission's decision."[223] Again in 1950, when Gordon Dean (1905–1958) replaced Lilienthal as head of the AEC, Dean went through the FBI file and cleared Oppenheimer "without a shadow of a reservation." Dean read all new additions to the file until June of 1953, still feeling "no reservations."[219]

From now until 1954 Robert's engagements oscillate between Princeton and Washington. I need to split these activities in two rather than follow their almost parallel timelines. I begin with Princeton.

CHAPTER 14

OPPENHEIMER'S EARLY YEARS AS INSTITUTE DIRECTOR

Soon after the director-elect had settled in his Institute office, as had his new secretary—her name was Eleanor Leary, she had been secretary of Supreme Court Justice Felix Frankfurter (1882–1965), a friend of Robert—he had his first enlightening contacts with the faculty, when he and Aydelotte watched Veblen wrest a room from the School of Economics for a mathematics professor. When Oppenheimer mentioned the possibility of supplanting the School secretaries and their helpers with a stenographic pool, he quickly reversed his field when he realized that academicians become as pleasantly inured to the custodial care of a good secretary as do businessmen and bureaucrats.[224]

Further enlightenment about the real nature of his new position—and the retiring director shared his chagrin—came in that faculty meeting when he referred to the Institute for Advanced Study as "an educational institution." Professors Alexander and Einstein protested that if they had thought of it as an educational institution they would not have come to it; it was a research organization. Aydelotte was as surprised as was Oppenheimer. The word educational was relegated to silence until the new director could study the founding documents and the laws under which the Institute had been incorporated. Those were the first examples for Robert to see how great men can devote themselves to piddling matters.

In December 1947, Oppenheimer, now director, opened his first report to the Trustees with the observation that he was beginning "to get a feeling for how things are at the Institute." The minutes continued:

The Director said he found the School of Mathematics a healthy and flourishing concern. With the very generous help already given to physics, he expressed the hope that that too will flourish.

But in the other schools, perhaps because of a certain insularity in their efforts, the Director felt there are troubles. Very eminent scholars feel that their work is not appreciated; no one seems able to answer the question of why what is going on. The Director saw no solution in blanket rules. He expressed doubt that all members of the School of Economics were in any strict sense interested in or qualified for "advanced study." And in the case of the School of Humanistic Studies there are obviously areas of great fruitfulness beyond the Hellenistic studies in which the Institute is already committed.

There are many fields, in the Director's opinion, in which a beginning could be made. He pointed to two main classifications of effort: (1) the application of scientific methods to fields in which there is really pioneering, and (2) the encouraging of work by men to whom experience in the creative arts has brought deep insight. . . . [He] outlined no specific program for such efforts. His suggestion was that there be opportunity for exploring new fields outside and beyond the specific areas of the schools, which in some cases have narrow interests. For this purpose he asked that there be members who are not members of the schools.

To accomplish his plan, he asked the Trustees to establish a General Fund of $120,000 on a five-year basis. This should be used for stipends, memberships and work not at present part of the activities pursued at the Institute. He suggested an Advisory Committee for the use of the Fund. He expressed the hope that in this way the Institute may carry out its functions in a more experimental way; and thus a coordinate community of scholars may be created.[225]

The Board approved his plan, and appropriated from surplus $20,000 to be used during the next year. It was to be known as the Director's Fund. It was a bold and beautiful plan, and promised to enable the director to break the mold in which the young Institute for Advanced Study was already firmly set.

To the best of my recollection, the first person to come to the Institute with support from the Director's Fund was the poet Thomas Stearns Eliot (1888–1965), who was at the Institute for most of the fall term of 1948. I had read and liked some of his poetry, none more than his *Old Possum's Book of Practical Cats*, the basis for *Cats*, one of the greatest musicals of the 1980s. Naturally, I was dying to have conversations with Eliot but refrained from approaching him, less out of shyness than from an ingrained sense not to bother him with trivia. Yet we had one talk. One day, stepping into the Fuld Hall elevator on my way to the lunch room I found one person already in there: Eliot. I smiled politely then pushed the button. Then he spoke, saying, "This is a nice elevator." I replied, saying, "Yes, this is a nice elevator." That was all the conversation with Eliot I ever had.

While in Princeton, Eliot completed work on his play *The Cocktail Party*. Oppenheimer once said to me he thought that was the worst thing he (E.) ever wrote. While at the Institute, Eliot received word of his award of the Nobel Prize for Literature for 1948 "for having enriched modern poetry with his pioneering work." He left the Institute for Stockholm a few weeks before the end of term. It was Robert's hope to appoint Eliot for a five-year term as member; the faculty was opposed. He never returned.

Another of Robert's invitees was his friend Francis Fergusson, a literary critic and writer, who became cofounder of a series of seminars on literary criticism, named for the Princeton dean Christian Gauss (1878–1951), still held at the University.

In the autumn of 1950 George Frost Kennan (1904–2005) arrived at the Institute for the academic year, also supported by the Director's Fund. He was the author of a famous anonymous article (signed "Mr. X") which stated the policy of containment regarding the Soviet Union.[226] He was on leave from the State Department in order to study and write on American foreign policy of the past 50 years. The appointment went through in spite of serious criticism from the mathematics faculty, which did not consider the man to be a sufficiently pure scholar. In the event, Kennan stayed for five years, supported by liberal grants from the Ford Foundation. His studies were interrupted during 1952, when he served as United States Ambassador to the Court of Joseph Stalin.

Kennan and I developed friendly relations when we found out that we both played the guitar. Every now and then after lunch we would repair to my office, where I had brought one of my guitars. We would play in turn and sing, he Russian folk songs, I those from the West. He was a gentle man, a bit shy, I believe, but warmed up by music.

I conclude my account of the early uses of the Director's Fund by mentioning two psychologists. The first, who stayed through academic 1951–53, was David Levy (1892–1977), a noted psychiatrist who specialized in the relations between infant and mother. He told me how he made his preliminary diagnosis during the first visit of the pair. He would say to the mother: "What a fine baby you have." The motherly mother would reply, "Thank you," looking at the same time lovingly at the child. If, however, she would say "thank you" and look at Levy, then there might be problems. At his invitation I once went with him to his clinic in New York, where I could observe such interviews while sitting in an adjoining room and looking through a one-way transparent window. It was illuminating.

With the second psychologist (1951–52), Jerome ("Jerry") Bruner (1915–), a professor of cognitive psychology, I had numerous discussions on his methods of testing. After one of these, he suggested that I visit his laboratory at Harvard to take tests myself—which I did. I was set down before a lit, opaque glass screen. Jerry pressed a button that caused a picture to appear on the screen for a fraction of a second. Whereafter he asked me to describe what I had seen. Then he showed the same picture again for double the time, asking me to report whether I had seen further details. We went through a sequence of such pictures. Afterward Jerry told me that I was the fastest person he had ever tested. Of pleasant conversations with other Director's Fund visitors I remember those with the psychologist George Miller (1920–), who also became one of my squash partners, and with the linguist Noam Chomsky (1928–).

The Institute's professors found little pleasure (nor did I) and little pride in the accomplishments of Arnold Toynbee (1889–1975), who during 1947–1953 was occasionally at the Institute on a grant from the Rockefeller Foundation.

The freedom the promise of the Director's Fund offered was to suffer from the reporting of an interview that Robert gave to the *New York Times*[227] in which he expressed too openly, perhaps, his own hopes. He was quoted as saying: "First, we expect to invite people who have experience outside the academic field—in business or politics, for example. Second, we [intend to] explore areas which have hitherto not been regarded as subject for scientific investigation."

The reporter continued his own account as follows:

Suppose you could use this fund to invite as your salaried house-guests the world's greatest scholars, scientists and creative artists—your favorite poet, the author of the book that interested you so much, the European physicist with whom you would like to mull over some speculations about the nature of the universe.

That's precisely the set-up that Oppenheimer enjoys. He can indulge every interest and curiosity, because his interests and curiosities correspond with the whole range of science and culture, and that coincides in turn with the scope of the Institute.

Though there was no appearance of a reaction at the time, there could be little doubt that neither the faculty nor the trustees were of the same mind as the director was thus reported to be. Did he intend to reduce the faculty? Had he unlimited power to bring whom he would to the Institute, according to his intellectual whim? Could he call in nonacademic persons? Had he presumed to say that the "interests and curiosities" of the Institute's faculty corresponded with the whole range of science and culture? It is unlikely he thought so, even as a potential; as for the faculty as it existed, they were highly specialized scholars and scientists, only truly at home in their area of expertise. Robert might have taken the precaution to submit the article to them before publication. I consider it a token of his arrogance that he did not do so.

A second indiscretion followed half a year later when he gave an interview to a reporter of *Time* magazine.[228] It is the first time that (as we Americans say) Oppenheimer made the cover of that November issue, showing his picture against a background of a blackboard filled with formulae (which, incidentally, are not his but mine). I quote from the article: "Oppenheimer likes to tell about a Bible study group in Germany that had begun with *Genesis* and doggedly plowed clear through to *Ezekiel*. Asked an impressed visitor: 'Don't you find *Ezekiel* terribly difficult?' Replied one Bible student: 'Yes—but what we don't understand, we explain to each other.'" That reply, one of Robert's favorites, later often used by others as well, is also used as caption to his *Time* cover picture.

Other comments from the interview: Einstein was "a landmark but not a beacon" to modern physicists—correct but gratuitously cutting; the Institute was a place where men could "sit and think," but could only be sure of the sitting. Also,

> "I regard it as a very open question whether the Institute is an important place, and whether my coming will be of benefit." By last week, he had answered the first half of the question to his own satisfaction.
>
> His first visit to Europe in 20 years had helped do the trick. Attending scientific conferences in Brussels and Birmingham, Oppenheimer had learned how despairing the life of the intellect had become in postwar Europe. Viewed from Princeton, the Institute might have its shortcomings; viewed from Europe, it had something of the special glow of a monastery in the Dark Ages.
>
> Director Oppenheimer preferred to think of the Institute as an "intellectual hotel"—a place for transient thinkers to rest, recover and refresh themselves before continuing on their way. He wanted an international clientele at his Grand Hotel. Expatriate and exiled scholars have always been welcome at the Institute, but Oppenheimer had something different in mind: a continuous world traffic in ideas. For such foreign scholars as Denmark's Bohr and Britain's Dirac and Toynbee, Oppenheimer hoped to work out periodic repeat performances, so that they would never wholly lose touch either with the U.S. or with home base. Said Oppenheimer: "The best way to send information is to wrap it up in a person."
>
> The guest list at Oppie's hotel this year will also include Historian Arnold Toynbee, Poet T. S. Eliot, Legal Philosopher Max Radin—and a literary critic, a bureaucrat and an airlines executive. There was no telling who might turn up next: maybe a psychologist, a Prime Minister, a composer or a painter. Oppenheimer was just working up courage: "If a man is a full professor at Harvard, he may be a fool, but he's a respectable fool. In the world of action, criteria for acceptability are more confused."

The characterization of the Institute as an "intellectual hotel" was likely to wound the sensibilities of the faculty. That it did was shown when the director was constrained to refuse an interview with a reporter from the *Saturday Evening Post* in 1949, and with another from *Colliers* in 1950, on the ground that the faculty opposed further publicity. Mrs. Leary corresponded for Dr. Oppenheimer and said that the faculty believes there had been too much publicity about the Institute.

Robert's last position before coming to Princeton had been director of the Los Alamos Laboratory, where some 6,000 people had been doing his bidding. Now, in Princeton, he was lording it over just about 100 persons. As is clear from the preceding, he had not yet learned that running a small-sized show demands delicate procedures of a characteristically distinct nature.

I turn next to the changes in the faculty largely wrought by Oppenheimer during his early years at the Institute. As to the three economists on the faculty, after some discussion (occasionally heated), one resigned, the other two retired. In 1949 the schools of humanistic studies and of economics and politics were merged into one, with the new name School of Historical Studies.[229]

New faculty appointments were made. In 1947 the archeologist Homer Thompson (1906–2000) joined. He was especially renowned for his dig in the Agora, ancient Athens' marketplace, which he had discovered by following the footsteps of Pausanias (2nd century AD). This Greek traveler and geographer had recorded in *Book I* (of ten) of his "Description of Greece" the position of the marble stele that marks the entry to the Agora— rediscovered by Thompson by searching at the indicated place. The excavation of the Agora became Thompson's main life's work, assisted by his wife Dorothy and an able staff, headquartered at the *Amerikaniki Skoli* (American School of Archeology) in Athens, also for part of many years the home of the Thompsons themselves.

In 1948 Harold Cherniss (1904–1987) was appointed to the faculty. He was America's foremost expert on Plato and Aristotle. We became very good friends. I think with gratitude of my many visits to his office, where I was always welcome, and where we discussed all kinds of topics, including his and my work. I also had friendly relations with other new professors, Ernst Kantorowicz (1895–1963), a medieval historian, and Sir Ernest Llewellyn Woodward (1890–1971), a modern historian, both appointed in 1951; and with Kurt Gödel (1906–1978), the great logician (1953).

At about that time a new rank was introduced: permanent member, with indefinite tenure but not a professorship. The first appointed to this category was the mathematician Deane Montgomery (1909–1992)(in 1948), whom Veblen was grooming as his successor in leading the faculty. The next permanent members were the mathematician Atle Selberg (1917–) and yours truly, both in 1949. According to the faculty minutes of April 19, 1949, "The Director proposed to change the present status of Dr. Pais by a) converting his $6,000 annual grant to $8,000 annual salary, b) giving Dr. P. permanent status rather than the present five-year tenure. On motion, seconded and carried, the appointment as recorded was approved." From the letter Oppenheimer sent me the next day: "Your appointment . . . will now be, if you care to accept it, a permanent appointment extending to the age of 65. . . . Whatever the future may have in store for physics, for you or for the Institute, one thing needs now to be recorded. That is my own deep sense of gratitude and that of all your other colleagues that you have elected at this time to continue your work with us here."[230]

Before Oppenheimer's arrival, mathematicians had formed the strongest group at the Institute; this remained so during his tenure. A few numbers: between 1948 and 1953, there were some 300 mathematicians at the Institute, whose work produced more than 500 papers in learned journals of mathematics.[231]

The growth of the faculty and also of the number of temporary members demanded more funds for salaries, for fellowships, and for additional space: $400,000 for the erection of three modest buildings providing 60 additional offices, several seminar rooms, and freeing of space allowing the library in Fuld Hall to expand. Furthermore, the Institute contributed $500,000 toward the construction of the new Firestone Library at the University.

All these growing expenses were covered in part by increases in grants from foundations and government contracts, from $82,000 in 1947 to $181,000 in 1952. In addition, the income from the well-managed portfolio showed sizable growth, from $643,000 in 1948 to $848,000 in 1951. At the annual trustee meeting in 1949, the director expressed his appreciation to the trustee's Treasurer, and also announced the establishment of the Einstein Award, a gift of the Rosa and Lewis Strauss Memorial Fund in honor of the famous professor on his 70th birthday. Every three years $15,000 was to be given for outstanding contributions to mathematics and/or physics. I was present at the first award ceremony, when Einstein himself handed over the checks. To Julian Schwinger (1918–1995), one recipient, he said: "You have deserved it;" to Kurt Gödel, the other one: "You do not need it."

It would have greatly helped if the principal endowment could have been increased. Robert, however, considered it *infra dig* to engage in such plebeian activities as fundraising—which caused murmurs of disapproval from the faculty. As von Neumann once said to me, rich Jews would have crept on their knees and with open purses from New York to Princeton if only Oppenheimer would have asked them to contribute to the Institute's funds.

Among government contracts was one entered with the New York office of the Atomic Energy Commission, by which some of the research fellows came to the Institute for their work. The director and the faculty were suddenly confronted with a policy issue when Congress passed an appropriation bill with a rider providing that all such fellows must be cleared by the Commission after full investigation by the Federal Bureau of Investigation. The policy was repugnant to most scientists. Those who had testified at recent hearings were frank to say that any such restriction would have an adverse effect on students and young postdoctoral workers who might not want to have their families and friends disturbed by such inquiries, and might turn away from scientific careers that the government wanted as a matter of policy to facilitate.

The director promptly consulted the faculty, and informed the New York office of the Atomic Energy Commission that the Institute would not in future administer any such funds. He said in part: "In view of the nonsecret nature of our work and of the traditions of the Institute for Advanced Study, we should be unwilling to make any appointments to membership in the Institute conditional upon an investigation by the Federal Bureau of Investigation. We shall therefore make no further grants-in-aid, the funds for which would be derived from subjects contract. . . . I need hardly add that unless a new basis for the support of basic, unclassified work in the sciences can be developed, the Institute will be unwilling to renew the contract."[232]

I conclude my account of Oppenheimer's activities as director in the early years by mentioning two more professorial appointments.

In the autumn of 1950 Robert took the first step toward my own promotion to full professor, when he sent a written statement to the School of Mathematics professors. Forty years later I obtained a copy. It reads in part:

> The record of Dr. Pais' work in the last decade is almost a history of the efforts to clarify our understanding of basic atomic theory and the nature of the elementary particles. Pais first proposed the compensation theories of elementary particles, and much of his work has been devoted to exploring the success and limitations of these theories, and indicating the radical character of the revisions which will be needed before they can successfully describe the sub-atomic world. Pais has made important contributions to nuclear theory and to electrodynamics. He is one of the few young theoretical physicists who within the last decade have enriched our understanding of physics.

In January 1951 I received the following letter from Oppenheimer: "It gives me great pleasure to inform you that on the unanimous vote of the Faculty and the Board of Trustees of the Institute for Advanced Study you have been appointed a Professor . . . of physics. . . . This step is taken in appreciation of your past work, in high hopes for your work of the future, and with the full recognition of the value which your counsel will be in guiding the Institute's policies." On July 1, I became the Institute's third professor of physics, after Einstein and Oppenheimer. On October 9, 1951, Selberg, Montgomery, and I were present for the first time as regular members at a faculty meeting—too late to meet Einstein there. He had ceased attending in 1949.

Next to attending faculty meetings and pursuing science, I set myself a third, self-appointed task: the care and nursing of temporary junior physics members. These young people had come from their respective universities as the golden boys or girls, the best of the local crops. Now they found themselves in the company of similar golden kids from elsewhere. That, combined with the Institute's decompressed atmosphere—do what you like—was nothing less than a culture shock, as I knew so well from my own initial experiences. The result was what I came to call the November Depression, which almost invariably occurred after the excitement of arrival had worn off. It was during this time that I felt I had to keep a protective eye on the newcomers. I would drop in, ask them what they were doing and how it was going, tell them it takes some time to adjust to new surroundings, stress that this is a very peculiar place, that it takes time to get going here, and that they would be just fine in a while. That was the kind of support Oppenheimer was congenitally incapable of providing; nor did he try.

A fair number took this wisdom to heart and got their act together. Many of those have since risen to full professorships all over the world. Looking back on my Institute years, it is perhaps my greatest satisfaction to have helped the youngsters along in the beginning. There were also some who could not take it, who collapsed mentally. On rare occasions, one or two of these would simply pack up and vanish. As all of us know, starting a career is rarely easy.

I turn to the last of the early professorial appointments in the Oppenheimer years. It brings me to March 1955, at which time I was teaching at Columbia University, on leave from the Institute. There I got a phone call from Robert. He had recently put up George Kennan for a permanent Institute professorship in diplomatic history but had hit upon strong resistance from the mathematics faculty. He asked me for help in a forthcoming faculty meeting at which the matter would come up for formal discussion. Strictly, he had no right to do so, since I was on leave, but he sounded so desperate that I said I would come. It was an unpleasant meeting, the opposition tearing hard into the proposal on the grounds that Kennan's publications to date could not be called scholarly contributions. Things got rather nasty; I did not say much but afterward told Robert that I would talk privately with the mathematicians, who considered me reasonably unbiased. I tried to calm them down.

The matter ended the following November, when the appointment was approved with a vote of 13 for and 5 mathematicians against. This contretemps marked the beginning of a lasting hostility of the mathematics group toward Oppenheimer. As to Kennan, his appointment has proved to be fully justified. The books he wrote while at the Institute have received wide acclaim and numerous high honors.

In the next chapter I shall mention further appointments in physics.

CHAPTER **15**

OPPENHEIMER AND THE WORLD OF PHYSICS: 1946–1954

"Nineteen forty-six was the first year of peace. . . . The year was marked by the widespread if delayed publication of results of the key war projects in physics, and above all, by the return to their old laboratories of hundreds of war-experienced physicists, brimful of information about what had been done, and confident in their understanding of whole fields of technique which had been vague general possibilities in 1940. . . . Physicists went back, a little rusty, to the problems of the days before the war. Most of those problems were still there, for not much fundamental progress had been made during the War years. But gone was the reluctance to do big things, gone the sometimes valuable, sometimes hampering isolation of the research worker. . . . [One may hope that in] the years ahead the best of the old spirit will come to employ the great new tools which are the legacy of war."[233] So wrote a physicist in 1947. Elsewhere I have written[234] how right after war's end physics took a sharp turn, rather than continuing on earlier trodden paths, how there was an almost abrupt sense of novelty, in regard to instrumentation, new styles of cooperative experimental venture, discoveries of new forms of matter, and evolution of new theoretical methods.

"The Great Charismatic Figure"

During the war, which had of course interrupted Oppenheimer's research activities, he published only one physics paper,[235] a report on progress in cosmic-ray physics during 1936–1941. His total postwar scientific production was minimal as well: one paper on electrodynamics,[236] three on meson physics,[100,237,238] and one, his last, a digression into biophysics.[239] This limited research activity was the price he had to pay not only for having become an administrator but, far more importantly, for having become a much-sought-after consultant on matters of national policy. In spite of all these activities he did continue to write copiously in the postwar years, however, but—as we shall see later—in areas other than pure science, publishing about 120 papers on general subjects.

At this point I single out one of his papers, which straddles physics and broader topics. It is the eulogy that Robert wrote[240] after Einstein's death in 1955—in 1939 he had also given a radio address on the occasion of Einstein's sixtieth birthday[241]—from which I quote:

> With the death of Albert Einstein in April of 1955, physicists lost their greatest colleague. For two golden decades early in this century, the history of Einstein's discoveries is inseparable from the history of physics.
>
> Einstein started with the nineteenth-century developments of statistical mechanics and of electromagnetic theory as his inheritance. In the first year of his fully mature work, his paper on Brownian movement enlarged and defined statistical theory, and led to those insights into fluctuations which were to play so great a part in Einstein's contributions to quantum theory. In a second great paper he formulated with full incisiveness the hypothesis of light quanta, and irrevocably changed our understanding of physical processes on the atomic scale. In a third paper he made the special theory of relativity. . . .
>
> From then on, for the next decade, Einstein was to be preoccupied with the problems of inertia, of mass, of acceleration, and of gravity. He discovered first the identity of mass and energy, which was to be verified in detail only some twenty-five years later, and was to provide the basis for such fateful developments for man's whole history during and since the Second World War. He began to understand the import of the precise equality of inertial and gravitational mass, and to see in this the foundation for a geometrical theory of gravitation. He sought to preserve the logically necessary general covariance of the equations of physics, until this long effort was crowned with the discovery of the general theory of relativity and the field equations. He was almost at once able to define three crucial experiments, accessible through existing observational techniques, by which the novel implications of his theory could be compared with experience. In the forty years that have elapsed these have remained the principal and, with one exception, the only connections between the general theory and experience. The exception lies in the field of cosmology, where Einstein himself was the first to see wholly new approaches opened by the theory of relativity. More than any other great advance in physics, the general theory of relativity is the work of one man. Without him, it might have lain long undiscovered.
>
> During this whole period Einstein was very close to the rapidly evolving quantum theory of atomic phenomena. He reverted to the use of statistical arguments, and to the logical meaning of fluctuations, to discover the laws of emission and absorption of radiation, and to establish the connection between

the waves of de Broglie and the statistical laws proposed by Bose from the description of light quanta. As this period drew to a close with the discovery in 1925 of the quantum mechanics, and its more and more definite formulation, especially by Bohr, Einstein's role was to change. He found himself from the first disturbed and unsatisfied by the statistical and acausal character of the new mechanics, to the discovery of which he had made such great contributions.

In a long period of brilliant discussion and analysis, especially with Ehrenfest and with Bohr, he attempted again and again to show that the new mechanics, for all its vast agreement with experience, contained logical errors and inconsistencies. Yet, as example after example, upon analysis, only confirmed the harmony and consistency of the quantum theory, he was led to accept this; but to it he always coupled his unaltered conviction that this should not be the ultimate description of the atomic world, and that in an ultimate description acausal and statistical features must be eliminated.

Thus, for the last decades of his life he did not share in full the convictions or the interests of the great majority of his colleagues. Instead, with increasing single-mindedness, he turned his attention to the discovery of what would for him have been a basic and satisfying account of the atomic nature of matter. This was the program of the unified field. Here he sought to generalize the matter-free field equations of general relativity so that they might also account for electromagnetic phenomena. He sought equations whose solutions would correspond to local aggregations of mass and charge, and whose behavior would resemble the atomic world so well described by quantum theory. He was hard at work on this program until his death. It was a program that did not arouse the hope or indeed the active interest of many physicists; yet his knowledge of their work, and his judgment of it, remained firm and masterful; and he was never deceived by any of the proposed causal reinterpretations of atomic physics.

When the weather was good enough, Einstein would walk home from work. One day not long ago he said to me, "When it has once been given you to do something rather reasonable, forever afterward your work and life are a little strange." It had indeed been given him to do something reasonable. His presence among us stayed us from the worst folly, and touched those who knew him with the light of magnanimity.

It is true that Oppenheimer's postwar scientific output was not particularly memorable. Until practically the day he died he remained intensely interested in physics, however, keeping track of new developments. Especially during the first decade following the war, he became one of the world's leading directors—in the original meaning of the word—of physics, addressing audiences in but also far beyond, Princeton. I give two samples.

First, from his Richtmyer lecture[3] in 1947 (never published; I own a mimeographed copy):

As the preoccupations of the war years abate, we are able to take stock of ourselves and our work. It would be a picture altered by the late years: a picture of intense activity, of classrooms crowded as never before, of great machines abuilding by the score to give us radiations of high energy, of contradictions, puzzles and questions as deep and presently obscure as any that have ever faced physics, of unprecedented demands for our cooperation in the solution of practical problems of decisive importance to our country and the world, of overriding if often inarticulate concern that our works may never again be needed for the destruction of war. . . .

In the field of fundamental understanding, the situation must be regarded as woeful when judged by the classic standards of physics. We are a long way from the simplicity and universality of Newtonian mechanics, or of electrodynamics, or of quantum theory. No one has an understanding even remotely comparable to our understanding of electron dynamics of the interactions which manifest themselves in nuclear phenomena, the strong but by no means simple forces between nucleons, the spectacularly weak coupling between electrons and nucleons. . . . It may be that, long before these questions are answered, others will have replaced them; today they are part of the challenge of the atomic world.

There is a vast field of endeavor in putting to effective practical advantage the discoveries in connection with the release of atomic energy. This is a difficult and demanding field, full of interest on its own, and to which many of us will be committed in the years to come. But I think that the problems here lie rather far from fundamental physics, and that the important problems are probably not in the field of nuclear physics at all. . . .

Contemporary atomic physics, the physics of the great accelerators, the reactors, even in large part the cosmic rays, is, very much more than ever before, three things: it is the physics of teams, it is expensive physics, it is prized as vital to armament. These things have become so much more pronounced than they were two decades ago that they have made some changes in our ways of life.

We have seen the beginnings of an attempt to establish, precisely in the field of atomic physics and its applications, that cooperation between peoples and that order among nations that is our one hope of lasting peace. Many of us, over the past years, have in all ways that were appropriately open to us attempted to contribute to this effort, for which in the nature of things the government and people of the United States have borne the greatest responsibility. It is not proper, nor is it possible, for me to give a valid appraisal of the measure of success of these past efforts. It is perhaps proper to give renewed expression to what has been so eloquently said before: to the ultimate success we, as a fraternity, are dedicated. . . .

It will not be very long before these words that I have spoken today will seem like very trivial physics and very poorly inspired prophesy. There are rich days ahead for physics; we may hope, I think, to be living in one of the heroic ages of physical science, where as in the past a vast new field of experience has taught us its new lesson and its new order.

Second, in 1950, *Scientific American* devoted an issue to "The Age of Science: 1900–1950." It contains contributions by ten prominent scientists, chosen from a variety of branches of science. It was fitting that Oppenheimer should write its general introduction.[242] As Rabi has written:

For the first half of this century the scientific community of the United States, and more especially the physicists, did not lack for strong and respected leadership. . . . This leadership was generally accepted by the physicists, by the press and by the public at large. By 1946, with the end of the war and the retirement from activity of the older leadership, this mantle naturally fell on the shoulders of Robert Oppenheimer. Although other eminent scientists exerted strong influences, . . . Oppenheimer's leadership was recognized more universally, both at home and abroad, even though he held no high position and was not the recipient of extraordinary scientific honors.

This rise to public eminence and recognition was quite sudden and was not presaged by events preceding the war. At that time Oppenheimer's reputation and influence were centered around the small and close circle of physicists. As the wartime director of the Los Alamos Laboratory, he was bound to receive important public attention, but there were other directors of great laboratories, and other physicists, who shared equal esteem but did not become objects of such general interest. *Oppenheimer, after Einstein, emerged as the great charismatic figure of the scientific world*[11] (my italics).

I quote next from Oppenheimer's *Scientific American* paper:

[All ten reports] tell of a period of unparalleled advance of understanding, of new experience, new insight and new mastery. Indeed, for some of the sciences— for biochemistry, for physics, for genetics—the half-century now closing has been a time of splendor: of great men and great discoveries, of a real revolution in our knowledge of the world. For all it has been a time of extraordinary vitality and progress, extending and enriching what we know about the world, and unearthing, for every question answered, a host of new questions. Few of the authors, schooled by the surprises and wonders unfolded in the history of the last 50 years, hazard much of a preview of the history of the half-century to come; yet all speak with confidence of a future that will be worthy of a great past. . . .

All the reports are pervaded, though necessarily and properly with varying emphasis, by this sense of the dual role of science. The purpose and the fruits of science are discovery and understanding. Yet equally, though in a quite different sense, its purpose and its fruits are a vast extension of human resources, of man's power to control and alter the environment in which he lives, works, suffers and perishes. . . .

One cannot read these 10 reports . . . without being sensible of a darker shadow, quite outside this serene and active workshop of the human spirit, and yet somehow touching it. Scientific progress, which has so profoundly altered both the material and the spiritual quality of our civilization, is not the sole root of its present grave crisis. But few men can be doubtful of its decisive part. Hand in hand, the growth of science and of the practical arts has produced, is increasingly producing, an unparalleled revolution in human resources, resources that in some part have altered, and in far greater part can alter, the material condition of man's life. . . .

The order that characterizes the relations of one part of science with another is not primarily an hierarchal order. It is true that there have been attempts to sketch out possible hierarchies, designating, let us say, physics as more abstract than biology, or astronomy as more quantitative than anthropology. But it is doubtful whether such schemes have contributed much either to the growth of science or to its general understanding; certainly they do not describe at all the benign and tolerant symbiosis in which the sciences have flourished and nourished one another. Tolerance, open-mindedness and confidence in the resolution of conflict by further inquiry—these constitute the liberalism of the sciences in their relations with one another. These relations are rooted in many things, but not least in mutual respect and in a total, a deliberate candor. . . .

Harmony, even in science itself, is being destroyed or threatened in vast areas of the world today. Terror, orthodox recantation, hierarchy, secrecy—these words are full of grim omens for science and for liberty. A society which as a matter of principle invokes the measures for which these words stand betrays, whatever its protestations, science and the tradition that has nourished it. A society which invokes these measures (in the name of man's welfare, in fear or in folly) is in danger of death.

Increasingly, in these days of growing crisis, men have talked with earnest desperation of the application of scientific method to new areas, to problems of man's behavior and to human society. None of us knows or can foresee what progress individual genius and common effort may make possible in our understanding of these problems in the decades to come. Yet if the history of other sciences is a good guide, progress will come in only fitful and wayward response to man's needs, and will wait upon his insight, his patience and his invention.

Several aspects in these two contributions strike me as unusual. While having science as their main theme, they both blend that subject with reflections on the world at large, as for example in the Richtmyer lecture, where in one sentence Robert moves from unsolved problems in physics to "problems of decisive importance to our country and the world"; likewise in the *Scientific American* article: "[T]he growth of science . . . has produced . . . an unparalleled revolution . . . that . . . can alter the material conditions of man's life." I would suppose that those mixtures reflect on the time they were spoken or written, the beginning of the Cold War, but perhaps even more on Oppenheimer's dual role as leader in science and GAC adviser in political matters.

Note in particular how Robert writes of "the environment in which [man] lives, works, suffers, and perishes"; of "these days . . . [in which] men have talked with earnest desperation"; and especially of "a darker shadow, . . . outside this serene and active workshop of the human spirit and yet . . . touching it." Here he reveals, I believe, some of the "darker shadow" that has resided in his forever troubled soul. There is melodrama in such language—which we shall encounter time and again in what follows.

I now return to the Princeton scene.

Prominent physicists had visited the Institute long before Oppenheimer arrived. Niels Bohr had been there in 1938–39, Dirac in 1934–35 and fall of 1946; Kramers in the spring of 1947, just before Robert's arrival; Pauli in 1935–36 and the entire war period, 1940–46. All these men returned for visits during Oppenheimer's tenure, Bohr in the spring terms of 1948, 1950, 1953, and the fall of 1954; Dirac in academic 1947–48, 1958–59, 1962–63;

Kramers in the fall of 1951; Pauli in academic 1949–50 and the spring of 1954 and 1956. Oppenheimer's presence obviously added to their desire to come to Princeton; their presence obviously added to the allure of physics at the Institute.

Building Up Physics at the Institute

Upon Oppenheimer's arrival, a function and quality of the Institute developed that had not been there before, however. It became a center for theoretical physics, in fact during the next decade the world's premier mecca for theoretical physicists, who came flocking as temporary members.

Oppenheimer's outstanding talent for assembling the right people and stimulating them to great effort was the decisive factor, just as it had been at Los Alamos. Regular periods of residence for eminent physicists have continued to play an important role in the life of the Institute, but from the very start Oppenheimer brought to physics at the Institute a new emphasis on youth. In fact, on his arrival in Princeton, five research associates from Berkeley came with him as the first temporary physics members in the new style.[243] This is characteristic for the continuity as well as for the transition in Oppenheimer's activities.

Oppenheimer's main role as physicist now turned into directing the research of these youngsters rather than being a teacher in the conventional sense, for there is no such teaching at the Institute. To be sure, we had our seminars. They were lively—sometimes very lively. Robert's sharp insights played a major part in making them so. Yet his main contribution to the work and the style of the Institute was not merely the conducting of a seminar. His influence was far more important, more subtle perhaps, but no less inspiriting. He could convey to young men a sense of extraordinary relevance of the physics of their day and give them a sense of their participation in a great adventure. He could define and thereby enhance their dedication, by words such as these: "People who practice science, who try to learn, believe that knowledge is good. They have a sense of guilt when they do not try to acquire it. This keeps them busy. . . . It seems hard to live any other way than thinking that it was better to know something than not to know it; and that the more you know the better, provided you know it honestly."[244] To an unusual degree, Oppenheimer possessed the ability to instill such attitudes in the young physicists around him, to urge them not to let up.

Robert's predilections for young men was also manifest in his choices for appointments to Institute professors of physics. I introduce these next.

F. J. Dyson (1923–)

On January 29, 1948, Robert Oppenheimer and I took a train from Princeton to New York to attend the 1948 winter meeting of the American Physical Society, held that year at Columbia University. Our main interest was the session on quantum electrodynamics, the hottest topic in physics at that time.

One of the speakers[245] was a youngster from Cornell, where he had been working with Bethe and Feynman. As he proceeded, we nodded to each other: that kid is smart. His name was Freeman Dyson (1923–). He looked a bit unusual: stiff white collar, and light blue eyes that would stare piercingly at you. I recall my first impression: that fellow must be an eccentric, an opinion which I have never changed.

It is not so simple, however, to define what one means by eccentricity. In my view eccentrics are people with a strong sense of personal liberty, strong individuals whose actions never include acting, who have strange inclinations of their own that they are not afraid to express and on which they refuse to compromise.

Britain has perhaps produced more eccentrics than any other nation. No two of them are alike, of course. Think of Dame Edith Sitwell (1887–1964) or of Joshua Norton,[246] who emigrated to California, where in 1859 he proclaimed himself emperor of the United States, regularly attended the State Senate sessions, where a seat was always reserved for him, and where on his death in San Francisco huge crowds paid their last respects to their beloved monarch.

To get back to 1948, I seem to remember that Oppenheimer and I spoke with Dyson after his talk and invited him to spend one year at the Institute for Advanced Study, an offer which he accepted. In 1953 he returned to the Institute as a full professor. From that time dates my friendship with him, which lasts to this day. Freeman has remained at the Institute ever since, presently in the state of grace called emeritus. In 1957 he became a United States citizen.

Dyson was born in England, in 1923. His father, Sir George Dyson (1883–1964), was a composer of choral and orchestral music, and for 25 years the director of London's Royal College of Music. His mother was a lawyer by profession. He was educated first at Winchester College, then at the University of Cambridge. He takes pride in never having received a Ph.D. From 1943–45 he served as civilian at the Operational Research Center, RAF Bomber Command.

When in 1947 he arrived at Cornell he had, in his words, "a good mathematical background and little knowledge of physics."[247] His first ten publications were in fact all pure mathematics. He could not have found better teachers than Bethe, solid contributor to many branches of physics, and Feynman, only five years older than he, who was in the process of developing a reformulation of quantum mechanics that nobody but he himself could understand at that time. In 1989, Dyson called Feynman "half genius, half buffoon,"[248] but had realized at once that Feynman was a great scientist. Dyson's first physics contributions, fundamental and technically hard, were to establish the links between Feynman's formulation and the earlier one of quantum electrodynamics.[249] That work established him at once as one of the leading physicists of my generation. It had also been the subject of his January 1948 talk, when I had first seen him.[245]

Freeman has continued to make fine contributions to science, in quantum-field theory, in statistical physics, and other areas of physics, in mathematics, astronomy, and space technology. He has called his work at General Dynamics on Project Orion, the design for a nuclear-fueled spaceship, ultimately abandoned, his happiest days in science, presumably, I would guess, because Peter Pan was one of his favorite characters in his youthful readings.

Dyson has also published a number of books[247, 250–254] about science addressed to general audiences, fascinating in content and elegant in style. In those writings Dyson treats us to physics, engineering, genetics, the origins of life, extraterrestrial intelligence, science and religion, and moral issues related to science and politics. My own favorite is his autobiography,[247] in which I particularly admire his unsparing self-revelation, such as: "I was, and have always been, a problem solver rather than a creator of ideas."[247] When in 1960 he published an article in *Foreign Affairs*[255] arguing against a test ban on atomic weapons, he later called that piece "an attempt to salvage an untenable position with spurious emotional claptrap."[247] Be it noted that he is coauthor of a report that influenced President Clinton to endorse in 1995 the concept of a comprehensive test ban.

C. N. Yang (1922–)

Chen Ning Yang (all his friends call him Frank) was born in 1922 in China, in Hofei, in the province of Anhwei. He is the oldest of five children of Ko-Chuen Yang, professor of mathematics (Ph.D., Chicago 1928) at the Southwest Associated University in Kunming, one of the best Chinese universities, later professor at Fudan University in Shanghai. Frank and his family had to endure the devastating war in China (1937–1945). "In 1940 the house that my family rented in Kunming received a direct hit . . . [but] no member of the family was wounded . . . the family survived intact—lean, very lean, but healthy."[256]

Frank started his university studies at the Southwest Associated University. Later he went to Tsinghua University in the same city, where he received the M.Sc. degree in 1944.[257]

In August 1945 Yang left for the United States. "There being no commercial passenger traffic between China and the United States at that time, I had to wait several months in Calcutta for a berth in a troop transport. I finally reached New York in late November and went to Chicago around Christmas. January 1946 saw me enrolled as a graduate student at the University of Chicago,"[256] where Fermi's oeuvre and style made a lasting impression on him.[258] In Chicago he received his Ph.D. in 1948 under Edward Teller (1908–2003) with a thesis on angular distributions in nuclear reactions.[259]

Already in his thesis we find Yang engaged on a program of obtaining physical information that is largely independent of a detailed dynamical description but where extensive use is made of the invariance properties of the problem in hand. In a similar vein are his investigations on the parity[260] of the π^0 meson and on the reflection properties of fermion fields.[261] Those papers were written at the Institute, which Frank had joined as a temporary member soon after having gotten his doctorate.

Early in 1950, five-year Institute memberships were voted[262] for Frank and for Georg Placzek (1905–1955), another physicist, who had worked on atomic bomb projects at Chalk River, Canada, and Los Alamos. In 1952, the School of Mathematics legislated[263] that, while Dr. Yang might some day become a professor, Dr. Placzek could not, "unless circumstances now unanticipated intervene."

In 1952 Yang contracted the celebrated Ising disease, but unlike many of his fellow patients he pulled through by being able to compute the spontaneous magnetization of the two dimensional lattice.[264,264a] In 1956 he was promoted to full professor. Placzek did not make the grade. He left the Institute in 1955, and died later that year in Switzerland. I believe it was a suicide. Whether or not that was the case, it seems to me that to effectively dispose of a long-term membership as a stepping stone to a professorship is a grave if not an evil mistake.

T. D. Lee (1926–)

Tsung Dao Lee (T. D. to his friends) was born in 1926 in Shanghai, the third of six children. His father, Tsing Kong Lee, was an agriculturalist. As Frank had done, Lee began his studies at the Southwest Associated University. The two men first met in 1945, when Lee was a student and Yang a high-school teacher in Kunming.

T. D., like Frank, went to Chicago. It was there that, in 1946, their friendship started. Lee got his Ph.D. in 1950 under Enrico Fermi (1901–1954) for his work on the hydrogen content of white dwarfs.[265] His first papers[266] deal with astrophysical problems and with the theory of turbulence.

In 1950 Lee went to Berkeley as a lecturer. In the fall of 1951 Lee started a two-year period of membership at the Institute. From that time, Lee and Yang collaborated intimately and steadily for many years. Incidentally, their first joint paper, together with Rosenbluth, deals with weak interactions.[267] In 1953 Lee went to Columbia, where he became a full professor in 1956.

At Columbia, Lee published, in collaboration with others, on such subjects as Π-nucleon scattering[268] and multiple meson production,[269] and on polaron problems.[270] Of particular interest is his work[271] on the "Lee model," a rigorously soluble model of a field theory.

Lee was still at Columbia when the celebrated Lee-Yang paper[272] on parity-nonconservation was written (to which I shall return later). In 1960 he was appointed Institute professor.

This completes the introduction of the four young Institute physics professors, known in their time as the four musketeers.

Of Some Who Came and Some Who Went

I mention next, briefly, some of the other principal scientists who were at the Institute in the early postwar years, a few of whom who died during that period.

Hideki Yukawa (1907–1981)

Hideki Yukawa was a one-year Institute member in academic 1948–49 who, later in 1949, would receive Japan's first Nobel Prize "for having foreseen the existence of mesons in the course of his theoretical works concerning nuclear forces." He was a friendly but shy man, as was particularly noticeable when he gave seminars. Not only did he speak softly, but he would also turn his back to the audience and address the blackboard, pure torture for his listeners.

Sin-itiro Tomonaga (1906–1979)

Sin-itiro Tomonaga came to the Institute in the fall of 1949 for a year's stay. I remember him as soft-spoken, serene, ascetic in appearance, and as the most profound of all the Japanese physicists I have known. In 1965 he shared the Nobel Prize with Schwinger and Feynman "for their fundamental contributions in the domain of quantum electrodynamics which carry profound consequences for the physics of elementary particles." I was pleased to note that in his Nobel lecture[273] he included reference to my early work on QED.

David Joseph Bohm (1917–1992)

David Joseph Bohm and Oppenheimer crossed paths first in Berkeley, later (1947–1951) in Princeton, though he was never an Institute member. My mention here of Bohm is meant to serve as a prelude to the high drama involving Oppenheimer, to which I shall turn later.

When in 1941 Bohm, then a graduate student, arrived in Berkeley, Oppenheimer suggested that he should make proton-deuteron scattering the main topic of his thesis. He made significant progress with this work, which was written up, but never published because it was immediately classified. He was awarded his Ph.D. at Berkeley in 1943, apparently without writing a thesis, because the papers containing the work had also been classified.

When in 1943 Oppenheimer left for Los Alamos, he wanted Bohm to go with him, but was unable to get clearance. The official reason for the refusal was that he had many relatives in Europe. Indeed, 19 of his family eventually perished in the Nazi gas chambers. Meanwhile Bohm had joined the Communist Party in 1942, which he left nine months later, disillusioned by the petty squabbling and maneuvering among its members.

When after the war Oppenheimer returned to Berkeley, Bohm worked again with him for half a year, on questions of principle in quantum mechanics and QED. John Wheeler, who was visiting Berkeley at that time, became very interested in the work Bohm was doing and offered him a job at Princeton University. In 1947 Bohm became an assistant professor at Princeton at the same time as Oppenheimer became head of the Institute.

While at Princeton, Bohm became embroiled with the House Committee on Un-American Activities. In 1948 he was subpoenaed to testify before that Committee. In this context Bohm's brief membership in the Communist party presented a problem. At that period in United States politics, to admit being a one-time member was regarded as a crime. Therefore the possibility of self-incrimination became dramatically real. Bohm took legal advice and although he wanted to plead the First Amendment, he was advised to plead the Fifth, which he did. For a time nothing happened and it seemed as if everything was dying down, but with the outbreak of the Korean War, a hostile anti-communist attitude re-emerged.

In the summer of 1949 Bohm was subpoenaed for a second time, but now to appear before a grand jury. He did not testify, again pleading the Fifth

Amendment. In November a United States Marshall arrested him at his office for contempt of court. He was taken to Trenton but released on bail of $1,500. The next day he had a letter from the University suspending him from his duties, and was requested not to enter the University buildings again. His pay continued, as he was working on a short fixed-term contract.

In June 1950 he was called for trial in Washington. After giving testimony, but still pleading the Fifth, he was acquitted. Fortunately for Bohm, in the spring of 1950 the Supreme Court had agreed that it was acceptable to plead the Fifth in such cases and it was this ruling that ensured Bohm's final acquittal.

In all of this sorry saga Bohm was never accused of any misdemeanor against the State. Indeed, Bohm had no access to sensitive information, since he had remained at Berkeley and was not part of the team working for Oppenheimer at Los Alamos.

Bohm's contract at Princeton expired in June 1951 and, although he had the unanimous support of the Physics Department, the contract was not renewed. He was now in an invidious position and could not get a permanent position in the United States. He did get a temporary job in a small industrial laboratory in Florida, but a university post seemed out of the question. Einstein, who had had several discussions with Bohm on basic issues in quantum mechanics, discussed his situation with Oppenheimer with the view to offering to appoint Bohm as his research assistant, but that was opposed by Oppenheimer.

Here ends the story of the interactions between Bohm and Oppenheimer and starts the period—not described here[274]—of Bohm's worldwide peregrinations, from Brazil to Israel to Bristol to Birkbeck College in London, where he spent the last 30 years of his life.

Finally, I note what Oppenheimer said later about Bohm's short flirtation with the Communist Party: "Oppenheimer stated . . . that somehow he did not believe that Bohm's temperament and personality were those of a dangerous person and implied that his dangerousness lay in the possibility of his being influenced by others."[275] I knew Bohm personally and regard it out of the question that he could in any way have endangered the security of the United States.

John von Neumann (1903–1957)

John von Neumann was sworn in as Commissioner of the U.S. Atomic Energy Commission on March 15, 1955, and took a leave of absence from the Institute at that time. My own reaction to this move was puzzlement— but then Johnny had always been easily impressed by officialdom. Perhaps his virulent anti-Soviet position also played a role. I remember how shocked I was when once, in 1947, Johnny calmly said to me that the best way to handle the budding Cold War conflict would be to atom bomb the Soviet Union—that was before the Russians had their own bomb.

Five months after having received his AEC appointment, von Neumann was operated on for a small cancerous growth in his clavicle. He seemed to recover fully, but soon after became increasingly ill from a rapidly spreading cancer. In April 1956 he was taken to Washington's Walter Reed Hospital.

To ease his deeply disturbed spirits, Johnny sought guidance from a Catholic priest, Father Anselm Strittmatter, who, beginning in the spring of 1956, began to see him regularly. I was shocked when I heard this later. He had been completely agnostic for as long as I had known him. As far as I could see this act did not agree with the attitudes and thoughts he had harbored for nearly all his life.

On February 8, 1957, Johnny died in the Hospital, at age 53. On a sunny but freezing morning later that February, I went to the cemetery on Witherspoon Street in Princeton, to attend the burial of Johnny in a brief Catholic ceremony. Father Strittmatter said a short prayer, followed by a brief eulogy by Admiral Strauss.

Thus came to an end the life of a Jewish wunderkind from Hungary.

Oswald Veblen (1880–1960)

Oswald Veblen retired as Institute professor in 1950. Two years earlier he had spoken rare words of commendation about the "scientific work going on in physics [at the Institute] . . . in the joint Princeton-Columbia-Institute weekly seminars, which have been extraordinarily popular and stimulating."[276] After his retirement he remained active behind the scene in Institute politics, however, as for example in the opposition to Kennan's appointment. I collect a few more personal recollections of him.

Veblen had been present at a lecture on quantum field theory I had given at the Institute, in October 1946. So were Bohr, Dirac, Weyl, von Neumann, Wheeler, and Alfred North Whitehead (1861–1947), the renowned mathematician from Harvard, who had deep interests in the foundations of physics, and who was on a short visit. Some audience.

Once Veblen invited me for lunch at the Nassau Club. During the meal he asked me about my scientific education. I told him that it had serious gaps, especially in mathematics, due to years of isolation during the war. Veblen was not moved. It is an advantage, he said, to be left alone for some time, because that frees the mind for its own pursuits. I have remembered that.

One day in early 1947, Veblen asked my help in a delicate matter. He had received an indignant letter from the eminent Soviet theoretical physicist Vladimir Fock (1898–1974), in which it was alleged that a paper by a young member of the Institute that had come out in the November 1946 issue of the *Physical Review* had been plagiarized from an article by him.[277] Veblen asked me please to check that, which I did. My finding astonished me. The article was indeed a word-for-word translation of Fock's paper. I told Veblen, who took care of it. I do not recall the outcome of the case.

A propos mathematics. One day Veblen asked me to give him my opinion about a physics manuscript by a young mathematician. I took it with me, sat down, and began to read. The first sentence began something like, Consider a Banach space. I got scared and said to myself, I must get out of here. I had never even heard of a Banach space. I returned the paper to Veblen, telling him I was ashamed to confess that it went over my head. Not to worry, he replied.

A conversation about Einstein. Veblen clearly did not feel like discussing the great man's current research but made an interesting remark about Einstein's famous letter of August 1939 to Roosevelt, in which he drew the president's attention to the feasibility of atomic weapons. Veblen told me that earlier in 1939 he had received a visit from Leo Szilard (1898–1964) and Eugene Wigner, who wanted to ask his counsel on how to approach the president regarding the possibility of producing atomic bombs. Veblen suggested they involve Einstein, which they did, and that in turn led to the mentioned letter.

Another remark by Veblen that I recall: he told me that for many years he noted down titles of books he wanted to read, but not until his retirement; currently he was too busy with mathematics and administration. He cannot have read them all because, sadly, he turned blind in his late years. He died in 1960.

Veblen was a stout champion of the Institute all his years. His Norwegian descent was manifest in the often tough ways he could handle those who differed in opinion with him. But I have always liked him.

Oppenheimer as Leader of Conferences: 1947–1954

Shelter Island, June 1947

The Manhansett Indians called their 7,700-acre island, tucked between Long Island's North and South Forks, "Manhansack-aha-quash-awamock," which means island sheltered by islands. They made their living by fishing. It had been British property, sold in 1651 to Barbados sugar merchants who saw Shelter Island's oak as ideal for making barrels. (The island was then heavily wooded, as was most of Long Island at that time.) They paid 1,600 pounds of sugar for the island, which later changed hands many times. It is now a favorite resort area.[278]

From June 1 to 3, 1947, 21 physicists, one chemist, and one mathematician gathered at Shelter Island for a "Conference on the Foundations of Quantum Mechanics," sponsored and financed by the National Academy of Sciences. (Among those invited who did not attend was Einstein, who had declined for reasons of health.)[279]

On the afternoon of Sunday, June 1, nearly all conferees met at the American Institute of Physics, then located at 55 East 55th Street, New York. There we boarded a bus that would take us to Greenport on Long Island's North Fork. We anticipated that it would be a rather lengthy trip along the Old Montauk Road with its many stoplights. Neither the Long Island Expressway nor the Sunrise Highway existed as yet.

Unexpectedly the ride went much faster than we had thought. As we entered Nassau County, the bus was stopped by a police trooper on a motorcycle who stuck his head in and asked: "Are you the scientists?" Yes, we were the scientists. "Follow me," he said to the driver, escorting us to the tune of sirens, passing unhindered through red lights, until we came to Suffolk County, where other troopers took over. We had no clue as to what this meant and speculated about scientific security, which in those days tended to take bizarre forms. All was cleared up after a fine dinner, oysters and steaks, was served to us in Greenport and our host, the president of the local Chamber of Commerce, rose to give a short speech. He told us that, during the war, he had been a marine in the Pacific, and that he might well not have been alive had it not been for the atomic bomb. Not only the dinner but also the police escort had been tokens of his personal gratitude for what "the scientists" had meant in his life. After our meal, we were taken by ferry to Shelter Island, where another siren-shrieking police escort delivered us to the Ram's Head Inn, where we would stay the following days and hold our meeting. We had the place all to ourselves; the Inn, located on a western cove of the Island, had been opened ahead of its summer schedule to accommodate us.

In later years, one finds comments in letters by and interviews with participants to the effect that the Shelter Island Conference may well have been the most important event of its kind in their entire scientific career; this is also my opinion. A newspaperman who covered the proceedings put it like this:

> Twenty-three of the country's best known theoretical physicists—the men who made the atomic bomb—gathered today in a rural inn to begin three days of discussion and study, during which they hope to straighten out a few of the difficulties that beset modern physics.
>
> It is doubtful if there has ever been a conference quite like this one. . . . The conference is taking place with almost complete informality, aided by the fact that the scientists have the inn all to themselves and feel that there is no one to mind if they take off their coats and get to work.[280]

The official chairman of the meeting was Karl Darrow (1891–1982). As he noted in his diaries, however, "As the conference went on, the ascendancy of Oppenheimer became more evident—the analysis (often caustic) of nearly every argument, that magnificent English never marred by hesitation or groping for words (I never heard 'catharsis' used in a discourse on [physics], or the clever word 'mesoniferous' which is probably O's invention), the dry humor, the perpetually-recurring comment that one idea or another (incl. some of his own) was certainly wrong, and the respect with which he was heard."[281]

My own recollections confirm this. I had heard Oppenheimer speak before but had never yet seen him in action directing a group of physicists during their scientific deliberations. At that he was simply masterful, interrupting with leading questions (at physics gatherings interruptions are standard procedure), summarizing the main points just discussed, and suggesting how to proceed from there.

Oppenheimer's stature as a leader among men at that time was recognized not only by scientists, as the following story may illustrate.

> After Shelter Island Oppenheimer had to go to Harvard, where he was to receive an honorary degree. Arrangements had been made to fly him and a few colleagues by seaplane from Shelter Island to Boston. However, bad weather forced the plane to come down at the New London Coast Guard Station, which is not open to civilian aircraft. The pilot was very worried since they were not supposed to land there. They were met by a naval officer who was clearly furious and ready to read them the riot act. As they opened up and jumped out, Oppenheimer told his very nervous pilot, "Don't worry." Hand outstretched, he introduced himself to the ranting and raging officer with the statement: "My name is Oppenheimer." The bewildered officer queried: "The Oppenheimer?" To which came the reply: "An Oppenheimer!" After an "official" welcome in the officers' club, they were driven—with a military escort—to the New London railway station, where they boarded a train for Boston.[282]

Some time before the meeting, Darrow had asked Kramers, Oppenheimer, and Weisskopf to act as discussion leaders and to prepare abstracts for that purpose. These were distributed ahead of time to the participants. I have at hand a hectographed copy of Oppenheimer's abstract, entitled: "The foundations of quantum mechanics, outline of topics for discussion." It reads in full:

It was long ago pointed out by Nordheim that there is an apparent difficulty in reconciling on the basis of usual quantum mechanic formalism the high rate of production of mesons in the upper atmosphere with the small interactions which these mesons subsequently manifest in traversing matter. To date no completely satisfactory understanding of this discrepancy exists, nor is it clear to what extent it indicates a breakdown in the customary formalism of quantum mechanics. It would appear profitable to discuss this and related questions in some detail.

We might start this discussion by an outline of the current status of theories of multiple production. Some illuminating suggestions about these phenomena can be worked out in a semi-quantitative way, for instance on the basis of the neutral pseudoscalar theory of meson couplings. The suggested results appear to agree reasonably well as to energy dependence of multiplication, energy and angle distribution with the experimental evidence, which is admittedly sketchy. However, no reasonable formulation of theories along this line will satisfactorily account for the smallness of the subsequent interaction of mesons with nuclear matter. Similar difficulties appear when one attempts to make a theory involving couplings of meson pairs to nuclear matter. There are two reasons for these apparent difficulties. One is that in all current theory there is a formal correspondence between the creation of a particle and the absorption of an antiparticle. The other is that multiple processes are in these theories attributable to the higher order effects of coupling terms which are of quite low order, first or second, in the meson wave fields. The question that we should attempt to answer is whether, perhaps along the lines of an S matrix formulation, both these conditions must be abandoned to accord with the experimental facts.

It would be desirable to review the experimental situation with an eye to seeing how unambiguous current interpretations are.

The calculation of the multiple production of mesons is in some ways an extension of the treatment given by Bloch and Nordsieck of the radiation of electrons during scattering. The difficulties of a complete description of these phenomena appear in exaggerated form in the problem of meson production. It would therefore be profitable to review the present status of the theory of radiation reaction and of certain recent suggestions for improving the theory.

This is not the place to recapitulate the very important new physics reported at Shelter Island; that I have done elsewhere.[283] Let me note here only that the main news concerned experimental evidence for deviations from the predictions of the Dirac theory of the electron for the fine structure ("Lamb shift") and the hyperfine structure in the atomic spectrum of hydrogen;[284] and reports of new puzzlements in meson physics[285]—both topics close to Oppenheimer's prewar interests.

Oppenheimer's comment on the meeting, written[286] on the last day of the conference, summarizes fittingly, I think, the responses of all participants: "The three days were a joy to us and perhaps unexpectedly fruitful. . . . [We] came away a good deal more certain of the directions in which progress may lie."

The news of the Lamb shift may well have caused Robert to think back wistfully to his first paper (1930) on QED,[46] in which he had been the very first to point out that QED effects cause shifts of light frequencies as compared with the standard theory of that time—which is at the root of the Lamb shift. In that early paper an infinite shift had been diagnosed—one of the troubles of QED in the 1930s. The effect observed in 1947 had been finite, of course. I could not make that observation while at Shelter Island (nor did anyone else do so), because I did not know of that early Oppenheimer paper at that time. Now, half a century later, I do know it. Ignorance of history is a privilege of youth.

Three months after Shelter Island, I attended a conference in Denmark that also produced exciting news.[283] (Robert did not come there.) In Shelter Island it had been conjectured[285] that the meson puzzles could be explained if there were *two* kinds of mesons. In Copenhagen I learned that these two kinds (now called π and μ, the latter not now called a meson) had actually been found, in fact that this result had already been published in the May 24, 1947, issue of Nature,[287] *before* Shelter Island! None of us knew of that at our meeting.

Shortly after my return, Oppenheimer asked me to give a seminar on the Copenhagen meeting. I did so; it took place in the Institute's Common Room. A special seminar room was almost but not completely finished, in a new building still known as "Building D." I had been talking for maybe one minute, when in came Einstein and sat down. For a very brief moment I was tongue-tied. I experienced a sense of unreality at having to lecture to the century's greatest scientist. It passed, and I went on with an enthusiastic account of the Copenhagen results. I may note that it was the only occasion in all my Institute years that I saw Einstein present at a physics seminar given by someone other than himself.

Pocono, March/April 1948

Shelter Island provided the initial stimulus for the postwar developments in quantum-field theory: relativistically invariant computational methods and renormalization theory. Already, five days after our conference, Bethe wrote to Oppenheimer[288] that he had obtained a theoretical estimate for the Lamb shift "in excellent agreement with experiment."[289] While his calculation was manifestly incomplete, it showed that, without doubt, the shift was a higher order QED effect. The first "clean" result of the new era was Schwinger's evaluation of the electron's anomalous magnetic moment (December 1947).[290] Thus began the new era of QED, in which all the troubles of the 1930s regarding infinities were bypassed (not eliminated) by new calculational methods, known as the renormalization program.[291]

By winter 1948, so much had recently happened in physics that another conference in Shelter Island style was called for. Oppenheimer had heard that there was a hotel in the Pocono Mountains in Pennsylvania that might be suitable for holding such a meeting. One morning he and I took off in his car (a blue Cadillac convertible) to check out the place, which indeed turned out to serve the purpose. On March 30 and April 1, 1948, the meeting came to be held in Pocono Manor. Many of the Shelter Island participants returned; newcomers included Bohr, Dirac, and Fermi.

There exists no printed version of the proceedings, but I have lying before me a dittoed copy of notes (dated April 2) taken at the meeting by John Wheeler. It is a 100-page document recording contributions by 15 speakers (including one by yours truly).

Forty pages are devoted to a marathon talk by Schwinger, on QED of course, given on the first morning. It was a major tour de force in which he unveiled a detailed new calculus for dealing with renormalization. It strained the absorption capacity of his audience, which explains an inadvertent remark by Rabi that first afternoon: "Yesterday Enrico [Fermi] said . . ." Schwinger's lecture led to this comment by Oppenheimer: "Now it does not matter anymore whether things are infinite"; and this one by Rabi: "What the hell should I measure now?"

The next longest (12 pages) entry is by Feynman. It is his first version of the "space-time approach" to quantum field theory applied to renormalization. Already at the final session of Shelter Island he had tried to explain to us his alternative formulation which he had begun working on before the new QED effects had been unveiled at that earlier conference. Darrow had recorded in his diary about that talk: "Feynman [spoke] with a clear voice, great rush of words and illustrative gestures sometimes ebullient."[292] At that time no one could follow what he was talking about. This time, the speed with which Feynman could reproduce results also found by Schwinger convinced us that he was on to something—but still nobody could follow his argument.

On April 5, a few days after we were back, Oppenheimer sent off a letter to all conference members. I quote from my copy:

> When I returned from the Pocono Conference, I found a letter from Tomonaga which seemed to me of such interest to us all that I am sending you a copy of it. Just because we were able to hear Schwinger's beautiful report, we may be better able to appreciate this independent development. From that letter:
>
> > I have taken the liberty of sending you copies of several papers and notes concerning the reaction of radiation field in scattering processes and related problems, which my collaborators and I have been investigating for last six months. I should be much obliged if you would be so kind to look them over. I should like to take this occasion to relate the circumstances of their formation and the reason why I have made up my mind to send you these manuscripts.

What had happened was this. Around the same time, a similar development had been reaching maturity in Japan. Tomonaga of the University of Education in Tokyo (predecessor of today's University of Tsukuba) was leading his collaborators there and at the University of Tokyo in an effort to tackle the problem of renormalizability, without the benefit of direct experimental support such as the Lamb shift. Already in 1946 he had published a paper (in English) on a completely covariant formulation of QED,[293] whereupon he and co-workers applied this method to renormalization of scattering processes.[294] The news of the Lamb shift was first brought to Japan through the science columns of *Newsweek* magazine, September 29, 1947, issue. The Tomonaga group at once began systematic calculations of this effect,[295] achieving results that agreed with those found by Americans.

Oppenheimer at once called Tomonaga, suggesting that he promptly publish a summary of his findings in the *Physical Review*, which he did,[296] and inviting him to the Institute, to which he came.

Solvay, September/October 1948

From September 27 to October 2, 1948, the 8th Solvay conference was held at the University of Brussels, devoted this time to "Elementary Particles." Oppenheimer was assigned the task to report[297] on progress in QED. In his historical introduction he now did refer to his early paper[46] on the shifts of light frequencies that I mentioned previously, and also to my review (1948) of the theory.[298] Among very recent developments he mentioned the first attempts to apply renormalization to meson field theory, which did not work well. "Despite these discouragements, it would seem premature to evaluate the prospects without further evidence."[297]

Discussants of the paper included Dirac, who then and later expressed dislike of the renormalization approach; Bohr, "I must deeply sympathize with the approach by Oppenheimer"; and Pauli, who expressed disagreement with Dirac's remarks.

I also note that, as far as I know, Solvay 8 was the first international conference in which mention is made—very briefly—of new, heavier mesons, then believed to have mass of about 800m (m = electron mass).[299] I shall come back later to these new particles.

Old Stone, April 1949

I have before me a letter from Robert, dated March 17, 1949, addressed to all members of Pocono. It reads:

> Arrangements are now completed for our conference. The National Academy of Science has agreed again to sponsor our meeting; Oldstone-on-the-Hudson [an inn 60 km north of New York City] has been reserved for the nights of Sunday, April 10th, 11th, 12th, 13th, and 14th; we will start work on Monday morning and should have four full days together. You may come as late as you wish on Sunday evening. R.O.

It was the sequel to Pocono.

By the time of Old Stone, interests of theorists had largely shifted to the physics of π-mesons, which had just been found to be copiously produced by the Berkeley accelerator known as a synchrocyclotron. QED remained a major item on the agenda, however, and this time it was Feynman's show. He had meanwhile worked out his methods systematically, and had sent in his first paper on that subject a few days before Old Stone.[300] Feynman's version, simpler and far easier to apply than Schwinger's, now began its rapid and never-waning rise in popularity. It was also Dyson's show, in particular because he had managed to build the bridge between Schwinger's and Feynman's approaches.[249]

The third main theme at Old Stone was the application of renormalization methods to meson theories of nuclear forces, which looked very bad. In fact, fundamental advances in the field theory of nuclear forces would not emerge until the 1970s.

My last recollection of Old Stone concerns my participation in an evening poker game. Others who joined were von Neumann, who played anxiously, Oppenheimer, very cautiously, and Teller, flamboyantly.

Rochester I, December 1950

After the Old Stone meeting, Oppenheimer decided that the original purpose, to assess the current status and the prospects for further developments, had been accomplished. Thereupon Robert Marshak (1916–1992), recently appointed chairman of the Physics Department in the University of Rochester (New York State), took a new initiative, to the lasting benefit of the high energy physics community. It was his belief that profitable meetings of the kind just ended should be continued but should be more international in scope and have a better mix of experimentalists and theorists, especially in view of rapid developments in accelerator physics. The result was a series of seven annual conferences, beginning in 1950, with ever-growing attendance, all held in Rochester, New York, with financial support from local industry. During Rochester I, the 1950 meeting, the subject of quantum electrodynamics did not even come up (although Feynman was there). After these first seven conferences, the meetings continued in later years but were most often held in different places, in different countries. Nonetheless, they have for years later continued to be called Rochester Conferences.

Since no published record exists for Rochester I, it may be of some use to state that it was a one-day meeting held on December 16, 1950, with an attendance of about 50; that it consisted of morning, afternoon, and evening sessions chaired respectively by Pais, Oppenheimer, and Bethe, and that the topics discussed were accelerator results on the interaction of pions and nucleons with matter, notably the recently discovered neutral meson (π^0),[301] muon physics, and cosmic ray physics. During the meeting, Oppenheimer suggested a discussion on the new mesons, but nothing came of that. I am grateful to the late Robert Marshak for having made available to me an unedited transcript of that meeting.

Rochester II (January) and III (December) 1952

Attendance at Rochester I had been about 50. Rochester II (January 11–12, 1952) saw a doubling of the number of participants. Later ones in this series of meetings have seen ever-growing numbers of those present. John Polkinghorne (1930–) has given an excellent account of the first 20 of these meetings;[302] from II on there exist records.

I noted earlier that in 1948, at Solvay 8, there was brief mention of new particles. At Rochester II these were the "hottest item on the agenda."[303] At that meeting I made the first proposals for a theoretical understanding of these new objects "with the slightly proprietary encouragement of Oppenheimer. . . . [Pais's] idea of associated production was a capital one, as was the general intuition that the new particles were going to require new selection rules. . . . He received magisterial endorsement from Oppenheimer."[304] I am not responsible for the title of my paper as it appears in the proceedings:

"An ordering principle for megalomorphian zoology." That fickle title was the creation of Oppenheimer, who, by the way, was also the inventor of the term "megalopolis."[305]

1952 is the only year in which two Rochester conferences took place, III on December 18–20. The only Oppenheimer remark of that meeting perhaps worth recording here was a comment on a contribution presented by a young man: "It is not completely clear from his papers, it is not completely clear to him and not completely clear to anyone."[306]

IBM, April 1953

On April 7, the IBM electronic data processing machine was publicly shown for the first time. At that ceremony, Robert gave the opening address,[307] which he began as follows:

> When I was asked to talk, I had the impression that the phone had rung in the wrong office at the Institute, and I said, "Haven't you got the wrong number? Don't you want to talk to Dr. von Neumann down the hall?" "No," I was told, "He really knows too much about this subject."
>
> So it was clear to me that my task was limited. I am to talk about the meaning of the computers in research, in new understanding of the world; I am not to talk about the immense prospect of their contributions to the defense program, of their contributions to industry, of their contributions to the solution of practical problems.

I give excerpts from this elegant talk.

> More than two millennia ago, computation was playing a very remarkable part in the life of Babylonia. There had been developed a most sophisticated and refined mathematical treatment of the raw data on lunar eclipses, purely as a mathematical problem without any mechanical model, without anything that we could call celestial mechanics. The problem the chaps had was to predict the next lunar eclipse and the next one after that, into the future. They learned the art of numbers so well that these same methods were still in successful use in India in the last century; and this, remember, was without any notion of the laws of motion; it was just from a study of the numbers themselves. . . .
>
> The use of computation to extend understanding is [therefore] not new. It characterizes the whole of the scientific life in the last centuries. But there is something new about the high-speed computer. I want to oversimplify and almost parody what this is about by stressing one element of it. The high-speed computer, in certain areas, is a sort of substitute for experiment. It enables us to find out the connection between things in places where we have not the power (and I hope my examples will illustrate why) to make those deliberate, controlled changes in the state of affairs which are the normal way that we try to disentangle things.
>
> I think I can illustrate by taking three examples:
>
> The first is the perpetual problem of the weather. How does the atmosphere act? And this, as everyone knows, is a complex problem in strongly non-linear

hydrodynamics. Great progress is being made in using rough information about the state of the atmosphere today to know something about the state of the atmosphere tomorrow—and that this will be of practical importance I need hardly add.

What will come out of it, too, is that after the accumulation of experience, which in this case is not to take weather readings so much as to do calculations, and check them occasionally against weather readings to see whether you got the point of that particular situation, a new kind of order and simplicity will emerge, because we will know what makes a difference, we will know what is important, we will know what is trivial, we will know (even though I think it in this case unlikely), whether we have forgotten some very deep or surprisingly new point.

A second example, that is even more striking, is this: We from time to time get messages of immense stellar explosions which may have taken place some hundred million years ago. It is hard to do experiments with those things. No one can go back a hundred million years, and no one wishes to go out a hundred million years into space in order to learn what effect mankind, if he then survives, will see two hundred million years from now. And yet it is of great interest and excitement, and a challenge to man's imagination, to try to figure out what causes these great events. This is also a deeply non-linear problem, in all likelihood a problem where the fundamental laws are known, a problem where the mathematical unscrambling will be the payoff.

The third example is a more modest thing, but also in its way striking, and that has to do with the state of affairs, not in an exploding star, but in an atomic explosion. Here I think a whole new tradition of the use of computers and of computational methods has been built up. And even today, when there have been a large number of atomic explosions, the inside of an exploding bomb is not a cozy place to observe; a great deal of the normal experimentation is foreclosed by that and by the cost and cumbersomeness of the effort. Initially, there was a much stronger argument, in that we did not have enough stuff to make an explosion. Then the important proving grounds of atomic bombs were the paper proving grounds in which one tries to see what ought to be going on. It is a rare, though not an unheard of event, that what happens in Nevada and in the Pacific tells us something important and new, that had not been found in this immense prior effort at understanding. This has set, I think, one of the highest standards of analysis that has ever appeared in what we could call a generalized sort of engineering.

In all of these efforts, one hopes for a lot. One hopes, first of all, out of the wealth of experience to get a simple view of what is at first quite a complicated phenomenon. One hopes that mathematics will eventually catch up in its full analytic powers with the experience that the computers give. One hopes to find out what the important elements of the problem are, and whether models work. And one hopes, above all, to find out if one has been a fool and left out the mainspring of the phenomena one has tried to investigate. . . .

It seems clear to me that in the statistical problems of genetics and of population studies, as in studies of economic models, experiment is also going to be a very costly and perhaps a prohibitive thing; thus I would expect that in these fields, too, the availability of computers could be of unmeasured value.

This is a new tool. It is a new tool, as was the microscope. It is a new tool, as are the tracers, the radioactive tracers, which have so recently become available to all branches of science. It is, as such a tool, a monument to man's reason, in two ways: to its limitation, because without experience, without massive experience, we never get the point; to its power, because once we have experience, knowledge cannot regress, science can never be retrograde. It is a tribute to deep modesty, and to the mind's high splendor.

A Book Review, October 1953

As best I know, this is the first book review Robert published.[308] The book, by Gordon Dean (1905–1958), then Chairman of the United States Atomic Energy Commission, gives a survey of the American atomic energy program to date.[309] I only give the review's opening lines, to illustrate Oppenheimer's knack for working sophisticated literary allusions into writing about scientific matters. "The atom, like all that touches us deeply, has its Stephen Dedalus as well as its Bloom, its lovers of Shiva and its devotees of Vishnu." It is not very clear to me what these words are meant to convey. Perhaps it will be to you.

Japan, September 1953

This entry does not deal with Oppenheimer's presence but with his absence.

On September 13 I arrived in Tokyo, to attend the first postwar conference in Japan in which foreign scientists, some 60 of them, were to participate. Two Japanese colleagues fetched me from the airport. In the taxi to my hotel they informed me that our meeting was treated as an event of national importance. I was told that, some days earlier, lectures for the general public had been arranged to explain what the meetings would be about, and that people had started queing up at 7:00 AM to get in at 1:00 PM; also that a leading Japanese physicist had conducted two months of prior briefings with reporters of the Asahi press.

The two men delivered me to my hotel, saying that they would collect me from there in an hour to bring me to a banquet for foreign participants of the conference, courtesy of the Japan Chamber of Commerce and Industry. I went to my room to wash up. While doing so I listened to the radio, catching what was apparently a news program. I was astonished to hear several times the words Oppenheimer *san* and even more so to hear Pais *san*. When the two men returned to collect me, I asked if they could please explain what that was about. They informed me that at the last minute Oppenheimer had canceled his plan to attend and chair the scientific opening session, and that I had been chosen to replace him.

I knew what Robert's change of plans was about. Shortly before departing from Princeton, Robert had told me in strict confidence that he had been informed that trouble was brewing for him in Washington in connection with his role in the atomic energy program. That trouble was to erupt into the open eight months thereafter, as I shall later recount in detail.

After the conference meetings,[310] held in Tokyo and Kyoto, we were taken to excursions which included a visit to Hiroshima. American conference members (myself included) had felt quite uncomfortable regarding how we would be received there. Those worries turned out to be unfounded. Officials as well as men in the street treated us in most friendly and courteous ways—even though their city was still largely in ruins at the time of our visit. I wonder how Oppenheimer would have felt had he been able to join us there.

Rochester IV, January 1954

Oppenheimer presided over the opening session, held on Monday, January 25. it was the first of these meetings to be reported in *Physics Today*.[311] I too had been at the conference but only now, reading through its entire proceedings, did I realize how unusually quiet Robert had been at that time. The only comment I found made by him came after a young theoretician remarked that a certain theory gives nonsense: "Not nonsense, you get an answer different from experiment. (Laughter.)"[312]

It is quite probable that Oppenheimer's near silence at Rochester IV was caused by his being severely distracted because of the official charges filed against him the previous month, December 1953, by the AEC.

CHAPTER 16

FURTHER ON OPPENHEIMER THE MAN

Los Alamos Vignettes

In chapter 9 I referred to Bethe and Weisskopf for an account of Oppenheimer's role as leader of the Los Alamos enterprise. As repeatedly stated, since I had not been there myself, I do not feel competent to form a personal judgment of that role. I am further constrained because reminiscences by others on science at Los Alamos are of course restricted by rules on classified information as they existed at the time those recollections were written down. That last restriction does not, however, apply to the numerous reminiscences of Oppenheimer's personality, not only by physicists but also by others. Moreover, I am in a position to confront those readily with my own memories of the years immediately after the war. What follows next is therefore an excerpt of others' observations of Oppenheimer the man in Los Alamos.

Robert Wilson

Robert Wilson (1914–2000) has stated about meetings held in Berkeley in preparation of Los Alamos:

> [At one meeting] Rabi and Bacher (and perhaps others) had managed to talk Oppy out of his determination to have everyone in the new lab inducted into the army. Before that, as Oppy and I had traveled about the country on various missions connected with the Los Alamos project, we had argued fiercely about his suggestion of our becoming soldiers in uniform.

I argued the impracticality of scientists taking arbitrary orders from above—all the orders from above that I had seen for the past year had seemed a bit nonsensical. Nor are scientists at their best in unquestioningly following orders. I wondered if we could function at all in those circumstances. But Oppy would get a faraway look in his eyes and tell me that this war was different from any war ever fought before: it was a war about the principles of freedom and it was being fought by a "people's army," and we all belonged right in there with the "people." Now I can be as idealistic as the next guy, but I thought that he had a screw loose somewhere when he talked like that. I couldn't budge him on the subject, so I was relieved when the reason of others, stronger than I, prevailed. . . .

I nagged at Oppy all day about his indecisiveness. We insisted that decisions had to be made, that people had to know what to do, when to come to Los Alamos, that priorities had to be established, that we had to come to a realistic understanding of where we stood with the army people. We wanted a little organization, we wanted to know who was to be in charge of what, not just vague talk about the scientific problems nor the even vaguer ideas about democracy. There were immediate problems to be faced, and from our point of view Oppy was not facing up to them. . . .

Typically, the day's technical discussion drifted into the evening's socialities. The driest of dry martinis mixed by the hand of the master, sophisticated guests, gourmet food (but on the scant side), an amorphous buzz of conversation, smoke, alcohol—all these were the inevitable ingredients of an evening at the Oppenheimers. . . .

I was soon caught up by the Oppenheimer charisma, became a loyal and devoted lieutenant, a confidant, a friend (at least, until the postwar era when his personality seemed to change). Oppenheimer stretched me. His style, the poetic vision of what we were doing, of life, of a relationship to people, inflamed me. In his presence, I became more intelligent, more vocal, more intense, more prescient, more poetic myself. Although normally a slow reader, when he handed me a letter I would glance at it and hand it back prepared to discuss the nuances of it minutely. Now it is true, in retrospect, that there was a certain element of self-delusion in all that, and that once out of his presence the bright things that had been said were difficult to reconstruct or remember. Nor, as I left, could I quite decide what it was we had agreed to do. No matter, the tone had been established. I would know how to invent what it was that had to be done. . . .

Not all the problems to be worked out in setting up a laboratory and the village around it involved matters of high policy. A few hundred very individualistic people were soon living on the [Los Alamos] site, and very real problems concerning day to day needs of life became important too. At first Oppy tried to deal with these himself. Surprisingly to me, he was remarkably good at it, but the nature of the problems was such that Solomon himself would have had to choose only between a number of bad possibilities. Oppenheimer had more important matters to attend to, and for this reason he appointed a Town Council to take care of these knotty civil problems.[313]

Another, vital, group of problems concerned health hazards.

Life was not safe for those who worked in the Tech Area or at one of the remote sites. High explosives could detonate unexpectedly or cause skin rashes. High voltages, large currents, and toxic chemicals were commonly encountered in routine work. During the war, with its continual atmosphere of crisis, there was little time to worry about contaminated waste. Certainly Oppenheimer and his staff practiced safety and were concerned about the health of all employees. However, there was not a full understanding of the effects of contaminated waste or the ability to know fully how to treat such waste. Radiation from the . . . accelerators, or radioactive substances was another danger. Plutonium and polonium emitted ionizing radiation, and uranium was a chemical poison. However, during the first year little fissionable material existed at Los Alamos.

Aware of the danger from radiation, Oppenheimer . . . [created a Health Group, which] consisted mainly of hematology technicians who recorded radiation exposures and monitored potentially dangerous areas. The group was also responsible during 1943 for defining safe exposures to radiation hazards and establishing safe operating procedures. Keeping track of individual exposure proved difficult, for no one knew the size of a dangerous dose, how much radiation had been absorbed, or how to tell if a large dose had been absorbed.[314]

Hans Bethe

Oppenheimer had expected that he could continue to look after the theoretical work in Los Alamos as well as direct the laboratory. After a few months he was convinced that the theoretical work needed a separate head, and Bethe was chosen.

To the world outside physics, Oppenheimer is best known as the director of the Los Alamos Scientific Laboratory during the war. I had the good fortune to participate in an activity preparatory to the work at Los Alamos. In the summer of 1942, a small group met under Oppenheimer's leadership to discuss theoretical methods of assembling an atomic weapon. By that time it was very likely that Fermi's atomic pile would work, that Dupont would build a production reactor, and that useful quantities of plutonium would be produced. The separation of uranium-235 by the electromagnetic method, although extremely expensive, also seemed very likely to succeed: separation by gaseous diffusion was less certain. In any case, the committee in charge of the uranium project considered it advisable to begin a serious study of the assembly of a weapon. It turned out to be accurate timing. Some members of our group, under the leadership of Serber, did calculations on the actual subject of our study, the neutron diffusion in an atomic bomb and the energy yield obtainable from it. The rest of us, especially Teller, Oppenheimer, and I, indulged ourselves in a far-off project—namely, the question of whether and how an atomic bomb could be used to trigger an H-bomb. Grim as the subject was, it was a most interesting enterprise. We were forever inventing new tricks, finding ways to calculate, and rejecting most of the tricks on the basis of the calculations. It was one of the best scientific collaborations I have ever experienced.[315]

Bethe recalled elsewhere:

[Oppenheimer] understood immediately when he heard anything, and fitted it into the general scheme of things and drew the right conclusions. There was just nobody else in that laboratory who came even close to him in his knowledge.

There was human warmth as well. Everybody certainly had the impression that Oppenheimer cared what each particular person was doing. In talking to someone he made it clear that that person's work was important for the success of the whole project. I don't remember any occasion at Los Alamos in which he was nasty to any person, whereas before and after the war he was often that way. At Los Alamos he didn't make anybody feel inferior, not anybody.[316]

Edward Teller

Edward Teller first met Oppenheimer in 1937. The meeting, Teller says, was "painful but characteristic. On the evening I was to talk at a Berkeley colloquium, he took me out to a Mexican restaurant for dinner. I didn't have the practice in speaking that I've had since, and I was already a little nervous. The plates were so hot, and the spices were so hot—as you might suspect if you knew Oppenheimer—and his personality was so overpowering, that I lost my voice."[317]

Teller traveled to Berkeley, together with Bethe, to participate in the summer study (1942) that preceded Los Alamos. Bethe has remembered: "We had a compartment on the train to California, so we could talk freely. . . . Teller told me that the fission bomb was all well and good and, essentially, was now a sure thing. In reality, the work had hardly begun. Teller likes to jump to conclusions. He said that what we really should think about was the possibility of igniting deuterium as a fission weapon—the hydrogen bomb."[318] Teller had studied two thermonuclear reactions that fuse deuterium to heavier nuclei with release of binding energy. In Berkeley "the senior men turned their collective brilliance to fusion. They had not yet bothered to name generic bombs of uranium and plutonium. But from the pre-anthropic darkness where ideas abide in nonexistence until minds imagine them into the light, the new bomb emerged already chased with the technocratic euphemism of art deco slang: the Super, they named it."[319]

During the Berkeley summer study the two men had begun what another participant judged a "mental love affair." Teller "liked and respected Oppie enormously. He kept wanting to talk about him with others who knew him, kept bringing up his name in conversation."[320] Bethe has observed then and later that despite their many outward differences, Teller and Oppenheimer were,

> fundamentally . . . very similar. Teller had an extremely quick understanding of things, so did Oppenheimer. . . . They were also somewhat alike in that their actual production, their scientific publications, did not measure up in any way to their capacity. I think Teller's mental capacity is very high, and so was Oppenheimer's but, on the other hand, their papers, while they included some

very good ones, never reached really the top standards. Neither of them ever came up to the Nobel Prize level. I think you just cannot get to that level unless you are somewhat introverted.[321]

In the late summer of 1942, Oppenheimer became quite dubious about the idea of a Super, as is seen from his letter to Teller: "The suggestions that you make have by now for us [O. and Bethe] a pretty fantastic sound. . . . We are satisfied, however, with the uranium [bomb]."[322]

Teller, not dismayed, requested and received permission to head a group in Los Alamos' Theory Division for study of his hydrogen bomb idea, better called his obsession.

> The thermonuclear bomb seemed then a hopeful possibility not too much beyond the . . . bombs from uranium and plutonium. Making it his particular province, Teller became a familiar figure at the liquid-deuterium or cryogenics plant, Laboratory Y. Physicists there vividly remember the way his gentle smile illuminated the place, especially during coffee breaks. Watching him stir the entire group's sugar ration into his coffee cup, they wondered how a man could be so genuinely friendly and at the same time so ruthlessly self-absorbed. . . .
>
> During the continuing thermonuclear discussions [one participant recalled] I remember Teller's getting up to make a speech. He started out by saying he would give only qualitative factors. But when he warmed up, he laid out a few calculations which showed he had actually forgotten the factor of C^2, the velocity of light. I suppose that for a profusely inventive man any sort of figures could sometimes seem like a straitjacket.
>
> Oppenheimer looked musingly at the blackboard as though it had opened a new philosophical concept for him. He seemed to be pondering what sort of reasoning could operate with an error of a million per cent. "This idea of dealing only in qualitative factors makes an interesting approach," he said, "but should we go so far as to treat the velocity of light as unity?" . . . [The participant] could not tell whether Oppenheimer meant to make [a joke], but the rustle in the audience showed he had done so. Teller [reacted with] a convulsive start and a whitened face.[323]

Teller himself has written:

> One of the first buildings constructed at Los Alamos was designed to handle thermonuclear materials. Several of the gifted scientists recruited to work at the Los Alamos Laboratory signed on only because they were intrigued by the thermonuclear possibilities.
>
> The thermonuclear objectives of Los Alamos, however, were sidetracked during the laboratory's first year for two compelling reasons: Successful construction of an atomic bomb proved to be somewhat more difficult than anyone had expected, and it became obvious to me that our thermonuclear discussions of the summer before had been incomplete—so incomplete that the new theoretical questions I raised seemed unanswerable, and realization of a thermonuclear explosion seemed most doubtful. The Los Alamos Laboratory, justifiably, gave the highest priority to the field with the greatest promise of early success. Nearly

all of the laboratory's theoretical physicists turned their full attention to the atomic bomb project. No matter how difficult it might be, we knew we had to produce an atomic bomb before our enemies could do it. Work on thermonuclear reactions was all but suspended.[324]

Teller was aware of the urgency of the work on the uranium bomb. In 1943 he and Bethe had sent the following memorandum to Oppenheimer:

Recent reports both through the newspapers and through secret service, have given indications that the Germans may be in possession of a powerful new weapon which is expected to be ready between November and January. There seems to be a considerable probability that this new weapon is tubealloy [code name for uranium]. It is not necessary to describe the probable consequences which would result if this proves to be the case.

It is possible that the Germans will have, by the end of this year, enough material accumulated to make a large number of gadgets which they will release at the same time on England, Russia and this country. In this case there would be little hope for any counter-action. However, it is also possible that they will have a production, let us say, of two gadgets a month. This would place Britain in an extremely serious position but there would be hope for counter-action from our side before the war is lost, provided our own tubealloy program is drastically accelerated in the next few weeks.[325]

Teller again:

Despite the urgency of the situation, Oppenheimer during those years of struggle with atomic questions did not lose sight of the more distant possibilities. He urged me to continue exploring the thermonuclear field, even though it was beyond the immediate aim of the laboratory. This was not easy advice for him to give or for me to take. It is hard to work apart from others in a scientific community, especially when most people are working toward a goal of the highest interest and urgency. Oppenheimer, Fermi, and many of the most prominent men in the laboratory, however, continued to say that the work at Los Alamos would not be complete as long as the feasibility of a thermonuclear bomb remained in doubt. But until atomic success was verified at Alamogordo on July 16, 1945, the thermonuclear program was eclipsed by our country's vital need for an atomic bomb.

After Alamogordo, some of the best scientific minds in the laboratory were applied to thermonuclear problems. Fermi and Bethe were among those who associated themselves with the thermonuclear effort that had been dormant for so long. But their association ended in a few short weeks, before anything could be accomplished. Hiroshima, coming only three weeks after the Alamogordo test, filled many associates with a moral repugnance for weapons work. Fermi, Bethe, and dozens of others left Los Alamos. Even Oppenheimer, who had supported and urged the thermonuclear effort for years, turned his back on the project. Publicly he announced: "The physicists have known sin." Privately, on the day of Hiroshima, he came to my Los Alamos office for a long talk. He told me that we would not develop a hydrogen bomb. Before Nagasaki, before the war was over, Oppenheimer made it clear to me that he would have nothing further to do with thermonuclear work.[324]

Teller did make an important contribution to thermonuclear physics before the war was over, however, to wit to the basic theory of thermonuclear reactions in the atmosphere. He was coauthor of a report that showed that no danger existed that a thermonuclear test would set the atmosphere on fire. This report, LA-602, was circulated in August 1946; it was secret until February 1973, when it was declassified.

In 1983, long after Oppenheimer's death, Teller has written:

> Throughout the war years, Oppie knew in detail what was going on in every part of the Laboratory. He was incredibly quick and perceptive in analyzing human as well as technical problems. Of the more than ten thousand people who eventually came to work at Los Alamos, Oppie knew several hundred intimately, by which I mean that he knew what their relationships with one another were and what made them tick. He knew how to organize, cajole, humor, soothe feelings—how to lead powerfully without seeming to do so. He was an exemplar of dedication, a hero who never lost his humanness. Disappointing him somehow carried with it a sense of wrongdoing. Los Alamos' amazing success grew out of the brilliance, enthusiasm and charisma with which Oppenheimer led it.[326]

He could have saved himself misery if he had spoken in this vein at the Oppenheimer hearings in 1954 (to which I shall turn later).

Enrico Fermi

In the summer of 1944, when Fermi (1901–1954) became a permanent resident of the mesa, Oppenheimer, who wanted to give him an official title, made him an associate director of the laboratory and created a new division, F Division, that he placed under Fermi's direct jurisdiction. The general responsibility of F Division was to investigate problems that did not fit into the work of other divisions.[327] He remained in Los Alamos through December 1945.

> Out of curiosity in 1940, while visiting Berkeley to deliver a lecture, Enrico Fermi attended a seminar one of Oppenheimer's protégés led in the master's style. [Afterward he joked], "I am getting rusty and old. I cannot follow the highbrow theory developed by Oppenheimer's pupils anymore. I went to their seminar and was depressed by my inability to understand them. Only the last sentence cheered me up: it was, 'and this is Fermi's theory of beta decay.'"[328]

> Fermi, superb experimentalist that he was, contributed valuably to the program of experimental studies, defining with clarity problems that needed to be examined. For him the war work was duty, however, and the eager conviction he found in Los Alamos puzzled him. "After he had sat in on one of his first conferences here," Oppenheimer recalls, "he turned to me and said, 'I believe your people actually *want* to make a bomb.' I remember his voice sounded surprised."[329]

Richard Feynman

Feynman (1918–1988) notes:

> We were recruited . . . by Oppenheimer and other people, and he was very patient. He paid attention to everybody's problems. He worried about my wife who had TB, and whether there would be a hospital out here, and everything. It was the first time I met him in such a personal way; he was a wonderful man.[330]

Luis Alvarez

Luis Alvarez (1911–1988) was at Los Alamos in 1944–45. From his autobiography:

> Lawrence strongly supported Robert's appointment as director of Los Alamos in 1943, when some of Robert's closest friends were skeptical. "He couldn't run a hamburger stand," I heard one of them say. I was certainly surprised to learn of the appointment, but after working at Los Alamos later in the war I came to feel enormous admiration for the way Robert handled that terribly difficult job.[331]

Elsewhere, Alvarez recalled:

> Not long after I began working at Los Alamos, Robert Oppenheimer, obviously pleased to see me finally on his staff, assigned me to his steering committee, which governed the laboratory. It was composed of division heads and others like myself who had wide experience in war projects. Remembering the unworldly and long-haired prewar Robert, I was surprised to see the extent to which he had developed into an excellent laboratory director and a marvelous leader of men. His haircut almost as short as a military officer's, he ran an organization of thousands, including some of the best theoretical and experimental physicists and engineers in the world. The laboratory's fantastic morale could be traced directly to the personal quality of Robert's guidance.[332]

Robert Serber

Around Christmas 1941, just after Pearl Harbor, Serber (1909–1997) received a call from Oppenheimer, who wanted to come to Urbana (where Serber held a University post) to discuss a delicate matter. On a walk in the corn fields Robert told him that he would be appointed head of the atomic bomb project and asked Serber to be his assistant. So it came about that Serber and his wife were the first after Oppenheimer to be recruited for Los Alamos.

From his autobiography: "We weren't allowed to take any papers home or even to talk about our work outside the technical area. This policy, while largely dictated by security concerns, I think had another effect as well: it encouraged an active social life on the mesa. There were lots of dinner parties, dorm dances, and weekends in the beautiful country around Los Alamos."[333]

From later in the memoir: "on the day Paris was liberated, in August of 1944, Rabi happened to be around, and he and Viki Weisskopf decided the event wasn't being properly celebrated. They marched around the residential area bellowing the Marseillaise, inviting everyone to join the parade and it turned into a sort of holiday."[334]

Niels Bohr

On the evening of September 29, 1943, two German freighters docked in the port of Copenhagen for the purpose of transporting Danish Jews to Germany. Danish authorities had been forewarned. So it came to pass that earlier that same day, Bohr (1885–1962)—who was half-Jewish—fled Denmark to Sweden. On October 4 he was flown from there to England, where he joined the British atomic bomb effort.[335]

Serber has recalled:

> Late in December 1943, Niels Bohr and his son Aage arrived in Los Alamos bearing the aliases Nicholas and James Baker, and promptly became Uncle Nick and Jim. There was a story that just before coming to Los Alamos, in a Washington hotel, Bohr entered an elevator and found himself face to face with a woman he knew as the wife of the Austrian physicist Hans von Halban. He said, "Good evening, Mrs. von Halban." She answered, "I'm not Mrs. von Halban now; I'm Mrs. Placzek. Good evening, Professor Bohr." And Bohr replied, "I'm not Professor Bohr now; I'm Mr. Baker." Elsa Placzek's new husband was the Bohemian physicist George Placzek, who had visited the ranch one summer and was now a member of the British Mission to Los Alamos.
>
> On the last day of December 1943, a secretary stuck her head in my door (the offices had no phones) and said Oppie would like me to come to his office. When I entered, Niels and Aage Bohr, Bethe, Teller, and Victor Weisskopf were already there. Oppie handed me a scrap of paper that looked as if it had been carelessly ripped from a note pad. It bore a sketch, and he asked me what I thought the sketch represented. After a minute I handed it back and said it looked like a heavy water moderated nuclear reactor [a so-called pile]. He then told me that Bohr had gotten it from Heisenberg [who had given it to him during a visit—much discussed since—to Copenhagen]. The question was whether it could be interpreted as a weapon. The Los Alamos experts gathered in that room all agreed it was useless as an explosive, and Bethe and Teller left to write a report to that effect for Groves, with whom Bohr, himself no expert, had previously raised the question. On New Year's Day, Oppie wrote Groves an account of our meeting and enclosed the Bethe-Teller memorandum.[333]

The letter read:

Dear General Groves:

> I am enclosing a memorandum written by Bethe and Teller after the conference yesterday. Present at the conference were the Bakers, Bethe, Teller, Tolman, Weisskopf, Serber, Bacher, and, for a small part of the time as you know, Oppenheimer. The calculations referred to and described in the accompanying memorandum were carried out by Bethe and Teller, but the fundamental physics was

quite fully discussed and the results and methods have been understood and agreed to by Baker.

I believe that it would be appropriate to emphasize that the *completely negative findings* [my italics] reported in the accompanying memorandum apply to the arrangement of materials suggested by Baker and take into account all the physical elements which appeared important to him. No complete assurance can be given that with a new idea or a new arrangement, something along these lines might not work. It is, however, true that many of us have given thought to the matter in the past, and that neither then nor now has any possibility suggested itself which had the least promise. The purpose of the enclosed memorandum is to give you a formal assurance, together with the reasons therefore, that the arrangement suggested to you by Baker would be a quite useless military weapon.

Very sincerely yours,
J. R. Oppenheimer[338]

The accompanying memorandum begins as follows: "EXPLOSION OF AN INHOMOGENEOUS URANIUM-HEAVY WATER PILE. We propose to show that the explosion of an inhomogeneous pile will liberate energies which are probably smaller, and certainly not much larger, than those obtainable by the explosion of an equal mass of TNT."[339]

"It was clearly a drawing of a reactor," Bethe recalled after the war, "but when we saw it our conclusion was that these Germans were totally crazy— did they want to throw a reactor down on London?"[340]

Bohr's first visit to "Y" (code symbol for Los Alamos) lasted only a few weeks. Robert made sure that his contribution was a matter of record. On January 17 he wrote to Groves:

Dr. Baker has left today and I think it appropriate to report to you briefly on his visit.

1. On the technical side Dr. Baker concerned himself primarily with the correlation and interpretation of the many new data on nuclear fission and related topics which have been obtained by this project. He left with us a brief report on the theoretical understanding of these data. It has been the point of view of this laboratory that in matters of such great importance, and where theories were involved which were new and unproven, all important quantities would have to be determined by experimental measurement, and I believe this policy was and is sound. Nevertheless, the advantage of some theoretical insight into the phenomena is very great indeed in that it enables us to evaluate experiments critically, to determine the relative priority of experiments, and in general to reduce the amount of futile discussion and waste motion. For all these reasons the work that Baker did for us should prove of very great value in the months to come. Baker concerned himself very little with the engineering problems of our program although he is of course aware of their importance and their difficulty.

2. By arrangement with Chadwick and me, Baker is to remain on the British payroll and all his expenses are to be paid by the British. A change in this

arrangement will only be made if you or Dr. Chadwick see strong reasons to alter it.

3. I should like in a formal way to express my hope that Baker's collaboration with this project will continue, since it has been of great help to us and is likely to be so throughout the year.

4. By word and deed Dr. Baker has done everything he could to support this project and to indicate that he is sympathetic not only with its purposes and general method of procedure, but with the policies and achievements of the project's overall direction. I should like to make it quite clear that the effect of his presence on the morale of those with whom he came in contact was always positive and always helpful, and that I see every reason to anticipate that this will be true in the future.[341]

Groves, too, was sympathetic to Bohr's influence. "An urgent appeal from Oppenheimer to the General has resulted in the latter agreeing that Bohr can go back again to Y when he wishes to. Oppenheimer's hope is that Bohr will pay more and more frequent visits to Y, and ultimately settle down there."[342] So it came about that Bohr peddled back and forth between England and the United States, though he never settled at "Y."

Bohr's presence at Y contributed only marginally to the weapons project. "They didn't need my help in making the atom bomb," he later told a friend.[343] He did follow the bomb work with "the deepest admiration . . . for the magnificent endeavor carried on here in Y, with the greatest zeal and ingenuity,"[344] however, while correspondence with Oppenheimer shows that "I have thought about various aspects of nuclear problems."[345] Bohr's main concerns, from 1943 on, were the political implications of the new weapons. Oppenheimer has said later, "Bohr at Los Alamos was marvelous. . . . He took a very lively technical interest. . . . But his real function, I think for almost all of us, was not the technical one."[346] He and Bohr spent hours discussing Bohr's conviction that the successful development of an atomic weapon would require a radical change in international relations and that Britain and the United States must make a generous offer to share its control if they hoped to avoid a disastrous arms race. Lecturing in 1963 on "Niels Bohr and his Times," Oppenheimer recalled, "He made the enterprise seem hopeful. . . . [he spoke of] his own high hope that the outcome would be good, that the objectivity, the cooperation of the sciences, would play a helpful part, [all this was something] we all wanted to believe."[346]

Bohr's views deeply influenced Oppenheimer and a few others to whom he talked at Los Alamos. They became gospel to most Los Alamos scientists as soon as the successful test of July 16, 1945, relieved the pressure of work and freed them psychologically to ponder its meaning.

To conclude this Bohr vignette, I recount a story told by Oppenheimer. One day in the spring of 1950 Bohr, known for his mumbling speech, called on Secretary of State Dean Acheson (1893–1971) to discuss with him the contents of an open letter dealing with his political ideas concerning the atom that he planned to submit to the United Nations. The meeting began at, say, two o'clock, with Bohr doing the talking. At about 2:30, Acheson spoke to Bohr something like this, "Professor Bohr, there are three things I must tell you at this time. First, whether I like it or not, I shall have to leave you at three for my next appointment. Secondly, I am deeply interested in your ideas. Thirdly, up till now I have not understood one word you have said." Whereupon, the story goes, Bohr got so enraged that he waxed eloquent for the remainder of the appointment.

Young Wives' Tales

Elsie McMillan (1913–1997)

Returning from the commissary one day I found a soldier standing guard at my door. He saluted me and said, "Good afternoon, Mrs. Oppenheimer, the baby you left in the bedroom is quite all right." I replied, "Thank you very much, but I am not Mrs. Oppenheimer and I didn't leave a baby in my house." He said, "My God, I'm guarding the wrong house!" (We were next door neighbors.) Very shortly after that a fence went up around the Oppenheimers' home. The guards then had to patrol around the fence, and Kitty Oppenheimer and I felt very sorry for them because in winter at Los Alamos we had very dry cold weather; cold enough for icicles to reach from the roof of our one-story house to the ground. Kitty and I would sneak out and leave thermos bottles and sandwiches for the guards.

Los Alamos had a small hospital with only two bedrooms, a waiting room, a pharmacy, and an operating room which at first could not be used because we did not have the proper anesthetic for the altitude. . . .

At the guard gate, we all showed our passes, though of course we didn't need one for our two month old baby. On one occasion, so the story goes, Oppy came up to the gate and went whizzing through. He had a lot on his mind and just went full speed ahead; when the guard shouted at him he didn't pay any attention. Finally, when his tires were shot at, Robert backed up and pulled down his window and handed a crisp dollar bill to the guard saying, sorry sir.[347]

Bernice Brode (1901–1989)

The strangest feature of all to us was the security. We were quite literally fenced in by a tall barbed wire barricade surrounding the entire site and patrolled along the outside by armed MPs. In our first weeks we heard shots but never knew why. Actually we felt cozy and safe, free from robbers and mountain bears. We never locked our doors. In our second year, extra MPs were sent to guard the homes of the Oppenheimers and Parsons, making round-the-clock patrols. No one, not even the families themselves, could go in without a pass. If they had forgotten their pass, they had a hard time getting in. Some of the practical house-wives cooked up a scheme to use these MPs as babysitters in the immediate neighborhood. What could be safer than a man with a gun guarding the precious small-fry? The children were sure to be impressed and behave accordingly. Martha Parsons never hired a babysitter as long as the MPs remained around her house, and Kitty Oppenheimer once got real service when the guard came to the front door of the house she was visiting to tell her that little Peter was crying. Soon after, the sergeant in charge put his foot down, no more babysitting for his crack MPs! a group that was specially picked for duty at the number-one government project. The patrol outside the fence soon ceased except for an occasional mounted patrol. There was little temptation to conquer the fence and no one tried, except dogs and children, to dig holes underneath it. Rather the fence became a symbol. We felt protected and very important, and tended to act accordingly, griping at everything, including our fenced-in condition. Although we could leave the mesa at will with a pass, we did have to keep within the boundaries roughly defined by Albuquerque, Cuba, Las Vegas and Lamy, all in New Mexico. We would go to Mesa Verde, Denver, Carlsbad Caverns or El Paso, with special permission. We could not talk to strangers or friends on trips and it was common knowledge that we were being watched by the Army G-2 and the FBI. In general, we were not allowed to send children to camp or away to school. If they were already in school they could not come up for vacations. Our driver's licenses had numbers instead of names and were not signed. All our occupations were listed "Engineers" and our addresses as Post Office Box 1663, Santa Fe. With gas rationing in effect, most of the traffic between Lamy and Santa Fe and Taos was ours. All in all it looked more than mysterious to the state police when we happened to be caught for a traffic violation. One day on the Taos road a caravan of Army cars carrying a group of Nobel Prize winners and Deans of science, all traveling under false names, was flagged down. When the officer asked the names of the occupants, each refused as politely as possible to give it. "Tell that to the judge," retorted the police as he wrote out the summons, determined to teach the almighty Army a lesson. "I'm sorry, officer," ventured one of the men, "we can't appear either." Finally the Army driver soothed the irate officer with the promise to take the summons to his commanding officer, who would look after it. And it took this commanding officer and the governor of New Mexico to come to an understanding about this.

After Oppenheimer's daughter Toni was born, the sign "Oppenheimer" was placed over baby Tony's crib and people filed by in the corridor of Los Alamos hospital for days to view the boss's baby girl. General Groves complained about the rapid increase in the population which immediately increased the housing problem and eventually would increase the school troubles. Rumor had it that the General ordered the commanding officer to do something about it. It is not clear what, if anything, was ever done. Our population was young and vigorous and the babies were free, so what could the General expect? . . .

We were all cut down to size at Los Alamos and it was sometimes a sobering experience. Even Oppenheimer abandoned his former pattern of living. I remember the old days in Berkeley, when he would not accept a class before eleven in the morning so he could feel free to stay up late for parties, music, or ideas.

But at Los Alamos, when the whistle blew at 7:30—we had a factory whistle—
Oppy would be on his way to T and hardly anyone could beat him to it. When
Sam Allison [1900–1965] came to the site from Chicago he shared Oppy's office
for some time. Sam said his one ambition was to be sitting at his desk when
Oppy opened the door.[347]

Robert Oppenheimer

In his early years Oppenheimer felt inferior himself, had always felt for the
actions of his life, as he confessed many years afterward, "a very great sense
of revulsion and of wrong." At Los Alamos for the first time he seems to
have found alleviation of that loathing. He may have discovered there a
process of self-analysis that served him more comprehensively later in his
life: "In an attempt to break out and be a reasonable man, I had to realize
that my own worries about what I did were valid and were important, but
that they were not the whole story, that there must be a complementary
way of looking at them, because other people did not see them as I did. And
I needed what they saw, and needed them."[349] Certainly he found the more
traditional alleviation of losing himself in work.

Whatever his burden of morale and work in those years, Oppenheimer
also carried his full share of private pain. He was kept under constant surveillance, his movements monitored and his rooms and telephones bugged;
strangers observed his most intimate hours. His home life cannot have been
happy. Kitty responded to the stress of living at isolated Los Alamos by
drinking heavily. Eventually Martha Parsons, a daughter of Admiral William "Deke" Parsons, director of the Los Alamos Ordnance Division, took
over the duties of social leadership on the Hill. Army security officers
hounded the director of the central laboratory of the nation's most important secret war project mercilessly; at least one of them, Peer de Silva, was
convinced Oppenheimer was a Soviet spy. They interrogated him frequently,
fishing for the names of people he knew or believed to be members of the
Communist Party, hoping to trip him up. He invented circumstances and
volunteered the names of friends to protect his own, indiscretions that would
return in time to haunt him.

One example of the indignities Robert had to submit to: during the first
Los Alamos summer he heard from Jean Tatlock, the unhappy woman he
had loved before he met his wife. Loyally, even though she had been and still
might be a Communist and he knew himself to be spied upon, he went to
her; an FBI document coldly summarizes a security man's peepshow version
of that meeting: "On June 14, 1943, Oppenheimer traveled via Key Railway

from Berkeley to San Francisco on the evening of June 14, 1943, where he was met by Jean Tatlock who kissed him. They dined at the Xochimilcho Cafe, 787 Broadway, San Francisco, then proceeded at 10:50 PM to 1405 Montgomery Street and entered a top floor apartment. Subsequently, the lights were extinguished and Oppenheimer was not observed until 8:30 AM the next day when he and Jean Tatlock left the building together."[350]

The following letter by Groves to Robert shows that his life in Los Alamos was a kind of privileged prison:

> In view of the nature of the work on which you are engaged, the knowledge of it which is possessed by you and the dependence which rests upon you for its successful accomplishment, it seems necessary to ask you to take certain special precautions with respect to your personal safety.
>
> It is requested that:
> (a) You refrain from flying in airplanes of any description; the time saved is not worth the risk. (If emergency demands their use my prior consent should be requested.)
> (b) You refrain from driving an automobile for any appreciable distance (above a few miles) and from being without suitable protection on any lonely road, such as the road from Los Alamos to Santa Fe. On such trips you should be accompanied by a competent, able bodied, armed guard. There is no objection to the guard serving as chauffeur.
> (c) Your cars be driven with due regard to safety and that in driving about town a guard of some kind should be used, particularly during the hours of darkness. The cost of such guard is a proper charge against the United States.
>
> I realize that these precautions may be personally burdensome and that they may appear to you to be unduly restrictive but I am asking you to bear with them until our work is successfully completed.[351]

Nevertheless, at Los Alamos, Robert often went out of his way to make others feel privileged as well.

> [Robert] seemed to understand the uprooted feeling that afflicted newcomers, many of whom had left homes as pleasant as the Oppenheimers' own house in Berkeley. Dismayed by lack of privacy and recurrent milk, water, and power shortages, they were somewhat appeased by the knowledge that it was Oppenheimer who had included fireplaces and large closets in the original house plans. He no longer came to dinner bearing bouquets of flowers, the gesture for which he was famous among Berkeley hostesses, but he gave both employed and nonworking wives a sense that their presence and participation in the collective enterprise was important. He shared the anxiety over a rash of illnesses that afflicted the mesa as families from all over the country pooled regional germs and adjusted to local food and water and to the 7,300 foot altitude. When anxiety reached a peak in the autumn of 1943 with the death of a young chemist, wife of a group leader, from an unidentified form of paralysis, it was somewhat reassuring to know that Oppenheimer himself had been the first to visit the bereaved husband.[352]

Finally, two letters from Robert's private correspondence during the Los Alamos years.

In July 1943 he received a letter from President Roosevelt that said in part: "Whatever the enemy may be planning, American science will be equal to the challenge. With this thought in mind, I send this note of appreciation."[353] Oppenheimer replied:

> Dear Mr. President:
>
> Thank you for your generous letter of June 29th. You would be glad to know how greatly your good words of reassurance were appreciated by us. There will be many times in the months ahead when we shall remember them.
>
> It is perhaps appropriate that I should in turn transmit to you the assurance that we as a group and as individual Americans are profoundly aware of our responsibility for the security of our project as well as for its rapid and effective completion. It is a great source of encouragement to us that we have in this your support and understanding.
>
> Very sincerely yours,
> J. R. Oppenheimer[354]

In September 1945, Einstein wrote to Robert, telling him that it was "unthinkable that we can achieve peace without a genuine supranational organization to govern international relations."[355] Robert replied:

> Dear Dr. Einstein:
>
> Thank you for your good letter of September 29th. I am in complete agreement with the views expressed by you. . . .
>
> If I say "general agreement" I mean only this: the history of this nation up through the Civil War shows how difficult the establishment of a federal authority can be when there are profound differences in the structure and values of the societies it attempts to integrate. . . .
>
> The statements attributed by you to me are not mine; nor, as a matter of fact, have I ever seen them. I have known, of course, of the existence of such views, and have attempted where possible to point out their inadequacies. These views do not correspond to the advice which I, or my immediate colleagues, have given to the government of the United States. We have been concerned rather with the problem of initiating those negotiations which might establish confidence and form the basis for a real unity. We have, I believe, from the first recognized the essentially political character of this problem, and regarded the development of the atomic bomb as of incidental, but perhaps decisive, importance in two respects:
>
> 1) Focusing more sharply the attention of the public on the dangers of international anarchy (and in particular on the dangers of competitive armament between two all-powerful nations).
> 2) Providing a new and specific point of discussion where agreement might be less difficult to achieve.
>
> . . . Very many of my associates at Los Alamos are profoundly concerned with these problems and would be grateful for help.
>
> With every warm good wish,
> J. R. Oppenheimer[356]

More Personal Recollections

In all my life I have never known a personality more complex than Robert Oppenheimer. That explains, I think, why different people reacted to him in such extremely varied ways. I have known those who worshipped him and those who hated his guts. As said earlier, my own reactions to him were ambivalent. There have been times when I felt genuine affection for him, others when I felt compassion if not pity, still others when he deeply angered me by his conduct.

Word portraits of people are by their very nature subjective. This is not the first time I attempt such a sketch but never more than in the case of Oppenheimer have I felt the need to forewarn that far be it from me to claim to have all the qualifications for understanding this man, so gifted, so tortured, so sweet, so cruel.

It will be evident that an understanding in depth of the man will at least demand knowledge of his early years and family relations. I have spent many untold hours in private conversations with Robert in which, however, he never even alluded to his youth. Indeed, all those whose lives have been affected by having known him had to be aware of Robert's uncommonly strong, protective sense of privacy that was sometimes taken for inner aloofness. In his writings I have found only a single reference of a personal nature, when he tells how, some time in the 1920s, Dirac had taken him "to task with characteristic gentleness. I understand [Dirac had said] that you are writing poetry as well as working at physics. I do not see how you can do both. In science we say something that no one knew before in a way that everybody can understand. Whereas in poetry . . ."[357]

Oppenheimer's talents were manifest in the way he led the Institute's physics seminars. Also his shortcomings. He angered me by his arrogance if not cruelty when a youngster failed to clarify or missed a point, cutting him down with unnecessarily biting comments. There have been one or two occasions where I had to console one of them who afterward came sobbing into my office.

Nor, in the beginning, was I myself spared such treatments. It may have taken about a year until this came to an end, when I was able to muster the courage to say to him something like this: "Robert, I want you to know that I won't take any longer your unwarranted behavior." The outcome of this brief conversation was astonishing. Never, in all the many years thereafter when I was in close contact with him, did he again expose me to his rough stuff. I have also noticed a few other cases of Robert changing his tune when someone else let *him* have it.

It is fitting to record next the impressions of a (then) young man. Polking-horne has written:

> I have to confess that I never really cared for Robert Oppenheimer. He had clearly been an inspiring teacher in his prewar days at Berkeley. By the time I first met him he was battered by his treatment at the hands of the AEC over security matters. The need to retain his authority and standing in another sphere was doubtless part of the reason for his mandarin manner. Perhaps there was also a further cause. When he gave the Reith Lectures on the BBC the *Observer* newspaper published a profile of him. I recall its saying the Oppenheimer's secret sorrow was that he had not made a fundamental discovery in physics. By the very highest standards—and Oppenheimer would never have deigned to apply to himself standards less than these—that was true. I think he had that secret sorrow and that it drove him to attempt always to assert a superiority over those ordinary physicists with whom he came in contact. My most frequent encounters with him were a few years later when I spent a semester as a visitor at the Institute for Advanced study at Princeton. . . . I came to feel that his gnomic way of speaking, with its stream of epigrams, phrased to be maximally striking but minimally clarifying, was a device to put the listener at a disadvantage. He was a most uncomfortable man to be with.[358]

In all, my most cherished recollections of Oppenheimer are the untold number of hours we spent together, mostly in his office, talking about physics, politics, literature, or what have you. As is familiar to all who knew him and as can also clearly be seen in his more reflective writings, it is an integral part of the Oppenheimer style that he had more than a touch of the poet. He was a master of the language.

For many of us it was a joy to hear him discuss or paraphrase a subject, especially if the subject was somewhat familiar, for Oppenheimer's discourse was not for beginners. But to some his style was alien. It is too simple to say that Oppenheimer polarized his surroundings, but it is true that the reactions he evoked were never bland.

Never in all our discussions would I raise a question about classified subjects nor would he ever volunteer such information. I should note here that just outside his office there stood safes containing top secret documents, in front of which sat guards on 24-hour duty, each discreetly carrying a revolver. Also, as Robert told me, he knew that his phone was tapped and held it probable that his office was bugged.

From my discussions with Oppenheimer I have come away with great admiration for his talents of verbal expression, his mastery of the English language. I learned new turns of phrase from him. One trivial example I remember: at one point he said that something was "inspiriting." I knew of course the word inspiring but had never heard "inspiriting" before. Afterward I went to a dictionary, looked it up—and adopted it myself for occasional use.

I came to Robert whenever I had finished a piece of physics research. Every time I told him that I had found something new he at once briefly bit his nails. I have my own interpretation of this involuntary gesture, which I shall spare the reader since I cannot prove that I am right. Then I would go to the blackboard in his office, sketch what I had done, then sit down and listen as he eloquently played back what I had told, emphasize the strong points and note the weak ones. It was always a masterful summary. I realized quickly, however, that I should never discuss with him—as physicists often do with each other—the status of unfinished work that was causing me problems. That would only lead to confusion rather than clarification.

In private conversations Robert had uncommon powers of persuasion. I recall meeting a distinguished Institute faculty member one day, as he came out of Oppenheimer's office, shaking his head. I asked what was up. Something odd had just happened to him, he replied. "I had gone to see Oppenheimer regarding a certain issue on which I held firm opinions. As I left I found that I had agreed with the opposite point of view. . . ."

In those early years I knew him, Robert was strikingly handsome, as can best be seen from his photograph on the cover of *Life* magazine of October 10, 1949. That is the best picture of him I know—ever so much better than the ones taken later where he looks like a martyr. He wore expensive suits (never sports jackets) that looked sloppy on his haggard frame.

No martyrdom was yet in evidence in the years I now write of. In fact, the man was ablaze with power, as I particularly noticed when, in my presence, his secretary would knock on his door and say, "Dr. Oppenheimer, Senator Arthur Vandenberg (1884–1951) [Chairman of the Senate Foreign Relations Committee] is calling"; or "General Marshall is on the line." (I of course stepped out during such phone conversations.) Such calls electrified him.

I noted earlier that Oppenheimer was a very private person, not given to showing his feeling. I have witnessed a few occasions, however, of him doing just that.

Some time in 1949 I gave my first big party, in my Dickinson Street apartment. Robert and Kitty were among my guests. At one point I said, "Everybody sit on the floor, we are going to sing folk songs." Robert sat down too, his air of hauteur clearly indicating that he thought this was an absurd situation for him to be in. I got out my guitar and started playing and singing. A while later I happened to look at Robert. I was touched to see that his attitude of superiority was gone; instead, he now looked like a man of feeling, hungry for simple comradeship.

Another occasion. I had gone to the Garden Theatre, one of Princeton's two movie houses, to see *La Grande Illusion*, that marvelous movie about comradeship among men during the First World War. As I walked toward the exit after the show, I saw Robert and Kitty sitting in a back row. I could see that he had wept.

One last instance. One day I had organized a craps game in my apartment. When I saw Robert that afternoon I said to him, "Please join us this evening for the game, it will be an all-male affair." Whereupon he made a characteristic gesture. He pressed his upper arms against his body, holding both elbows with his hands, then said, "But I am not all male."

I cannot forget that response. Already then I was convinced that strong latent homosexuality was an important ingredient in Robert's emotional makeup, though, as stated earlier, there was no evidence whatsoever for active homosexual behavior from his side.

Robert properly considered it part of his obligations as director to invite new members to his house for afternoon cocktails. These poor people were not prepared for what was awaiting them. Robert would have concocted a pitcher of viciously strong martinis. I have seen members stumbling dead drunk out of the house. (One faculty member had renamed the director's house Bourbon Manor.) I never accepted such drinks, having always found the cocktail hour a barbaric custom.

Robert himself would join in the drinking. He invariably held his liquor well. Not so Kitty, who was an alcoholic as long as I knew her. Off and on Robert invited me for dinner at home, just with the family. One summer evening, after drinks, Kitty appeared with a bowl of vichyssoise from which she served us. It was delicious. After having finished our soup, Robert and Kitty indulged in a rather extravagant exchange about its superb quality. Fine, I said to myself, now let's get on with the dinner. But nothing else came, that soup *was* the dinner. I waited for a civilized period, then thanked my hosts and drove to town, starving, where I treated myself to two hamburgers.

I have caught glimpses of Robert's reactions to Kitty's drinking. On several occasions when he and I were talking in his office, I saw her staggering drunkenly toward the door of the office that gave out directly to the lawn. When Robert noticed her, all he would say to me was, "Don't go away." Those were moments when I hurt for him. It seems he did all he could to overlook those habits of hers.

Quite independently from her drinking I have found Kitty the most despicable female I have ever known, because of her cruelty. I shall give just one minor example. Every spring a dance evening was held at the Institute. At the end of one such occasion I went to Kitty, the hostess, to thank her. When I approached, she was talking to an Institute secretary. This is what I heard her say, "Mrs. T., for your next evening dress you should choose blue instead of the pink you are now wearing. Pink does not suit you at all." It caused me to tremble with rage but I said nothing. I just thanked her for the evening.

To an outsider like me, Oppenheimer's family life looked like hell on earth. The worst of it all was that inevitably the two children had to suffer. I have seen how Kitty and Peter did not get along well, and was not surprised when Peter left home for good in his late teens and broke all contact with his mother. Toni, the daughter, poor dear Toni, ended by taking her own life.

I conclude this chapter with an assessment by Rabi, who had known Oppenheimer since his stay in Zurich, and who had witnessed his Berkeley, Los Alamos, and Princeton years. His short characterization of Robert, the best I have seen, sheds incidental light on my earlier remark that Oppenheimer was unable to derive contentment from his notable and varied achievements:

> One often wonders why men of Oppenheimer's gifts do not discover everything worth discovering, why important problems are still left to solve. With the vast intellectual arsenal at his disposal there were important questions in physics in which Oppenheimer worked diligently, where he was very often on the track of the solutions, and where his taste in the selection of the questions was impeccable, and yet as in the case of quantum electrodynamics the definite solutions came from others. In pondering this subject it seems to me that in some respects Oppenheimer was overeducated in those fields which lie outside the scientific tradition, such as his interest in religion, in the Hindu religion in particular, which resulted in a feeling for the mystery of the universe that surrounded him almost like a fog. He saw physics clearly, looking toward what had already been done, but at the border he tended to feel that there was much more of the mysterious and novel than there actually was. He was insufficiently confident of the power of the intellectual tools he already possessed and did not drive his thought to the very end because he felt instinctively that new ideas and new methods were necessary to go further than he and his students had already gone. Some may call it a lack of faith, but in my opinion it was more a turning away from the hard, crude methods of theoretical physics into a mystical realm of broad intuition. . . .
>
> In Oppenheimer the element of earthiness was feeble. Yet it was essentially this spiritual quality, this refinement as expressed in speech and manner, that was the basis of his charisma. He never expressed himself completely. He always left a feeling that there were depths of sensibility and insight not yet revealed. These may be the qualities of the born leader who seems to have reserves of uncommitted strength.[11]

CHAPTER 17

ATOMIC POLITICS IN THE EARLY POSTWAR YEARS

The release of atomic energy constitutes a new force too revolutionary to consider in the framework of old ideas.

President Truman in his message to
Congress of October 3, 1945

1945–1946

Here and there in the preceding I have recorded snippets of Oppenheimer's opinions and activities regarding political aspects of atomic energy: his first correspondence with the secretary of war and his reply on accepting the certificate of appreciation for the work in Los Alamos, from the secretary of war; his credo; and his involvement with the May-Johnson and the McMahon proposals, as well as his appointment to the GAC. I recall a few dates mentioned earlier.

October 3, 1945

Truman's message in which he requested the establishment of the AEC. Note that in his policy statement he mentioned not only this domestic issue but also managed to fuse it with international aspects. The latter would turn into a long inconclusive meander.

August 1, 1946

Truman signs the Atomic Energy Act into law.

October 1946

Lewis Strauss is appointed member of the AEC.

December 1946

Oppenheimer is appointed to the General Advisory Committee of the AEC. Well before joining that body he had begun to express opinions on policy matters, however.

Already, while at Los Alamos, Robert had been one of the first to recognize that a nuclear detection system should be established and so recommended while he was still with the Manhattan District.[364] Shortly after Truman's October 1945 address, he wrote an article[365] that may be considered a response to the president's message, in which he (O.) stated that atomic weapons "call for and by their existence will help to create radical and profound changes in the politics of the world."

About those weapons he wrote:

> The interior of an exploding fission bomb is, so far as we know, a place without parallel elsewhere. It is hotter than the center of the sun; it is filled with matter that does not normally occur in nature and with radiations—neutrons, gamma rays, fission fragments, electrons—of an intensity without precedent in human experience. The pressures are a thousand billion times atmospheric pressure. In the crudest, simplest sense, it is quite true that in atomic weapons man has created novelty. . . .
>
> [I]t will cost enormously less to destroy a square mile with atomic weapons than with any weapons hitherto known to warfare. My own estimate is that the advent of such weapons will reduce the cost, certainly by more than a factor of ten, more probably by a factor of a hundred. In this respect only biological warfare would seem to offer competition for the evil that a dollar can do . . . Ton for equivalent ton, atomic explosives are vastly cheaper than ordinary explosives . . . Costs might be several hundred times less, possibly a thousand times less. . . . [T]he power of destruction that has come into man's hands has in fact been qualitatively altered by atomic weapons.[366]

The main message in Oppenheimer's brief article deals with his views on how this alteration will profoundly influence the world of politics and how this in turn will inevitably affect the role in which science and its practitioners will play in the world at large.

> In these problems a common approach, in which national interests can play only a limitedly constructive part, will be necessary if a solution is to be found at all. Such an approach has been characteristic of science in the past. In its application to the problems of international relations there is novelty . . .
>
> The injection of the spirit of the scientists into this problem of atomic weapons, in which it has been clear from the first that purely national ideas of welfare and security would doubtless prove inadequate, has been recognized, if not

clearly understood, by statesmen as well as by scientists. The emphasis that has been given—in the statements of the President and in the agreed declaration of the heads of state of Britain, Canada, and the United States—to the importance of the reestablishment of the international fraternity and freedom of science is an evidence of this recognition. . . .

The vastly increased powers of destruction that atomic weapons give us have brought with them a profound change in the balance between national and international interests. The common interest of all in the prevention of atomic warfare would seem immensely to overshadow any purely national interest, whether of welfare or of security. At the same time it would seem of most doubtful value in any long term to rely on purely national methods of defense for insuring security. . . . The true security of this nation, as of any other, will be found, if at all, only in the collective efforts of all.

It is even now clear that such efforts will not be successful if they are made only as a supplement, or secondary insurance, to a national defense. In fact it is clear that such collective efforts will require, and do today require, a very real renunciation of the steps by which in the past national security has been sought. It is clear that in a very real sense the past patterns of national security are inconsistent with the attainment of security on the only level where it can now, in the atomic age, be effective. It may be that in times to come it will be by this that atomic weapons are most remembered. It is in this that they will come to seem "too revolutionary to consider in the framework of old ideas."

In these lines I recognize the influence on Robert of his long conversations with Bohr in Los Alamos on international aspects of atomic policy. (I know of Bohr's thoughts on these matters from my own talks with him.) Oppenheimer had in fact asked Bohr's permission (which was given) to quote his "classic statement of the feelings with which scientists approach the new situation."[367] Incidentally, Oppenheimer had been the first American scientist whom Bohr had contacted after his escape from Denmark.[368]

The Acheson-Lilienthal Plan

> The natural sciences have fundamentally extended the range of questions about which man has to make decisions.
>
> Oppenheimer[369]

The year 1946 marks the beginnings of serious efforts toward atomic policy, both national and worldwide. All these early attempts have turned out to be fruitless. Now, with the advantage of hindsight, one can clearly see how inevitable these failures had to be. That, however, does not diminish their interest as part of the Oppenheimer saga, rather on the contrary, it seems to me. Let us see what came to pass.

In January 1946 the General Assembly of the United Nations adopted a resolution calling for the establishment of the United Nations Atomic Energy Commission (UNAEC). Part of its charge: "The Commission shall make specific proposals for extending between all nations the exchange of basic scientific information for peaceful purposes." They should also see to it that atomic energy should be confined to peaceful purposes, eliminating atomic weapons from national armaments, and effectively safeguarding complying states.

The UNAEC organized a scientific and technical subcommittee. The Dutch physicist Hans Kramers, friend of Oppenheimer as well as of myself, was elected its chairman (which explains why Kramers was in New York in 1946, where he introduced me to Oppenheimer).

Meanwhile, earlier that January, Dean Gooderman Acheson (1893–1971), then undersecretary of state, had been asked to chair a committee to formulate United States atomic policy that should guide future American representatives at the United Nations. It was an excellent choice. Acheson was a man with a sharp mind, who disbelieved in his own omniscience and had an experienced respect for both committee process and staff support. Members of his committee were Vannevar Bush, James Conant (1893–1978), leading statesman of science, John J. McCloy (1895–1989), assistant secretary of war from 1941–1945, and, of course, General Groves. Typically, Acheson objected; he had not a clue of atomic matters but was reassured when told that most of his committee members knew a lot.[370]

Acheson chose as his assistant Herbert S. Marks (1907–1960), a young lawyer who had understood the urgency of the problem better than most nonscientists. It was Marks who made the decisive suggestion that the committee Byrnes had appointed was too grand to work the problem through for itself. Let there be a board of consultants with the necessary time and technical skills, and let its chairman be David Lilienthal (1899–1981), then the chairman of the Tennessee Valley Authority, where Marks had worked for him. Lilienthal had made the TVA a symbol of effective public enterprise; at 45 he was able, articulate, energetic, optimistic, ambitious, and decent. Oppenheimer, then still at the University of California, agreed to serve on this advisory panel.

Lilienthal has remembered how on January 22, 1946, he met Oppenheimer:

Late in the evening we went out to the Shoreham [Hotel, in Washington] and saw Oppenheimer, who had just come in by plane from California. First time I had seen him. The setting was curious, too: a newly decorated room, very fancy, with a bed in the room, eight feet wide, and the atmosphere hardly that of a physics laboratory or an atom bomb assembly plant. We had a couple of drinks. He walked back and forth, making funny "hugh" sounds between sentences or phrases as he paced the room, looking at the floor—a mannerism quite strange. Very articulate.[372]

From the AEC history:

The work of education [of the Acheson committee] began Monday morning, January 28, in quarters the OSRD had arranged—the loft-like top floor of the American Trucking Association Building across Sixteenth Street. . . . There for two days . . . Oppenheimer put his colleagues through a short course in nuclear physics. . . . [I]t was the first time the panelists had been exposed to the physicist's extraordinarily fluent, lucid speech. Starting with the most basic concepts, he told how plutonium was produced and how the neutron bombardment of thorium offered the prospect of deriving important quantities of the fissionable isotope U-233. He described the various isotope-separation processes and what it took to build a reactor. . . . He explained the physics and ordnance of the uranium and plutonium bombs, observing that the effort required here was relatively small. It was the fissionable material itself that demanded heroic exertions.[372a]

Already on the evening of the first day, Lilienthal wrote in his diary:

No fairy tale that I read in utter rapture and enchantment as a child, no spy mystery, no "horror" story, can remotely compare with the scientific recital I listened to for six or seven hours today. Seated in a prosaic office . . . I heard more of the complete story of the atomic bomb, past, present, and immediate future, than any but a few men have yet heard. It was told well, technically, dispassionately, but interspersed with stories of the decisions that had to be made, the utter simplicity and yet fantastic complexity of the peering into the laws of nature that is the essence of this utterly bizarre and, literally, incredible business. There were things that have never been even hinted at that are accomplished, or virtually accomplished, facts, that change the whole thesis of our inquiry, and of the course of the world in this generation.[373]

How adulatory Lilienthal was of Oppenheimer is seen from a letter by him: "He is worth living a lifetime just to know that mankind has been able to produce such a being. We may have to wait another hundred years for the second one to come off the line."[374] Groves, who found himself at odds with the Lilienthal-Oppenheimer axis, was to view their relationship through jaundiced eyes. "Everybody genuflected," he complained. "Lilienthal got so bad he would consult Oppie on what tie to wear in the morning."[371]

On January 31, Oppenheimer revealed his own thoughts.

For some time, the outlines of an international control agency had been taking shape in his mind. He had not revealed his thinking at the first meetings of the consultants. It was better, he judged, to wait until his associates possessed the fundamental information necessary to understand his plan. Now he enthusiastically sketched a vision of an international agency that would have important developmental functions.[374a]

His starting point was that an exclusively negatively defined control, decoupled from controlled research and development, would cause great difficulties. He compared such a kind of control with an international policy authority that goes after lawbreakers by means of a "cops and robbers" scheme. It seemed clear to him that in such a procedure the robbers would always have the advantage because they would always know more than the cops. "I fear that the cops will never know about new methods—only the robbers will."[375]

Therefore, he continued, it is essential to merge development *and* control in one committee, also because there was pitiably little to inspect outside the United States, Great Britain, and Canada. Furthermore, there are areas like tracer studies for medical and biological purposes that do not need to be controlled. Domains to be supervised, he argued, are research, development, and use of uranium and of atomic explosives. He also emphasized that possible conflicts regarding development of atomic energy for industrial purposes need to be supervised by an authority with technical competence.

Oppenheimer's ideas found immediate resonance. During February the Board of Consultants set about "working hard as the very devil on the atomic bomb report."[376] There was agreement to present an informative document to the Acheson Committee that should not settle on one specific control plan—that should be left to the parent committee. The result was the so-called "Acheson-Lilienthal report," though it was largely the work of Oppenheimer himself. Its core idea: "International control implies an acceptance from the outset of the fact that our monopoly cannot last. . . . It is essential that a workable system of safeguards remove from individual nations or their citizens the legal right to engage in certain well-defined activities in respect to atomic energy which we believe will be generally agreed to be intrinsically dangerous because they are or could be made steps in a production of atomic bombs."

On March 7 the Acheson and Lilienthal committees met at Dumbarton Oaks in Georgetown for the presentation of the report. Lilienthal announced, "This, gentlemen, is our recommendation of a plan for security in a world of atomic energy."[377] The report was received seriously and positively.

So far so good.

But two days earlier the Cold War had begun.

On March 5, Winston Churchill (1874–1965) gave a speech at Westminster College, in Fulton, Missouri, after receiving an honorary degree. With typical oratorical skills, Churchill introduced the phrase "Iron Curtain" to describe the division between Western powers and the area controlled by the Soviet Union. As such the speech marks the onset of the Cold War. A few lines from this address:

> From Stettin in the Baltic to Trieste in the Adriatic an iron curtain has descended across the Continent. . . . In a great number of countries, far from the Russian frontiers and throughout the world, Communist fifth columns are established and work in complete unity and absolute obedience to the directions they receive from the Communist center. . . . [They] constitute a growing challenge and peril to Christian civilization. . . . From what I have seen of our Russian friends and allies during the war, I am convinced that there is nothing they admire so much as strength, and there is nothing for which they have less respect than weakness, especially military weakness.

I have always admired, perhaps revered, Churchill for his acts and even more for his words during the Second World War. I was shaken, however, when I first read his Fulton speech. Not that what he said was wrong but his language appeared to me to be politically tactless and tasteless. Nor was he the only one to harbor such opinions at that time. For example, four days after this speech, Lilienthal wrote of "the constant fear of a long, bitter period of antagonism and strain and perhaps war with the Russians"[378]—but that was in his private diary. Churchill could at least have waited until the United Nations had come forth with a policy statement.

Meanwhile much more serious news had become public. Lilienthal again, in his diary: "In the meantime, the situation in respect to a rational dealing with the problem has been deteriorating, though it is by no means hopeless. I refer to the announcement of Russian spies and what not issuing from Canada."[376] This is what happened.

> Saturday, February 16, brought news from Ottawa of the arrest of twenty-two persons in an investigation of the disclosure of secret information, reportedly about atomic energy, to unauthorized persons, including members of a foreign mission. Although Canadian officials at first denied that atomic energy data were involved, it was clear by Tuesday that some "bomb secrets" had reached the Soviet embassy. The news stunned Washington. To those who had come to think of the "secret" as the nation's most valuable possession, the reports represented a threat to American security. For others, the evidence of Russian perfidy shattered the hopes for international peace and understanding. . . .
>
> [On February 21] General Groves explained [to a Congressional committee] what had not yet been released to the press, that Alan Nunn May [1911–2003], a British physicist assigned to the Canadian atomic energy project, had transmitted to Soviet agents some information about the American effort. During three visits to the Chicago Metallurgical Laboratory in 1944, May had seen most of the research and development work at the laboratory, learned something of the design, construction, and operation of the Hanford piles, and received very limited information about the production of fissionable materials and weapons.[379, 380]

On March 17, the Acheson committee approved the Acheson-Lilienthal plan. That evening Acheson handed a copy to Secretary of State James ("Jimmy") Byrnes (1879–1972), accompanied by a covering letter signed by all members. The plan was made public on March 28. Two days later, Oppenheimer sent a copy to Bohr, along with a letter[381] in which he told that even in their gloomy moments they did not succeed quite in thinking how difficult it would get to be. "This report is not all it should be. . . . For what is good in it, it should be dedicated to you." Bohr replied,[382] "to give expression for the deep pleasure it was to read this report. . . . From page to page I recognized your broad views and refined power of expression."

American physicists tended to be less sanguine about Oppenheimer at that time. When they met him they felt,

> that he was no longer quite one of them. Some were no doubt susceptible to the glamour that now surrounded him, but it was his best friends, in particular, who grew cold towards him. One of Oppenheimer's former favorite pupils relates, "When Oppie started talking about Dean Acheson as simply 'Dean,' and actually referred to General Marshall, as merely 'George,' I knew that we did not move in the same circles any more and that we had come to the parting of the ways. I think that his sudden fame and the new position he now occupied had gone to his head so much that he began to consider himself God Almighty, able to put the whole world to rights."[383]

The Baruch Plan

On the evening of March 17, when Acheson had come to see Byrnes, he could not suspect what job message was awaiting him: he was told that the day before, the 75-year-old financier Bernard Baruch (1870–1965) had been appointed as United States spokesman at the United Nations on the international control of atomic energy. Acheson protested vehemently but in vain against this choice.[384] Lilienthal in his diary: "When I read this news last night, I was quite sick. We need a man who is young, vigorous, not vain, and whom the Russians would feel isn't out simply to put them in a hole, not really caring about international cooperation. Baruch has none of these qualifications."[385] Years later Oppenheimer said, "That was the day I gave up hope, but that was not the day for me to say so publicly."[386]

Searching for scientific advisers, Baruch first fell back on the Acheson committee. Groves accepted, Bush and Conant declined. Bush told Baruch to his face that he was used to working in "higher echelons" and did not relish his group of "Wall Streeters."[388] Because of Oppenheimer's feelings about Baruch, Acheson took him to see Truman. "Hesitant and cheerless, he seemed so different from his reputation that Truman wanted to know what was the matter. 'I feel we have blood on our hands,' Oppenheimer mumbled. 'Never mind,' said Truman, 'it'll all come out in the wash'. . . . 'When will the Russians be able to build the bomb?' asked Truman. 'I don't know,' said Oppenheimer. 'I know.' 'When?' 'Never.'"[389] Truman found Oppenheimer's statements offensive. Later he said to Acheson: "Don't you bring that fellow around again. After all, all he did was make the bomb. I'm the guy who fired it off."[389]

In the event, Oppenheimer also declined to serve as Baruch's adviser, though he and Acheson's camp bickered with Baruch and his supporters for weeks.

On May 16, 1946—before Baruch first addressed the United Nations—Oppenheimer delivered a lecture on "Atomic Explosives" before the George Westinghouse Centennial Forum in Pittsburgh. His talk was meant "to add a few comments which may help to supplement the [Acheson-Lilienthal] report that was made public."[390] Parts of his address follow:

> In this proposal we attempted to meet, and to put into a constructive context, two sets of facts, both long recognized, and commonly regarded as contributing to the difficulty, if not to the insolubility, of the problem.
> The first of these facts is that the science, the technology, the industrial development involved in the so-called beneficial uses of atomic energy appear to be inextricably intertwined with those involved in making atomic weapons. . . .
> The heart of our proposal was the recommendation of an International Atomic Development Authority, entrusted with the research, development, and exploitation of the peaceful applications of atomic energy, with the elimination from national armaments of atomic weapons, and with the studies and researches and controls that must be directed toward that end.

Among peaceful applications he mentioned:

> There has even been a little talk of possible beneficent applications of atomic explosives, such as the blasting of polar ice or the possible control of major natural phenomena such as tornados, earthquakes, eruptions. There is enough energy in atomic explosives to give these vague suggestions an air of plausibility; even the weapons so far used release an energy about one thousandth of that in the San Francisco earthquake. But of course the forces produced by an atomic explosion have a very different sort of order from those involved in the great natural phenomena of quakes and of tornadoes; and the radiation and radioactivities that accompany any major atomic explosion must at least complicate its application to benign purposes. If men are ever to speak of the benefits of atomic energy, I think these applications will at most play a very small part in what they have in mind. . . .

The same raw material, uranium, is needed for the use of atomic energy for power as for atomic bombs. . . . Thus a mere prohibition on the activities of nations in the field of atomic energy sufficiently incisive to inspire confidence that, if enforced, it would prevent rapid conversion to atomic armament, would at the same time close this field to the exploitation of any of its benefits. This fact, which further technical developments appear unlikely to invalidate, has long been regarded as an almost decisive difficulty on the path of international control. It might have appeared so to us, too, if there had not been a greater one. For even if the course of development of atomic energy for peace were entirely distinct from its development for war, even if it were universally agreed that there were no peaceful applications of atomic energy worthy of interest or of effort, we should still be faced with the fact that there exists in the world today no machinery for making effective a prohibition against the national development of atomic armaments . . . [This is] the second of the great difficulties [mentioned before] . . .

What relation does the proposal of an International Atomic Development Authority, entrusted with a far-reaching monopoly of atomic energy—what relation does this proposal of ours have to do with these questions? It proposes that in the field of atomic energy there be set up a world government, that in this field there be renunciation of national sovereignty, that in this field there be no legal veto power, that in this field there be international law. How is this possible, in a world of sovereign nations? There are only two ways in which this ever can be possible: one is conquest, that destroys sovereignty; and the other is the partial renunciation of that sovereignty. What is here proposed is such a partial renunciation, sufficient, but not more than sufficient, for an Atomic Development Authority to come into being, to exercise its functions of development, exploitation and control, to enable it to live and grow and to protect the world against the use of atomic weapons and provide it with the benefits of atomic energy.

Whatever else happens, there is likely to be a discussion of the control of atomic energy in the United Nations Commission set up for that purpose . . .

If any great note of confidence or gaiety has invested these brief words, it would be a distortion of the spirit in which I should have wished to speak to you. No thoughtful man can look to the future with any complete assurance that the world will not again be ravaged by war, by a total war in which atomic weapons contribute their part to the ultimate wreck and attrition of this our Western civilization. My own view is that the development of these weapons can make, if wisely handled, the problem of preventing war, not more hopeless, but more hopeful, than it would otherwise have been, and that this is so not merely because it intensifies the urgency of our hopes, but because it provides new and healthy avenues of approach.

On the morning of June 14, 1946, Baruch led the United States delegation into the hastily converted gymnasium of Hunter College in the Bronx where the first meeting of the United Nations Atomic Energy Commission was taking place.

Oppenheimer sat with other members of the United States section and sadly watched as the battle lines of self-interest were drawn up with the Russians. His vision, which he believed had the irresistible appeal of sanity, he saw crushed there.

In his opening remarks, General Secretary Trygve Lie (1896–1968) found it of particular significance that the earlier director of Los Alamos was present, the man "who built the bomb and then tried to find ways to get it under control."[391]

A little after 11 AM, Baruch stepped to the rostrum. "We are here to make a choice between the quick and the dead, that is our business," he began. The Baruch plan included much of the Acheson-Lilienthal plan but differed from it on four essential points. First, he demanded total disarmament, not just control over atomic weapons. Secondly, he anticipated prompt punishment for certain violations of the proposals. Thirdly, the ownership of the atomic authority should remain in private hands. Lastly, the most important difference with Acheson-Lilienthal, and Baruch's most controversial new point, "It might as well be admitted here and now that the subject goes straight to the veto power contained in the U.N. Charter so far as it relates to the field of atomic energy. . . . There must be no veto [regarding atomic issues]." As a closing remark Baruch dramatically paraphrased Abraham Lincoln (1809–1865): "We shall nobly save, or meanly lose, the last best hope of earth. The way is plain, peaceful, generous, just—a way which, if followed, the world will forever applaud."[392]

Lilienthal has recalled Oppenheimer's immediate reaction to the Baruch plan: "Met J. R. O. last night, just in from New York; talked until 1:30 this morning. He is really a tragic figure; with all his great attractiveness, brilliance of mind. As I left him he looked so sad: 'I am ready to go anywhere and do anything, but I am bankrupt of further ideas. And I find that physics and the teaching of physics, which is my life, now seems irrelevant.' It was this last that really wrung my heart. Here is the making of great drama; indeed, this *is* great drama."[393]

The Russian response also came rapidly. On June 19, Andrey Gromyko (1909–1989), permanent representative on the Security Council, announced that he wanted a flat prohibition on the possession, production and use of atomic weapons, and stated that the Soviet Union would never accept any change in the veto. Later he would add that his country could not accept the Baruch plan "either as a whole or in their separate parts."

On July 1, 1946, two weeks and two days after Baruch's speech, a United States fleet was riding at anchor in the lagoon of Bikini Atoll in the Pacific. On the skydeck of the U.S.S. *Appalachia* military experts, congressmen, foreign observers, and a group of accredited journalists were awaiting the test shot, named Able, of an atomic bomb, the first postwar shot of its kind. At 9 AM a B29 bomber dropped the weapon. The pyrotechnics were spectacular, the blast less than expected—which, perhaps, may explain a fine pun of that time: It doesn't Bikini difference Atoll. A second shot (July 25), named Baker, exploded underwater and was more visible and more impressive.

The timing of these events was bizarre, to put it mildly. Here was the United States testing the atomic bomb with one hand and seeking its control with the other. Actually, the timing was set by the need to act before scientists returned to their university posts and while Congress was still in session.[394]

Be it noted that, the preceding May, Oppenheimer had written to Truman to express his reservations about the usefulness of these tests and to record his refusal to help with their preparation;[395] also that he served on the president's evaluation committee for Operation Crossroads.[396]

On October 19, 1946, Robert Oppenheimer met with Secretary of Commerce Henry Wallace. Wallace's diary states: "I never saw a man in such an extremely nervous state as Oppenheimer. He seemed to feel that the destruction of the entire human race was imminent. . . . He wanted to know if I thought it would [be] any good for him to see the President. I said yes. . . . He says that Secretary Byrnes' attitude on the bomb has been very bad. It seems that Secretary Byrnes has felt that we could use the bomb as a pistol to get what we wanted in international diplomacy. Oppenheimer believes that that method will not work. . . ."[397]

Within weeks the Baruch plan was gravely ill, and in less than six months it was dead.

> By December Baruch had run out of patience and forced a vote. The language of the resolution was moderated in deference to other friendly delegations, but in essence it endorsed the American position. Gromyko remained adamant. The resolution was passed by a vote of 10 to 0, the Russians and Poles abstaining. To Baruch the vote was a resounding endorsement. But to him and to his government it was also the end of the road for any real hope that the plan would be accepted. Baruch resigned in early January, and there is no record that from that day forward anyone near the top of the Truman administration had any hope, or made any effort, for agreement.[398]

Desultory discussions on atomic matters continued throughout 1947 and 1948 but with steadily decreasing expectations. On May 17, 1948, the UNAEC recommended the suspension of its own activities.

1946 as the Highest Point of Oppenheimer's Political Contributions

By the end of 1946 a chapter in international postwar atomic politics had come to its conclusion. For Oppenheimer it marked the year of his most important political contributions—even though these failed to have the desired effect.

In 1954 he reflected on why the Russians could not accept the Acheson-Lilienthal plan:

> It would have meant that the Russian Government gave up control over things going on involving their citizens on their territory. It would have permitted free intercourse between Russian nationals and people of the rest of the world. It would have meant that there could be no Iron Curtain. . . . I think that any attempt at that time to establish control along these lines would, if accepted by the Soviets, have so altered their whole system and so altered their whole relations with the Western World that the threat which has been building up year after year since could not have existed. I think that no one at that time could with much confidence believe that they would accept these proposals. I think it was important to put them forward, and it was also important not to express too much doubt that they might be accepted.[399]

Oppenheimer reminisced again about 1946 shortly before his death: the negotiations should have been handled under other assumptions than were made then, since at that time the United States was the only atomic power. The Soviet distrust should have been understandable. The Russians believed that the American plan had no other purposes than securing its monopoly and building more bombs as long as we considered that necessary, while Russia should make public its uranium stock and should put its use of the ore in the hands of the international control authority.

These reflections of Oppenheimer do much to explain why the Cold War started in 1946. It should not be forgotten, however, that American attitudes also constituted a major contributing factor. "The concept that the United States was ahead and could stay ahead by keeping its know-how to itself took deep root in this year . . . [as did] the tensions between the fear of the atom and reliance upon its protection. That tension reappears in every judgment that political leaders have made. In 1946 it was what finally divided a Baruch from an Oppenheimer."[400]

In view of Oppenheimer's obvious despair at that time, one should wonder why, late in 1946, he did not retire from the enervations of the political scene. The reasons are complex. First, he could not find any more appeal in continuing research and conventional teaching because of the interruptions caused by the war. Secondly, he continued to believe in his powers to convince others of his views and continued to rely on his abilities to influence events because of his insider position. In 1948 he wrote to Bohr of his hopes to remain "of [political] use,"[401] that is, that he could continue to sway events as adviser to political bodies. Thirdly, and most importantly, I believe, was the fact that he was emotionally drawn to the political game, like a mosquito is drawn to the killing flame. Yet all his later political activities pale by comparison to his 1946 work on the Acheson-Lilienthal plan, which might well have carried his name also. And so, in December 1946, *after the failure of the Baruch plan*, he accepted membership in the GAC—where he failed in his efforts to give priority to the development of reactors for peaceful purposes over continuing weapons production.

On and on his political efforts went. From 1947 to 1952 he was chairman of the Committee on Atomic Energy of the Joint Research and Development Board, overseeing research on techniques for detecting nuclear explosions. He served on the panel that evaluated and confirmed the report by early scientific-detection experts that the Soviets had broken the United States monopoly on nuclear weapons by testing a device of their own on August 29, 1949. Serving in a similar capacity, he endorsed the 1951 findings of the United States detection system that the Soviets had conducted their second and third nuclear tests. He was a member of the Naval Research Advisory Committee from 1949 to 1952 and the Science Advisory Committee, Office of Defense Mobilization, from 1951 to 1954. He served on the secretary of state's Panel on Disarmament in 1952 and 1953. And this enumeration of his services is probably only part of these kinds of contributions.

As chairman of the GAC he argued for proposals that the AEC would play a leading role in fundamental nuclear research, advocating that the Commission support such work in universities and other institutions, thus helping to initiate the enormous growth of science resulting from government-university cooperation. He was a strong advocate for making fundamental scientific information available to scientists at home and abroad for use in basic research.

In June 1947, Lilienthal wrote about a meeting between the GAC and the AEC, to which he had meanwhile been appointed chairman: "Robert Oppenheimer summarized the committee's views on questions we submitted to them for their opinion, in an hour's statement that was as brilliant, lively, and accurate a statement as I believe I have ever heard. He is pure genius. Even these great brains joined in the amazement and delight we all felt with this wonderful piece."[402]

Oppenheimer's Public Expressions on Atomic Policy: 1947–1948

With the sad outcome of the United Nations' deliberations behind him, Oppenheimer began efforts to explain to general audiences what, in his view, were the problems and prospects in the field of atomic policy. I mention next some of his opinions dating from 1947–48, as recorded in three articles. The main theme of the first is international security; of the second, peaceful applications of atomic energy; of the third, a historical perspective.

The first is from a lecture[403] given on September 17, 1947, in Washington to a group of officers in the armed services, the Foreign Service and the State Department:

> There are three planes on which we have more or less explicitly asserted that we would like to achieve security: One is international control; this is the official policy of the United States. It is a very far-reaching control which would eliminate the rivalry between nations in this field, which would prevent the surreptitious arming of one nation against another, which would provide some cushion of time before atomic attack, and presumably therefore before any attack with weapons of mass destruction, and which would go a long way toward removing atomic energy at least as a source of conflict between the powers. . . .
>
> Second, there is the path of technical superiority, which has a dual purpose. By this superiority I mean that we should always be in the forefront as far as ideas, management and development are concerned—we should as much as possible avoid being taken by surprise as far as technical development goes, we should know our business and have an active and flourishing group of people working in the field of atomic energy. This has a dual function—on the one hand of giving us the opportunity of maintaining a freedom of maneuver in this field which we would entirely lose if we were outstripped or surprised by some foreign effort, and in the second place, it is regarded—and I think rightly regarded—as a strong deterrent to aggression against us.
>
> The third plane is the plane of actual strength, which in this field—and this field is clearly not separate from others—has itself a number of elements which need to be spelled out. It means among other things effective, maximumly effective, defense against probable methods of delivery of atomic weapons, proper and necessary dispersion for survival in the event of attack, proper schemes for the necessary and probably extremely difficult effort of mobilization; it means having effective and ready means of retaliation; it means a detailed strategic coordination for the use of our atomic facilities. . . .
>
> You may think it strange that I have included the achievement of international control as one of the things to keep in mind in planning atomic activities. This I think . . . is the only way in which this country can have a security comparable to that which it had in the years before the war. It is the only way in which we will be able to live with bad governments, with new discoveries, with irresponsible governments such as are likely to arise in the next hundred years, without living in fairly constant fear of the surprise use of these weapons, and their surprise development. . . . The whole notion of international control presupposes a certain confidence, a confidence which may not be inconsistent with carrying a gun when you sit down to play poker, but at least is consistent with sitting down to play poker. . . .
>
> To those who would say that this is no time to be thinking of long-term things, or that it is sheer madness, with the "world as it is" to dream about international control, or again to those others who say that there is no security except in inter-

national control and that any other precautions are useless, I would quite profoundly disagree; to them I should like to tell a final story. It is a story of Confucius.

One day in a clearing in the forest, Confucius came upon a woman in deep mourning, racked by sorrow. He learned that her son had just been eaten by a tiger; and he attempted to console her, to make clear how unavailing her tears would be, to restore her composure. He left, but had barely reentered the forest, when the renewed sounds of weeping recalled him. "That is not all," the woman said. "You see, my husband was eaten here a year ago by this same tiger." Again Confucius attempted to console her and again he left only to hear renewed weeping. "Is that not all?" "Oh, no," she said. "The year before that my father too was eaten by the tiger." Confucius thought for a moment, and then said: "This would not seem to be a very salutary neighborhood. Why don't you leave it?" The woman wrung her hands. "I know," she said. "I know; but, you see, the government is so excellent."

From a second article, "Travelling to a land we cannot see,"[404] originally published in early 1948:[405]

[I]n the summer of 1945 . . . it became fully apparent that atomic weapons and the large-scale release of atomic energy were not only realizable, but were about to be realized. Even at that time a good deal of thought had gone into what subsequently came to be known as the peaceful use of atomic energy. . . . It was clear to us that the forms and methods by which mankind might in the future hope to protect itself against the dangers of unlimited atomic warfare would be decisively influenced just by the answer to the question "Is there any good in the atom?" From the first, it has been clear that the answer to this question would have a certain subtlety. The answer would be "yes," and emphatically "yes," but it would be a "yes" unconvincing, conditional, and temporizing compared to the categorical affirmative of the atomic bomb itself. . . .

Only two classes of peaceful applications of atomic energy were then apparent. To the best of my knowledge, only two are apparent today. One is the development of a new source of power; the other is a family of new instruments of research, investigation, technology and therapy.

Of the former, it was clear two years ago, and it is clear today, that although the generation of useful power from atomic sources would assuredly be a soluble problem and would under favorable circumstances make decisive progress within a decade, the question of the usefulness of this power, the scale on which it could be made available, and the costs and general economic values, would take a long time to answer. . . .

[N]o honest evaluation of the prospects of power in 1945 could fail to recognize the necessity of intensive development and exploration. Equally, no honest evaluation could give assurances as to the ultimate outcome beyond those general assurances which the history of our technology justifies. Certainly no evaluation at that time, nor for that matter today, could justify regarding atomic power as an immediate economic aid to a devastated and fuel-hungry world, nor give its development the urgency which the control of atomic armaments would be sure to have once the nature and ferocity of the weapons had been made clear to all.

With regard to the use of tracer materials, of radioactive species, and of radiations for science, the practical arts, for technology and medicine, we were in a better position to judge what might come. The use of tracer materials was not new. The last decade—the 1930's—had seen increasingly varied and effective applications of them. The use of radiation for the study of the properties of matter, for diagnosis, and for therapy was likewise not new. Several decades of hopeful and bitter experiences gave us some notion of the power and limitations of these tools. What was held in store by the development of atomic reactors and of new methods for the handling of radioactive materials and the separation of isotopes, was a much greater variety and a vastly greater quantity of tracer materials, and a far higher intensity of radiation, than had been available in the past. That this would be a stimulus to physical and biological study was clear; that its value would in the first instance depend on the skillful development of chemical, physical, and biological techniques, and that this development even under the circumstances would be a gradual and continuing one, we knew as well.

Thus, our picture of the peaceful uses of atomic energy was neither trivial nor heroic: on the one hand, many years, perhaps many decades, of development—largely engineering development—with the purpose of providing new sources of power; on the other hand, a new arsenal of instruments for the exploration of the physical and biological world, and in time, for their further control, to be added to the always growing arsenal of what scientists and engineers have had available.

Three other matters were clear at that time. On the one hand, the development of atomic power could not be separated from technological development essential for and largely sufficient for the manufacture of atomic weapons. On the other hand, neither the development of power nor the effective and widespread use of the new tools of research and technology could prosper fully without a very considerable openness and candor with regard to the technical realities—an openness and candor difficult to reconcile with the traditional requirements of military security about the development of weapons of war. To these general considerations we should add again: although the peaceful use of atomic energy might well challenge the interest of technical people, and appear as an inspiration to statesmen concerned with the welfare of mankind, it could not make a direct appeal to the weary, hungry, almost desperate peoples of a war-ravaged world. Such an appeal, if made, could hardly be made in honesty.

In this article, Oppenheimer also reiterated his views on the politics of atomic armament. These I shall not quote here in extenso; only the concluding remarks will be reproduced here. In these one finds his characteristic blend of despair and hope.

The view sketched above of the international aspects of the problems of atomic energy is a history of high, if not provably unreasonable hope, and of failure. . . . It is necessarily denied to us in these days to see at what time, to what immediate ends, in what context, and in what manner of world, we may return again to the great issues touched on by the international control of atomic energy. Yet even in the history of recent failure, we may recognize elements that bear more generally on the health of our civilization. We may discern the essential harmony, in a world where science has extended and deepened our understanding of the common sources of power for evil and power for good, of restraining the one and of fostering the other. This is seed we take with us, travelling to a land we cannot see, to plant in new soil.

Thirdly, from the address "The open mind"[406] given on December 11, 1948, before the joint session of the Rochester Association of the United Nations and the Rochester Foreign Policy Association:

> We have a natural sympathy for extending to foreign affairs what we have come to learn so well in our political life at home: that an indispensable, perhaps in some ways *the* indispensable, element in giving meaning to the dignity of man, and in making possible the taking of decision on the basis of honest conviction, is the openness of men's minds, and the openness of whatever media there are for communion between men, free of restraint, free of repression, and free even of that most pervasive of all restraints, that of status and of hierarchy.
>
> In the days of the founding of this republic, in all of the eighteenth century which was formative for the growth and the explicit formulation of our political ideals, politics and science were of a piece. The hope that this might in some sense again be so, was stirred to new life by the development of atomic energy. In this it has throughout been decisive that openness, openness in the first instance with regard to technical problems and to the actual undertakings underway in various parts of the world, was the one single essential precondition for a measure of security in the atomic age. Here we met in uniquely comprehensible form the alternatives of common understanding, or of the practices of secrecy and of force. . . .
>
> We need to start with the admission that we see no clear course before us that would persuade the governments of the world to join with us in creating a more and more open world, and thus to establish the foundation on which persuasion might so largely replace coercion in determining human affairs. We ourselves have acknowledged this grim prospect, and responded by adopting some of the very measures that we had hoped might be universally renounced. With misgivings—and there ought to be misgivings—we are rearming, arming atomically, as in other fields. With deep misgivings, we are keeping secret not only those elements of our military plans, but those elements of our technical information and policy, a knowledge of which would render us more subject to enemy coercion and less effective in exercising our own. . . .
>
> When the time is run, and the future become history, it will be clear how little of it we today foresaw or could foresee. How then can we preserve hope and sensitiveness which could enable us to take advantage of all that it has in store? Our problem is not only to face the somber and the grim elements of the future, but to keep them from obscuring it. . . .
>
> In that other agony, the Civil War, where the foundations of our government were proved and reaffirmed, it was Lincoln who again and again struck true the balance between power and reason. By 1863, the war and the blockade had deepened the attrition of the South. They had also stopped the supplies of cotton to the English mills. Early that year Lincoln wrote a letter to the working men of Manchester. He wrote:
>
>> . . . It is not always in the power of governments to enlarge or restrict the scope of moral results which follow the politics that they may deem it necessary for the public safety from time to time to adopt.
>>
>> I have understood well that the duty of self-preservation rests solely with the American people; but I have at the same time been aware that

favor or disfavor of foreign nations might have a material influence in enlarging or prolonging the struggle with disloyal men in which the country is engaged. A fair examination of history has served to authorize a belief that the past actions and influences of the United States were generally regarded as having been beneficial toward mankind. I have, therefore, reckoned upon the forbearance of nations. . . .

Fifteen months later, a year before Lincoln's death, the battle had turned. He could say:

. . . When the war began, three years ago, neither party, nor any man, expected it would last till now. Each looked for the end in some way, long ere today. Neither did any anticipate that domestic slavery would be much affected by the war. But here we are; the war has not ended, and slavery has been much affected—how much needs not now to be recounted. . . .

But we can see the past, though we may not claim to have directed it; and seeing it, in this case, we feel more hopeful and confident for the future. . . .

It is in our hands to see that the hope of the future is not lost, because we were too sure that we knew the answers, too sure that there was no hope.

CHAPTER **18**

OF THE FIRST SERIOUS ENEMIES AND OF THE FIRST RUSSIAN A-BOMB

In Which the First Clouds Appear

Oppenheimer had emerged from the war as an American hero. In 1945 he had been considered for nomination to a California Congress seat.[407] In 1946 the War Department had called him "a man of boundless energy, rare common sense, great personal charm, and possessing tremendous organizational abilities."[408] In a White House press release (also from 1946), he was described as "an outstanding theoretical physicist with the broadest insight into all the problems in the development of atomic energy . . . a very helpful citizen . . . [who had the confidence] of the armed services."[408] President Truman wrote of him: "More than any other man, Oppenheimer is to be credited with the achievement of the completed bomb."[409]

Robert had paid a price for his glory, however. A friend from that time described him as "probably the most famous man in the world today . . . [but looking] more emaciated . . . [with] drawn and tired features . . . [and whose] emotional resources and nervous system had been strained almost to the breaking point."[410] Another friend has also described his looks, "His hair cut like a monk's, skin-tight."[411] That was what fame had cost him. Tides were about to turn, however.

Small signs on the far horizon can be harbingers of a heavy thunderstorm. So it went in Oppenheimer's postwar years. The first clouds appeared in 1947. The storm broke loose over him in 1954. In those years several irreconcilable issues were to place him at loggerheads with some extremely powerful and vindictive men who would silence his voice.

163

Early in 1947 American scientists began appealing to the AEC to permit distribution of isotopes to European colleagues. The GAC (headed, it will be remembered, by Oppenheimer at that time) heartily concurred, noting that it would have the effect abroad of restoring confidence in American science. On May 31, 1947, Oppenheimer made a presentation of this issue before the AEC that was highly praised by Lilienthal.[412] The majority of the AEC members were in favor of the proposal but one dissented: Lewis Strauss, who opined that distribution of isotopes abroad would be a breach of security. Nor did he believe that doing so would bring goodwill abroad. By a vote of four to one the Commission decided to send a positive recommendation to the State Department.[413]

In June 1949, Oppenheimer appeared before the House Committee on Unamerican Activities (HUAC). When asked about the political backgrounds of some of his Berkeley students, his answers were protective, with one exception. When queried about Bernard Peters (1910–1993), also an ex-student, "whom he had years ago described to the security officer at Los Alamos as 'quite a Red' and a 'crazy person,' he did not back away from these remarks but instead underwrote them firmly. In so doing, he was to anger a sizeable section of the scientific community" (including me).[413a]

The Committee members went on to inquire about the Communist Party membership of Robert's brother Frank. Audaciously, he asked them to withdraw the question. Astoundingly, they did.

A week later, on June 13, Oppenheimer testified before the Joint Committee on Atomic Energy (JCAE). This committee was investigating the charge by one of its members, Senator Bourke Hickenlooper (1896–1971), that the AEC was guilty of "incredible mismanagement." Robert was now about to enter a political battle whose scope he could not have foreseen.

The year before, the secretary of defense had started cost-cutting measures in the three armed services, which now competed against each other for funding. They felt threatened by the actions of Lilienthal, the GAC— and Oppenheimer. That was the background against which Congress initiated an investigation, headed by Hickenlooper, to look into alleged waste of money on certain AEC projects. One key issue involved the export of radioactive isotopes to foreign researchers, an issue of particular importance to the paranoid Strauss.

Strauss had an ally in Hickenlooper, who was united with him in his opposition to isotope exports. On June 9, Strauss testified before the JCAE that the export of isotopes to the allies might be of some military value and, therefore, he was against their export.[416] Four days later, Senator Hicken-looper announced before the Joint Committee that "when we furnish iso-topes" to other nations "we are embarking on a program which I believe is . . . inimical to our national defense. . . ."[417] Later that day, Oppenheimer testified before the committee on the same subject, and demolished the arguments of both Strauss and Hickenlooper,[418] in the process humiliating the former.

David Lilienthal watched as Oppenheimer "dismissed" Strauss's objections "with a swift rapier thrust, just passing it off as not really worthy of much consideration. . . ." Oppenheimer had "made fun" of Strauss's opposition, and Gordon Dean remembered "the terrible look on Lewis's face."[419]

An examination of the correspondence between Strauss and Oppenheimer reveals that until this incident Strauss wrote to Oppenheimer frequently, and as "Dear Robert." After 1949, there was just one letter from Strauss, and it began with "Dear Dr. Oppenheimer."[420]

June 1949 had been a bad month for Oppenheimer. He had angered colleagues because of the Peters affair, and by his notorious arrogance had made his first serious enemies.[421]

A few addenda.

Richard Rhodes remarks:

> More elementally than political differences, Strauss seems to have been repelled by what he characterized as Oppenheimer's immorality. When Edward Teller, some years later, wanted to write that Oppenheimer had been "magnificent," Strauss rebuked him waspishly: "Is a man magnificent who is what JRO was by his own admission in respect to his veracity and personal morals? (Did Ernest Lawrence ever tell you what he did in the Tolman household?) Some other word maybe, Edward, but not magnificent."[422]

Strauss was referring to the affair Oppenheimer had with Ruth Tolman, the wife of Caltech senior physicist Richard Tolman. Tolman was not only one of Oppenheimer's closest colleagues, but when Tolman was part of Conant's team at OSRD during the war, responsible for atomic energy matters, Oppenheimer always stayed at the Tolman house when in Washington.

Rhodes also notes: "Oppenheimer's friend Joseph Alsop, the influential journalist and columnist, would write of Strauss a few years later[423] that he was a 'natty, energetic, ambitious, and intelligent man' who was 'all pliability' with his 'chiefs' but who 'likes no argument' from 'equals and subordinates. . . . One of his fellow commissioners has said of him, "If you disagree with Lewis about anything, he assumes you're just a fool at first. But if you go on disagreeing with him, he concludes you must be a traitor.'" With such a man as Strauss, Alsop concludes, 'Oppenheimer was fated from the first to get on badly.'"[422]

In 1947 Oppenheimer's troubles had not yet reached the general public, however, which continued to be treated to tidbits of the famous man. A sample from *Life* magazine in December 1947:

> The new director has a sharp, selective mind, and his friends sometimes feel that he wins arguments too quickly. He and his family live in an 18-room, white colonial house near Fuld Hall, and Oppenheimer stops work at about 6:30 every evening to go home and play with his children, Peter, 6, and Katherine, 3. On Sundays he and his wife, who was a biologist, take the children out to hunt four-leaf clovers. Mrs. Oppenheimer, whose thinking is also direct, keeps her children from cluttering the house with four-leaf clovers by making them eat all they find right on the spot.[424]

The First Soviet A-Bomb

When Oppenheimer returned to Princeton in September 1949, he was greeted with the news that the Soviets had exploded an atomic bomb. This is what happened.

On September 3, a teletype alerted the headquarters of the Air Force's Long Range Detection System that a WB-29 weather reconnaissance plane on routine patrol from Japan to Alaska had picked up some measurable radioactivity. A filter paper, exposed for three hours at 18,000 feet over the North Pacific east of the Kamchatka Peninsula, had produced slightly more than the number of radioactive counts per minute necessary to constitute an official "alert." Another test revealed fission fragments.

As one example of scientists' reactions, this is what Rabi said in 1954: "I was astonished that it came that soon. I will tell you this was a peculiar kind of psychology. If you had asked anybody in 1944 or 1945 when would the Russians have it, it would have been 5 years. But every year that went by you kept on saying 5 years."[426]

Back to September 1949. A committee of outstanding physicists was appointed to examine the evidence, joined on the 19th by Oppenheimer. Their findings: the hundreds of samples collected across a broad portion of the northern hemisphere showed good correlation in the composition and age of the fission products, and their wide dispersal led to the conclusion that they had come from a single, large fission reaction. It was still not possible to fix the exact time and location of the detonation, nor to determine conclusively the composition of the device, but there was no reluctance on the

Abraham Pais and J. Robert Oppenheimer at the Institute for Advanced Study, Princeton, ca. 1950. *Courtesy Ida Nicolaisen*

Above
Robert's birth certificate. Notice that his full original name, despite Robert's later denials, is "Julius Robert Oppenheimer." *Courtesy NYC Municipal Archives*

Left
Robert (left) and his brother Frank. *Frank Oppenheimer. AIP Emilio Segrè Visual Archives*

Robert's records in the Ethical Culture School, showing both "J. Robert" and "Julius Robert." *Courtesy the Ethical Culture Fieldston School*

Kammerlingh-Omnes Lab, Leiden 1926. L–R front row: Uhlenbeck, Honl, Florin, student, Fokker, Kramers, Goudsmit; L–R back row: Niessen, Dirac, student, Oppenheimer, Polak, student, Mrs. Ehrenfest, Ehrenfest, Wolfjer. *AIP Emilio Segrè Visual Archives, Uhlenbeck Collection*

Oppenheimer, I. I. Rabi, Mott-Smith, Pauli at Lake Zurich, 1930s. *AIP Emilio Segrè Visual Archives*

SEPTEMBER 15, 1935   PHYSICAL REVIEW   VOLUME 48

Note on the Transmutation Function for Deuterons

J. R. OPPENHEIMER AND M. PHILLIPS, *University of California, Berkeley*
(Received July 1, 1935)

We consider the effect of the finite size and ready polarizability of the deuteron on the probability of transmutations involving the capture of the neutron. These have as a consequence that the Coulomb repulsion of the nucleus is less effective than for alpha-particles or protons, and that the corresponding transmutation functions increase less rapidly with deuteron energy. We treat the collision by the adiabatic approximation and obtain quantitative results for this energy dependence which are in good agreement with experiment.

MANY elements can be rendered radioactive by deuteron bombardment, the reaction involving the capture of a neutron and the liberation of a proton:

$$_nA^m + H^2 \rightarrow {}_nA^{m+1} + H^1. \qquad (1)$$

Four reactions of this type have been studied in detail by Lawrence, McMillan and Thornton.[1] The transmutation functions which are found increase smoothly with deuteron energy, but the increase is far less rapid than we should expect on the basis of the familiar considerations of Gamow[2] on the penetration of charged particles through the potential barrier of the nuclear Coulomb field. To account even roughly for the observations on this basis, we are forced to assume that the Coulomb potential breaks down at very large distances ($\sim 1.5 \times 10^{-12}$ cm for copper). The transmutation function is thus anomalous when compared to that for protons and alphaparticles, and it is natural to associate this anomaly with the structure of the deuteron, particularly its low stability. We wish to show in this paper that when this is taken into account, it does in fact provide a satisfactory explanation of the experiments.

For neutron capture to be possible the neutron must have an appreciable probability of coming within the range of the nuclear forces. But this condition can be satisfied even when the center of mass of the deuteron lies beyond the range of these forces. It is this possibility which leads to an explanation of the fact that even with such a

highly charged element as copper nuclear transmutations can occur for deuteron energies of the order of 2 MV.

The quantitative treatment of the corresponding collision problem is complicated, not only by our ignorance of the detailed forces involved, but by the complete inapplicability of ... proximation. For the velocity o ... not large compared to the int ... proton and neutron; the effectiv ... of the deuteron is long compar ... We have thus to use the adiabati ... the relative motion of proton ar ... proximately given by the solut ... equation when the distance of t ... of the deuteron from the nucle ... the center of mass moves in an e ... which is the energy $\mathcal{E}(X)$ ... and the perturbation which ind ... impacts of the transmutation is ... kinetic energy neglected in this ... mation. In fact the cross section ... tation is then given, with a prop ... of the wave functions, by

$$\sigma = 1/h^3 |\int \int dp dm \bar{\psi}_f(p, n)$$
$$\times [h^2/4M\Delta_x + W - I - \mathcal{E}(X)$$

Here p and n are the coordinate ... neutron, $x = p - n$ their relativ ... the coordinates of the center of ... measured from the nucleus as o ... is the approximate adiabatic w ... the initial state (normalized to ... wave function for the final sta ... neutron is captured and the pr ... with a considerable kinetic energ ... are kinetic energy, binding ener ...

[1] Lawrence, McMillan and Thornton, preceding article. We are greatly indebted to the authors for the opportunity of seeing their experimental results, and for many helpful discussions.
[2] Gamow, *Atomic Nuclei and Radioactivity* (Oxford University Press, 1931).

MARCH 1, 1930   PHYSICAL REVIEW   VOLUME 35

NOTE ON THE THEORY OF THE INTERACTION OF FIELD AND MATTER

BY J. R. OPPENHEIMER
BERKELEY, CALIFORNIA
(Received November 12, 1929)

ABSTRACT

The paper develops a method for the systematic integration of the relativistic wave equations for the coupling of electrons and protons with each other and with the electromagnetic field. It is shown that, when the velocity of light is made infinite, these equations reduce to the Schroedinger equation in configuration space for the many body problem. It is further shown that it is impossible on the present theory to eliminate the interaction of a charge with its own field, and that the theory leads to false predictions when it is applied to compute the energy levels and the frequency of the absorption and emission lines of an atom.

THE relativistic theory of the interaction of electrons and protons with each other and with the electromagnetic field has been developed in two papers.[1] The theory is developed in close analogy to the corresponding classical theory: the field is on the one hand determined by the configuration of the charges; and the motion of the charges is affected by the field. The interaction between two charges is not then, on this theory, expressed directly as a function of the configuration of the charges, but as the effect on each of the charges of the field induced by the other. On the classical theory this procedure involves grave difficulties, because each charge reacts also with its [ow]n proper energy of this interaction is, for point charges infinite; [depe]nds upon the motion of the charge. On the classical theory one [av]oid this difficulty by ascribing to the elementary charges a finite [... w]as not possible to carry through the theory in a way that was not [ ]arbitrary; nor was it possible to make the work relativistically [... O]ne of the purposes of the present paper is to see in how far these [...p]ersist in the quantum theory, and in what measure they render [t]he application of the theory.

[... re]capitulate briefly the main points of divergence between the [qua]ntum theoretic treatment and the classical theory. In the first [... sta]te of the matter is here represented, not by a trajectory, but by a [...o]n. Further, the Hamiltonian for the matter is that derived from [...li]near wave equation, and not from the quadratic wave equation [...]follow from the classical relativistic Hamiltonian. Finally, both [...]waves and the electromagnetic waves are quantized, the matter

[... Heisen]berg and W. Pauli, Zeits. f. Physik 56, 1 (1929); ibid. in press. The second [... p]apers is referred to in this work as I.C. I am greatly indebted to Professor [... and] Professor Pauli, not only for the opportunity of seeing their work before its [... bu]t also for their very valuable criticism and advice.

---

densed neutron phase would start at the center. By reason of the greater density of the condensed phase, the star will begin to collapse. The details of this process are difficult to analyze without knowing the change of density and the heat of condensation (latent heat of evaporation). If the latter one can be neglected then the regular energy liberation in the stellar interior, collapsing can go on until a very thin neutron atmosphere is left around the condensed neutron core. This hypothesis affords a

concrete physical basis for Zwicky's[6] suggestion that the supernovae originate from the sudden transition of an ordinary star to a centrally condensed one. It is obvious that a detailed analysis of this problem must await a great deal more experimental data concerning the physical properties of the neutron.

I should like to express my thanks to Dr. Rupert Wildt for helpful discussions on the subject.

[6] F. Zwicky, Astrophys. J. 88, 522 (1938).

SEPTEMBER 1, 1939   PHYSICAL REVIEW   VOLUME 56

On Continued Gravitational Contraction

J. R. OPPENHEIMER AND H. SNYDER
University of California, Berkeley, California
(Received July 10, 1939)

When all thermonuclear sources of energy are exhausted a sufficiently heavy star will collapse. Unless fission due to rotation, the radiation of mass, or the blowing off of mass by radiation, reduce the star's mass to the order of that of the sun, this contraction will continue indefinitely. In the present paper we study the solutions of the gravitational field equations which describe this process. In I, general and qualitative arguments are given on the behavior of the metrical tensor as the contraction progresses: the radius of the star approaches asymptotically its gravitational radius; light from the surface of the star is progressively reddened, and can escape over a progressively narrower range of angles. In II, an analytic solution of the field equations confirming these general arguments is obtained for the case that the pressure within the star can be neglected. The total time of collapse for an observer comoving with the stellar matter is finite, and for this idealized case and typical stellar masses, of the order of a day; an external observer sees the star asymptotically shrinking to its gravitational radius.

I

RECENTLY it has been shown[1] that the general relativistic field equations do not possess any static solutions for a spherical distribution of cold neutrons if the total mass of the neutrons is greater than $\sim 0.7 \odot$. It seems of interest to investigate the behavior of nonstatic solutions of the field equations.

In this work we will be concerned with stars which have large masses, $> 0.7 \odot$, and which have used up their nuclear sources of energy. A star under these circumstances would collapse under the influence of its gravitational field and release energy. This energy could be divided into four parts: (1) kinetic energy of motion of the

particles in the star, (2) radiation, (3) potential and kinetic energy of the outer layers of the star which could be blown away by the radiation, (4) rotational energy which could divide the star into two or more parts. If the mass of the original star were sufficiently small, or if enough of the star could be blown from the surface by radiation, or lost directly in radiation, or if the angular momentum of the star were great enough to split it into small fragments, then the remaining matter could form a stable static distribution, a white dwarf star. We consider the case where this cannot happen.

If then, for the late stages of contraction, we can neglect the gravitational effect of any escaping radiation or matter, and may still neglect the deviations from spherical symmetry

[1] J. R. Oppenheimer and G. M. Volkoff, Phys. Rev. 55, 374 (1939).

Some of Robert's early papers.
Courtesy American Physical Society

Four future presidents of the American Physical Society—including two future Nobel laureates—taking time off from the June 1938 American Physical Society meeting to visit the San Diego Zoo. L–R: Robert Serber, Willy Fowler, Robert, and Luis Alvarez. *AIP Emilio Segrè Visual Archives*

Robert (third from left) at Los Alamos, with Richard Feynman (second from left, facing camera). *Los Alamos National Laboratory. AIP Emilio Segrè Visual Archives*

On a trip to select a site for the Trinity test, with Major W. A. ("Lex") Stevens. *AIP Emilio Segrè Visual Archives*

WEST POINTER LED ATOM-BOMB STAFF

General Groves, Fourth in 1918 Class, Coordinated Work of Many Technicians

Conferring at Oak Ridge, near Knoxville, Tenn., site of one of the government bomb projects. Left to right: Sir James Chadwick, Great Britain; Maj. Gen. Leslie R. Groves, in charge of the entire program; Dr. Richard C. Tolman, Office of Scientific Research and Development, Washington, D. C., and Dr. H. O. Smyth, project consultant.

The New York Times (U. S. Army)

Special to The New York Times.

WASHINGTON, Aug. 6—Under Maj. Gen. Leslie R. Groves, 48 years old, who stood fourth in the West Point class of '18, the War Department assembled a brilliant staff of the scientists, engineers and organizers from all parts of the country to direct the atomic-bomb experiment to a successful climax.

The first assistant to General Groves was Brig. Gen. Thomas F. Farrell, 53, a veteran Army officer, born in New Brunswick, N. J., who has described himself as "handy man" for the director in executing plans for the project. The chief engineer was Col. Kenneth David Nichols, 37, an indefatigable researcher, born in Cleveland. Col. Franklin T. Matthias, also 37, who heads the division of the project at Hanford and Richland Village, Wash., brought to the experiment a facility for organization.

Dr. J. Robert Oppenheimer, 41, in charge of the atomic laboratory in New Mexico, is a physics professor at the University of California and a leading scientist in the structure of the atom. Dr. Richard C. Tolman, 64, dean of the Graduate School of the California Institute of Technology, was General Groves' scientific adviser and Dr. James B. Conant, 52, president of Harvard, also served as a counselor.

Was Deputy Chief of Construction

General Groves was deputy chief of construction under Gen. Thomas M. Robbins in the Washington office of the Chief of Engineers when he was assigned to the atomic research development in the summer of 1942. In that capacity he aided in all military construction in the United States. Expenditures for that purpose ran to $600,000,000 a month. He also supervised the erection of the huge Pentagon across the Potomac from Washington. His scientific researches had previously dealt with anti-aircraft searchlights and allied equipment.

General Groves was born in the manse of the First Presbyterian Church in Albany, of which his father was minister. The father became an army chaplain just before the Spanish-American War and the son first saw army life in many stations over the country where his father served tours of duty.

He left the Massachusetts Institute of Technology in 1916 to enter West Point. After his graduation he attended the Engineers School at Fort Humphries, Va. He later held engineer assignments in Hawaii, Galveston, Tex., and Nicaragua. He holds a Nicaraguan decoration for work done after the Nicaraguan earthquake in 1931. He became a brigadier general in September, 1942. He is married and has two children, one of whom, Lieut. Richard H. Groves, graduated from West Point in June.

Veteran of Five Battles

General Farrell is described as a "fast-talking, fast-moving" hero of five major engagements of the First World War. He joined the atomic-bomb project last February, after having served as chief engineer in charge of construction in the China-Burma-India theatre for fourteen months.

He was educated in Troy, N. Y., schools, and graduated in engineering from the Rensselaer Polytechnic Institute there in 1912. He was with an engineering party on the New York State Barge Canal for nine months, then spent four years in Panama on canal construction.

After having resigned from the regular Army in 1926, he was Commissioner of Canals and Waterways for the State of New York and then served as Chief Engineer of the State Department of Public Works until February, 1941, when he returned to active duty in the Army. He and his family live in Albany.

Colonel Nichols, who first met General Groves in Nicaragua, has supervised the organization of the atomic research project since the summer of 1942. From Oak Ridge, Tenn., he has controlled the operations of the Clinton Engineer Works. He also supervises the Hanford Engineer Works in Washington.

A former instructor at West Point, from which he was graduated fifth in his class in 1929, he was the third person to be appointed to the project. He was educated in Cleveland until he went to West Point. Later he attended Cornell University for his degree in civil engineering. His background includes special studies in hydraulic engineering in this country and Germany.

Colonel Matthias, assigned to the Hanford project at its inception, was born in Glidden, Wis. He attended and later taught at the University of Wisconsin, whose faculty he left in 1935 to become a construction engineer with the Tennessee Valley Authority. In 1939 he was in charge of engineering work on a rock-dredging and bank-protection project on the Tennessee River near Pickwick Dam, Tenn.

Dr. Oppenheimer was born in New York and graduated from Harvard in 1925. He later attended Cambridge and received his Ph. D. from the University of Goettingen in Germany in 1927. A fellow of the American Academy of Physical Society, the American Philosophical Society and the National Academy of Sciences, he has contributed studies on the nature of matter, electricity and radiation and the constitution of the stars.

Dr. Tolman, who was born in West Newton, Mass., graduated from the Massachusetts Institute of Technology. During the first World War he was a major in the Chemical Warfare Service. He is a recognized authority on ionization, colloids, relativity of motion, metallic conductors, cosmology and relative thermo-dynamics.

Dr. J. Robert Oppenheimer
Associated Press Wirephoto

Dr. James B. Conant
The New York Times Studio

Dr. A. H. Compton
The New York Times

Prof. Harold Urey
The New York Times

Dr. Enrico Fermi
The New York Times

Dr. Neils Bohr
Associated Press

Dr. Vannevar Bush
Associated Press

George L. Harrison
The New York Times

Prof. Ernest Lawrence
Associated Press

Robert enters the world stage. *Front page © 1945 by The New York Times Co. Reprinted with permission*

Participants at the 1947 Shelter Island conference. L–R standing: W. Lamb, Jr., K. K. Darrow, V. Weisskopf, G. E. Uhlenbeck, R. E. Marshak, J. Schwinger, D. Bohm. L–R seated: J. R. Oppenheimer, A. Pais, R. P. Feynman, H. Feshbach. *Courtesy of Archives, National Academy of Sciences*

Robert on the cover of *Time*; the equations in the background are by Abraham Pais.
TIME Magazine © November 8, 1948 Time, Inc. Reprinted by permission.

Robert with Tony and Peter and his dog Buddy. *Mrs. J. Robert Oppenheimer, courtesy AIP Emilio Segrè Visual Archives*

Robert Oppenheimer, Paul Dirac, and Abraham Pais in discussion at the Institute for Advanced Study, Princeton, ca. 1950. *Courtesy University Libraries, Florida State University, Tallahassee, Florida*

Excerpts from the hearing on
Robert's security clearance, April 1954

Dr. GRAY. An investigation of Dr. J. Robert Oppenheimer conducted under the provisions of section 10 (b) (5) (B) (i–iii) of the Atomic Energy Act of 1946 has revealed certain information which casts doubt upon the eligibility of Dr. Oppenheimer for clearance for access to restricted data as provided by the Atomic Energy Act of 1946. This information is as follows:

Q. Didn't you say that X had approached 3 people?
A. Probably.
Q. Why did you do that, Doctor?
A. Because I was an idiot.

Q. You spent the night with her, didn't you?
A. Yes.
Q. That is when you were working on a secret war project?
A. Yes.
Q. Did you think that consistent with good security?
A. It was, as a matter of fact. Not a word—it was not good practice.

Q. Now let us go back to your interview with Colonel Pash. Did you tell Pash the truth about this thing?
A. No.
Q. You lied to him?
A. Yes.

"Because of these associations that I have described, and the contributions mentioned earlier, I might well have appeared at the time as quite close to the Communist Party—perhaps even to some people as belonging to it. As I have said, some of its declared objectives seemed to me desirable. But I never was a member of the Communist Party. I never accepted Communist dogma or theory; in fact, it never made sense to me. I had no clearly formulated political views. I hated tyranny and repression and every form of dictatorial control of thought. In most cases I did not in those days know who was and who was not a member of the Communist Party. No one ever asked me to join the Communist Party.

J. Robert Oppenheimer Papers, Manuscript Division, Library of Congress, Washington, D.C.

Q. Now, a question which is the corollary of that. Do you or do you not believe that Dr. Oppenheimer is a security risk?

A. In a great number of cases I have seen Dr. Oppenheimer act—I understood that Dr. Oppenheimer acted—in a way which for me was exceedingly hard to understand. I thoroughly disagreed with him in numerous issues and his actions frankly appeared to me confused and complicated. To this extent I feel that I would like to see the vital interests of this country in hands which I understand better, and therefore trust more.

In this very limited sense I would like to express a feeling that I would feel personally more secure if public matters would rest in other hands.

Q. He was certainly more of a professional than you were; wasn't he, Colonel?
A. In what field?
Q. The field he was working in, security.
A. No.
Q. No?
A. No.
Q. He was a graduate of West Point; wasn't he?
A. Certainly. I am a graduate of VMI. too. You want to fight about that?

Or to put the question in another way, I ask you whether it is not a fair inference from your testimony that your story to Pash and Lansdale as far as it went was a true story, and that the fabrication may have been with respect to the current version.

A. Let me take the second part of your question first.
Q. Yes.
A. The story I told to Pash was not a true story. There were not three or more people involved on the project. There was one person involved. That was me. I was at Los Alamos. There was no one else at Los Alamos involved. There was no one in Berkeley involved. When I heard the microfilm or what the hell, it didn't sound to me as to this were reporting anything that Chevalier had said, or at that time the unknown professor had said. I am certain that was not mentioned. I testified that the Soviet consulate had not been mentioned by Chevalier. That is the very best of my recollection. It is conceivable that I knew of Eltenton's connection with the consulate, but I believe I can do no more than say the story told in circumstantial detail, and which was elicited from me in greater and greater detail during this was a false story. It is not easy to say that.

Now, when you ask for a more persuasive argument as to why I did this than that I was an idiot, I am going to have more trouble being understandable.

A. I do feel strongly that Dr. Oppenheimer at least to the extent of my knowledge is loyal. I am extremely disturbed by the current hysteria of the times of which this seems to be a manifestation.
Q. You think this inquiry is a manifestation of hysteria?
A. I think——
Q. Yes or no?

The WITNESS. That the suspension of the clearance of Dr. Oppenheimer was a very unfortunate thing and should not have been done. In other words, there he was; he is a consultant, and if you don't want to consult the guy, you don't consult him, period. Why you have to then proceed to suspend clearance and go through all this sort of thing, he is only there when called, and that is all there was to it. So it didn't seem to me the sort of thing that called for this kind of proceeding at all against a man who had accomplished what Dr. Oppenheimer has accomplished. There is a real positive record, the way I expressed it to a friend of mine. We have an A-bomb and a whole series of it, * * * and what more do you want, mermaids? This is just a tremendous achievement. If the end of that road is this kind of hearing, which can't help but be humiliating, I thought it was a pretty bad show. I still think so.

Mr. GRAY. We now conclude this phase of the proceedings. I think that I have already indicated to Dr. Oppenheimer that if we require anything further, he will be notified.

We are now in recess.

(Thereupon at 1 : 30 p. m., the hearing was concluded.)

Herblock cartoon commenting on the hearing. *Courtesy the Herb Block Foundation*

Robert at the wedding of Abraham Pais, 15 December 1956. *Courtesy of Ida Nicolaisen*

Facing page, top   Bohr, MacMillan, and Oppenheimer at CERN, in Geneva, Switzerland, for the inauguration of the proton synchrotron, 1960. © *CERN. Reprinted with Permission*

Facing page, bottom   Fermi Award: "Presented to J. Robert Oppenheimer for especially meritorious contributions to the development, use, or control of atomic energy," December 2, 1963. *AIP Emilio Segrè Visual Archives, Fermi Film Collection*

Robert at a physics conference, probably 1966. *AIP Emilio Segrè Visual Archives*

part of the panel to accept the conclusion in Oppenheimer's draft that the observed phenomena were "consistent with the view that the origin of the fission products was the explosion of an atomic bomb" on August 29.[427]

Teller later said, "This answer worried me even more than the Russian explosion."[430]

I add brief remarks on the history of the Russian A-bomb.

Moscow News (an English weekly written in Moscow) of April 12, 1988, contains the first publication in full of a letter to Stalin written in April 1942 by Georgy Flerov. Before the war Flerov, later director of a laboratory at the Joint Institute for Nuclear Research in Dubna, had discovered the spontaneous fission of uranium-235, together with Konstantin Petrzhak. Flerov wrote his letter, addressed "Dear Iosif Vissarionovich." After having noted that recent physics journals from the United States, Britain, and Germany contained no reference whatever to fission, he had correctly inferred that scientists in those countries were up to something. He pleaded with Stalin to take an initiative "concerning the feasibility of the uranium problem."[431]

Stalin did not take action until mid-August 1945, however—after Hiroshima. In a meeting with leading politicians and scientists, he said, "A single demand of you, comrades—provide us with atomic weapons in the shortest possible time. You know that Hiroshima has shaken the whole world. The equilibrium has been destroyed [*ravnovesie narushilos*]. Provide the bomb—it will remove a great danger from us."[432]

CHAPTER 19

OF THE SUPERBOMB AND OF SPY STORIES

Varia: 1947–1949

In this section I record a variety of topics from the years 1947 to 1949 that led up to October 1949, the time that marks the beginning of Oppenheimer's serious involvement with the issue: shall the United States build a super, a hydrogen bomb, or shall it not?

Already before the Russians had exploded their first A-bomb, Oppenheimer had become known for his hard-headedness and strongly anti-Soviet attitude, a viewpoint that resulted from his reactions to repeated Soviet obstruction of the internationalization of atomic control and disarmament under United Nations' auspices. Speaking to those scientists who were content with the United States' superiority in atomic weapons, Oppenheimer said: "No Government can adequately meet its responsibilities for defense if it rests content with wartime results of this project [Los Alamos]."[433] He had warned the administration in 1944 of Soviet designs in the Far East, and disagreed with those scientists who felt that the international control of the atom would bring complete security. His attitude toward Soviet obstruction of the international control of atomic energy at the United Nations evolved from a mild distrust to a deep resentment.[434] He even went so far as to advise the Truman administration to abandon the United Nations' negotiations on atomic energy control because of the Soviet refusal to adopt the Baruch Plan.[435] As a consultant to the United Nations Atomic Energy Commission during 1946 and 1947, Oppenheimer warned of possible Soviet attempts to secure vital information, and attributed the failure of international control to "the pro-grammatic hostility and institutionalized secretiveness" of the Soviets, as well as their frequent use of the term: "No!"[436]

While the Soviet Union's intransigence became more obvious to many Americans, and the future prospects of Soviet atomic capabilities became more manifest, Oppenheimer called for an effective defense against attack and for a "ready means of retaliation." Regarding the available United States supply of atomic weapons, he said that we "cannot sit on it, however adequate, with any total assurance of superiority in this field," and warned how "dangerous complacency could be with regard to work in this field."[437] In 1948, he wrote, "Whatever our hopes for the future, we must surely be prepared, both in planning and in the development of weapons, and insofar as possible in our 'force in being,' for more than one kind of conflict."[438]

Meeting Teller at a party right after the war, Oppenheimer had said to him, "We have done a wonderful job here [at Los Alamos] and it will be many years before anyone can improve on our work in any way."[439] This perhaps indicates that in 1949 he, too, was surprised at the speed with which the Russians had managed to make their first test bomb.

On June 12, 1946, "Report of Conference on the Super" was issued as a classified document. (A heavily censored version was declassified in 1971.[440]) The conference was attended by three members of the British team at Los Alamos.[441] One of these was the German-born theoretical physicist Emil Klaus Fuchs (1911–1988), known in Los Alamos as "penny-in-the-slot-Fuchs," because he only spoke when spoken to.[442]

From November 14–17, 1947, a conference of United States, British, and Canadian scientists and officials was held in Washington, for the purpose of establishing a common declassification policy. Those attending included Oppenheimer, Fuchs, and Donald McLean (1913–1983), a representative of the British Embassy in Washington.[444] Shortly afterward I met Fuchs, for the only time, as he stepped out of Oppenheimer's Princeton office.

In 1947, the struggle began to establish air power as the preponderant force in military planning. But throughout 1947 and 1948, Oppenheimer's advocacy of a balanced force concept, combining conventional forces with air retaliatory strength, still met with agreement by Defense Secretary James Forrestal (1892–1949), who stated that "we can not rest our security on any one arm, weapon, or plan."[445] However, with the establishment of President Truman's Air Policy Committee on January 13, 1947, a concerted effort was made to increase our nuclear air power capabilities. The resultant report gave great encouragement to the advocates of air power.[446]

In 1948, a battle erupted between the Air Force and the Navy over which service was to be invested with the job of strategic bombing. The Navy tried to promote the idea of a super carrier for the task, while the Air Force insisted that the B-36 bomber was the answer. Air Force chief of staff General Carl Spaatz (1891–1974) demanded that the control of atomic weapons be assigned to his office. Secretary Forrestal agreed, but warned: "I do not believe that air power alone can win a war."[447] The Air Force did win the battle through its persistence.

So intense was the struggle over the B-36 that Forrestal remarked that there were "fundamental psychoses" surrounding the use of air power, especially the "psychosis of the Air Force that the Navy is trying to encroach upon the strategic air prerogatives of the Air Force."[448] He expressed his concern over "one of the real difficulties" that was "becoming more manifest every day: the gap in the Air Force of wise and experienced leadership in the upper ranks. Ten or even five years from now they will be all right . . . but for the immediate future they have a problem."[449] The Air Force had tended to argue that they had the strategic answers from the beginning,[450] and this attitude was to cause Robert Oppenheimer serious trouble. Following the creation in 1947 of the Air Force as a separate branch of the military establishment, its top brass had got hold of Oppenheimer's FBI file and "started telling its contents to any officer or civilian employee who might conceivably ever come into contact with him."[451]

The Strategic Air Command (SAC), established in 1948, evolved into the principal nuclear retaliatory United States striking force. Curtis LeMay (1906–1990), one of the toughest American generals, became its commander. He purportedly said, after learning of the feasibility of the H-bomb: "Give me more bombs; give me more powerful bombs; then stand out of my way, Moscow." When an Air Force colonel read a report to LeMay on the plentifulness of atomic bombs, LeMay said: "That's stupid. It's crazy. He [the colonel] ought to be locked in a box and dropped to the bottom of the sea." LeMay's face had turned beet red.[452]

Even after it was proven that an unlimited number of atomic bombs could be made available to the Air Force—by late 1949 the United States had a stockpile of about 200 A-bombs[453]—LeMay still did not concede that some bombs should be given to the Tactical Air Command; "instead, he tripled his own requirements."[454] LeMay apparently believed that all fissionable material "by right" belonged to SAC, because he thought that there was no such thing as enough.[455] LeMay once told a visitor that SAC was a "wonderful and complex and beautiful instrument," and it was a "solemn responsibility to tamper with the tuning of this instrument."[456] Oppenheimer's activities within the Defense Department would be viewed by the Air Force as a deliberate tampering with the effectiveness of its strategic air arm.[421]

It is well to remember that the Russian A-bomb was not the only scary news at that time. Other sensational, seemingly inexplicable tidings had further contributed to bring America into a state of terrible uncertainty. In February 1948, the Communist coup in Czechoslovakia had succeeded. On June 24, 1948, the Russians had started their blockade of Berlin (lifted July 1949). In the 1948 presidential elections, anti-Communism became a central political issue. On January 25, 1949, Alger Hiss (1904–1996), a high State Department official, was sentenced to five years in prison for perjury. On October 1, 1949, a week after Truman's public announcement of the Russian A-bomb, the People's Republic of China was officially inaugurated, becoming the most populated Communist nation in the world, with 500 million people, one fifth of the world's population.

"There was no panic in the [U.S. in late 1949, but] the fears and tensions of the Cold War were greatly amplified."[457]

Shall the United States Develop the Super?

In early October 1949 the AEC called for a special meeting of the GAC, to be held as soon as possible. They requested advice on the question whether or not they should immediately initiate an all-out effort to develop the Super and what its military worth would be in relation to fission weapons.

On October 21, a week before that GAC meeting, Oppenheimer sent a letter[459] to James Conant, a fellow GAC member, which reads in part:

> On the technical side, as far as I can tell, the super is not very different from what it was when we first spoke of it more than 7 years ago: a weapon of unknown design, cost, deliverability and military value. But a very great change has taken place in the climate of opinion. On the one hand, two experienced promoters have been at work, i.e., Ernest Lawrence and Edward Teller. The project has long been dear to Teller's heart; and Ernest has convinced himself that we must learn from Operation Joe that the Russians will soon do the super, and that we had better beat them to it. . . . Ernest spoke to . . . some at least of the joint chiefs. The joint congressional committee, having tried to find something tangible to chew on ever since September 23rd, has at last found its answer. We must have a super, and we must have it fast. A subcommittee is heading west to investigate this problem at Los Alamos and in Berkeley. The joint chiefs appear informally to have decided to give the development of the super overriding priority, though no formal request has come through. The climate of opinion among the competent physicists also shows signs of shifting. . . .

What concerns me is really not the technical problem. I am not sure the miserable thing will work, nor that it can be gotten to a target except by ox cart. It seems likely to me even further to worsen the unbalance of our present war plans. What does worry me is that this thing appears to have caught the imagination, both of the congressional and of military people, as the answer to the problem posed by the Russian advance. It would be folly to oppose the exploration of this weapon. We have always known it had to be done; and it does have to be done, though it appears to be singularly proof against any form of experimental approach. But that we became committed to it as the way to save the country and the peace appears to me full of dangers.

In explanation of this letter, note that as early as September 1945, the Scientific Panel to the Interim Committee of the War Department reported that "the very feasibility of a super bomb does not appear now, on theoretical grounds, as certain as the fission bomb appeared certain, on theoretical grounds, when the Los Alamos Scientific Laboratory was started."[460] Indeed, it was not until June 1951 that a feasible approach to the production of the hydrogen bomb was perfected, revealed at Oppenheimer's Princeton office on June 16–17, 1951.[461] (I shall come back shortly to this crucial advance.) Until that time all Teller's efforts, begun in 1942, had led absolutely nowhere. In those years Teller's work had been based on the idea that the essential ingredients for the bomb, deuterium and tritium, had to be kept under pressure at more than 400 degrees below zero to remain in their liquid state.[462] Nor could this kind of bomb be loaded easily into an aircraft—which explains Robert's picturesque allusion to an ox cart. He understood that the bomb was a weapon of unknown design, cost, deliverability, and military value, as things stood in 1949. Moreover, if a crash program were to be undertaken on an H-bomb, the manufacture of tritium and plutonium needed for the bomb would have to be drained from the existing fission bomb program, along with the already limited supply of neutrons, manpower, and funds.[463]

Robert's critique of the status in 1949 of hydrogen bomb construction was entirely justified. It was not the only reason why he was anti-Super at that time, however. Alvarez, another pro-Super physicist, has recalled what Oppenheimer had said to him a week after the letter to Conant: "He said that he did not think the United States should build the hydrogen bomb, and the main reason that he gave for this if my memory serves me correctly, and I think it does, was that if we built a hydrogen bomb, then the Russians would build a hydrogen bomb, whereas if we did not build a hydrogen bomb, then the Russians would not build a hydrogen bomb."[464]

In those first months of its existence, the General Advisory Committee was a very real revitalizing force for the whole atomic energy programme. It revived

the reactors at Hanford, which had burned out and stopped producing plutonium. At Oak Ridge the immensely costly electromagnetic separation plants
which had served a valuable function in the wartime race against time were shut
down. Los Alamos was relieved of its routine production line work so that the
physicists there could concentrate on the sophistication of the bomb design.
Two new laboratories, at Brookhaven and Argonne, joined Los Alamos in this
basic research and under the watchful eye of the GAC grew in size and prestige
to match Los Alamos.

For physics at least, the period under Oppenheimer and his Committee was
something of an age of enlightenment. There was money, there was equipment,
and there was an atmosphere of expansionism. . . .[465]

How Oppenheimer actually ran this committee was, in the years ahead, to
become an important question particularly as many of their decisions were to
be the center of controversy. In essence, the critics and victims of the Committee believed that Oppenheimer manipulated it to his own ends but, from within,
this seemed to be anything but the case.

> He was not an original [Isidor Rabi said]. Most of the real ideas came
> from others but he could open doors and present them. Give
> Oppenheimer the glimmering of an idea and he'd present it most beau-
> tifully. Far from bending us to his viewpoint, he took other people's
> views, absolutely. Then he'd make them more acceptable, more clear,
> more persuasive and this sort of thing made him a wonderful front.

> There was a good deal of talk about how he had swayed or hypno-
> tized or improperly influenced the General Advisory Committee, says
> John Manley. I was there and I knew he didn't do any such thing. I
> can't imagine any nine people who'd be more insistent on each mak-
> ing up his own mind for himself. What happened was that he at all
> times had the national interest at heart and never did anything or wanted
> to do anything except in the national interest *as he saw it*, and they could
> tell this as well as I could.

Nobody was ever to disagree about the sincerity of Oppenheimer's actions,
but there were to be many who would question his interpretation of the "national interest." [Probably his oft-quoted remark: "In some sort of crude sense
which no vulgarity, no humor, no overstatement can quite extinguish, the physicists have known sin; and this is a knowledge which they cannot lose"[466] may
not have sat well with the military.] Over the next few years Oppenheimer was
going to learn the hard way the price of having an independent mind in the
political world.[467]

The GAC special meeting, perhaps the most important one in its history,
began at 2 PM on October 28, 1949—four days after the cornerstone for the
U.N. building in New York had been laid. Its report, almost entirely declassified, became public in 1974. It consists of three parts,[469] following a
letter of transmittal by Oppenheimer, all of it drafted and edited on October 30 in a matter of a few hours.

The first part deals with what may be called—such is the speed of history—conventional, fission-type atomic weapons. It says in part: "We are not satisfied that the present scale [of production of fissionable material] represents either the maximum or the optimum scale. . . . The GAC recommends [to the AEC] an intensification of efforts to make atomic weapons available for tactical purposes."

This statement is of particular interest since it shows that the suggestion often made, that Oppenheimer was opposed to nuclear weapons of any kind, is incorrect. He did believe in the need for such weapons as long as there did not exist an international agreement on atomic arms control.

From part two, dealing with the Super:

> It is notable that there appears to be no experimental approach short of actual test which will substantially add to our conviction that a given model will or will not work, and it is also notable that because of the unsymmetric and extremely unfamiliar conditions obtaining, some considerable doubt will surely remain as to the soundness of theoretical anticipation. Thus, we are faced with a development which cannot be carried to the point of conviction without the actual construction and demonstration of the essential elements of the weapon in question. This does not mean that further theoretical studies would be without avail. It does mean that they could not be decisive. A final point that needs to be stressed is that many tests may be required before a workable model has been evolved or before it has been established beyond reasonable doubt that no such model can be evolved. Although we are not able to give a specific probability rating for any given model, we believe that an imaginative and concerted attack on the problem has a better than even chance of producing the weapon within five years.

Given the fact that, at the time of that GAC meeting, the concepts about the Super were still in the "ox-cart" stage, this is a very positive statement. It contradicts what would be said a few years later about Oppenheimer, cosigner of this statement: that he painted a falsely gloomy picture of the possibilities of producing the Super.

Part two continues with estimates of the Super's effects:

> A second characteristic of the super bomb is that once the problem of initiation has been solved, there is no limit to the explosive power of the bomb itself except that imposed by requirements of delivery. . . . Taking into account the probable limitations of carriers likely to be available for the delivery of such a weapon, it has generally been estimated that the weapon would have an explosive effect some hundreds of times that of present fission bombs. This would correspond to a damage area of the order of hundreds of square miles, to thermal radiation effects extending over a comparable area, and to very grave contamination problems which can easily be made more acute, and may possibly be rendered less acute, by surrounding the deuterium with uranium or other material. It needs to be borne in mind that for delivery by ship, submarine or other

such carrier, the limitations here outlined no longer apply and that the weapon is from a technical point of view without limitations with regard to the damage that it can inflict.

It is clear that the use of this weapon would bring about the destruction of innumerable human lives; it is not a weapon which can be used exclusively for the destruction of material installations of military or semi-military purposes. Its use therefore carries much further than the atomic bomb itself the policy of exterminating civilian populations. . . . It is clearly impossible with the vagueness of design and the uncertainty of performance as we have them at present to give anything like a cost estimate of the super. If one uses the strict criteria of damage area per dollar and if one accepts the limitations on air carrier capacity likely to obtain in the years immediately ahead, it appears uncertain to us whether the super will be cheaper or more expensive than the fission bombs.

Part three deals with the heart of the matter: Should the Super be developed?

Although the members of the Advisory Committee are not unanimous in their proposals as to what should be done with regard to the super bomb, there are certain elements of unanimity among us. We all hope that by one means or another, the development of these weapons can be avoided. We are all reluctant to see the United States take the initiative in precipitating this development. We are all agreed that it would be wrong at the present moment to commit ourselves to an all-out effort toward its development.

We are somewhat divided as to the nature of the commitment not to develop the weapon. The majority feel that this should be an unqualified commitment. Others feel that it should be made conditional on the response of the Soviet government to a proposal to renounce such development. The Committee recommends that enough be declassified about the super bomb so that a public statement of policy can be made at this time.

Two addenda follow. From the first, signed by five of the GAC members, including Oppenheimer:

We have been asked by the Commission whether or not they should immediately initiate an "all-out" effort to develop a weapon whose energy release is 100 to 1000 times greater and whose destructive power in terms of area of damage is 20 to 100 times greater than those of the present atomic bomb. We recommend strongly against such action.

We base our recommendation on our belief that the extreme dangers to mankind inherent in the proposal wholly outweigh any military advantage that could come from this development. Let it be clearly realized that this is a super weapon; it is in a totally different category from an atomic bomb. The reason for developing such super bombs would be to have the capacity to devastate a vast area with a single bomb. Its use would involve a decision to slaughter a vast number of civilians. We are alarmed as to the possible global effects of the radioactivity generated by the explosion of a few super bombs of conceivable magnitude. If super bombs will work at all, there is no inherent limit in the destructive power that may be attained with them. Therefore, a super bomb might become a weapon of genocide. . . .

The existence of such a weapon in our armory would have far-reaching effects on world opinion: reasonable people the world over would realize that the existence of a weapon of this type whose power of destruction is essentially unlimited represents a threat to the future of the human race which is intolerable. Thus we believe that the psychological effect of the weapon in our hands would be adverse to our interest.

We believe a super bomb should never be produced. Mankind would be far better off no to have a demonstration of the feasibility of such a weapon until the present climate of world opinion changes. . . .

In determining not to proceed to develop the super bomb, we see a unique opportunity of providing by example some limitations on the totality of war and thus of limiting the fear and arousing the hopes of mankind. . . .

The second addendum, signed by Fermi and Rabi, is even more strongly worded. It says in part:

By its very nature it cannot be confined to a military objective but becomes a weapon which in practical effect is almost one of genocide.

It is clear that the use of such a weapon cannot be justified on any ethical ground which gives a human being a certain individuality and dignity even if he happens to be a resident of an enemy country.

The fact that no limits exist to the destructiveness of this weapon makes its very existence and the knowledge of its construction a danger to humanity as a whole. It is necessarily an evil thing considered in any light. . . .

On December 2–3 the GAC reconvened to review the question of the Super once more. Oppenheimer reported to the AEC that no member of the GAC wished to change his opinions expressed in the earlier meetings. The AEC members' views were mixed. Chairman Lilienthal agreed with the GAC conclusions,[471] but Strauss was pro Super, as he expressed in a letter to Truman:

I believe that the United States must be as completely armed as any possible enemy. From this, it follows that I believe it unwise to renounce, unilaterally, any weapon which an enemy can reasonably be expected to possess. I recommend that the President direct the Atomic Energy Commission to proceed with the development of the thermonuclear bomb, at highest priority subject only to the judgment of the Department of Defense as to its value as a weapon, and of the advice of the Department of State as to the diplomatic consequences of its unilateral renunciation or its possession.[472]

The final AEC vote was 3 to 2 against.

Most physicists were against. I have already mentioned the principal ones who were pro Super. To those I should add Von Neumann, whose efforts consisted mainly in "talking [the] ear off" Oppenheimer.[473]

On the afternoon of January 31, 1950, President Truman publicly announced his decision to go ahead with the development of the hydrogen bomb:

It is part of my responsibility as Commander-in-Chief of the armed forces to see to it that our country is able to defend itself against any possible aggressor. Accordingly, I have directed the Atomic Energy Commission to continue its work on all forms of atomic weapons, including the so-called hydrogen or super-bomb. Like all other work in the field of atomic weapons, it is being and will be carried forward on a basis consistent with the over-all objectives of our program for peace and security.

This we shall continue to do until a satisfactory plan for international control of atomic energy is achieved. We shall also continue to examine all those factors that affect our program for peace and this country's security.[474]

Later that day, a newspaper columnist spotted Oppenheimer standing alone and morose on the sidelines of a party. "You don't look jubilant," he said to him. After a long pause Oppenheimer replied: "This is the plague of Thebes."[474a]

I didn't know what that oracular statement meant, so I looked for it in an encyclopedia. I believe that this is what Robert had in mind: in 302 AD a legion of soldiers from Egyptian Thebes was sent by Emperor Maximianus to fight the Christians in Gaul. The legion refused to fight and was slaughtered near St. Maurice in Canton Wallis. June 22, "the day of the 10,000 knights" is the day held in sacred memory of that event. Very Robert.*

Some consequences of the Truman decision:

The Air Force framed an alliance with Senator Hickenlooper to oust Lilienthal because he had opposed the Super. Lilienthal resigned of his own accord in 1950, however. He was succeeded by Gordon Dean, who, in turn, was followed in 1953 by Strauss.[476]

The Air Force chief of staff appointed Vannevar Bush over Oppenheimer as chairman of an Air Force committee to study the uses of the H-bomb, because he "lacked trust in Robert Oppenheimer,"[477] since he (O.) refused to place exclusive reliance for U.S. defense on the deterrent effect of the H-bomb.

In 1952, Teller got his own weapons laboratory at Livermore, fifty miles inland from Berkeley.

Emil Klaus Julius Fuchs et al.

From Lilienthal's journal, February 2, 1950: "The roof fell in today, you might say. . . . The news . . . will be out tomorrow when [Klaus Fuchs] is arraigned in London. . . . [A]s the President is reported to have said to [an aide], tie on your hat." From the entry of February 3:

---

*One wonders, however, whether Oppenheimer was not simply referring to the plague that afflicts Thebes in *Oedipus*.—RPC

I got to the office at about 9 . . . to find an agitated bunch. The word was on the radio, the British had it at twelve o'clock *their* time . . . six o'clock ours. I was as calm as I can remember being; insisted we put into the statement the strongest language about what Fuchs knew and was part of: "a wide area of the most vital weapons information," including Fuchs's attendance at a 1947 declassification conference [mentioned earlier] with the British.

The Joint Committee had set a meeting for 10:30, with a good attendance. . . . When called on, I told the story in terms of what he [Fuchs] knew, emphasized this was no periphery guy, or a courier, or a dumb spy, but a scientist who knew most of the weapons stuff because he had helped work out many of the most difficult of the problems. I poured it on: there wasn't a bright light in the whole picture. This had a good, sobering effect. They were most courteous, . . . asked what advice I had. I said, "This is bad; but let's not panic the country; keep your shirt on, don't wallow in it. And let's hope this won't so disturb the Los Alamos outfit, or investigations so harass everyone that the new super program is held up."[478]

The news about Fuchs had actually reached the United States a week before Lilienthal heard of it. Already on January 27 a Counselor of the British Embassy had informed the undersecretary of state of the affair.[479] The president did not learn of Fuch's espionage until February 1,[480] the day *after* he had made his hydrogen bomb announcement, which explains Strauss's flattery of the President. "The recent word from the FBI . . . only fortifies the wisdom of your decision."[481] The congressional JCAE members recognized the seriousness of the perfidy but did not indulge in recrimination. A year later they reported, a bit too dramatically: "Fuchs alone has influenced the safety of more people and accomplished greater damage than any other spy not only in the history of the United States but in the history of nations."[482]

I next sketch briefly Fuchs's life[483] up till the time of his confession at age 38.

Fuchs was born in 1911 in a Rhine valley village south of Frankfurt, and brought up in a poor, strictly pious Quaker home. He saw tragedy in his early years: the suicide of his mother, and of his elder sister, a Communist, who jumped in front of a train when she was about to be arrested by Nazis. He studied physics and mathematics at the Universities of Leipzig, then Kiel, where he joined the Communist Party.

After the burning of the Reichstag in 1933, he went underground, then fled to Paris. "I was sent out by the Party."[484] From there he found his way to Edinburgh, where "he did some excellent work in the electron theory of metals."[485] In May 1940 he was interned on the Isle of Man as an enemy alien, and from there was shipped to a Canadian army camp. During all that time he had "complete confidence in Russian policy."[486] Intercession by friends made possible his return to England in December 1940. In 1941 he started atomic bomb work in Birmingham, directed by Rudolf Peierls (1907–1995).

"When I learned of the purpose of the work I decided to inform Russia,"[486] and made contact with a secretary of the Russian embassy in London. In August 1942 he became a British citizen.

In December 1943 Fuchs arrived in New York as a member of a British team of scientists engaged in atomic bomb work. Before leaving England his Russian connection had told him when and where in New York to meet with a new contact person, code named Raymond. His real name was Harry Gold (1910–1972), born Heinrich Golodnitsky, in Switzerland, who had become a naturalized American citizen. He was a middleman who reported to a Soviet supervisor. Gold met with Fuchs a number of times before Fuchs left for Los Alamos in late 1944. In subsequent contact with Gold he informed him of the design and method of construction of the plutonium bomb and of the implosion device used for its explosion. He also told him of the Trinity test a month before the event. In Albuquerque, near Los Alamos, Gold also contacted another American, David Greenglass (1922–), who handed him the drawings of the implosion lens which he had stolen from Los Alamos, for which Gold gave him five hundred dollars. It should be noted that Fuchs always waved aside Gold's offers of money. His spying was motivated by idealism.

During their last meeting, on September 19, 1945, Fuchs gave Gold vital information on the two bombs exploded over Japan, their size and content and how they were detonated. They did not meet again. On June 16, 1946, Fuchs left Los Alamos for good. A few weeks later he arrived at Harwell to take up his position as head of the theory section. He was the only scientist there deeply involved with atomic weapons.

In early 1947 Fuchs felt the draw to Moscow again and once more made Russian contacts, to whom he was able to give details about British plutonium production.

After Truman's announcement of the Russian A-bomb, U.S. intelligence had already begun to explore the possibility that espionage had contributed to the timely Soviet success. Intercepts of KGB messages led the FBI to conclude that Fuchs was the prime suspect, on whom they opened a case file[487] on September 22, 1949—the day before Truman had announced the news of the Russian bomb. After carefully considering the FBI information, Prime Minister Atlee authorized a circumspect interrogation, for which, curiously enough, Fuchs himself provided a convenient pretext.

In mid-October Fuchs approached the security officer at Harwell for advice on a personal problem. Could his father get into difficulty because he had accepted a professorship in theology at the University of Leipzig, in the Russian Zone? In the course of that discussion the officer asked him if he had not passed information to a Soviet official in New York. "I don't think so," said Fuchs, with a look of surprise. Whereupon he was told that there existed information showing that he was guilty of espionage on behalf of the Soviet Union. Fuchs persisted in denying this several times, until January 13, 1950, when he told the officer that he had decided to confess. On February 2 he was formally arrested in London, after having pleaded guilty of espionage in Birmingham, New York, Boston, and Harwell. His confession also included information about the Super, about which he, jointly with Von Neumann, had in 1946 produced a top-secret "Disclosure of Invention," or patent. He was arraigned on February 3.

The news made headlines throughout the world. Publicly Oppenheimer said of the physicists: "We were a pretty glum bunch."[488] I remember what Oppenheimer privately said to me that week: "I hope that Fuchs will have told the Russians all we know about the Super, because that will set them back several years." I could of course not ask at that time what Robert meant by that. Now I know: Fuchs's only knowledge, at that time, was the "ox-cart" model.

Six days later, on February 9, Joseph McCarthy (1908–1957), the junior Senator from Wisconsin, gave a speech in Wheeling, West Virginia, in which he claimed to have a list of 205 Communists who worked in the U.S. State Department. So began the dark days of McCarthyism.

One day in February 1950 Fuchs stood trial in Old Bailey, before Lord Goddard, the lord chief justice, who pronounced: "The maximum sentence which Parliament has ordained for [your] crime is fourteen years imprisonment, and that is the sentence I pass upon you." The trial had lasted exactly one hour and twenty minutes.

On February 12, 1951, Fuchs was deprived of his British nationality. On June 22, 1959, he was released from Wakefield prison, having served nine years. On the same day he was placed on a Polish airliner for East Berlin, where, on arrival he said in a press conference that he would "work for the new society." He was granted East German citizenship and appointed Deputy Director, later Director, of the East German Institute for Nuclear Physics at Rossendorf near Dresden. He died in 1988.

In concluding this spy story, I note what happened to some others of those involved.

On May 23, 1950, Harry Gold was arrested in Philadelphia. Fuchs positively identified him on the day after Gold's arrest and after he (G.) had signed his confession. On December 9 he was brought up for sentencing and was convicted to 30 years in prison, the maximum admissible sentence. He was released on parole in 1965. He had been awarded the Order of the Red Star of the USSR, which entitled him to free bus rides in Moscow, where he never went.

David Greenglass was arrested in New York on June 16, after Gold had identified him the preceding June 4 from a photograph. On the front page of the June 24 *New York Times* one will find a picture of Greenglass being escorted in handcuffs from a New York court. On April 6, 1951, he was sentenced to 15 years in prison but was released in 1960.

In passing his sentence the judge had said to Greenglass: "You repented and you brought to justice those who enlisted you in this cause." What this loathsome man had managed to do was to give testimony about having told Julius (1918–1953) and Ethel Rosenberg (1915–1953) scientific secrets of which he in fact had no inkling. This was a main contributory cause of the arrests of Julius, on July 17, 1950, and of Ethel, the following August 11.

This is what happened in the next few years.

On June 7, 1951, the press reported that Donald Maclean, one of the "Cambridge five," and conversant with secret atomic matters, had defected to the Soviet Union. On March 5, 1953, the *New York Times* reported the deaths of Stalin and, the next day, that the Tennessee legislature had adopted this resolution: "Whereas Josef Stalin is dead, long live America"—a typical sample of Cold War silliness.

On June 19, 1953, the Rosenbergs, Julius and Ethel, convicted of atomic espionage, went to Sing Sing's electric chair. Whatever they were guilty of, their execution was a blemish on the United States.

In September 1943 the Security Officer at Los Alamos had written to his superior in San Francisco: "The writer wishes to go on record as saying that J. R. Oppenheimer is playing a key part in the attempt of the Soviet Union to secure, by espionage, highly secret information which is vital to the Soviet Union."[489] This totally unfounded allegation—about which more later—explains why I felt the need to add the present section on espionage. It is meant to give a sense of the climate of intense suspicion which would soon develop around Oppenheimer.

Finally, a personal note. Some time in mid-1950 I received a letter from Peierls, sent from Birmingham, in which he offered me the position of head of the theory division, vacant after Fuchs's arrest. I replied that I felt much honored by his offer but had to decline. One reason was that it would require me to become a British subject. The other was that I had never been involved with projects related to atomic weapons and did not wish to do so now.

CHAPTER 20

THE NEW SUPER

The Teller-Ulam Invention

Stanislaw Marcius Ulam (1909–1984), a brilliant Polish-born mathematician, was a staff member at Los Alamos from 1943 until 1967. In the beginning of that period, he had been working primarily, without major success, on devising schemes for a workable hydrogen bomb. Then, in January 1951, his wife remembered: "Engraved on my memory is the day when I found him at noon staring intensely out of a window in our Santa Fe living room with a very strange expression on his face. Peering unseeing into the garden, he said, 'I found a way to make it work.' 'What work?' I asked. 'The Super,' he replied. 'It is a totally different scheme, and it will change the course of history.'"[490] Not even Teller had anticipated Ulam's idea. Years later, Bethe has written: "The new concept was to me, who had been rather closely associated with the program, about as surprising as the discovery of fission had been to physicists in 1939."[491]

As we learn from a report[492] on work at Los Alamos on thermonuclear weapons in the years 1946–1950, in the months that followed Truman's January 1950 directive that work on the Super should proceed, the prospect of actually being able to build a hydrogen bomb became less and less likely. Ulam had undertaken calculations of the amount of tritium that would be needed for ignition of the classical Super. The results were spectacular and discouraging: the amount needed was estimated to be enormous. In the summer of

1950 more detailed and thorough calculations by other members of the Los Alamos Theoretical Division confirmed Ulam's estimates. This meant that the cost of the Super program would be prohibitive. Also in the summer of 1950, Fermi and Ulam calculated that liquid deuterium probably would not burn—that is, there would probably be no self-sustaining and propagating reaction. Barring surprises, therefore, the theoretical work to 1950 indicated that every important assumption regarding the viability of the classical Super was wrong. If success was to come, it would have to be accomplished by other means.

By 1951 one important and, in the event, very useful idea had been put forward, however. It had been realized by then that a salt-like compound of a lithium isotope and deuterium, lithium six deuteride (Li^6H), could serve as a fuel alternative to liquid deuterium. That variant came to be known as the "dry bomb." Lithium, a soft, silvery-white metal, atomic number 3, was already in use in the American bomb program in the form of lithium fluoride slugs, which were irradiated in the Hanford reactors to produce tritium, superheavy hydrogen (symbol T). Lithium in a bomb would pick up neutrons (n) from the reaction

$$D + D \rightarrow He^3 + n + 3.27 \text{ MeV}$$

where D = deuterium, heavy hydrogen, and 1 MeV is an energy unit (million electron volts), 6.25×10^{12} MeV = 1 joule. The neutrons collide with lithium to yield

$$Li^6 + n \rightarrow He^4 + T + 4.78 \text{ MeV},$$

and the principal fusion reaction follows:

$$D + T \rightarrow He^4 + n + 17.5 \text{ MeV}.$$

The advantage of using lithium in a thermonuclear device would be at least twofold: it would generate tritium at hand, reducing or eliminating the need for incorporating expensive reactor-bred tritium into the design; and it was a solid at room temperature and did not require maintaining within a bomb temperatures at several hundred degrees below zero (with all the elaborate bottling and insulating that would entail) as liquid deuterium did—no more ox-cart!

Turning now to Ulam's major idea of January 1951, I should note first of all that details of that development remain classified and therefore not known to me, since I have no access to classified information. Qualitative aspects have been widely disseminated, however, and can in fact be found by visiting the Internet. I can therefore convey at least some highlights.

In December 1950, Ulam had made a proposal for a new *fission* weapon, entirely independently of the thermonuclear program. His suggestion was to use the hydrodynamic, mechanical shock of an ordinary fission bomb to compress to a very high density a second fissile core, the idea behind this two-stage fission device being that fissionable materials could be used more economically this way.

Ulam's breakthrough of January 1951 was to use a similar two-stage procedure for compressing and igniting a thermonuclear bomb. He recognized that the burning of thermonuclear fuel would be more efficient if a high density were achieved throughout the fuel prior to raising its temperature, rather than the classical Super approach of just raising the temperature of uncompressed liquid deuterium to the point, it was hoped, when it would sustain thermonuclear burning. In Ulam's way a relatively small fission explosion can ignite an arbitrarily large amount of thermonuclear fuel.

Ulam has recalled Teller's reaction when he went to tell him of his new idea: "For the first half hour [he] did not want to accept the new possibility [but] after a few hours he enthusiastically took up the suggestion . . . when he found a parallel version to what I had said, perhaps more convenient."[493] Teller's alternative, a good idea, was to use *electromagnetic radiation* coming from the primary, rather than the mechanical shock it produces (from generated neutrons) to compress the thermonuclear secondary. The advantages of radiation over mechanical shock are that it works faster and gives longer sustained compression.[494]

The resultant scheme, staging, implosive fuel compression before ignition, has become basic for all hydrogen bombs which have subsequently been built. It is variously known as the Teller-Ulam invention, also as the New Super.

> Afterward Teller would variously deny, acknowledge and claim credit for Ulam's contribution. Ulam would consistently acknowledge Teller's part but quietly insist upon his own. Others . . . confirm, as [Lothar] Nordheim [1899–1985] wrote in 1954 to the *New York Times*, that "a general principle was formulated by Dr. Stanislaw Ulam in collaboration with Teller, who shortly afterward gave it its technically practical form. . . ." [Teller] came to dislike being called "the father of the H-bomb," but asserted his paternity in 1954. . . : "It is true that I am the father in [the] biological sense that I performed a necessary function and let nature take its course." Bethe sifts the evidence the other way. . . . "I used to say that Ulam was the father of the hydrogen bomb and Edward was the mother, because he carried the baby for quite a while."[495]

When the GAC met in March 1951, it was felt that "much more work was needed to see whether the new member of the thermonuclear family would survive."[498]

Concerning that further work, Teller has remarked: "We needed a significant test [which had] to play the role of a pilot plant."[499] About the first of these tests, the George shot, part of the Greenhouse series, fired on May 9, 1951, it was been poetically written: "The largest fission explosion to date [about 200 kilotons] succeeded in igniting the first small thermonuclear flame ever to burn on earth."[500] That flame was generated by a small DT capsule, weighing less than an ounce, which yielded 25 kilotons—twice the force released over Hiroshima.

The first test of a large thermonuclear device took place on November 1, 1952. It was the Mike shot in the Ivy series, executed on Eniwetok atoll in the Pacific. Its main objective was to verify the Teller-Ulam configuration. Yield: 10.4 megatons, 1,000 times as large as the Hiroshima bomb. It created a fireball more than 3 miles across (Hiroshima: 0.1 miles), erased the entire atoll, lifted 80 million tons of solid material in the air, would have obliterated all of the five New York boroughs. It was still an "ox-cart" device, using liquid deuterium. One reason for this was that it was much easier for theorists to calculate the burning of deuterium than the complex chain-like process involved in the explosion of LiD.

On March 1, 1954, the first large American hydrogen *bomb* was exploded during operation Castle, Bravo shot. Previous tests had operated with devices not, as with Bravo, with bombs adaptable for delivery by aircraft. (That device weighed 23,500 pounds and could fit into a B-47.) It was the first time that LiD fuel was used. Bravo's yield was 15 megatons, the biggest weapon ever exploded by the United States, 1,000 times as large as the Hiroshima bomb. With the Bravo shot, the feasibility of lightweight solid-fuel thermonuclear weapons was proved. Vast quantities of tritium would not be needed after all.

Meanwhile, on August 8, 1953, Georgiy Malenkov (1901–1979), successor to Stalin (who had died in 1953), had announced in a major speech before the Supreme Soviet that "the United States of America has long ceased to have a monopoly in the matter of the production of atomic bombs" and added spectacularly, "The United States has no monopoly in the production of the hydrogen bomb either." Four days after that statement, the Russians indeed exploded a hydrogen test device, not a true H-bomb, named Joe 4 in the United States, with a yield comparable to Mike. On November 23, 1955, a true Soviet thermonuclear was dropped from an aircraft in a test. The Cold War had heated up considerably.[503]

As will be seen in the next chapter, the Super played a major role in the drama of the Oppenheimer hearings. The present brief account of that weapon's history is meant to provide the necessary background for those later events. The following concluding comments of this section have nothing to do with Oppenheimer, however. They are here included to round off this book's tale of atomic weapons.

The British exploded their first Super in 1957 (what follows happened after Oppenheimer's death), the Chinese in 1967, the French in 1968.

By 1997 the United States had produced (the following in round numbers) 70,000 nuclear weapons of 70 major types. By then there were 9,600 weapons of 10 major types in the U.S. arsenal, which is officially named "Enduring Stockpile."

The U.S. Senate ratified the START II treaty on nuclear weapons in 1997; the Russian Duma followed suit three years later, in 2000. After signing, the United States began to reduce its nuclear stockpile, with further reductions to come in subsequent years.

The Atmospheric Test Ban Treaty, signed in Moscow on August 5, 1963, halted all further atmospheric tests by both superpowers.

On March 31, 1976, the Soviet Union and the United States agreed to limit the maximum yield of underground tests to 150 kilotons.

With the signing of the Comprehensive Test Ban Treaty in September 1996, the United States, along with the other nuclear powers, made a legal commitment never to test nuclear devices again. It remains to be seen whether this treaty will ever go into full force because of opposition by rogue nations.

Oppenheimer's Views on the Super

In 1944, while still directing the completion of the A-bomb, Oppenheimer wrote to a colleague: "I should like to put in writing . . . the recommendation that the subject of initiating violent thermonuclear reactions be pursued with vigor and diligence, and promptly."[504] I have already mentioned a few of his postwar thoughts on that subject, his letter to Conant[459] and the addendum to the October 1949 GAC report which he cosigned.[469] Both these comments were critical and negative—not surprising because they date back to the years when efforts at building hydrogen bombs were still following the wrong track. Opinions changed to cautious optimism after the Teller-Ulam invention, as is seen from the record[498] of the GAC meeting held in May 1951, and turned quite positive after the Greenhouse test the following May.

In June 1951, the new design idea and the calculations supporting it were presented to a wider group in a meeting held in Oppenheimer's office at the Institute for Advanced Study at Princeton.[461] In attendance were members of the AEC and of the GAC, plus Teller and other staff and consultants of the Los Alamos laboratory. It was immediately recognized by this wider audience that the new idea was the way to go. About that meeting, Robert has later written: "The outcome of the meeting, which lasted for 2 or 3 days, was an agreed program and a fixing of priorities and effort [regarding the Super]. This program has been an outstanding success."[505] Teller has recalled of that meeting, "Dr. Oppenheimer warmly supported this new approach . . . and . . . made a statement to the effect that if anything of this kind had been suggested right away [i.e., at the time of the 1949 H-bomb debate] he would never have opposed it."[506] Oppenheimer himself remembered, "The program we had in 1949 was a tortured thing that you could well argue did not make a great deal of technical sense. It was therefore possible to argue also that you did not want it even if you could have it. The program in 1951 was technically so sweet that you could not argue about that. The issues became purely the military, the political and the humane problem(s) of what you were going to do about it once you had it."[507]

Regarding the humane problems, ever since 1949[469] Robert has unalterably expressed himself against the use of the Super. When asked in 1954: "At what time did your strong moral convictions develop with respect to the hydrogen bomb?", he replied, "When it became clear to me that we would send to use any weapon we had[508] . . . even [though] from a technical point of view it was a sweet and lovely and beautiful job, I have still thought it was a dreadful weapon."[509]

Oppenheimer's Participation in Panels: 1950–1953

In the years 1950–1953 a series of special study projects were instituted. These owed their origins largely to the Korean War, which had broken out in June 1950. I give a brief survey of those panels in which Oppenheimer took part, either as member or as consultant.

The Long Range Objectives Panel

The Long Range Objectives Panel was established in late 1950 to reexamine the relation of nuclear weapons to foreign policy and military strategy. This panel was chaired by Oppenheimer, who himself invited Alvarez to join, so as to give balance to views on the Super. Army and Air Force generals also participated. The committee's report cited the Korean War as evidence for the fact that limited wars were possible and also noted that general war with Russia could happen.[510]

Project Gabriel

Project Gabriel, begun in early 1951, deals with the number of nuclear weapons that can be detonated without causing health hazards. In the spring of 1952, Oppenheimer wrote its draft report.[511]

Project Charles

Project Charles, also started in 1951, a study of the feasibility of a continental air defense system, in which Oppenheimer participated. This study resulted in the establishment of *Project East River*, which was undertaken to examine civil defense problems, including the effects of biological, chemical, and radiological warfare on civilian population centers. Oppenheimer served on this project, too, and helped formulate a memorandum, dated April 12, 1952, which urged the necessity of building an air defense system that provided a one-hour warning against atomic attacks on U.S. urban centers.[512]

Project Vista

United States air support in Korea had been notoriously inefficient. Fear of similar wars in the future provoked thinking within the military on the use of tactical nuclear weapons. Oppenheimer urged further "development of weapons systems so that one can use atomic bombs [and] can deliver them in more than one way, and so that one can make them for a variety of targets and uses and situations."[513]

Thoughts like these led to Project Vista, set up in January 1951 at Cal Tech, to study ground and tactical warfare. Oppenheimer was one of the participating scientists. The resulting report proposed improvements in communications, tactical missiles, tank killers, intelligence handling systems, anti-submarine devices, troop carrier aircraft, tactical nuclear and non-nuclear weapons which could be delivered accurately in any weather, interceptors, and support aircraft. Part of the draft report was written by Oppenheimer.[514,515] The report urged holding SAC in reserve during the initial phases of war, and splitting up the atomic arsenal among the three armed services.[515]

Reactions to the report were intense. One Air Force general wrote to Oppenheimer: "Your recommendations . . . have impressed me always in their wisdom."[516] Most responses were strongly negative, however: "Later attacks on Oppenheimer ... seem to have grown out of his association with Project Vista."[517] Air Force Secretary Thomas Finletter (1893—1980) gave direct orders not to use Oppenheimer as a consultant in any further studies and to keep classified Air Force information away from him.[518] He and most Air Force generals were enraged by the suggestion to assign a second-ary role to SAC and to share atomic weapons with the Army and Navy.

The Research and Development Board of the Defense Department, con-sisting of Oppenheimer and a few other distinguished scientists, took their Vista recommendations to General Eisenhower, NATO commander in Europe. On December 4, 1951, the scientists met with Eisenhower; the general was impressed with their recommendations. He favored publishing portions of the Vista Report, and approved of the scientists' additional sug-gestions that atomic weapons combined with amphibious operations should be used in Korea, that military people who knew atomic weapons should be brought into SHAPE (Supreme Headquarters Allied Powers Europe), and that restrictions on our allies, in connection with plans to use atomic weapons, should be loosened.[519]

On December 6, Oppenheimer and the other scientists presented a memo-randum to nine officers at Air Force headquarters in Europe. After his re-turn to Washington, he urged the secretary of defense to send technicians who were expert in the use of tactical nuclear weapons to Europe, and to include the allies in the formulation of war plans.[519] Oppenheimer further suggested that the United States maintain its ground strength and tactical forces in Europe, but underplay the use of long-range bombers to avoid alienating the Russians, who resented U.S. air base encirclement.[520]

The visit to Eisenhower "marked the beginning of an attack by certain people identified with strategic air operations," who were "motivated by fear that if a program for tactical use of atomic weapons was adopted this would mean that money essential for strategic air would be diverted to other purposes."[517]

It is quite evident that Oppenheimer's role in Vista enforced the Air Force's resentment of his advice and created several new enemies for him.

Project Lincoln

Project Lincoln, the culmination of *Charles* and *East River*, was established in early 1952 at MIT, with a staff of 1,600 people, including 350 scientists, and with an annual budget of $20 million. Oppenheimer was one of the senior physicists who participated.

In August 1952, a Project Lincoln memorandum urged the immediate
expansion of the air defense system, including the establishment of early
warning radar stations along the arctic circle and throughout Canada, electronic processing equipment, and a network of missile and jet interceptor
batteries around urban population centers and military installations. Air
Force and Defense Department representatives were on hand during the
next two days to examine the proposals. Initial estimates of the cost of the
proposal's implementation reached $50 billion.[520] Since the very inception
of the Lincoln Project, Air Force Secretary Finletter had asked his chief
scientist, David Griggs, to "keep an eye" on the project and to "report to
him" any "net loss" to the Air Force in its findings.[521] The Air Force apparently feared that if the Lincoln air defense proposals were enacted, they
would divert vital funds from SAC. Nevertheless, in the last few months of
the Truman administration, the pleas of the Lincoln Project scientists began to be acknowledged.[522]

Throughout 1952, journalists Joseph and Stewart Alsop criticized the over-
dependence of the nation's defense on the retaliatory power of the Strategic
Air Command, at the expense of an effective air defense system,[523] raising
concern that the articles by the Alsops were "similar to" the Lincoln Summer Study Group conclusions, in recommending a "Maginot Line type of
concept in which we depend on air defense rather than on our retaliatory
capability."[524] Joseph Alsop met frequently with Oppenheimer throughout
1952, and in December, the Alsops gained access to the Summer Study Group
summary conclusions.[525]

As the result of Oppenheimer's participation in *Lincoln*, he made more
powerful enemies within the Air Force who viewed his activities and advice with extreme suspicion and resentment. Their strong feelings were
motivated by a genuine belief that Oppenheimer's proposals would jeopar-
dize essential appropriations for SAC.

1952: Oppenheimer Leaves the General Advisory Committee

In the summer of 1952, Oppenheimer announced that he would not accept
reappointment to the GAC. On September 17, he received the following
letter:[526]

> Dear Dr. Oppenheimer: Having in mind your strong desire, which you ex-
> pressed to me last month, to complete your service on the General Advisory
> Committee to the Atomic Energy Commission with the expiration of your

present term, I note with a deep sense of personal regret that this time is now upon us.

As Chairman of this important committee since its inception, you may take great pride in the fact that you have made a lasting and immensely valuable contribution to the national security and to atomic energy progress in this Nation. It is a source of real regret to me that the full story of the remarkable progress that has been made in atomic energy during these past 6 years, and in which you have played so large a role, cannot be publicly disclosed, for it would serve as the finest possible tribute to the contribution you have made.

I shall always be personally grateful for the time and energy you have so unselfishly devoted to the work of the General Advisory Committee, for the conscientious and rewarding way in which you have brought your great talents to bear upon the scientific problems of atomic energy development and for the notable part you have played in securing for the atomic energy program the understanding cooperation of the scientific community.

As director of the Los Alamos Scientific Laboratory during World War II, and as chairman of the General Advisory Committee for the past 6 years, you have served your country long and well, and I am gratified by the knowledge that your wise counsel will continue to be available to the Atomic Energy Commission on a consultant basis.

I wish you every future success in your important scientific endeavors.

Very sincerely yours,
Harry Truman

Two months before receiving this gracious letter, Robert had written to his brother, "By August 1 my six years on the Gen. Advisory Committee are over; they have seemed long. Physics is complicated & wondersome & much too hard for me except as a spectator; it will have to get easy again one of these days, but perhaps not soon."[526a]

CHAPTER 21

ATOMIC POLITICS IN THE EARLY 1950S

The Doctrine of Massive Retaliation

Throughout most of the Truman administration, military leaders had been reluctant to have an air defense system worked out in any detail. The *Vista* proposal for a secondary role of SAC had been considered too controversial, as had the *Lincoln* proposals for air defense. It was not until January 1953, when the Republican Eisenhower administration took over, that a definite defense policy was enacted, named "The New Look," sanctioned by newly elected Joint Chiefs of Staff.

The new government was run like a business enterprise, droves of businessmen joined the Cabinet. The administration's balanced budget proponents decided against a continental air defense system, and opted instead for an Air Force equipped with hydrogen bombs, which would involve fewer expenditures and was cheaper to maintain than a large standing Army and Navy. Accordingly, Eisenhower ordered the Pentagon to assume that if the United States got into war it would be fought with nuclear weapons and that priority in budgetary funds be given to the Air Force. So came into being "massive retaliation" as the central doctrine and so was SAC established as the most significant force in military planning.[527] In his State of the Union Message of January 1954, Eisenhower recognized air power doctrine as official U.S. policy. The American people were assured that SAC, rather than a continental air defense system, would protect them from atomic attack, that in fact air retaliatory power was to be the only response to communist aggression.[528] Vice President Richard Nixon put it like this: "Rather than let the Communists nibble us to death all over the world in little wars we would rely in the future primarily on our massive mobile retaliatory power."[529]

Other voices ranged from caution to severe criticism, however. In 1954 the Air Force Chief of Staff conceded that "one grand-scale atomic blow by the Soviets on our industrial and population centers could be decisive if allowed to be conducted without interference."[530] *Fortune Magazine*, though allied with the Air Force in requesting more funds for SAC, estimated that in a surprise attack on the United States, only 15 to 20 percent of the attacking Soviet bombers could be shot down in daylight, and only 1 percent at night.[531]

Various Democrats sharply attacked the administration's overreliance on airpower. Ex-Secretary of State Acheson called the policy "a fraud upon the words and upon the facts." Adlai Stevenson wondered: "Are we leaving ourselves the grim choice of inaction or thermonuclear holocaust? Are we, indeed, inviting Moscow and Peiping [Beijing] to nibble us to death?"[532]

Even Eisenhower himself had reservations: "What should we do if Soviet *political* aggression, as in Czechoslovakia, successfully chips away exposed portions of the free world? . . . Such an eventuality would be just as bad for us as if the area had been captured by force. To my mind, this is the case where the theory of 'retaliation' falls down."[533]

Operation Candor

No concept could be more alien to the proposal for a continental defense system, laid down in the report on *Project Lincoln* (see the preceding chapter), than massive retaliation. Several scientists, deeply disturbed by the government's ideas, decided to launch a crusade for their views on continental defense, and chose Oppenheimer as their principal spokesman.

Robert accepted, though he understood his vulnerability to attack in taking such a position. As early as December 1951, when his visit to Eisenhower to promote the Vista Project proposals provoked attacks against him, he wrote: "I could propose . . . concentration upon a vast expansion of U.S. national military forces, and my judgment or my narrow military mind might be impugned in some quarters, but my loyalty and patriotism would go unquestioned."[534] In December 1952, he left several proposals for air defense with Eisenhower, then president-elect, including summaries of *Projects Charles, East River, Lincoln,* and *Vista.*

In January 1953, the State Department's Disarmament Committee, which Oppenheimer chaired, presented its report to the Eisenhower administration. Two of the committee's five recommendations included a demand for public candor and a continental defense system. The report initiated the campaign known as *Operation Candor*, which urged the administration to present to the American people the facts of the destructive power of nuclear weapons, the approximate relative sizes of the nuclear stockpiles of the United States and the U.S.S.R., and the nature and results of nuclear warfare.[535] The committee believed that if these general facts were made available to the American public, then the need for a continental defense system would become immediately apparent.

Oppenheimer, feeling a sense of urgency about the adoption of an air defense system, spoke before the Council on Foreign Relations in New York City on February 17, 1953. He warned that "our twenty-thousandth bomb" would "not in any deep strategic sense offset" the Soviet Union's "two-thousandth" atomic bomb, and criticized the U.S. war plan as "a rather rigid commitment" to the use of nuclear weapons "in a very massive, initial, unremitting strategic assault on the enemy," with "relatively little done to secure our defense against the atom." He also warned against overdoing secrecy: "[The nation does] not operate well when the important facts, the essential conditions which limit and determine our choice are unknown, [or] are known, in secrecy and fear, only to a few men. . . . Follies can occur . . . whenever the men who know the facts can find no one to talk to about them, when the facts are too secret for discussion, and thus for thought."

On the following May 22, Oppenheimer met with the president to discuss *Operation Candor*.[536] Eisenhower invited him to present his views on the National Security Council (NSC) meeting of May 27. At that gathering he "had everybody spellbound—except the President, who thanked him very much for what he had to say, but waited until he had left the room before [deciding] what should and should not be done."[537]

On June 19, with the NSC still split over what to recommend, Oppenheimer published his February 17 address in *Foreign Affairs*. On the same day the *New York Times* and the *Washington Post* came out with summaries of the article. In July it was reprinted in full in the *Bulletin of the Atomic Scientists*.[538] In an interview, Robert said: "If this issue of candor were cleared up . . . the people of the United States would not be talked out of reasonable defense measures. . . . [Eisenhower] is the only person to transcend the racket or noise, mostly consisting of lies, that have been built up about this subject of the strategic situation of the atom."[539,540] Scientist allies supported his crusade for candor. For example, one wrote that the United States "had acquired a 'glass jaw' because of its vulnerability to atomic attack."[541]

In July 1953, Oppenheimer summarized his own view of the international tensions, using an analogy that would long outlive him: "The atomic clock ticks faster and faster. We may anticipate a state of affairs in which two great powers will each be in a position to put an end to the civilization and life of the other, though not without risking its own. We may be likened to two scorpions in a bottle, each capable of killing the other, but only at the risk of his own life. . . . This prospect does not make for serenity."[542]

To the Air Force, anyone identified with *Operation Candor* "quickly became highly vulnerable not only to criticism but to smear."[543] Oppenheimer was the obvious choice for main target. In 1953 he was at the peak of his influence, holding five government posts, and having access to information on the atomic stockpile, U.S. strategic and tactical airforces and intelligence estimates of Soviet air power.[544] Within the Air Force "vindictive elements . . . set out to eliminate [him] as the leader of a defense philosophy which they conceived as inimical to theirs."[545] It was not sufficient to eliminate him from his consultant's posts. He had to be destroyed. The time was ripe for men who former President Truman has called "crude and sinister" and "witch hunters."[546]

The Opening Salvos of the Attackers

I have mentioned earlier that in 1949 Oppenheimer had made powerful enemies. Yet during the next following years this did not lead to any actions of consequence against him. Those began in 1953, the first year of the Republican administration under Eisenhower, also the year when witch hunts on alleged communists in government began in earnest.

This sad story began with the unveiling of presidential executive order 10450, on April 27, 1953.[547] Under its terms, a government employee had not only to be adjudged "loyal" in order to serve his country; his background had to be such that his employment by the government was "clearly consistent with the interests of national security." For most federal agencies, new and broader screening criteria were put into effect. Security officers were given wider authority to screen out job-holders and applicants with "derogatory information" in their dossiers. All federal agencies, including such nonsensitive departments as Agriculture and Interior, were given the power summarily to suspend suspected "security risks," a power formerly reserved to agencies having a connection with national defense.

The cases of some 19,000 civil servants whose "full field" investigations had turned up "derogatory information," but who had been cleared under the old Truman loyalty program, were to be "readjudicated" under the new, more severe screening standards.

May 1953

Fortune Magazine publishes an anonymous article entitled: "The Hidden Struggle for the H-bomb." The subheading describes it as "The Story of Dr. Oppenheimer's persistent campaign to reverse U.S. military strategy."[548] As the public learns only months later, its author is Charles Murphy, who served as an Air Force reserve officer with Secretary Finletter.

Murphy's article begins dramatically: "A life-and-death struggle over national military policy has developed between a highly influential group of American scientists and the military." This dispute involved disagreements with Air Force officials over the role of airpower in nuclear war. The "prime mover among the scientists," always according to Murphy, was Oppenheimer, who had "no confidence in the military's assumption that SAC as a weapon of mass destruction is a real deterrent to Soviet action" . . . and who was asking the United States "to throw away its strongest weapon for defense."

The article, rife with insinuations and oversimplifications, closes with Murphy's conclusion that scientists should have no voice in defense planning: "There [is] a serious question of the propriety of scientists to settle such grave national issues alone, inasmuch as they bear no responsibility for the successful execution of war plans."

Reactions to the article are intense. Examples: Lilienthal calls the *Fortune* piece "another nasty and obviously inspired article attacking Robert Oppenheimer in a snide way. . . . Even a gossip columnist signs his gossip, and takes personal responsibility."[549] Admiral Parsons finds the article replete with "fantastic distortions [that show] how unhealthy it is to have most of the reading public unable to project such an article against the facts [and worries about] the anti-intellectualism of recent months. . . . We might be at the eye of the hurricane."[550]

June 5, 1953

Oppenheimer's consultant's contract with the AEC is extended for one year beyond its June 30 expiration date. "That June 5 was perhaps the most fateful date in Robert Oppenheimer's life."[551] As Strauss wrote later: "It was this contract which involved the AEC in the clearance of Dr. Oppenheimer and which required that the Commission, rather than some other agency of the Government, be made responsible to hear and resolve the charges against him."[552]

June 20, 1953

The Department of Defense implements Reorganization Plan Number 6, which effects, among other changes, the dissolution of that Department's Research and Development Board, of which Oppenheimer was a member. A year later Defense Secretary Charles ("Engine") Wilson was asked in an interview why he dropped Oppenheimer at that time. He replied: "We dropped the whole board. That was a real smooth way of doing that one [referring to O.] as far as the Defense Department was concerned."[553]

July 3, 1953

Strauss becomes the third chairman of the AEC.

July 7, 1953

Strauss initiates steps to organize the removal of all classified documents in Oppenheimer's Princeton files.[554] Seven months earlier, the AEC had removed some 32 linear feet of paper from Oppenheimer's vault, leaving only material immediately relevant to his work as consultant.

July 1953

Oppenheimer publishes his thoughts on Operation Candor,[542] and lectures in Brazil to members of the National Research Council, speaking of the beauty of physics and its promise to humanity.

August 1953

Murphy responds to Oppenheimer's article on Candor with another article in *Fortune*, entitled: "The atom and the balance of power," signed this time,[555] and more temperate and accurate than his previous one. It includes one picture, a portrait of Strauss (with whom Murphy had been in touch for some time) with the caption: "Strauss believes in keeping a tight lid on information about atomic weapons."

August 20, 1953

It is made public that the Soviets have exploded their first thermonuclear device.

November 12, 1953

A registered letter addressed to J. Edgar Hoover (1895–1972), director of the FBI, is received at the FBI offices in Washington; copies are received by the members of the JCAE. The letter was written by William Liscum Borden, former staff director of that Joint Committee, who knew Senator McCarthy[556] and Lewis Strauss.[557] The key phrases of this letter are these: "The purpose of this letter is to state my own exhaustively considered opinion, based upon years of study of the available classified evidence, that more probably than not J. Robert Oppenheimer is an agent of the Soviet Union. . . . For some years he has been in a position to compromise more vital and detailed information affecting the national defense and security than any other individual in the United States."[558]

On what evidence did Borden base his grave charge? Where had he obtained that evidence? His information came from the government's massive investigative dossier on Oppenheimer. This file, a four-and-a-half foot stack of reports, had been amassed in the course of eleven years' minute surveillance of the scientist's life, private as well as public. Oppenheimer's telephone had been tapped. His office and home had been bugged. His mail had been opened. Even so intimate an event as a night spent with a former fiancée had not escaped the watchful eyes of government agents.[559]

Borden listed, in four categories, the evidence for his charges:

1. The evidence indicating that—
   (a) He was contributing substantial monthly sums to the Communist Party;
   (b) His ties with communism had survived the Nazi-Soviet Pact and the Soviet attack upon Finland;
   (c) His wife and younger brother were Communists;
   (d) He had no close friends except Communists;
   (e) He had at least one Communist mistress;
   (f) He belonged only to Communist organizations, apart from professional affiliations;
   (g) The people whom he recruited into the early wartime Berkeley atomic project were exclusively Communists;
   (h) He had been instrumental in securing recruits for the Communist Party; and
   (i) He was in frequent contact with Soviet espionage agents.

2. The evidence indicating that—
   (a) In May 1942, he either stopped contributing funds to the Communist Part or else made his contributions through a new channel not yet discovered;
   (b) In April 1942 his name was formally submitted for security clearance;
   (c) He himself was aware at the time that his name had been so submitted; and

(d) He thereafter repeatedly gave false information to General Groves, the Manhattan District, and the FBI concerning the 1939–April 1942 period.

3. The evidence indicating that—
(a) He was responsible for employing a number of Communists, some of them nontechnical, at wartime Los Alamos;
(b) He selected one such individual to write the official Los Alamos history;
(c) He was a vigorous supporter of the H-bomb program until August 6, 1945 (Hiroshima), on which day he personally urged each senior individual working in this field to desist; and
(d) He was an enthusiastic sponsor of the A-bomb program until the war ended, when he immediately and outspokenly advocated that the Los Alamos Laboratory be disbanded.

4. The evidence indicating that:
(a) He was remarkably instrumental in influencing the military authorities and the Atomic Energy Commission essentially to suspend H-bomb development from mid-1946 through January 31, 1950.
(b) He has worked tirelessly, from January 31, 1950, onward, to retard the United States H-bomb program;
(c) He has used his potent influence against every postwar effort directed at obtaining larger supplies of uranium raw material; and
(e) He has used his potent influence against every major postwar effort toward atomic power development, including the nuclear-powered submarine and aircraft programs as well as industrial power projects.

From such evidence, considered in detail, the following conclusions are justified:

1. Between 1929 and mid-1942, more probably than not, J. Robert Oppenheimer was a sufficiently hardened Communist that he either volunteered espionage information to the Soviets or complied with a request for such information. (This includes the possibility that when he singled out the weapons aspect of atomic development as his personal specialty, he was acting under Soviet instructions.)
2. More probably than not, he has since been functioning as an espionage agent; and
3. More probably than not, he has since acted under a Soviet directive in influencing United States military, atomic energy, intelligence, and diplomatic policy.

It is to be noted that these conclusions correlate with information furnished by Klaus Fuchs, indicating that the Soviets had acquired an agent in Berkeley who informed them about electromagnetic separation research, during 1942 or earlier.

This letter contains several falsehoods (notably items 1(i), 4 (b, e). Otherwise it contained no substantial evidence that had not long been known and accepted in official circles. Yet, as we shall see shortly, it suddenly prompted the government to move against Oppenheimer.

November 1953

McCarthy discloses that a Harvard physics professor (whom he later identified as Wendell Furry, an earlier collaborator of Oppenheimer[69]) had pleaded the Fifth Amendment in refusing to answer questions about his previous communist connections and activities. Since Professor Furry's actions affected Harvard's reputation, this matter was of concern to Robert Oppenheimer, as chairman of the Harvard physics department's "Visiting Committee." To various of Furry's colleagues, he expressed "rather strong feelings about the fact that Furry had been for really a . . . long time a member of the Communist Party." To some, including Furry himself, he vigorously deplored the physicist's invoking the Fifth Amendment.[560]

November–December 1953

Robert and Kitty were in Europe at the time the Borden letter arrived at the FBI. They visited Copenhagen briefly, also Paris, where they dined with Haakon Chevalier, a friend of Robert from Berkeley days (about whom more later). The main purpose of this trip was Robert's delivery of the Reith lectures, a series of six, broadcast by the BBC. He was received enthusiastically, although he was told that some thought him "hopelessly obscure." Some listeners seemed to be more taken with the eloquence of his delivery than the contents of his speech. Robert himself regarded them as one of the most important presentations of his life.[561]

When in December the Oppenheimers returned to the United States, Robert found an urgent message to call Lewis Strauss as soon as possible. Grave trouble was awaiting him. I knew from him that he had been expecting that for some time (see end of Chapter 15) but did not know what the details were.

CHAPTER 22

IN WHICH THE EXCREMENT HITS THE VENTILATOR

The Oppenheimer-Strauss Meeting: December 1953

Replying to Strauss's message, Robert agreed to meet with him at 3:30 PM December 21 at Strauss's office in AEC headquarters, where the two men were joined by Kenneth Nichols, the Commission's general manager.

In that meeting, Strauss handed Robert an eight-page letter written by Nichols which contained references to his associates as far back as the 1930s, his contributions to leftwing causes, his brother's and wife's membership in the Communist Party, and, most startling, the charge that he had tried to stop or delay the development of the hydrogen bomb. It ended with the statement that the AEC was to suspend Robert's clearance. I quote from the letter:[562]

> It was reported that in 1945 you expressed the view that "there is a reasonable possibility that it [the hydrogen bomb] can be made," but that the feasibility of the hydrogen bomb did not appear, on theoretical grounds, when the Los Alamos Laboratory was started; and that in the autumn of 1949 the General Advisory Committee expressed the view that "an imaginative and concerted attack on the problem has a better than even chance of producing the weapon within 5 years." It was further reported that in the autumn of 1949, and subsequently, you strongly opposed the development of the hydrogen bomb; (1) on moral grounds, (2) by claiming that it was not feasible, (3) by claiming that there were insufficient facilities and scientific personnel to carry on the development, and (4) that it was not politically desirable. It was further reported that even after it was determined, as a matter of national policy, to proceed with development of a hydrogen bomb, you continued to oppose the project and declined to cooperate fully in the project. It was further reported that you departed from your proper role

as an adviser to the Commission by causing the distribution separately and in private, to top personnel at Los Alamos of the majority and minority reports of the General Advisory Committee on development of the hydrogen bomb for the purpose of trying to turn such top personnel against the development of the hydrogen bomb. It was further reported that you were instrumental in persuading other outstanding scientists not to work on the hydrogen-bomb project, and that the opposition to the hydrogen bomb, of which you are the most experienced, most powerful, and most effective member, has definitely slowed down its development.

In view of your access to highly sensitive classified information, and in view of these allegations which, until disproved, raise questions as to your veracity, conduct and even your loyalty, the Commission has no other recourse, in discharge of its obligations to protect the common defense and security, but to suspend your clearance until the matter has been resolved. Accordingly, your employment on Atomic Energy Commission work and your eligibility for access to restricted data are hereby suspended, effective immediately, pending final determination of this matter.

The letter stated further that "to assist in the resolution of this matter, you have the privilege of appearing before an Atomic Energy Commission personnel security board." Strauss added verbally that this would be an in-camera hearing before an independent three-man board, also that, alternatively, Oppenheimer could at once request that his consultant's contract be terminated—which would close the matter then and there.

Robert was stunned.

He had been granted security clearances in 1943, 1947, 1950, and as late as a few months earlier, on June 5, 1953, when all derogatory information against him, stated in the Nichols letter, had been known in government circles—including his position regarding the hydrogen bomb. As he was to say to a newspaper reporter, only a few months later: "There is a story behind my story. If a reporter digs deep enough he will find that it is a bigger story than my suspension."[563] Later, looking back on that day, he said: "It was like Pearl Harbor—on a small scale. Given the circumstances and the spirit of the times, one knew that something like this was possible and even probable, but still it was a shock when it came."[564]

When Robert asked how much time he had to think the matter over, Strauss replied that he could only give him until the next day to make up his mind.[565] When he asked if he could take a copy of Nichols's letter with him, Strauss refused on the grounds that it would be unwise to circulate the unsigned letter.[565] Oppenheimer did receive a copy of the letter, sent to Princeton, dated December 23,[566]—two days after the session with Strauss, which lasted only half an hour. During that short meeting Strauss, who has recorded his own recollections of that encounter,[568] did not mention the

Borden letter to him.[569] Also on December 23, Nichols sent a confidential letter to all American Army, Navy, Air Force and AEC installations which read: "The clearance of Dr. J. Robert Oppenheimer for access to Restricted Data and other classified information has been suspended. The *fact* that this clearance has been suspended is presently classified information."[570]

Shortly after noon the next day Nichols called Oppenheimer in Princeton to ask whether he had reached a decision. Oppenheimer had not had time to recover from the blow of the previous day's meeting, much less give very much thought to the decision, but Nichols insisted upon an answer that afternoon. From Oppenheimer's point of view, it was one thing to resign under pressure when one's services were no longer wanted or needed, but quite another to be forced out by the security system, sacrificing both integrity and honor while leaving the charges unchallenged. He decided to accept the Commission's statement of charges with all the risks and uncertainties it entailed.

Even before Oppenheimer accepted the statement of charges, Strauss inquired whether the FBI could set up a "full-time surveillance" of Oppenheimer, which would have required agents to monitor Oppenheimer's every movement and contact around the clock. Hoover objected that such an operation would be too costly in manpower and money, but he did order the FBI office in Newark, New Jersey, to maintain a "spot check" on Oppenheimer. This meant assigning two agents to follow Oppenheimer and members of his family when they left his residence and to observe visitors. Hoover also authorized taps on Oppenheimer's home and office telephones; these were installed on January 1, 1954. The Newark office reported that the taps made the spot check quite efficient and permitted the FBI to plan surveillance operations when Oppenheimer indicated that he planned travel outside the Princeton area.[567]

Eisenhower Erects a "Blank Wall"

As noted, Robert was unaware of the Borden letter at the December 21 meeting with Strauss, nor could he know of the impact of that letter on the highest levels of government, which I shall relate next. He would undoubtedly have been aware, however, of a public statement which forcefully demonstrated the political climate of the times: In his January 7, 1954, State of the Union Message, Mr. Eisenhower told Congress that the new and more stringent security-screening standards he had promulgated in the preceding April had brought about the dismissal of more than 2,200 federal employees.[571]

Now to the aftermath of the Borden letter.[572] After receiving that letter, FBI Director Hoover had Oppenheimer's file data compiled into a summary report, which was completed on November 18. Nine days later, Hoover sent Strauss a copy of Borden's letter and the new FBI summary report, "supplementing information previously furnished to you concerning Dr. J. Robert Oppenheimer. . . ." Hoover pointed out to Strauss that "the accusations made by Mr. Borden concerning Dr. Oppenheimer have previously been investigated by the Federal Bureau of Investigation. . . ."[573] However, according to JCCAE member Senator Clinton P. Anderson (1895–1975), Strauss "insisted that opposition to the weapon [H-bomb] was evidence of disloyalty to the country." Strauss "now proposed to treat" Borden's charges "as something new and spectacular."[574]

The 67-page FBI summary report contained eight parts, dealing successively with Oppenheimer's private life and nongovernment career through 1947; the various Communist Front groups to which he contributed money from 1938 to 1942; interviews about his activities before he joined the Manhattan Project with people who "described O. as having radical or liberal views but none considered him disloyal to the United States"; his relations with Haakon Chevalier, to which I shall turn later; a report by two paid FBI informants who stated that he had been present at a Communist Party meeting in Berkeley, in July 1941, the FBI inquiry concluding that "in July 1941 O. was not in California"; O.'s comments on alleged Communist Party members employed at Los Alamos; and interviews with 26 O. associates at Los Alamos, who "all advised that O.'s loyalty to the United States is unquestioned."

All information mentioned thus far was known to the AEC and the JCCAE when Robert was cleared in 1947 and 1950. The last (21) pages of the report introduced a new element, however, by examining his advice and views on defense issues, the central theme being Oppenheimer's alleged role in the development of the hydrogen bomb, the only issue that was raised after these earlier clearances.

On April 4, 1952, "a prominent scientist," who wished to remain anonymous, told the FBI that he "previously had the utmost confidence in the loyalty" of Oppenheimer, but "he is now doubtful. . . ." He stated that Oppenheimer "had opposed the development of the H-bomb," had "attempted to influence" others "to oppose it," and had been "impeding the progress of the work on the H-bomb" as GAC chairman. The scientist "could not specifically recall the names of the individuals whom Oppenheimer had persuaded not to work on the H-bomb." Another unnamed scientist felt that "it would be extremely wise not to reappoint" Oppenheimer to the AEC. This view "was not based on security reasons but was based on his belief that Oppenheimer lacked the necessary enthusiasm for the [H-bomb] program." Four scientists, however, told the FBI that they had never been approached by anyone trying to influence them not to work on the H-bomb. According to these scientists, Oppenheimer had "done absolutely nothing to in any way impede the program."

By far the longest and most damaging testimony given to the FBI was that of Edward Teller. Teller stated that, as early as 1945, "Oppenheimer recommended that all work on the H-bomb and the Los Alamos Project be discontinued." Oppenheimer, according to Teller, "delayed, or attempted to delay the development of the H-bomb. . . ." To Teller, Oppenheimer should have "gotten behind the program or resigned his position on the General Advisory Committee." He felt that "opposition to the H-bomb definitely slowed down its development," and kept the United States from amassing an H-bomb stockpile. Teller viewed Oppenheimer as "the most experienced, the most powerful, and the most effective member of the opposition." He concluded that Oppenheimer did not have "any disloyal thoughts or influences," but expressed his *personal hope that Dr. Oppenheimer would be relieved of his responsibilities . . . connected with military preparedness*" (my italics) because of his "record of having given mistaken advice in past years."

On November 30, Hoover sent copies of the Borden letter and the FBI report to Strauss and to the president. Presidential adviser C. D. Jackson has recalled that Hoover also sent copies "to one additional person, the last person I would have selected, namely, Engine Charlie Wilson." Jackson characterized Defense Secretary Wilson as a "simple valve-in-head character," who "practically exploded with terror" when he received the Borden letter. Wilson "clapped on his hat, and rushed to the White House to see the President, clamoring for action," and "requesting permission to notify all defense installations that J. Robert Oppenheimer's clearances" be "withdrawn and that he was the next thing to a spy, etc."[575]

On December 3 Eisenhower called for a meeting in his office to consider Oppenheimer's status. Among those present were Strauss, Attorney General Herbert Brownell (1904–1996), and Defense Secretary Wilson (1890–1961). In their discussion, the Borden letter was not a crucial consideration, because Eisenhower recalled that the letter "didn't have anything new that we could see." To Eisenhower, there was "never a question of Oppenheimer being a 'Soviet agent,' nor was disloyalty raised in my hearing, in the accusations." The one piece of evidence that was seriously considered was the FBI summary report of November 18.

Strauss considered opposition to the development of the H-bomb as "evidence of disloyalty to the country." The AEC chairman possessed "virtually the unlimited confidence of President Eisenhower. . . ."[574] By not emphasizing that he had been one of the AEC commissioners who cleared Oppenheimer on essentially the same evidence in 1947 and 1950, Strauss misled the president, and made Oppenheimer "a hostage to political expediency. . . ."[574]

The president was against Operation Candor, and did "not intend to disclose the details of our strength in atomic weapons of any sort. . . ."[576] Eisenhower remembered the May 27 NSC meeting at which Oppenheimer urged greater candor in telling the public about atomic weapons. He "did not completely trust" the physicist, and "just didn't feel comfortable with Oppenheimer," who supposedly had "almost hypnotic power over small groups." Although the president never considered Oppenheimer to be a "Soviet agent," or disloyal, he did think that "too many very great secrets would be available to him, if we renewed his clearance." Eisenhower "just wouldn't do it."[577] He was also informed that security officers wanted Oppenheimer's case reviewed.

Whereupon Eisenhower "decided that no matter what anyone's personal feelings or beliefs" about Oppenheimer's "guilt or innocence, or whether he was or was not a security risk," a "'blank wall' would have to be erected between Oppenheimer and atomic data until such time as it would be possible to dig into the situation."[578] The administration had concluded the first major step in completely removing a dissident civilian adviser who had expressed heretical views on defense policy. Oppenheimer had been successfully attacked for being the 'strong protagonist' for air defense and candor. Since he was out of the country, Strauss decided on December 4 to stall the implementation of the "blank wall" until Oppenheimer returned.

Later, when the president's "blank wall" order became public, the Washington *Post*'s cartoonist, Herblock, depicted Eisenhower and Strauss separated by a wall from Oppenheimer, the scientist who had created so many of the secrets he was now supposedly being denied—all observed by a puzzled Uncle Sam wondering "Who's Being Walled Off From What?"[579]

This concludes my account of events preceding Robert's meeting with Strauss on December 21, 1953. I turn next to what happened shortly after that day.

Preparations for the Hearings

On December 22 Oppenheimer wrote to Strauss regarding the option he (S.) had proposed: resign immediately. The main part of his reply follows; it is dated December 22:

> Dear Lewis . . . You put to me as a possibly desirable alternative that I request termination of my contract as a consultant to the Commission, and thereby avoid an explicit consideration of the charges on which the Commission's action would otherwise be based. I was told that if I did not do this within a day, I would receive a letter notifying me of the suspension of my clearance and of the charges against me, and I was shown a draft of that letter.
>
> I have thought most earnestly of the alternative suggested. Under the circumstances this course of action would mean that I accept and concur in the view that I am not fit to serve this Government, that I have now served for some 12 years. This I cannot do. . . . Faithfully yours.[580]

About a week later, the AEC Commissioners agreed unanimously to institute the regular procedures of the Commission to determine the veracity or falsity of the charges. These "regular procedures" were the Personnel Security Boards appointed by the general manager to inquire into an employee's suitability for one of the various grades of security clearance.[581]

Oppenheimer now set about to obtain competent legal assistance in his confrontation with the Commission. To this end he and Kitty consulted, in late December, with Herbert Marks (1907–1960) and Joseph Volpe, both erstwhile general counsels for the AEC, both on good terms with him. (Marks's wife Anne had served as Robert's personal assistant and secretary at Los Alamos.) Far from complacent about his situation, Oppenheimer would have been even more concerned had he known that Strauss and Nichols were privy to his every move in selecting counsel. When the FBI agent in Newark first began to pick up conversations about legal matters, he called his supervisors in Washington to ask whether the tap should be continued "in view of the fact that it might disclose attorney-client relations." He was assured that the tap was appropriate because Oppenheimer was involved in a security case, not a criminal action; moreover, the FBI's chief concern, the agent was informed, was to learn immediately of any indication that Oppenheimer was planning to flee the country. Under the circumstances the surveillance was "warranted."[582]

A recollection by an AEC official shows the extraordinary length to which those buggings went: "There was a detailed account of what transpired in his conversation with Volpe. How they got to know about it, I don't know, presumably by some form of bugging, but whether they had something planted in anticipation that he would go there or whether they had equipment which enabled them to bug it instantaneously or what I don't know. Anyway, then there was a similar thing when he left Volpe's office and went to Herb Marks's office—there was a similar account of that conversation."[583] An FBI memo dated February 2 stated: "We do feel that Strauss should be again cautioned concerning the use of the information we furnish him which was obtained from the technical surveillance because if information should leak from AEC that the Bureau has such coverage, Oppenheimer and his attorneys will undoubtedly use it for propaganda purposes."[584]

It took Oppenheimer almost two weeks, with Marks's help, to assemble his legal staff. His chief counsel would be Lloyd Kirkham Garrison (1897–1991), of the New York firm of Paul, Weiss, Rifkind, Wharton, and Garrison, whom Oppenheimer knew as a member of the board of trustees of the Princeton Institute. He has been described as Lincolnesque in appearance and mild of manner, who liked reading philosophy and birdwatching. Garrison's early impressions of Oppenheimer:

> From the beginning he had a quality of desperation about him—in his appearance and in his manners. I think we all felt oppressed by the atmosphere of the time but Oppenheimer particularly so. . . . I found him enigmatic, fascinating of course, with those most beautiful blue eyes, but he was hard to be intimate with. We saw so much of each other that it was always a little surprising to me that we didn't have any of that feeling of comradeship you might have expected from sharing an ordeal of this sort. Cold is too strong a word, he wasn't cold but he kept his distance.[585]

Meanwhile the AEC had decided that an outside attorney should handle the case for the Commission. On the advice of the Department of Justice, Strauss chose for this assignment Roger Robb, who had a private law practice in Washington and had prosecutorial experience as an assistant U.S. attorney. The contrast between the leading attorneys was striking: Robb, tough conservative, at home in the rough-and-tumble atmosphere of the courtroom; Garrison, mild-mannered, almost saintly, a comparative stranger to the merciless world of adversary courtroom proceedings.

The AEC requested an "emergency Q clearance" for Robb, which he received in eight days, unusually fast. Garrison first broached the matter of *his* clearance on January 18, at a meeting with Strauss and Nichols. After further deliberation he decided to forgo clearance, reasoning that nonclearance might minimize the amount of secret material included in the hearing material that might inhibit whatever appeal to the courts might later be necessary. On further reflection Garrison became so troubled that on March 26 he renewed his request for clearance, but was now told that this was not possible before the hearing had ended. What Robb had gotten in eight days, Garrison could not get in eight weeks. Moreover, the AEC had failed to respond to a single of the 19 questions posed by Marks on February 12.

Thus did the hearings develop into a lopsided contest between the Commission's fully documented version and Oppenheimer's ability to recall in detail events that had occurred a decade or more earlier.[586]

One final item showing the AEC's prejudices. Garrison was advised that the members of the hearing board would spend a full week before the hearings studying the investigative materials and talking with Robb. When Garrison asked to be accorded the same privileges as Robb, the Commission rejected this suggestion.[587]

On February 15 a special meeting was held of the trustees of the Institute for Advanced Study. There was only one item on the agenda: the Institute's director wished to advise the trustees of the charges leveled against him by the United States Government, and to proffer his resignation.

The board voted unanimously to voice its complete confidence in its director and to refuse any consideration of his resignation.

Of the 15 members of the board, two were absent that day: Harold F. Linder and Lewis L. Strauss.[588]

James Reston, of the *New York Times,* had wind of the story as early as January and had persistently sought the facts from Oppenheimer. Days before the hearing was due to open, Reston insisted the story could not hold much longer, so Garrison turned over the full texts of the Nichols and Oppenheimer letters to the reporter. Reston held off publishing, until April 13, the day after the hearing had opened, when the article was picked up by every agency, newspaper, and radio station across the nation.

On June 12, 1954, Nichols sent a letter to the AEC members, from which I quote: "On December 23, 1953, Dr. J. Robert Oppenheimer was notified that his security clearance had been suspended, and informed of his right to a hearing under AEC procedures. By telegram dated January 29, 1954, Dr. Oppenheimer requested that he be afforded a hearing and on March 4, 1954, after requesting and receiving three extensions of time, he submitted his answer to my letter of December 23, 1954."[589]

I quote next from Oppenheimer's March 4 letter:

Dear General Nichols: This is in answer to your letter of December 23, 1953, in which the question is raised whether my continued employment as a consultant on Atomic Energy Commission work "will endanger the common defense and security and whether such continued employment is clearly consistent with the interests of the national security."

Though of course I would have no desire to retain an advisory position if my advice were not needed, I cannot ignore the question you have raised, nor accept the suggestion that I am unfit for public service.

The items of so-called derogatory information set forth in your letter cannot be fairly understood except in the context of my life and my work. This answer is in the form of a summary account of relevant aspects of my life in more or less chronological order, in the course of which I shall comment on the specific items in your letter. Through this answer, and through the hearings before the personnel security board, which I hereby request, I hope to prove a full basis upon which the questions posed by your letter may be resolved.[590]

The letter continues with a long, detailed resumé of his activities in the prewar period, the war years, and the postwar period (all described in the preceding), and ends as follows: "In preparing this letter, I have reviewed two decades of my life. I have recalled instances where I acted unwisely. What I have hoped was, not that I could wholly avoid error, but that I might learn from it. What I have learned has, I think, made me more fit to serve my country."[591]

In response to Oppenheimer's request for a hearing, the AEC established a three-member Personnel Security Board (PSB). President Eisenhower chose Gordon Gray as the chairman, and the Commission picked Ward V. Evans and Thomas A. Morgan. Gray had served as secretary of the Army in the Truman administration, and was the president of the University of North Carolina. Evans was a chemistry professor at Loyola University, and Morgan was a businessman and the former president of the Sperry Gyroscope Company. The opening date for the hearing was set at April 12, 1954.

On April 5, Robb briefed the PSB on the file data, and continued to brief them for the rest of that week. The three-man panel read through over 3,000 pages of material derived from AEC, FBI, and Manhattan Engineering District records. The information contained testimony and Air Force documents relating to Oppenheimer's position on the H-bomb, tactical nuclear weapons, air defense, and government candor. Oppenheimer's attorneys were never shown this material or given the opportunity to provide the board with a balanced perspective.

Years later, in 1963, a reporter wrote: "Long before the hearing itself started, almost from the week his clearance was revoked, Oppenheimer says, he had no 'real hope of other than the actual outcome—once a thing like that has been started, they can't *not* go through with it to the end; and they couldn't let me win.'"[592]

Oppenheimer and McCarthy

At the 1952 Republican convention, Senator McCarthy received an ova-
tion when he called for a "rough" anti-communist drive.[593] After the Republican victory, he was promoted from ranking minority member of the Senate's
Investigation Committee to chairman, with broad powers—including the
choice of those to be investigated.

Robert was an obvious McCarthy target. Already in 1952 he (McC.) had
called on Edgar Hoover to discuss the possibility of starting an investigation of Oppenheimer, hinting at bipartisan support for such a move.[594]
McCarthy in fact came close to the Oppenheimer issue when, a week before the hearings were about to begin, he said in a nationally televised speech:
"If there were no Communists in our government, why did we delay for
eighteen months—delay our research on the hydrogen bomb, even though
our intelligence agencies were reporting, day after day, that the Russians
were feverishly pushing their development on the hydrogen bomb? Our
nation may well die because of that eighteen-month delay. And I ask who
caused it? Was it loyal Americans—or was it traitors in our government?"[595]
This charge met with bipartisan rebuttal.[596]

The day after the hearing opened he told a reporter: "Oppenheimer's
suspension was long overdue—it should have taken place years ago. . . . I
think it took considerable courage to suspend the so-called untouchable
scientist—Oppenheimer. . . . I gave Strauss credit for that."[588]

Both the White House and the AEC were wary and enervated by
McCarthy's exploitation of the Oppenheimer case.

Strauss was scared that McCarthy was waiting in the wings. To Senator
Anderson's astonishment, Strauss said at a JCCAE meeting that "he would
have to turn the [O.] file over to McCarthy [who] would have to be molli-
fied."[597] Eisenhower, who loathed McCarthy and wanted to discredit him,
was afraid that the senator might raise the accusation against Oppenheimer.
I could even imagine (but for this I have no proof whatsoever) that Robert's
decision *not* to resign may have been influenced in part by the fear that in
that case the Senator from Wisconsin would be after him.

Why *did* McCarthy in fact *not* get into the act, in a case that he would
have considered juicy?

Senator McCarthy assigned one of his staff members to work on "the
Oppenheimer case" for a time, but the senator refrained from any probe of
Oppenheimer or the H-bomb program because, he later recalled, he had
"*assurances from top Administration officials* that this matter would be gone into in

detail" (my italics). Congressional employees intimate with these affairs were given to understand that the principal "top Administration official" responsible for saving Robert Oppenheimer from a McCarthy investigation was the vice president of the United States, Richard M. Nixon. "We decided we were not the committee to go into it. It was not a matter for open hearings, [since] it definitely involved security. . . . we got some pretty high assurances that it would not be neglected."[588]

The Oppenheimer hearings started when McCarthy's influence was at its peak. His decline began ten days later, on April 22, 1954, when Senate hearings began concerning McCarthy's accusations directed against the U.S. Army for coddling an alleged communist sympathizer. The following December 2, he was formally censured by the Senate for conduct "contrary to Senate traditions." Thereafter he never regained power. He died in 1957.

CHAPTER **23**

IN WHICH THE NEWS OF THE
HEARINGS IS MADE PUBLIC

How Einstein and I First Heard

In the *New York Herald Tribune* edition of Sunday, April 11, 1954, there appeared a column by Joseph Alsop (1910–1989) and his younger brother Stewart (1914–1974), entitled "Next McCarthy target: the leading physicists." The next morning, the *Christian Science Monitor* published an article with a similar heading: "Senator stalks A-Scientists."

The Alsop column began by stating that the junior senator from Wisconsin was "getting ready to play his ace in the hole. . . . McCarthy will, of course, carefully time his ace-in-the-hole in order to smother the smell of the McCarthy-Army mess." The authors write of the "truly monumental naiveté about political matters" shown in their youth by some physicists, referring in particular to "one extremely distinguished American physicist, who made great contributions to the American atomic program, [who] is known in his younger years to have committed acts of political folly unworthy of a five-year old child. He is certainly not alone." That one, of course, was Robert, whom the Alsop brothers knew and liked well. I may note, first, that I did not read that Alsop column on the day it came out, being a *New York Times* and not a *Herald Tribune* reader; secondly, that the quoted columnists were apparently unaware that, already at the time of their writing, it had been decided that McCarthy would not play a direct role in the Oppenheimer affair.

On the evening of that same Sunday I was working in my office at the Institute when, at about 10 o'clock, my phone rang. A long distance operator from Washington, D.C., asked to speak to Dr. Oppenheimer. (I should explain that this call reached me because the Institute switchboard was closed on Sundays, and I had one of the few direct outside lines.) I replied that Oppenheimer was out of town; I knew, in fact, that he was in Washington that day. The operator asked next to be connected with Dr. Einstein. I told her that Einstein was not at the office and that his home number was unlisted. Whereupon the operator told me that her party wished to speak to me. The person who came on the line introduced himself as Henry Raymont, director of the Washington Bureau of the United Press. He told me that the Oppenheimer case would be all over the papers on Tuesday morning. He was eager for a statement by Einstein as soon as possible.

I realized that pandemonium on Mercer Street the next morning might be avoided by a brief statement that evening and so said that I would talk it over with Einstein and would call back in any event. I drove to 112 Mercer Street and rang the bell; Helen Dukas, Einstein's secretary, let me in. I apologized for appearing at such a late hour and said it would be good if I could talk briefly with the professor, who meanwhile had appeared at the top of the stairs in his bathrobe and asked, "Was ist los?" ("What is going on?") He came down and so did his stepdaughter Margot. After I told him the reason for my call, Einstein burst out laughing. I was a bit taken aback and asked him what was so funny. He said the problem was simple. All Oppenheimer needed to do, he said, was go to Washington, tell the officials that they were fools, and then go home. On further discussion, we decided that a brief statement was called for. We drew it up, and Einstein read it over the phone to the UP director in Washington.[598]

That done, Mr. Raymont asked Einstein what he thought the impact of the coming events would be on the scientific community. Listening in on this conversation on another phone, I heard Einstein take a deep breath. Before he could begin to talk, I broke in, saying that it was best that Einstein's statement should do for the moment, and that further comments could wait. My reason for doing so was that I could easily imagine Einstein making remarks on the fools in Washington, like he had done to me—which to me did not appear at all apposite at that time. Raymont reacted by thanking both Einstein and me. End of conversation.

And so it came about that it was I who first informed Einstein of the upcoming Oppenheimer hearings. That evening was also the first time that I myself heard that news. Earlier remarks by Robert had given me intimations that something was brewing, but not before had I known what was now about to happen. I should further note most of the details of what led up to the hearings, described in the preceding, have become clear to me only in the course of preparing this book, about half a century, after the event.

I conclude this account of Einstein's early awareness of the Oppenheimer case with a few further remarks.

Shortly after the news broke, statements from a number of outstanding scientists were published. Einstein's contribution was limited to a single sentence: "The systematic and widespread attempt to destroy mutual trust and confidence constitutes the severest possible blow against society."[599]

During the same period, Einstein replied to a correspondent in New York who had written him about the Oppenheimer case: "It is best not to be too excited. Fear and stupidity have generally been the origin of most human actions. We can only continue to strive for honesty and independence of thought."[600]

Was Einstein's initial response—to tell Washington officials that they were fools and then go home—correct? Of course it was, even though his suggestion would not and could not be followed. I remember once attending a seminar by Bertrand de Jouvenel in which he singled out the main characteristic of a political problem: it has no answer, only a compromise. Nothing was more alien to Einstein than to settle any issue by compromise, in his life or in his science. He often spoke out on political problems, always steering to their answer. Such statements have often been called naive. In my view, Einstein was not only not naive but highly aware of the nature of man's sorrows and his follies. His utterances on political matters did not always address the immediately practicable, and I do not think that on the whole they were very influential. However, he knowingly and gladly paid the price of sanity. Oppenheimer's description, "There was always with him a wonderful purity at once childlike and profoundly stubborn,"[601] shows the writer's talent for almost understanding everything.

Finally, the day after the evening's events just described, Helen Dukas was preparing lunch when she saw cars in front of the house and cameras being unloaded. In her apron (she told me), she ran out of the house to warn Einstein, who was on his way home. When he arrived at the front door, he declined to talk to reporters.

First Newspaper Comments

When Mr. Raymont called me that Sunday evening, he told me not just that the news would be in the next Tuesday papers but also that the *New*

York Times would carry 17 columns in their April 13 edition—a number I noted in my diary. I do not know for certain how he had obtained such detailed information but have a good guess.

As already mentioned, James Reston of the *Times* had been aware for some time that something was brewing. He had been in touch with Oppenheimer and Garrison. The latter had spoken with Lilienthal, who already in January had written in his diary: "So it will be all over the place. Surprising that it hasn't before this."[602]

True to his promise, Reston held off publishing until the hearings had started. One finds his article in the *Times* edition of April 13, beginning on the front page, followed by four full pages inside—17 columns in all, as I had been told. It will be clear that Raymont's information must have come from someone on the *Times* staff; also that the article had been typeset over the weekend but held until after the hearing had opened on Monday, April 13.

On the most prominent position of the *Times* front page one will find a two-column picture of a meditative Oppenheimer in his Princeton study, under the headlines: "Dr. Oppenheimer suspended by A.E.C. in security review; scientist defends record; hearings started; access to secret data denied nuclear expert—red ties alleged."

Reston wrote in his article: "In view of the fact that the *Times* was in possession of most of the facts, Dr. Oppenheimer made the statement of charges and his reply available to the *Times* so that the record of the case could be written from the actual documents." Thus one finds in the article the full texts of the December 23, 1953, letter by Nichols to Oppenheimer, and of the lengthy March 4, 1954, reply by Robert (which Reston had obtained the previous April 9.)[603]

The *Times* news was picked up by newspapers worldwide. The first of these was probably the New York *Daily News*, which on the afternoon of that same April 13 came out with one of its superheavy headlines: "Oppenheimer A-bomb chief suspended; U.S. Board studies charges of scientist's commie ties."

I select from my vast collection of newspaper clippings some representative comments from other papers.

The *Washington Post*, April 14, front page headline: "Ike bars atomic secrets from Dr. Oppenheimer." From its editorial (page 14): "If men are to be accused of disloyalty for the honest and open expressions of opinions which later come to be considered mistaken, then only sycophants can survive in government."

The *New York Post,* April 14, editorial:

He [O.] is a man blessed by fortune with every endowment and tortured by fortune with every mischance. . . . After the war he became the symbol of the newly-canonized nuclear physicist, young and intense and quite beyond the comprehension of the ordinary. . . . A man accepts the challenge of alchemy, he labors and helps make gold out of dross; and, when he has finished, men hate him in his triumph as they would have forgotten him in his failure.

The *New York Herald Tribune,* April 13:

The fact that Dr. Oppenheimer has been charged on security grounds has been known in the higher circles of the scientific community for weeks. The reaction in these circles, in which, of course, Dr. Oppenheimer is intimately known, is significant. A committee has been formed . . . to raise money for Dr. Oppenheimer's defense. The response has so far been remarkable—the most distinguished scientists in the country, including rivals who have by no means always seen eye to eye with Dr. Oppenheimer, have been eager to contribute.

Same paper, editorial, April 16:

The action of President Eisenhower in suspending, during re-investigation, the security clearance of the great nuclear scientist, Dr. J. Robert Oppenheimer, who has done as much as any man in the world to give America the atomic bomb, is reassuring to the whole nation. It shows that the Administration is resolving all borderline doubts on the side of prudent safety.

It shows that there isn't a smitch of oh-there-can't-be-anything-wrong-here thinking in the executive handling of security decisions.

It shows that the Administration does not need to be harassed by Congress to do its own job under orderly and fair procedures.

It shows that the Administration is not lightly accepting past clearances as any substitute for its own responsibility when, even as in Dr. Oppenheimer's earlier clearance, it had the participation of the President's trusted chairman of the Atomic Energy Commission, Lewis L. Strauss, who shared Mr. Eisenhower's view that both old and some new questions concerning Dr. Oppenheimer must be restudied.

New York World Telegram, April 16:

Dr. J. Robert Oppenheimer is discouraging his fellow scientists from demanding that the loyalty charges against him be aired publicly, it was learned today.

Many colleagues and friends of the physicist are opposed to the present secret hearings before a special security board of the Atomic Energy Commission.

They would like to see a public investigation—preferably before the House-Senate Atomic Energy Commission—so the nation would be able to weigh the charges of procommunism against Dr. Oppenheimer's record in development of the atomic bomb.

Fears Blurring of Issues.

But an informed source revealed Dr. Oppenheimer does not favor this course. He fears it might develop into a sensational trial in which the issues could become blurred.

The *New York Times* of April 18 contains reports by regional correspondents on the reaction in their respective areas.

Excerpts follow.

New England

Most editorials called for caution pending the shedding of further light. Dr. Oppenheimer personally was termed an "uneducated intellectual," and was characterized as being politically naive.

Mid-Atlantic States

After the initial shock, residents of this area took a wait-and-see attitude in the case of Dr. Oppenheimer. There was a general feeling that it was better to have the allegations produced in full, along with Dr. Oppenheimer's reply, than to have them the subject of rumor and possible misinterpretation. Many, however, found it hard to understand why the A.E.C. had waited so long to start a full investigation.

The Southeast

The general feeling of the man in the street is that President Eisenhower acted wisely in suspending Dr. Oppenheimer. However, the consensus seems to be that in view of the fact it was known that he had associated with Communists in the past, further action in the case is hardly required.

McCarthy has few partisans and enjoys little prestige in the Deep South, and the Oppenheimer ouster has done little, if anything, to raise his stock.

The Midwest

Calling Dr. Oppenheimer a "political innocent," the Eisenhower-supporting *Chicago Daily News* said: "The Oppenheimer files have been hashed over repeatedly, and it will take new evidence to carry much weight. Unless that is forthcoming, we would think the statute of limitations had run on pre-war political follies."

The incident did nothing to raise Senator McCarthy's stock among the public as a whole, but it gave satisfaction to the proclaimers of the Wisconsinite's "infallibility."

The Southwest

Texans appear to have adopted an attitude of "wait and see" regarding the allegations against Dr. Oppenheimer.

Even some of the pro-McCarthy newspapers have adopted a cautious approach to the disclosures. One of these is the *Houston Chronicle*, which observed that the Oppenheimer case "should be handled soberly, intelligently and without political flamboyance."

On the whole the Administration has been credited with acting wisely in suspending Dr. Oppenheimer until the facts in the case can be proved.

The Mountain States

Reaction to suspension of Dr. Oppenheimer and investigation of charges against him ranged from sharp incredulity to "I told you so" attitudes in this area.

Fully 50 percent of persons queried on the Oppenheimer case feel "McCarthy opened this up" through his television appearance charging an eighteen-month delay in H-bomb development. There seems no doubt the Senator's backing has been strengthened by the airing of the charges against Dr. Oppenheimer about his past associations and H-bomb attitude.

Pacific Coast

The Oppenheimer case was greeted editorially in this region with some applause for the scientist for electing to combat the charges against him, with some demand for a factual inquiry without smear or whitewash; with some appeal to the public to withhold judgment until the investigation was complete and a decision rendered.

In spite of editorial appeals for caution in judgment, there appeared to be a tendency for "headline readers" to prejudge the case without giving Dr. Oppenheimer even a slight advantage.

Incidentally, the whole subject was greeted with silence by most of Dr. Oppenheimer's former Berkeley colleagues. Sideliners on the California campus analyzed the prevailing attitude as: "What of value could we contribute by sticking our necks out?"

New York Times, April 30. Under the heading: "Oppenheimer case divides physicists,"

Colleagues of Dr. J. Robert Oppenheimer in the American Physical Society, are divided in their views as to whether the war-time scientific director of the atomic bomb project should have been subjected to a hearing on his being a possible security risk.

The existence of diametrically opposing views among his own colleagues was revealed here today at the opening of the annual meeting of the American Physical Society, of which Dr. Oppenheim is a past president, and at a meeting tonight under the auspices of the Washington Chapter, Federation of American Scientists.

Questioning of representative physicists from various parts of the country brought to light the existence of three distinct points of view: those who believe that Dr. Oppenheimer will be cleared and reinstated; those who expect an unfavorable decision, finding him to be a "security risk"; and those who actually believe that his opposition to the hydrogen bomb must be taken as "proof" of disloyalty.

There is still another group that does not question his loyalty, and does not even hold that he is in any way a security risk; while at the same time it regards his suspension as an adviser to the Atomic Energy Commission pending the outcome of the hearing, was fully justified.

As a leading scientist expressed it: "We dismiss generals if they make mistakes, and sometimes even court-martial them. Why should scientists who give bad advice not be given the same treatment?"

Same paper, same day, heading:

President praises Oppenheimer, but says inquiry was required.

President Eisenhower expressed today his admiration and respect for the professional attainments of Dr. J. Robert Oppenheimer. However, the President said the allegations against the scientist as a security risk made necessary the new investigation of him.

The President took personal responsibility for the Administration decision to raise—in the words of the Atomic Energy Commission—a "blank wall" between Dr. Oppenheimer and the secret information he helped to unlock as director of the research team that built the first atomic bomb. The scientist has been suspended as an adviser to the commission.

It was the proper responsibility of the Executive branch to investigate the allegations against Dr. Oppenheimer, President Eisenhower said, as he disclaimed in answer to a question at his news conference any attempt to interfere with the investigative function of Congress.

The President then volunteered that he had known Dr. Oppenheimer and had certainly admired and respected the scientist's very great professional and technical attainments. But this was the kind of thing that must be gone through with, he said.

President Eisenhower was asked whether the re-examination of the allegations against Dr. Oppenheimer by a special commission panel had been started to avoid a public hearing in the Congress.

The reply by the President was that he was not trying to interfere with the proper execution of Congress' duties. As he had said many times, the President added, such investigations fell squarely on the shoulders of the Executive Branch.

He had acted on that responsibility when the case was brought to him, he said.

Later, in April, national magazines began to devote articles to the case.

Time Magazine, April 26, begins with a quote from Oppenheimer, taken from an interview dating from 1948:

You have no idea how repugnant this is—to go over my life. It is impossible to be completely candid. It's an art and it takes technique, and you have to learn it. If you've lived a life that isn't free and open with people, it's almost impossible to unsnarl it, to unravel the ball of twine.

It continues with excepts from Oppenheimer's March 4 letter to Nichols.

Oppenheimer's letter shone with literary brilliance; the strength of his personality leaped out from the page. It was especially moving to men and women in the same age bracket as Oppenheimer (he is 50). Many men ten years older or ten years younger did not fully understand him. His letter was an account of a strange period of history, the decades 1920–1950—not so much of their strange events but of even stranger states of mind. His story was an extreme example of what had happened in that period to a large body of the world's intellectuals.

About his student years:

He decided that physics was his first interest, but he did not enter into that austere and noble priesthood, as some did, without exposure to the world of ideas that lay beyond and around it. At Harvard, the youth who had already met Sophocles, and who was later to be bewildered and surprised by the evil in the world, discovered Dante and pored over French literature.

About the case:

That he opposes [Eisenhower's] policy does not mean that Oppenheimer is disloyal. Indeed, the Vice President of the U.S., Richard Nixon, last week went out of his way to express his belief in Oppenheimer's loyalty. But Oppenheimer's kind of politics and his peculiar power arouse violent antagonism.

A sense of moral responsibility concerning war is not limited to atomic scientists. Most generals have that sense and so do most nonscientific civilians at the top layers of Government. They do not feel it as "a sense of sin." Most of them have borne this sense of responsibility as citizens, soldiers, or officials for many years. This fact does not make them more right or more loyal than Oppenheimer. Or less so.

It is possible—and for thousands of years men have known this—to develop pride out of a sense of guilt. Many of the military and civilian officials whom Oppenheimer opposed sensed in him an arrogant desire to take into his own hands the destiny of society. Perhaps they were wrong to think this of him. Even if they were right, disloyalty may not be the relevant accusation. However he came to his present ordeal, J. Robert Oppenheimer's life is a bitter parable of a bitter time.

Life Magazine, April 26, carried an article headlined: "U.S. ponders a scientist's past," which started out as follows.

Silently and impassively, a thin, thoughtful man wearing a porkpie hat and accompanied by a policeman and three lawyers walked with hurried step last week through the shabby back door courtyard of a Washington office building.

The almost furtive entrance gave the scene an appropriate air of mystery, for the secret questioning of the man was of profound national importance. The porkpie hat identified the man as J. Robert Oppenheimer. . . .

Whatever the truth of the charges and whatever the outcome of the inquiry, the situation which involved one of the nation's most brilliant scientific minds was in itself a national tragedy.

With these lines we enter the scene of the hearings.

SUPPLEMENTAL MATERIAL
BY ROBERT P. CREASE

CHAPTER 24

"OPEN BOOK": THE HEARING IN THE MATTER OF J. ROBERT OPPENHEIMER

The chief puzzle surrounding Robert Oppenheimer's security clearance hearing is why it had not happened earlier.

Despite Truman's approval of the Super project in 1950, its supporters had neither forgiven nor forgotten Oppenheimer's opposition. As Cold War anxieties rose, many key H-bomb supporters had grown increasingly anxious about his continued influence on atomic weapons development. Oppenheimer was neither the only eminent scientist to oppose the Super nor the only one to do so on moral grounds: in 1949, Compton, Conant, Fermi, and Rabi, among others, had signed on to documents that articulated powerful practical and moral objections to the Super's development. But this did not cause its proponents to question the integrity of these scientists, nor to fear that they were spies. Oppenheimer was different. No one else with that much access and influence had that much of a leftwing past. No one else with that much of a leftwing past had that much access and influence. Oppenheimer's opposition to the Super's development coupled with his past leftwing activities to magnify the suspicion and determination of his adversaries. Their fear of each intensified their fear of the other.

Oppenheimer thus became the largest object in the cross-hairs of nuclear weapons proponents such as Lewis Strauss and anti-communist crusaders such as FBI Director J. Edgar Hoover.

It was not that Oppenheimer continued to harbor any leftist leanings; indeed, he had become known as anti-Soviet after witnessing Soviet intransigence toward international control of atomic energy in reaction to the

Acheson-Lilienthal plan. Rather, his increased vulnerability was due to the more intense scrutiny his previous activities, and his steps to conceal them, attracted in the new hypersensitive Cold War climate. Oppenheimer thus experienced his earlier "leftwanderings," in Lawrence's words, and his coverups thereof, to be an increasingly burdensome albatross. Political controversies can reach a threshold at which key individuals or institutions are pushed into a "fishbowl" phase, when every aspect of their present and past behavior becomes exhaustively scrutinized, and every potentially damning thing is examined from the most damning angle possible. This was about to happen to J. Robert Oppenheimer. His fishbowl would be exceptionally transparent, given over a dozen years of FBI and Army Intelligence gathering on him with interviews and informants, personal surveillance and wiretaps. And in the aftermath of the trial, the contents of that fishbowl would become unusually public. His life, Garrison would remark at the end of the hearing, would become an "open book."

Why it took so long for his powerful enemies to act has to do with what Stanford historian Barton Bernstein has called Oppenheimer's "exceptionalism," or special protection within the Truman administration, in which he had high friends.[1] Foremost among these was Acheson, Oppenheimer's new Groves, who stood ready to save Oppenheimer from his missteps. Moreover, the fishbowling still had failed to produce gold-plated evidence of either Communist Party membership or perjury. Lacking hard evidence, Oppenheimer's opponents dared not move against someone with that high a public profile and political reputation. Failure would risk retaliation, and permanent delegitimization of the cause.

In 1953, with Eisenhower's ascension to the presidency, this began to change. That June 5, Oppenheimer's consultancy contract with AEC was extended by one year, to June 30, 1954. A month later, another fateful event: Lewis Strauss, still determined to reduce Oppenheimer's power, became chairman of the AEC. In August, yet another: the Soviet Union exploded its first H-bomb. These events—and in particular the last, which would be alluded to in the coming hearing in language such as "the current crisis" and "the present crisis"—generated a new sense of power and urgency among Oppenheimer's antagonists. Some, including Senator Joseph McCarthy, were eager to investigate Oppenheimer right away. Strauss and Hoover demurred, fearing to make a martyr of Oppenheimer and alienate the physics community, whose support they thought essential for the looming nuclear arms race. Better to ease Oppenheimer out by working behind the scenes. This had been the tactic, for instance, that they had used just a few months previously to ease out Carroll Wilson as the general manager of the AEC. Strauss was also reluctant to press for an investigation, for he was politically sophisticated enough to realize the possibility of a backlash that could destroy him.

But a series of events conspired to frustrate this scheme. Chief among them was the Borden letter. Though nearly all its charges were old, except those concerning Oppenheimer's opposition to the Super development, it came on the heels of the Presidential Order of April 1953 tightening security requirements. Furthermore, Eisenhower was worried that any appearance of indulging Oppenheimer would leave his administration vulnerable to a flank attack by Senator Joseph McCarthy. When word of Borden's letter reached Eisenhower, who by now was convinced that Oppenheimer was "at least a liar,"[2] the President directed Strauss to establish, for the time being, a "blank wall" between Oppenheimer and atomic data. Certain of Strauss's advisers wanted to solve the problem by simply canceling Oppenheimer's consultancy contract, fearing a "test of strength" with the Commission, but Nichols and General Counsel William Mitchell argued for termination of the security clearance. Strauss, emboldened by the new, less tolerant climate, agreed.[3] But he still hoped that Oppenheimer would resign, and at the December 21 meeting at which he and Nichols informed Oppenheimer of the suspension of his clearance, they made clear their preference for resignation rather than a hearing.

Oppenheimer could have accepted that suggestion and spared himself an experience that would surely be grueling and humiliating at best. But Oppenheimer by now was deeply attached to his power and influence. He was confident of his ability to prevail over those who were less intellectually quick than he was; which is to say, over everyone else. Finally, not only was he accustomed to regard himself as essentially a public custody (as one of his high school teachers once remarked), so were other influential scientific leaders, who despite the controversies and occasional betrayals of previous years still vested him with leadership. Weisskopf wrote him before the trial: "Somehow Fate has chosen you as the one who has to bear the heaviest load in this struggle. I know that you are suffering from this, and any man would in view of such enormous strain. On the other hand, I would not know of any better man to bear this load. As a matter of fact, if I had to choose whom to select for the man who has to take this on, I could not but choose you. Who else in this country could represent better than you the spirit and the philosophy of all that for which we are living."[4]

To have accepted the judgment without a fight was not in keeping with a public custody. Hence Oppenheimer's letter, on March 4, requesting a hearing on his security clearance suspension. This required the AEC to empanel a Personnel Security Board (PSB), to conduct a hearing and make a recommendation to the five AEC commissioners.[5] By 1954, several scientists—mostly physicists and chemists involved in atomic research—had undergone such hearings. A tried and true, and generally successful, defense strategy was to bring in prominent friends to testify to your character and ability, and to be impressive yourself. Oppenheimer was well positioned to do this. He selected the prestigious Lloyd Garrison, whose ancestors included the famous abolitionist William Lloyd Garrison, as his chief counsel. The two then put together what historian Gregg Herken has called a "strategy of notables,"[6] a list of scientists and administrators to testify on Oppenheimer's behalf, all of whom had worked with Oppenheimer. Of the 31 who would ultimately testify, 10 were former and present members of the GAC, five former AEC commissioners (including the two former chairmen prior to Strauss), three present or future Nobel laureates, two security officers at Los Alamos, and General Groves himself. Oppenheimer and Garrison had little reason to suppose that this lineup—representing, in effect, the intellectual establishment of the day—plus Oppenheimer's inimitable performance, would not suffice to prevail at the hearing. Said one reassuring colleague: "Just give them the standard JRO."[7]

But Strauss, now forced into a confrontation, knew his adversary only too well, and feared Oppenheimer's power and influence. No doubt his determination was reinforced by the stark personal clash: Strauss, from a poor background and unashamed to profess himself a religious Jew, versus Oppenheimer, born into wealth, highly educated, and having all but denied his Jewish heritage. Strauss, too, was smarting over many insults, that much-cited congressional hearing over the isotope issue merely a synecdoche for many others. Strauss set about to make sure that this would be no standard PSB.

As the AEC chairman, Strauss skillfully wielded his power and influence with the agency's General Manager Nichols to oversee selection of the PSB members. On January 1, 1954, with the attorney general's approval, Strauss had Oppenheimer put under surveillance, to include wiretaps on home and office telephones, and then extended the surveillance to opening his mail.[8] Even Oppenheimer's movements and conversations were reported, meaning that the AEC counsel had advance knowledge of every step taken by Oppenheimer and his lawyers.

The fact that it was a hearing appeared to be in Oppenheimer's favor, for it suggested that the AEC's counsel would face more constraints, and his less, than in a civil trial. But Strauss and his allies would exploit ambiguities in the process to put him at a decided disadvantage. There was no shared understanding, from beginning to end, of terms such as "security risk" and "loyalty." (For "loyalty," as Oppenheimer had written three years previously, in response to a former associate who was appealing for help with his own clearance hearing, "is a hard thing to document.") There were different understandings, too, of the criteria by which to evaluate someone: the "zero tolerance" or "Caesar's wife" standard, according to which even the slightest risk was unacceptable; and the "whole man" standard, in which a person's entire record—good and bad—would be evaluated, the relative value of the person to the program counted, and "calculated risks" acceptable.[9] The presence of these different understandings made it unclear what Oppenheimer had to do to defend himself.

Moreover, Strauss took other steps to make sure this would be no standard PSB hearing. Wanting to encourage more of a prosecutorial atmosphere than at other PSB hearings, he went outside the AEC's staff to recruit as the agency's chief counsel Roger Robb, who had extensive trial experience as an assistant U.S. attorney. Robb's powers were vastly extended and enhanced, while Garrison's were restricted. Robb was given clearance, Garrison was not. Robb refused to supply advance notice of his witnesses, while Garrison gave advance notice of his. Robb received transcripts of each day's proceedings immediately, Garrison several days later. Robb had the PSB supplied with transcripts of the secret wiretaps made of Oppenheimer and with 3,000 pages of material from AEC, FBI, and MED records—with the contents of the fishbowl, which tilted the Board against Oppenheimer before the hearing began—while Oppenheimer and his attorneys were denied access. Oppenheimer was even denied access to documents he had helped write.

In violation of the AEC's own security clearance procedures,[10] Robb was able to consult with the Gray panel, was in fact treated as the panel's (rather than the AEC's) counsel, and sometimes shared meals with panel members. Robb was also allowed to work closely with the FBI in gathering information and preparing for the trial. Throughout spring 1954, the FBI pursued every available lead to squirrel up evidence of Oppenheimer's contradictions and false statements. Meanwhile, Strauss, Robb and the other AEC counsel recruited and interviewed witnesses. This was unprecedented. Their work was so promising that when Rabi and Wigner each tried to broker a compromise in which Oppenheimer would resign his contract in return for withdrawal of the charges, Strauss was confident enough to refuse.

Robb still had to prepare carefully. Winning this case, Robb told people, was "most important to him," and he "did not intend to give up without a strong fight."[11] Oppenheimer's by-now familiar persona was "a master at innuendo and evasive answers," as one FBI report put it.[12] Robb armed himself against this persona, set traps for it, even lay in wait for it, throughout the four weeks of the hearing. He was equipped with documents and transcripts that Oppenheimer could not consult—some he did not even know about—which Robb would spring on Oppenheimer and his notables. It was not an inquiry, not an attempt to seek information: Robb and the AEC already had virtually all the information they wanted, and what they still needed they knew they could not get from Oppenheimer. Rather, it was a set-up: Robb set out to display Oppenheimer's already fully documented mistakes in the worst possible light, to exhibit all the contradictions in previous testimony, and maximize the threat that this posed. When asked whether Oppenheimer had not demonstrated himself to be too clever and agile to fall into the standard prosecutorial traps, Robb replied, "Maybe so, but then he's not been cross-examined by me before."[13]

The standard JRO would be all but helpless against this PSB.

The Hearing: April 12–May 6, 1954

The hearing opened on April 12, 1954, in Room 2022 of a drab, two-story AEC building in Washington, D.C. It was conducted as a confidential hearing, and participants were assured their words would remain secret. Today, mountains of material exist on this episode, which has inspired books (including one by Philip M. Stern, *The Oppenheimer Case: Security on Trial*, devoted mainly to the trial itself), articles, commentaries, reviews, plays, and movies. The transcript was published shortly after the hearing, then republished a year and a half later with an introduction and supplementary material, and recently reissued in an abridged version. It is not fun reading: there are no citations of Sanskrit or Greek, no sudden disclosures of deep truths, no dagger-like verbal thrusts, no brutal putdowns. Oppenheimer, indeed, comes off startlingly poorly, often confused, clumsy, and lacking a knowledge of his own motives.

Why? "He was a wonderful actor, in a sense," Rabi once said. "He could assume the character that was expected of him in the milieu in which he was. Always overdoing it, to some degree . . . a lot of his life was playing a role."[14] But this was a different milieu. Robb would run the hearing like a trial where the details were of the essence—who said what to whom and when—and he would take all the time in the world to get these details on the table, to display them as fully as possible, and to review them more than once. Knowing that his adversaries had fishbowled him, but not knowing exactly what they had seen, Oppenheimer had to speak extremely—and abnormally—cautiously lest he compound the damage he had created in episodes that already littered his past. It would be easy for an experienced criminal prosecutor to trap him in contradictions and apparent misstatements. Moreover, Oppenheimer was best when dramatizing himself in front of a receptive audience. His self-dramatization would be utterly ineffective before an audience with no incentive to be seduced. Being the supplicant was not a role he had any experience playing.

Gray opened the hearing on Day One by reading into the record Nichols's letter of the previous December, mentioning the requirement in the Atomic Energy Act of 1946 charging the commissioners to determine the "character, associations, and loyalty" of the individuals who work for the commission, and referring specifically to Section 10 of the Act referring to the requirement that AEC employees not endanger "the common defense and security," as well as the Executive Order of the previous April requiring that an individual's employment be suspended if information exists that employment would "not be clearly consistent with the interests of the national security."[15] When Gray finished reading Nichols's letter, he read Oppenheimer's reply. Garrison then made an opening statement. After the lunch break, Oppenheimer took the stand and Garrison led him through questioning and read more documents into the record. The first notable, Mervin J. Kelly, president of the Bell Telephone Laboratory, showed up on Day Two, followed by more Oppenheimer. The flavor of the event, however, did not begin until Day Three, when Robb began to question Oppenheimer for the first time. Stern describes the contrast between them aptly, if a bit hyperbolically: "Oppenheimer's career had been devoted largely to the laboratory and the classroom, Robb's to the courtroom. Robb's professional skill lay in toe-to-toe combat, Oppenheimer's in intellectuality and soft persuasiveness. Oppenheimer was often preoccupied with the distant past and future; Robb, in his career, dealt mainly with the here-and-now. The gulf between the two was epitomized on two occasions that day: when Oppenheimer made references to Friedrich Engels and Niels Bohr, Robb in both instances was obliged to ask, "Who?" Now their lives had intersected: the consummate intellectual was face to face with the master cross-examiner."[16]

The encounter, however, was not taking place on level ground, for the rules of the game were all in favor of the cross-examiner. Oppenheimer's strength was to grasp the essence of a situation quickly, before anyone else, even if that meant omitting a few details. Again and again, Robb would in effect test Oppenheimer's unaided memory, leading him into contradictions with documents and (sometimes secret) transcripts which Robb would spring on Oppenheimer, Garrison, and the notables. Again and again, Robb would insinuate that these contradictions were more deliberate, extensive, and sinister than they actually were. He would do the same with Oppenheimer's witnesses, and would not hesitate to treat some of the most eminent scientists and governmental leaders "after the manner of a county prosecutor cornering a petty thief."[17]

The aim would be to make Oppenheimer appear a continued risk to the "national security." To Strauss and his allies, Oppenheimer's opposition to the Super had made him a risk; without that opposition, the trial would not have happened. But Oppenheimer's opposition to the Super looked uncomfortably like a policy difference. The risk would therefore have to be anchored in some of Oppenheimer's leftwanderings. Though these were in the past, they were made to look more threatening through highlighting what Strauss would call Oppenheimer's "falsehoods, evasions, and misrepresentations." This, plus an appeal to the zero tolerance criterion, would justify not reinstating his clearance.

In an interview that third day of the hearing, Defense Secretary Charles E. Wilson likened Oppenheimer to a bank teller with a criminal record. It was an excellent analogy for understanding the AEC counsel's strategy. For a few people, simply having a criminal record (leftist past) would be sufficient to disqualify a person from handling money (military secrets). What would be far more convincing to a much broader audience, however, would be to point out implausibilities and inconsistencies in the bank teller's *current* explanations of that record, suggest that the criminal tendencies persist into the present—or at least some uncertainty about the matter—and argue that zero tolerance of such tendencies was the only prudent course. Thus Oppenheimer's hearing would turn on more than the fact that his actions in the 1930s, when the Soviet Union was a United States ally and leftist causes had one kind of niche in academic life, could be made to appear quite differently in the 1950s, when leftist causes could be made to seem much more threatening, with the Soviet Union a mortal enemy and in possession of potentially world-destroying weapons. Rather, it was that his falsehoods, evasions, and misrepresentations could be made to appear as manifesting an ongoing character weakness that posed a continued risk in using him as an adviser privy to military secrets. No risk however small, it would be argued, was worth taking on a matter as important as national security in a time of peril.

At the beginning of that encounter on Day Three, Robb set about eliciting Oppenheimer's unaided recollections of his previous actions and claims concerning several Communist Party members, including Rudy Lambert and three former Oppenheimer students, Giovanni Lomanitz, Bernard Peters, and Joseph Weinberg. Robb was laying traps. Regarding Lambert, the trap would turn on whether Oppenheimer had lied when he claimed, in 1943, not to know what Lambert looked like; regarding Lomanitz and Weinberg, whether Oppenheimer had known that these former students of his were communists when he sought to have them employed in the Manhattan Project; regarding Peters, the trap concerned an embarrassing episode in which Oppenheimer told a HUAC committee meeting that this former student had communist leanings, then appeared to disavow this testimony after it became public. Later, on the basis of documents and wiretaps already in Robb's possession, Robb would demonstrate that Oppenheimer's statements were incorrect, and imply duplicity. Robb was in no hurry to spring the traps—only to make sure they were well set. And Oppenheimer had given him plenty of material to work with.

Late in the afternoon, Robb brought up the subject of Oppenheimer's June 1943 rendezvous with Jean Tatlock. By this time, Oppenheimer clearly sensed how thoroughly Robb was apprised of his activities, and Robb's exacting and relentless examination, coupled with uncertainty about just how much Robb knew—not to mention the anxiety of discussing this intimate event in court in his wife's presence—made the ordinarily confident and eloquent Oppenheimer stumble.

Q. You spent the night with her, didn't you?
A. Yes.
Q. That is when you were working on a secret war project?
A. Yes.
Q. Did you think that consistent with good security?
A. It was, as a matter of fact. Not a word—it was not good practice.[18]

But Robb's main coup that day concerned the so-called "Chevalier incident."

Haakon Chevalier was a leftist French professor who, in the 1930s, was at the center of a well-organized political discussion circle at Berkeley in which Oppenheimer participated. At the hearing, Oppenheimer called it a discussion group. Chevalier called it as a "secret unit" of the Communist Party whose members for safety reasons did not have open party membership.

Documents that have surfaced recently in the Soviet archives and discussed by Gregg Herken in his book, *Brotherhood of the Bomb,* reinforce the impression that Soviet contacts viewed this group as a secret unit, and Oppenheimer as an unlisted party member in it.[19] (These documents do not show any evidence of him spying.) On the one hand, as Herken notes and as a careful reading suggests, the documents are full of overinflated claims by the agents who sent them. The agents were anxious to impress their bosses, especially by as important a figure as Oppenheimer (whom they called the "big shot"), and were known to grossly exaggerate contacts and activities. The documents do not prove that Oppenheimer was a Communist Party member. And if the criterion for Communist Party membership is the existence of a membership card bearing one's name, one may say with almost complete confidence that such proof does not exist. On the other hand, Party membership was not always clear, intentionally or not. Bart Bernstein once proposed the following criterion for Party membership: if one joined a group all of whose other members *thought* they were thereby members of the Communist Party. By this admittedly but deliberately vague criterion the evidence leans toward the legitimacy of calling Oppenheimer a party member. Ironically, the FBI's efforts to look for black and white evidence of something inherently murky nearly made Oppenheimer look entirely innocent of the charge that he was a communist, for a membership card was the one thing he did not have.

The "incident" occurred sometime in the winter of 1942–1943; thus, after Robert had been chosen to head the Los Alamos laboratory but before it actually opened. Chevalier and his wife Barbara came to dinner with Robert and Kitty at their Eagle Hill home. At one point, Barbara and Kitty were playing a duet on the piano and Robert went into the pantry to mix drinks; Haakon followed him and a discussion ensued in which Haakon told Robert that their mutual friend George C. Eltenton had a means of getting technical information to the Soviets, an apparent invitation to pass on secrets, which Robert refused.

At first, Oppenheimer kept this episode to himself. Months later, he mentioned it to Army intelligence but refused to divulge the name of the person contacting him. In the following years, he told several different versions of the episode, and at the hearing would say that his earliest had been "a cock-and-bull story":

> *Version number 1* (August 26, 1943, Berkeley), told to security officer Boris Pash: Oppenheimer says that Eltenton had approached three members of the Manhattan Project through intermediaries, but does not mention Chevalier.

Version number 2 (Dec. 12, 1943, Los Alamos), told to General Groves: Oppenheimer says the intermediary is Chevalier, and that Frank Oppenheimer was the one contacted.

Version number 3 (April 14, 1954), told at the hearing in response to Robb's questioning: Oppenheimer says that Chevalier said that Eltenton had "means of getting technical information to Soviet scientists," and "I thought I said, 'But that is treason,' but I am not sure."

Version number 4 (after the hearing), which Kitty and Robert told Oppenheimer's secretary Verna Hobson as the "real" story, who later relayed it to Pais:[20]

HC came in. K saw that something was up. She didn't want R to be alone with HC and so went in the kitchen too. When HC spoke up, it was *Kitty* who said that would be treason. R never let on to that, in order to protect K.

Added Hobson:

R relied on Kitty for practical & political judgment. After HC meeting in the kitchen R told K of his intent to tell the "original" cock & bull story to the security people. K said *that won't do.*[21]

At the hearing, Robb elicited Oppenheimer's version of the story, his confession that the earliest version had been a "cock-and-bull story," then dwelt on it some more:

Q. Did you tell Pash the truth about this thing?
A. No.
Q. You lied to him?
A. Yes . . .
Q. Didn't you say that X had approached three people?
A. Probably.
Q. Why did you do that, Doctor?
A. Because I was an idiot.[22]

Robb had what he wanted: Oppenheimer's frank admission to having lied. This was a key part of the convicted bank teller strategy, for it invited the question: If he had lied once, why not again? But Oppenheimer had also stumbled badly after Robb's request for an explanation. Oppenheimer might have said something to the following effect: "I was trying to protect a dear friend, and was then prideful and arrogant enough to think that I could get away with it." This would have rung true, bolstered perception of his integrity, and countered the convicted bank teller strategy. Instead, Oppenheimer produced another evasion. It was one thing to call onself an idiot in informal company as a brush-off to change the subject, and another to do so in a legal context where one's character was the issue.

Later that evening, Robb told his wife, "I've just seen a man destroy himself."[23] But back in the hearing room, he relentlessly hammered away at Oppenheimer, dwelling on and dramatizing the lie.

> Q. Isn't it a fair statement today, Dr. Oppenheimer, that according to your testimony now you told not one lie to Colonel Pash, but a whole fabrication and tissue of lies?
> A. Right.
> Q. In great circumstantial detail, is that correct?
> A. Right.

Oppenheimer's evasions did not bother some people in physics circles; for Rabi, indeed, they manifested Oppenheimer's childlike streak. "He could tell sort of stories like that, in this harmless kind of way," Rabi once said, referring to the Chevalier incident. "I didn't take a very strong view of that because I found it somewhat endearing that he had clay feet."[24] But hardliners like Strauss did not find Oppenheimer's clay feet endearing; a clay-footed man was the very definition of someone whom they wanted out of classified circles. Over the next three weeks of the hearing, Robb would repeatedly use Oppenheimer's admission about the Chevalier incident to deflate not only Oppenheimer, but nearly all of the notables who came to deliver encomiums on his behalf. Robb would point again and again to those clay feet, asking how one could be sure they had hardened up; and even if they had hardened up whether there wasn't a danger that they might return; and whether Oppenheimer's lameness in accounting for them didn't show that he still had them.

For instance, the Chevalier incident loomed in the background during the testimony of the first pro-Oppenheimer witness, General Leslie R. Groves. Strauss met with Groves before the trial, and passed on to Robb suggestions as to what questions to ask, and what Groves's answers would be. Under Garrison's questioning, Groves painted a flattering portrait of Oppenheimer, calling him a hard worker—"he worked harder at times than I wanted him to, because I was afraid he would break down under it." Then came Robb's questioning:

> Q. General, in the light of your experience with security matters and in the light of your knowledge of the file pertaining to Dr. Oppenheimer, would you clear Dr. Oppenheimer today?

Groves first gave his interpretation of the provision of the Atomic Energy Act requirement that persons with access to restricted data should not "endanger the common defense or security," and that its investigations should include "character, associations, and loyalty," then added, "In this case I refer particularly to associations and not to the associations as they exist today but the past record of the associations. I would not clear Dr. Oppenheimer today if I were a member of the Commission on the basis of this interpretation."

Later that day, Oppenheimer returned to the stand. Robb questioned him further about his associations, and sprang his traps about Lambert, Lomanitz, Peters, and Weinberg. The results illustrated the core of the convicted bank teller strategy, and clearly made an impression on Gray. For the next day, Friday, Gray asked Oppenheimer whether he had not been caught in a conflict between "loyalty to an individual," that is, to his friends, and "a broader obligation," that is, to his country, and how he would handle this conflict in the future. In the case of at least Peters, Gray seems to have found Oppenheimer's reply evasive.

Pro-Oppenheimer witnesses who appeared on Friday included former AEC Commissioner T. Keith Glennan, former MIT president Karl T. Compton, and John Landsdale, Jr. Landsdale was an important witness, as the former head of Security and Intelligence for the Manhattan District, and one to whom Oppenheimer had told the earliest version of the Chevalier "cock-and-bull" story. But Robb skillfully used the incident to blunt Landsdale's positive judgment of Oppenheimer.

> Q. Colonel Landsdale, as a lawyer are you familiar with the legal maxim, "Falsus in uno, falsus in omnibus"?
> A. Yes; I am. Like all legal maxims, it is a generalization, and not of particular significance when applied to specifics.
> Q. When you are trying a jury case and the veracity of a witness is in question, do you request the court to give an instruction on that subject?
> A. Oh, certainly; don't you?
> Q. Certainly, I want to know that you do.
> A. The instruction usually is that the jury may, but does not have to, take that as an indication, and the judgment is to be exercised in the particular case.
> Q. And when you are trying a jury case and you examine a witness on the opposite side and you demonstrate that he has lied, don't you argue to the jury from that that they should disregard his evidence?
> A. You are speaking now as to what I as an advocate do?
> Q. Yes.
> A. It depends on circumstances; usually I do.
> Q. Sure. Any lawyer worth his salt would.
> A. Particularly if it is my belief.
> Q. Yes, sir.
> Robb That is all.[25]

Landsdale, however, was one of the few witnesses who could spar effectively with Robb. After Landsdale testified that the Chevalier incident was the only time that he knew of Oppenheimer lying to him, and that Oppenheimer's "veracity is good," and Robb pointed out that Los Alamos security officer Peer de Silva had a considerably harsher view of Oppenheimer's veracity than Landsdale's, the two had the following exchange:

Q. He [de Silva] was a professional; was he not?
A. Oh, yes . . . we were all professionals.
Q. He was certainly more of a professional than you were; wasn't he, Colonel?
A. In what field?
Q. The field he was working in, security.
A. No.
Q. No?
A. No.
Q. He was a graduate of West Point; wasn't he?
A. Certainly. I am a graduate of VMI, too. You want to fight about that?[26]

It was one of the few times a witness succeeded in making Robb back down. It was also a demonstration of a might-have-been; how a more experienced prosecutorial lawyer might have handled Robb. Garrison, a gentleman accustomed to civil battles in appellate courts before important judges, was the wrong person for the kind of battle being pressed.

In 1979, Pais met the 81-year-old Garrison at his Park Avenue law office, finding him "friendly and courteous . . . a gentleman, strong but not tough" whose "light blue eyes can be friendly but also hard." In an hour and a half long meeting, Pais "did much talking for the purpose of drawing him out." but was generally unsuccessful, with Garrison often citing "the lawyer-client aspect of his relationship with RO," the fact that he still felt "that the episode was a very painful one" and that "when it was over he wanted to make a clean break with it and cease involvement." Pais did get Garrison to speak about how, once each day's hearings were over, he and Oppenheimer would go to the house of Garrison's law partner Randolph Paul, where Oppenheimer and Kitty were staying, and talk about the day's events. (For a while, the children were sent to Rochester, New York, in the care of Louis Hemplemann, who had been the pediatrician at Los Alamos, and his wife.) In these and other social settings after the trial, Garrison told Pais, no closeness developed between the two men. On one trip together, probably between Princeton and New York, Garrison tried to engage Oppenheimer on something other than the hearings—on "the mysterious forces in the universe"—but Oppenheimer did not respond.[27] Pais noted to himself after the interview, "My impression is that he had deep feelings for the cause of justice and also for RO as a person. Yet that in the course of the events he (G.) had looked into abysses he would rather forget from now on. His principal comment on the hearings was: 'They slayed him—inch by inch.'"[28]

It would have taken remarkable foresight for Garrison to have prepared for the kind of warfare taking place in Room 2022. Assuming the hearing to be fair, he went out of his way at first to avoid challenges that might offend the judges and thus wound up failing to protect his client properly. Even if he had known just how rigged the hearing was, Garrison would not necessarily have been successful, for Oppenheimer had mined his own terrain. Still, Landsdale's cross-examination revealed how someone who was less a gentleman, who was strong and tough, might have contested every one of those inches.

At the end of Week One, Robb and Strauss were thrilled. Robb thanked FBI agent Bates for the "thoroughness and promptness with which the FBI had answered each and every request." Strauss told Bates that he was "most happy" with the way that the hearings were going and remarked that "if this case is won it is primarily due to the excellent job the FBI has done," expressing appreciation for the "close cooperation" between the AEC and the FBI in preparing for the case.[29]

Most of Week Two was devoted to more Oppenheimer notables: former AEC chairman Gordon Dean, Institute member and government adviser George Kennan, former AEC chairman Lilienthal, former Harvard University President Conant, Nobel laureate Enrico Fermi, former AEC Commissioner Sumner T. Pike, future Nobel laureate Norman Ramsey, Nobel laureate and GAC Chairman I. I. Rabi, Los Alamos lab director Norris Bradbury, MIT chemistry department chairman Walter Whitman, former GAC member Hartley Rowe, Caltech president Lee DuBridge, General Electric administrator Harry Winne, and the wartime director of the Office of Scientific Research and Development Vannevar Bush. (A few other pro-Oppenheimer notables, including John J. McCloy, Robert Bacher, and John von Neumann, would appear in third week, as would Kitty Oppenheimer.) Several said they shared Oppenheimer's thinking on the hydrogen bomb; Conant, for instance, remarked that if one took the view that opposition to it made one ineligible for atomic energy work then that would apply to him, for "I opposed it strongly, as strongly as anybody else on that committee."[30] Others argued that loyalty was best judged, not by applying rules, but by those who knew and worked alongside a person. Kennan said of Oppenheimer's previous associations with the likes of Chevalier: "I suppose most of us have had friends or associates whom we have come to regard as misguided in the course of time, and I don't like to think that people in senior capacity in Government should not be permitted or conceded maturity of judgment to know when they can see such a person or when they can't. If they come to you sometimes, I think it is impossible for you to turn them away abruptly or in a cruel way, simply because you are afraid of association with them, so long as what they are asking of you is nothing that affects your government work."

Kennan added that this was a matter of "Christian charity." Of course, others saw more arrogance than charity in Oppenheimer's cavalier associations. As Rabi said later, "[H]e had such complete confidence in his reputation and integrity and accomplishment that he felt he could . . . go and sup with Stalin."[31]

But Robb repeatedly and effectively used the Chevalier strategy to blunt the force of their judgments. At times, the tactics were dirtier. Documents had been secretly removed from Lilienthal's files, meaning that the former AEC chairman did not see these documents while preparing for his testimony in Oppenheimer's favor, leaving him vulnerable to an ambush by Robb.

There were a few dramatic moments, including the appearance of I. I. Rabi. Rabi was as sharp-tongued as Oppenheimer, more politically savvy, and unafraid to talk back. He had nothing to hide, and was liked by President Eisenhower. Rabi was even more cantankerous than usual, having spent the previous evening over a pitcher of martinis with AEC Commissioner Pike, having assumed that he would be testifying in the afternoon as scheduled, but having been rudely awakened by an early-morning call saying that he had to testify right away and would not have time to sleep it off. "[Oppenheimer] is a consultant, and if you don't want to consult the guy, you don't consult him, period. Why you have to then proceed to suspend clearance and go through all this sort of thing, he is only there when called, and that is all there was to it. So it didn't seem to me the sort of thing that called for this kind of proceeding at all against a man who had accomplished what Dr. Oppenheimer has accomplished. There is a real positive record. . . . We have an A-bomb . . . and what more do you want, mermaids?"

This last became a famous quip often cited in physics circles for years afterwards in bitter remembrance. "I don't think it [the remark] was from the resources of a classical education," Rabi would recall years later. "[I]t was a disrespectful remark to make under those circumstances. . . . I was so annoyed, so angry with them, with those people sitting in judgment of a man who was so much better than any of them. . . ."[32]

One of the few moments of insight that occurred during the testimony was provided by John von Neumann who in 1949 had been a strong H-bomb supporter. When Robb raised the Chevalier episode, von Neumann said,

Look, you have to view the performance and the character of a man as a whole. This episode, if true, would make me think that the course of the year 1943 or in 1942 and 1943, he was not emotionally and intellectually prepared to handle this kind of a job; that he subsequently learned how to handle it, and handled it very well, I know. I would say that all of us in the war years, and by all of us I mean all people in scientific technical occupations, got suddenly in contact with a universe we had not known before. I mean this peculiar problem of security, the fact that people who looked all right might be conspirators and might be spies. They are all things which do not enter one's normal experience in ordinary times. While we are now, most of us, quite prepared to discover such things in our entourage, we were not prepared to discover these things in 1943. So I must say that this had on anyone a shock effect, and any one of us may have behaved foolishly and ineffectively and untruthfully, so this condition is something ten years later, I would not consider too serious. This would affect me the same way as if I would suddenly hear about somebody that he has had some extraordinary escapade in his adolescence. I know that neither of us were adolescents at that time, but of course we were all little children with respect to the situation which had developed, namely, that we suddenly were dealing with something with which one could blow up the world. Furthermore, we were involved in a triangular war with two of our enemies had done suddenly the nice thing of fighting each other. But after all, they were still enemies. This was a very peculiar situation. None of us had been educated or conditioned to exist in this situation, and we had to make our rationalization and our code of conduct as we went along. For some people it took 2 months, for some 2 years, and for some 1 year. I am quite sure that all of us by now have developed the necessary code of ethics and the necessary resistance.[33]

The first anti-Oppenheimer witnesses appeared on Week Three. It was unprecedented for witnesses against a subject to appear at a hearing. Strauss and Robb had arranged for eight: four University of California scientists who had worked on the Manhattan Project (Luis Alvarez, Wendell Latimer, Kenneth Pitzer, and Edward Teller), two individuals from the Air Force (General Roscoe Wilson and David Griggs), Pash, and William Borden. Strauss and Robb had sought more, including the influential physicist and Nobel laureate Ernest Lawrence, who initially agreed but, fearful of antagonizing Oppenheimer's powerful friends, withdrew at the last minute, citing an attack of ulcerative colitis—probably a classic example of a psychosomatic illness brought on by stress. Several witnesses mentioned that their appearance was not voluntary, but that they were appearing under orders of others—including, in one case, AEC General Manager Nichols himself. The testimony of these witnesses (except for Pash) was mainly devoted to Oppenheimer's positions on the hydrogen bomb and various other national defense programs with a nuclear component, such as the Vista Project and the Strategic Air Command. Several witnesses admitted that they had been direct and virulent opponents of Oppenheimer on various policy matters, with Griggs even confessing that he "may not be fully capable of objectivity" on such issues.[34] One remarkable piece of Griggs's testimony was his claim to having seen Zacharias write the acronym "ZORC" on a blackboard at a meeting of the Scientific Advisory Board in Cambridge, which allegedly stood for the first initials of four scientists

(Zacharias, Oppenheimer, Rabi, and Charlie Lauritsen) who were trying to make an argument against the need for offensive nuclear weapons.

Edward Teller appeared on Wednesday April 28. Like Oppenheimer, Teller was a controversial and contradictory figure who inspired deep passions. He has been called "the most politically influential scientist of the twentieth century."[35] Yet he was the antithesis of the conventional image of the paragon scientist. He was prickly and sensitive. He had a famously selective memory, especially when it came to contributions by others. He regarded his weapons work as a duty. He often used political considerations to trump technical objections to his favorite projects. But in Lawrence's absence, Teller was key to the anti-Oppenheimer forces, as the only scientist among their witnesses of Oppenheimer's scientific caliber.

Having been fortunate enough to have escaped Nazi Germany, Teller wrote in his *Memoirs*, "I had the obligation to do whatever I could to protect freedom." But he often interpreted "protect" to mean stigmatizing colleagues who insufficiently shared his political enthusiasms. Philip Morrison, Robert Serber, and Steven Weinberg were among the eminent U.S. physicists whose careers Teller denounced or otherwise tried to harm careers in retaliation for their political views.

Before Los Alamos, "there was great love between Teller and Oppenheimer."[36] The love continued for some months after the laboratory opened, with Oppenheimer having individual meetings with Teller once a week—highly unusual for the busy director. Oppenheimer clearly appreciated both Teller's contributions and his prickliness.[37] The love soon soured. In his *Memoirs*, Teller claims to pinpoint the moment "that the relationship between us changed" to a remark Oppenheimer made at the beginning of the Manhattan Project to the effect that, while scientists have to cooperate with the likes of Groves, "the time is coming when we will have to do things differently and resist the military."[38] This is unconvincing, an example of Teller's penchant for zealously interpreting off-hand remarks by associates as policy statements. More plausible sources of Teller's animosity are the fact that Oppenheimer appointed Bethe head of the Theoretical Division rather than Teller, and Oppenheimer's insistence during the Manhattan Project that the scientists focus on the matter at hand rather than Teller's pet project, a thermonuclear bomb—a resentment which, after the war, matured into open hostility with Oppenheimer's opposition to the Super.

In *Memoirs*, Teller writes that he arrived in Washington for the hearing prepared to say that Oppenheimer should be cleared, but changed his mind when Robb showed him portions of the transcript of the hearing thus far.[39]

This is one of many points of variance between Teller's words and the historical record. Teller was instrumental in providing Nichols and Strauss with harmful information against Oppenheimer; in Nichols's letter to Oppenheimer of December 23, detailing the allegations against him, extensive excerpts from Teller's FBI interview (based on what was said to be a "prominent scientist") show up in three of the four paragraphs concerning his alleged opposition to the Super. In March 1954, Teller told Robb "that Oppenheimer has given a great deal of bad advice in the matter of the H-bomb, and that in the future his advice should not be taken and he should never have any more influence" and that "he hoped Oppenheimer's clearance would not be lifted."[40] In his testimony Teller went on at length about Oppenheimer's lack of contributions to and support for the hydrogen bomb project. But by far the most dramatic, and often-cited, of Teller's statements was the following: "I would like to see the vital interests of this country in hands which I understand better, and therefore trust more."

Few people, it is safe to say, understood Oppenheimer—Fermi, for instance, on his deathbed after a visit from Teller told Yang that "I always understood Edward, but I did not always understand Oppenheimer."[41] But Oppenheimer inspired in Teller a particular aversion. Surely the most significant clue to this is Teller's mention, in *Memoirs*, of his childhood fear of the dark. Oppenheimer, one of the most enigmatic historical figures of the twentieth century, had a profound and intense dark side. He surely must have terrified Teller, a man with no tolerance for mystery, no sympathy for the ambiguous aspects of human nature.

Teller's testimony, while not decisive, was the psychological coup de grace of the prosecution. It was only the most spectacular play of a game whose rules were stacked against Oppenheimer. Teller, coached by Robb, was the perfect player: authoritative, sincere, and able to insinuate effectively what he could not state truthfully. The Oppenheimer trial would cast a long shadow over Teller's life and career—acquaintances describe him often returning obsessively to Oppenheimer in extended conversations—which he neither would, nor should, ever escape.

Week Three ended with the appearance of William Borden, the final anti-Oppenheimer witness. Over Oppenheimer's attorneys' objections, he proceeded to read his letter of November 7, 1953, that had triggered the hearing, which accused Oppenheimer of being "more probably than not . . . an agent of the Soviet Union." It was the first Oppenheimer or Garrison knew of this letter, though—against any rudimentary notion of fairness—the Board had been in possession of it all along. After a few perfunctory questions by Robb, the hearing adjourned for the weekend.

Week Four began with Garrison announcing that Borden would not be cross-examined. Over the weekend, Oppenheimer's attorneys had argued whether to do so, but finally decided that, in view of an assurance Gray had made that the Board had "no evidence" for the principal allegations of the letter, cross-examining Borden would be counter-productive and draw yet more attention to Oppenheimer's vulnerabilities. Borden thus stepped down from the witness stand without testifying, his letter seemingly discounted by both sides. "It was as if the match that had ignited the fire had been snuffed out," remarks Stern. "Yet the fire burned on."[42]

"That is all the testimony we have to offer, Mr. Chairman," Robb said. Gray then made a crucial remark to Garrison. Much of the testimony had dwelt on matters that Nichols had not mentioned in his December 23, 1953, letter, such as Oppenheimer's actions with respect to Vista and the Strategic Air Command. Gray now said these issues had become "material to the matters under consideration by this board," indicating an expansion of the scope of the hearings to matters of policy. Yet Garrison did not object, ceding yet more territory he might have contested.

Gray then called Oppenheimer back for more questioning. He wasted no time in broaching Oppenheimer's biggest vulnerability: "I want now to go back to the so-called Chevalier incident." Reminding Oppenheimer of its various versions, Gray asked how one could tell which story was the fabrication and which the truth. Oppenheimer's rambling and unenlightening reply showed weariness and even touches of resignation. "Now, when you ask for a more persuasive argument as to why I did this than that I was an idiot, I am going to have more trouble being understandable. I think I was impelled by 2 or 3 concerns at that time. One was the feeling that I must get across the fact that if there was, as Landsdale indicated, trouble at the Radiation Laboratory, Eltenton was the guy that might very well be involved and it was serious. Whether I embroidered the story in order to underline that seriousness or whether I embroidered it to make it more tolerable that I would not tell the simple facts, namely, Chevalier had talked to me about it, I don't know. . . . [I]t was a matter of conflict for me. . . . I wish I could explain to you better why I falsified and fabricated."

Oppenheimer was followed, the next day, by Vannevar Bush, whom Oppenheimer's attorneys had called back to rebut an allegation that cast doubt on President Truman's confidence in Oppenheimer. Kitty Oppenheimer was recalled. Zacharias—the "Z" in ZORC—and Lincoln Laboratory director Albert Hill each appeared to counter Griggs's story about that episode. Then, on Wednesday, Oppenheimer himself returned. In the cross-examination, Robb posed a stunning question. "Doctor," he said, "do you think now that perhaps you went beyond the scope of your proper function as a scientist in undertaking to counsel in matters of military strategy and tactics?" Robb was challenging, in effect, not only Oppenheimer's authority to address social issues such as military policy, but that of any scientist. This challenge went unanswered.

As the lunch recess drew near, and the time for Garrison's summation, Gray brought up a point relating to the Chevalier episode, and remarked, "I think Dr. Oppenheimer's counsel ought to know that the board considers that an important item." Gray then agreed to Garrison's request to postpone continuation of the hearing until the next morning to allow him more time to prepare.

Shortly after the hearing recommenced on its final day, May 6, 1954, Garrison stood up to make his summary. At last he was in his element, in an appellate role, able to make a sustained case for his client, free of the haggles over technicalities that had consumed and bloodied him for three and a half weeks. And though he spoke from hurriedly-assembled notes, he rose to the occasion with an eloquent, two-hour long speech. The legal framework in which the charges raised by General Nichols have to be evaluated, Garrison said, is provided by two documents, the Atomic Energy Act of 1946 and Executive Order 10450. The first speaks of dangers to "the common defense and security," the second to "the interests of the national security." The "basic question" of the case of J. Robert Oppenheimer, Garrison said, "is whether in the handling of restricted data he is to be trusted. That, it seems to me, is what confronts this board, that bare, blunt question."

In deciding that issue, Garrison continued, the relevant guidelines speak of "character, associations, and loyalty." "Certainly loyalty is the paramount consideration. If a man is loyal, if in his heart he loves his country and would not knowingly or willingly do anything to injure its security, then associations and character become relatively unimportant." He then shrewdly produced an AEC decision in the 1948 security clearance hearing of Frank Graham, who, like Gray, had been president of the University of North Carolina. Though Graham "has been associated at times with individuals or organizations influenced by motives or views of Communist derivation," the AEC decision read, it must be recognized "that it is the man himself the Commission is actually concerned with, that the associations are only evidentiary, and that commonsense must be exercised in judging their significance."

In judging the man himself, Garrison said, in returning to "the basic acid question" before the board, "the most impelling single fact . . . is that for more than a decade Dr. Oppenheimer has created and has shared secrets of the atomic energy program and has held them inviolable . . . for more than a decade Dr. Oppenheimer has been trusted, and . . . he has not failed that trust. That in my judgment is the most persuasive evidence that you could possibly have."

What, then, is behind this case against him? Two items stand out, Garrison said: Oppenheimer's 1949 opposition to the H-bomb development, and his "leftwing associations and related incidents through 1943." The short response to the first, Garrison said, is that it involves "simply an honest difference of opinion"; to the second, that the essentials were known to General Groves and to the AEC itself when it cleared him in 1947. In his lengthier response to the first, Garrison pointed out how absurdly Machiavellian a portrait Oppenheimer's opponents had painted. Could it really be true, Garrison asked, that Oppenheimer's advice, "unlike that of every other member of the GAC, was motivated by a sinister purpose to injure the United States of America, and to help our enemy," adding that "the mere utterance of that proposition is somehow shocking to me." Even Oppenheimer's fiercest critics questioned his wisdom, not his loyalty. Given all his efforts on behalf of the U.S. defense and nuclear weapons program, "it is fantastic to suppose that . . . he should be harboring a motive to destroy his own country in favor of Russia." Whatever evidence for a "pattern of opposition" to this program has, indeed, fallen apart. "This whole H-bomb controversy, all of the rest of these things, Vista, Lincoln, and all the rest of them, that we have been talking about, except as indicating an affirmative attitude, as I believe, toward the strengthening of the United States, have nothing to do with the question of Dr. Oppenheimer's clearance unless you are willing to believe . . . the unthinkable thought . . . that in spite of everything he had done to help this country from 1945 on, he suddenly somehow became a sinister agent of a foreign power."

Turning to his lengthy answer to the second item, the question of Oppenheimer's leftwing associations, Garrison said he would address the Chevalier incident in some detail because of the importance that Gray himself had given it.

> Now, this whole Chevalier incident has, I am convinced, assumed undue importance, and must be judged in perspective. It has been so extensively analyzed here in cross-examination, in the reading of transcripts of interviews of 11 years ago, the hearing of a recording, Colonel Pash's presence here, it is almost as if this whole Chevalier case brought into this room here at 16th and Constitution Avenue in 1954 had happened yesterday in the setting of today, and that we are

judging a man for something that has happened almost in our presence. I get that illusion of a foreshortening of time here which to me is a grisly matter and very, very misleading. This happened in 1943. It happened in a wholly different atmosphere from that of today. Russia was our so-called gallant ally. The whole attitude toward Russia, toward persons who were sympathetic with Russia, everything was different from what obtains today. I think you must beware above everything of judging by today's standards things that happened in a different time and era.

Garrison reminded the board of the judgments of Groves and Landsdale, who by virtue of their perspective in time and place were able to trust Oppenheimer even after the Chevalier incident. Garrison also elaborated at length Oppenheimer's AEC clearance hearing of 1947. He appealed to the depth and thoroughness with which Oppenheimer's witnesses knew him, and to the intangible nature of trust, which Garrison saw as lying at the core of security: "Every one of these men who has appeared here have been men who have worked with Dr. Oppenheimer, who have seen him on the job and off the job, who have formed judgments about character which is the way human beings do judge one another. How do we learn to trust one another except by knowing each other? How can we define the elements of that trust except to say, 'I know that man,' 'I have worked with that man?' That is what it comes down to. How else can you express it? These men have known him and have worked with him, and have lived with him."

Garrison reminded the board of the high estimation that these men had of Oppenheimer. Then he turned back to how the board might go about evaluating "the acid question" of trust:

Here he is now with his life in one sense in your hands, and you are asked to say whether if he continues to have access to restricted data he may injure the United States of America, and make improper use of that. For over a decade that he has had this position of sharing in the atomic energy information, never a suggestion of an improper use of data. His life has been an open book. . . . I beg of you, as I wind up now my conclusion, to take the straightforward commonsense judgment that the Commission took in the case of R. Graham, and look at the whole man. "It must be recognized that it is the man himself that the Commission is actually concerned with. Associations are only evidentiary, and commonsense must be exercised in judging their significance." There is the whole thing in a nutshell. . . . The thing that I would most urge you not to do, in addition to not bringing 1943 into 1954, is to get chopped up into little compartments of categories that will give to this case a perfectly artificial flavor of judgment, that you will treat it in the round and the large with the most careful consideration of the evidence, and then treat it as men would treat a problem of human nature, which can't be cut up into little pieces.

Reaching his conclusion, Garrison said,

> There is more than Dr. Oppenheimer on trial in this room. I use the word "trial" advisedly. The Government of the United States is here on trial also. Our whole security process is on trial here, and is in your keeping as is his life—the two things together. There is an anxiety abroad in this country, and I think I am at liberty to say this to you, because after all, we are all Americans, we are all citizens, and we are all interested here in doing what is in the public interest, and what is best for our country. There is an anxiety abroad that these security procedures will be applied artificially, rigidly, like some monolithic kind of a machine that will result in the destruction of men of great gifts and of great usefulness to the country by the application of rigid and mechanical tests. America must not devour her own children, Mr. Chairman and members of this board. If we are to be strong, powerful, electric, and vital, we must not devour the best and the most gifted of our citizens in some mechanical application of security procedures and mechanisms.

Observing that Oppenheimer was "a very complicated man . . . a gifted man . . . unique, sole, not conventional, not quite like anybody else that ever was or ever will be," he urged them "to exercise the greatest effort of comprehension" in judging "the whole man." "I am confident . . . that when you have done all this, you will answer the blunt and ugly question whether he is fit to be trusted with restricted data, in the affirmative. I believe, members of the board, that in doing so you will most deeply serve the interests of the United States of America, which all of us love and want to protect and further. That I am sure of, and I am sure that is where the upshot of this case must be. Thank you very much."

Garrison's speech—moments of it, anyway—are the only moving and eloquent part of the proceedings. But it was delivered to the wrong audience, and it motivated nothing in the way of response or discussion. Gray spent a few moments reviewing what would come next: the Board would send its findings to Nichols, who would write to Oppenheimer, who in the event of a negative finding could appeal to the five AEC commissioners. Gray then declared, "We are now in recess." And so, on May 6, the nineteenth day of the hearing, the Gray panel adjourned and its three members took a break, returning to their homes.

Findings, Appeal, Decision: May 17–June 29

The Gray panel members reconvened on May 17. Gray and Morgan voted not to reinstate Oppenheimer's clearance, while Evans dissented. The panel members then wrote up their findings for Nichols.[43]

Aware that this document, dated May 27, would become public and fuel a controversy already swirling about the trial, Gray and Morgan reassured "the people of our country" of its fairness. Noting that policies and actions "taken in the interests of national security" can potentially "pose a threat to our ideals," they nodded to Garrison in saying that "this case puts the security system of the United States on trial." Not to worry, it passed with flying colors. The hearing, they wrote, was conducted "in calmness, in fairness, in disregard of public clamor and private pressures, and with dignity." More: "We believe that it has been demonstrated that the Government can search its own soul and the soul of an individual whose relationship to his Government is in question with full protection of the rights and interests of both," that is, "within the frameworks of the traditional and inviolable principles of American justice." No mention was made of the numerous differences between the procedures of Oppenheimer's hearing and those of an ordinary civil trial, or between Oppenheimer's hearing and any other PSB hearing thus far, or even between Oppenheimer's hearing and a hearing conducted according to the AEC's own regulations governing such procedures.

How had they proceeded? Gray and Morgan again alluded to Garrison and his appeal to use the "whole man" criterion when they said they had not considered the matter "a fragmented one either in terms of specific criteria or in terms of any period in Dr. Oppenheimer's life, or . . . loyalty, character, and associations separately." Tellingly, though, they described their task as to address "the whole question"—by which they meant, national security. This allowed them to reject (with a meaningless qualification) the "whole man" approach in favor of zero tolerance: "There can be no tampering with the national security, which in times of peril must be absolute, and without concessions for reasons of admiration, gratitude, reward, sympathy, or charity. Any doubts whatsoever must be resolved in favor of the national security."

Of which they had plenty. At pains to prevent Oppenheimer's martyrdom, Gray and Morgan raked over the specifics. They sprinkled the letter with references to Oppenheimer's "deep devotion to his country," twice said he was "a loyal citizen," and remarked that he "seems to have had a high degree of discretion reflecting an unusual ability to keep to himself vital secrets." Nevertheless, they carefully recited every one of Nichols's 24 allegations, with evidence to show that, with a single exception, all were true or substantially so. That one—#17, involving Oppenheimer's alleged appearance, in the summer of 1941, at a Communist Party meeting at his house at 10 Kenilworth Court in Berkeley—was "inconclusive." Moreover, they added concerns not mentioned in Nichols's letter, in particular a meeting between Oppenheimer and Chevalier as recently as December 1953.

Oppenheimer, they decided, was vulnerable to the zero tolerance strategy in four different respects: in his present inability to account satisfactorily for his past duplicities, coverups, and evasions; in his current associations with supposedly risky individuals notably Chevalier; in his alleged "susceptibility to influence;" and in his opposition to the Super. This last continued to have special status. While it had been the driving force behind the hearing, and had some potential of manifesting Oppenheimer's supposed weakness toward national security, it had to be delicately handled lest the hearing appear to be punishment for a policy difference. Thus Gray and Morgan worded their discussion of it carefully. They said that the Board was "unable to make a categorical finding" concerning whether Oppenheimer had slowed down its development, and did "not find that Dr. Oppenheimer urged other scientists not to work on the program" as Teller had claimed. Still, "enthusiastic support on his part would perhaps have encouraged other leading scientists to work on the program," and his leading role in the opposition "did delay the initiation of concerted effort which led to the development of a thermonuclear weapon." This wording invited much sarcasm and ridicule among Oppenheimer's supporters, many of whom wondered aloud whether national security was really safer in the hands of an enthusiast such as Teller, who was known to champion politically attractive but technically unfeasible systems—high-tech Maginot lines.

Gray and Morgan therefore concluded that Oppenheimer's "continuing conduct and associations have reflected a serious disregard for the requirements of the security system," he exhibited "a susceptibility to influence which could have serious implications for the security interests of the country," his conduct with respect to the Super program was "sufficiently disturbing as to raise a doubt as to whether his future participation . . . would be clearly consistent with the best interests of security," and he "has been less than candid in several instances in his testimony before this Board."

Evans's dissent was a surprise. Before the hearing, he had had a reputation for voting against clearances. During it, his interventions had been tame and noncommittal, though at one dinner his anti-Semitic tirade had troubled Gray, who worried about discredit to the Board should Evans's attitude leak out. At the end of the hearing, Gray contained his surprise on receiving a draft of Evans's conclusion, but noted that it was badly written. Again fearing discredit should the Board's one document favorable to Oppenheimer be poorly written, Gray asked Robb to improve it. Robb did so, but not too much. Evans's minority report is still clumsy and pedestrian, agrees with much of the majority opinion, skirts arguing with the rest, and its most memorable sentence—"I personally think that our failure to clear Dr. Oppenheimer will be a black mark on the escutcheon of our country"—is an embarrassing cliché, though it was often quoted by Oppenheimer allies.

After receiving a copy of the Board's letter to Nichols, Garrison composed a sharply worded letter of rebuttal. On June 12, Nichols sent his own even more sharply worded recommendation to the five AEC commissioners, without showing it to Oppenheimer or Garrison. Security was all-important given the current crisis involving "the horrible prospects of hydrogen bomb warfare if all-out war should be forced upon us." Nichols invoked the zero tolerance principle, writing that it was not sufficient to find a person loyal, for "substantial deficiency in any one of the three factors—character, associations, or loyalty" may be found to "endanger the common defense or security."

And he found deficiencies galore in Oppenheimer's record. Regarding character: the Chevalier episode shows that Oppenheimer is "not reliable or trustworthy," that he is guilty of "deliberate misrepresentations and falsifications," that his conduct is "dishonest" and "criminal." Regarding associations: his record shows that he "was deeply and consciously involved with hardened and militant Communists at a time when he was a man of mature judgment . . . a Communist in every respect except for the fact that he did not carry a party card." Next to these findings, and the framework in which Nichols was considering them, it mattered little that he wrote that the record shows "no direct evidence" that Oppenheimer "is disloyal to the United States." Nichols, like Gray and Morgan, carefully added a section clearly labeled "Finding of Security Risk Is Not Based on Dr. Oppenheimer's Opinions," saying that while he found "no sinister motives" in Oppenheimer's attitude toward the hydrogen bomb, his lack of "enthusiastic support" was "disturbing." Therefore "Dr. Oppenheimer's clearance should not be reinstated."

By the time Nichols sent his recommendation to the commissioners, an ironic deadline loomed: on June 30, Oppenheimer's 1-year contract as an AEC consultant would expire and the entire issue would become moot. The five Commissioners—Strauss, Joseph Campbell, Thomas E. Murray, Eugene Zuckert, and Henry DeWolf Smyth—knew it would not only be absurd, but invite ridicule, to permit the proceedings to overstep that date, and worked furiously to complete their work. On June 29, they announced that they had voted, 4–1, against restoring Oppenheimer's clearance.

They released their decision in a document that had a majority opinion, three concurring opinions, and a dissent (Smyth's). The authors of the majority opinion, like Nichols, pointed out that disloyalty was "only one" basis for disqualification for employment by the AEC, the other two being "substantial defects of character and imprudent and dangerous associations." And they had found not only that his "falsehoods, evasions, and misrepresentations" pointed to "fundamental defects" in Oppenheimer's character, but also that, even after the war, he has had "persistent and continuing association with Communists."

Smyth wrote a direct and thoughtful reply: "With respect to the alleged disregard of the security system, I would suggest that the system itself is nothing to worship. It is a necessary means to an end. Its sole purpose, apart from the prevention of sabotage, is to protect secrets. If a man protects the secrets he has in his hands and his head, he has shown essential regard for the security system."

Smyth added: "In my opinion the conclusion drawn by the majority from the evidence is so extreme as to endanger the security system."[44]

It is tempting to cite the various criteria that the Commissioners said they used to make their decision, to point out contradictions between these and criteria invoked by Gray and Nichols at different times throughout the proceedings, and then say that this demonstrates the unfair handicap Garrison had in trying to defend Oppenheimer. This would miss the point: shifting criteria of "loyalty" and "risk" shed only partial light on the mismatch between the inquiry and the result, for one needs to appreciate what Bart Bernstein calls the "deeper politics" of the hearing "that helps explain the final results."[45] A more important clue is found in the way that the AEC's decision and the various concurring opinions therein, like the Board's findings and the general manager's recommendation, protest too much in downplaying the role of Oppenheimer's opposition to the hydrogen bomb. This issue had occupied a large part, perhaps a fifth, of the hearing. And notes and letters by Strauss and others during and after the hearing—including one from Bradbury to Strauss warning of the reaction in the scientific community to a finding that this opposition had hurt Oppenheimer—reveal the continuing sensitivity and even fear of overplaying Oppenheimer's opposition to the Super program lest it provoke a backlash in the scientific community that would hurt the weapons program.

Eisenhower was pleased, and the day the decision was released called Strauss to congratulate him on his actions in the matter, which had prevented McCarthy from becoming involved—indicating the deeper politics that had worried the president.

The FBI continued, even intensified, its surveillance and investigations during the hearing and its immediate aftermath. "[I]n view of the importance of this case in the public eye and its importance to other agencies, we must be doubly alert to cover every possible aspect with whatever additional investigation is necessary."[46] The FBI files reveal frenzied attempts to investigate whether Zacharias wrote "ZORC" on the blackboard, whether Oppenheimer had on his recent trip to Paris contacted the science attaché at the U.S. embassy on behalf of Chevalier, whether the nickname "Opje" had any "special significance" (upon noting that Chevalier had addressed Oppenheimer that way),"[47] and whether there was any proof that Oppenheimer was really present at 10 Kenilworth Court in the summer of 1941.

Strauss and the FBI considered pursuing further legal action against Oppenheimer, probably to involve the Kenilworth Court episode, but ultimately dropped it. They had solved their Oppenheimer problem. Oppenheimer was not only out of government circles, but in a way that put a substantial dent in the claim to martyrdom and headed off rebellion in the scientific community. This was due to several factors: to the release of the transcript, which showed that Oppenheimer was no saint; to Eisenhower's Atoms for Peace initiative, which meant that one could do atomic energy work without becoming an accomplice of the defense establishment; and to the fact that Oppenheimer had, after all, been more statesman than physicist for the past dozen years. The American Physical Society grumbled, saying it was "deeply disturbed" by the case, and predicted that the decision "will have an adverse effect upon the utilization of scientists in the Government,"[48] but not much more came of it. For Strauss and his allies, the hearing had succeeded beyond their wildest dreams.

On Wednesday April 14, the day after the hearing became public, IAS Board chairman Herbert Maass announced that Oppenheimer would remain director. But Pais and some other IAS faculty members, worried, began circulating a draft of a formal statement of support. This was thought urgent, for Strauss was a member of the board, and formally at least Oppenheimer's directorship had to be renewed annually. The draft came to have what Pais would call an "involved" history as its authors attempted to satisfy some faculty members who wanted the statement strengthened and others who wanted it weakened.[49] Eventually, everyone agreed, and the 26 permanent members and professors emeriti of the Institute issued the following statement: "Dr. Oppenheimer has performed for this country services of another kind, more indirect and less conspicuous but nevertheless, we believe, of great significance. For seven years now he has with inspired devotion directed the work at the Institute for Advanced Study, for which he has proved himself singularly well suited by the unique combination of his personality, his broad scientific interests and his acute scholarship. We are proud to give public expression at this time to our loyal appreciation of the many benefits that we all derive from our association with him in this capacity."

The fears were not groundless. In July 1954, the Chairman of the Board of Trustees called Strauss saying that he intended to call a special meeting of the Board of Trustees for that month "and if Oppenheimer would not submit his resignation, it would be requested."[50] Fearing that the action might be interpreted as vindictiveness on his part, Strauss convinced him to put off the meeting to early fall.[51] By the time that meeting eventually took place, Strauss was anxious to appear magnanimous and in favor of Oppenheimer's reconfirmation as director.

A passionate, ambitious man, Oppenheimer was surely deeply wounded by being stripped of his ability to influence power. One FBI entry: "Oppenheimer is reported to be very depressed at the present time and has been illtempered with his wife."[52] But he revealed nothing of that in his public statements. "He had a talent for self-dramatization," Dyson wrote, "an ability to project to his audience an image larger than life, to bestride the world as if it were a stage."[53] Post-hearing, the role Oppenheimer discovered himself playing changed. He was more aware than ever that he bore what James Baldwin, in another context, called "the burden of representation"—that his statements were not those of just another scientist, but political or social statements that were more than about him, and addressed to a historical audience. Oppenheimer's first public reaction to the hearing, June 29, was what one would expect of a public custody: he refused comment. "Dr. Henry D. Smyth's fair and considered statement, made with full knowledge of the facts, says what needs to be said. Without commenting on the security system which has brought all this about, I do have a further word to say. Our country is fortunate in its scientists, in their high skill, and their devotion. I know that they will work faithfully to preserve and strengthen this country. I hope that the fruit of their work will be used with humanity, with wisdom and with courage. I know that their counsel when sought will be given honestly and freely. I hope that it will be heard."

This set the tone for Oppenheimer's later comments. He made only brief, offhand remarks about the hearing, and in those seemed to be all but detached from it. He once described the hearing as a train wreck, as if he were only one passenger and had not helped build the rails or run the train. On another occasion he denied a reporter's suggestion that he was a tragic figure, saying the tragic sense came from the "chorus," or those around him—again, that he was not a protagonist.[54] On still another occasion he told a reporter there was a story behind the story. There surely was, but he himself had been a key player in it. Reporters repeatedly pressed him for personal thoughts about what he had undergone, in vain. In mid-December 1954, Oppenheimer recorded an interview on Edward Murrow's television program, "See It Now." He was neither asked about, nor spoke about, the recent hearing only a half year before.

One senses that Oppenheimer's refusal to talk in the confessional mode was deliberate. It was as if he was aware of his forthcoming historical role as a martyr, that he was as an actor on the world stage, that all he had to do was to step back and let it this story unfold, and that the confessional mode was unnecessary to this role and could only sully it. This made him less prone to the petty animosities, defensiveness, and score-settling that permeate, say, Teller's autobiography. Oppenheimer was always addressing, in the words of his Los Alamos farewell address, "what has happened to us," and never "what has happened to me"—thus the unsettling serenity, the disturbing selflessness, in his public comments thenceforth.

One of the few times he said more than a few sentences about the hearing occurred near the end of his life, in 1964, in Geneva. At the end of a talk, he suddenly seemed to veer toward the personal. A decade ago, he told his listeners, the Atomic Energy Commission held a lengthy hearing on his trustworthiness, and the transcript was published, leading many to say his life had become an open book. "That was not really true. Most of what meant most to me never appeared in those hearings. Perhaps much was not known: certainly much was not relevant." Nevertheless, he continued, the experience prompted him to imagine what it would be like for one's life to be an open book: "I have come to the conclusion that if in fact privacy is an accidental blessing, and can be taken from you, if it is worth anyone's trouble, for a few dollars, and a few hours, it [having one's life an open book] may still not be such a bad way to live. We most of all should try to be experts in the worst about ourselves; we should not be astonished to find some evil there, that we find so readily abroad and in all others. We should not, as Rousseau tried to, comfort ourselves that it is the responsibility and the fault of others, that we are just naturally good; nor should we let Calvin persuade us that despite our obvious duty we are without any power, however small and limited, to deal with what we find of evil in ourselves."[55] And when we do, he continued, we should neither fall prey to the temptation to blame that evil on others, nor to imagine ourselves helpless to combat it.

This was vintage Oppenheimer—a brief and opaque personal reference, a loose appeal to learned thinkers, a leap to a perspective so grand that he the puny participant becomes of no real significance, a total absence of reflection about his own role in the events he had just touched on, a trace of melodrama and sentimentality—all this topped off with an optimism that rings just a little false, as befits a statement issued by a public custody.

"We seem to be finished with this horror, pro tem at least," Kitty wrote at the beginning of July, 1954. It had been a strain on the entire family. During the hearing, Toni had answered the telephone and held off reporters at the house. Kitty had been plagued with bouts of pancreatitis. She also had concerns about the health and welfare of her parents, "Franz" and "Mutti," who lived in a small town in Pennsylvania, about a hour's drive from Princeton. Franz was a "short, bald, bespectacled, gentle figure," while Mutti, preferred to be treated as a "grand dame."[56] Everyone hoped to get away quickly, though Robert's commitments kept him around for several weeks. Kitty sat about planning a six-week vacation in the Virgin Islands. She contacted Ted Dale and family, a friend in the U.S. Virgin Islands who owned a hotel, the Comanche, where the Oppenheimers had occasionally stayed, and a boat by the same name which they had occasionally chartered. "Everyone in the family is thinking of the Caribbean, which means the Comanche. Could we charter the Comanche for about three weeks?"[57]

The aftermath of the hearing generated numerous temptations for Oppenheimer to postpone the vacation, and he also worried about rumors that he would flee the country, but felt that since the Virgin Islands were U.S. territory he could travel there without causing too much disturbance. Still, as a precaution, on July 17 he sent a letter to Hoover mentioning his plan to leave "with my family for St. Croix in the U.S. Virgin Islands for a three or four week period of rest and sailing."[58] But he was annoyed when Kitty wired information about the planned charter, aware that the communication would certainly be picked up by the FBI—it was, of course—and possibly deny him what modicum of privacy he was seeking to retain.[59]

The Comanche turned out to need repair, but another boat was found. And on 19 July the family left for the Virgin Islands.

CHAPTER 25

NO FINAL JUDGMENT

After the verdict, Oppenheimer later told a reporter, one option was to seek to show "that what was put out as a final judgment about me wasn't *the* final judgment."[1]

At this he succeeded without much trying. Different judgments about the Oppenheimer hearing began circulating as soon as it got under way. These judgments came from reporters, scientists, academics, government officials, and the public; they were embodied in telegrams, letters, speeches, articles, editorials, books, poems, plays, movies, and public debates and controversies.

First Judgments

The spinning of the Oppenheimer hearing started even before it began, when Garrison and Oppenheimer gave *New York Times* reporter James Reston a copy of the letter of charges and a reply three days before the hearing. On Monday, on the hearing's first day, Garrison called Reston to say he could break the news. Kitty called Kay Russell to contact the Hemplemanns to prepare the children.[2] On Tuesday, Reston's story appeared on the front page of the *New York Times*; the Alsop brothers also wrote about the story in the *Herald Tribune*.

The AEC responded with a press release portraying Strauss as handling the Oppenheimer case responsibly. By the next day, other administration officials and congressmen weighed in on the suspension of Oppenheimer's clearance, including Senator McCarthy ("long overdue"). Thus began a media battle that Strauss and his allies waged with as much dedication as they did the trial itself. For the moment, both sides worked around the barrier posed by the hearing's confidentiality.

The first week of the hearing, Oppenheimer's home, the Institute, and Garrison's law office were deluged with telegrams of support from friends and strangers.

> ALL OF US IN PRINCETON TODAY WANT TO EXPRESS OUR ADMIRATION FOR YOUR CONDUCT IN THIS ORDEAL. BOTH AS YOUR COLLEAGUES AND AS YOUR FRIENDS WE ASSURE YOU THAT NOW AS EVER YOU HAVE OUR FIRM CONFIDENCE, OUR DEEP DEVOTION, AND OUR STAUNCH LOYALTY.
>
> > HAROLD CHERNISS, BRAM PAIS, FREEMAN DYSON, KURT GODEL, MARSTON MORSE, ATLE SELBERG, ERNST KANTORWICZ, ERWIN PANOFSKY

> ILLEGITIMI NON CONUNDUM EST
> [Don't let the bastards get you down]
> > L J KAHN

> HAVE DEEP RESPECT FOR YOUR STAND. SINCEREST REGARDS AND GOOD WISHES FROM
>
> > DESER EDEN GIESEY NEWTON SIEGERT THIRRING COEASTER DYSON KINOSHITA NAMBU SHEPHERDSON SACHS GAFFNEY LOWE

> I AM SO ASHAMED OF MY COUNTRY THAT I DON'T KNOW WHAT TO DO
> > JONATHAN ANDERSON 405 WEST 46 ST NYC

> 100 MILLION AMERICANS DEPLORE CHARGES AGAINST YOU BY CHEAP CONNIVING POLITICOS IN WHITE HOUSE. STAND YOUR GROUND NO MATTER WHAT COST AND TAKE TO OFFENSIVE THESE MEN ARE BASICALLY COWARDS AND YOU KNOW HOW TO HIT THEM
> > LOUIS ALTER

> UTTERLY SHOCKED AND DISTRESSED AT THE NEWS STOP WE ARE SURE ALL INTELLECTUALS WILL BE PROUD TO BACK UP YOUR COURAGEOUS STAND
>
> > CHIH LI AND FRANK [Yang][3]

Most of these telegrams, sent by friends who revered and trusted Oppenheimer, assumed that of course he would prevail. The few worriers included Rabi, who knew enough about the government and the AEC to fear it, and

Ruth Tolman, who knew Oppenheimer as a man who concealed potentially damaging secrets.

The spinning intensified after the Gray panel released its findings to Nichols on Thursday, May 27. Garrison gave a copy of the decision, Evans's dissent, and his own rebuttal to Reston, who reported the news in a front page story the next Wednesday, June 2. Later that week, annoyed by remarks in the *Times*, Strauss called Reston to pitch his side of the story, and the result was a Reston article on Monday, June 7 much more favorable to Strauss and less to Oppenheimer. This elicited more leaks: Oppenheimer released his December 22 letter to Strauss; Nichols released a letter he had sent the previous week to Garrison; and "both sides began peeling away at the concealing cover of secrecy" that hitherto had cloaked so much of what was happening.[4] Reporting the story began to depend on who leaked what to whom and with what slant. *Time* complained that leaks by "handout" were distorting coverage.[5]

Telegrams to Oppenheimer continued to express disbelief, but confidence that he would eventually triumph.

> THIS IS DISILLUSION BUT ROBERT AND KITTY IT MAY NOT HURT YOU STOP UNDERSTAND YOU APPEAL AND AM GLAD YOU DO THIS MADNESS CANNOT LAST ALL MY BEST WISHES ACCOMPANY YOU BOTH
>
> BRAM[6]

On June 11, AEC Commissioner Zuckert accidently left a sheaf of documents about the hearing on a train. Fearing they would soon make the front page of the *New York Times*, Strauss prepared to release the entire transcript. Though the documents turned up safe and sound, in the lost-and-found at Boston's South Station, Strauss became convinced that releasing the transcript would help him and damage Oppenheimer. He persuaded the other commissioners to go along, despite the assurances of confidentiality given to all witnesses. The transcript—over half a million words and 992 pages—was cleansed of material potentially damaging to national security and published in the astoundingly short time of two days. It was ready at 6 PM on June 15, and sent to reporters (and to every member of Congress), with the proviso that no stories appear for 18 hours, to give journalists time to read and digest. But right-wing radio commentator Fulton Lewis, a client of Roger Robb, broke the embargo by using the material on his program less than an hour after receiving it, evidently aided by a "cheat sheet" guiding him to select passages in the transcript prepared by Strauss's allies, and other news services felt forced to follow suit.[7]

Two weeks later came the Commission's ruling:

OPPENHEIMER LOSES APPEAL TO A.E.C., 4 TO 1
                                —*New York Times,* June 30, 1954.

Most editorials, even some in ordinarily liberal publications, supported the decision. This reflected the increasingly edgy Cold War climate, Oppenheimer's own flawed performance in the transcript, and Strauss's clever management of information about the hearing. Though publication of the transcript appeared to have lifted the "concealing cover of secrecy," this was far from the case; deeper concealments remained. From the transcript alone it was impossible to see the extent to which the hearing had been handicapped against Oppenheimer; or what Bernstein has called the "deeper politics" that had motivated it; or the perversity with which the Chevalier episode had been used. And even if one did know of such things, the transcript only made more complex the identity of J. Robert Oppenheimer, and the meaning of the event. The *Washington Post* said of the transcript, "It is about the length of the Bible, has a plot more intricate than *Gone With the Wind* and has half as many characters as *War and Peace*. . . . It reflects on the troubled social and political world about us perhaps more deeply and disturbingly than any other book published during the cold war. . . . It is quite possibly the raw material for dozens of future dramatists, novelists and social philosophers."[8] Yet what was one to make of that raw material?

The AEC, meanwhile, published a booklet of the "Texts of Principal Documents and Letters" of the Oppenheimer case, heavily laden with the documents unfavorable to Oppenheimer and light on favorable ones. Garrison's request that such documents be included were rebuffed.[9]

Across the Atlantic, Chevalier read of the hearing for the first time, and turned against Oppenheimer ("He'd have to be a saint not to," Rabi once noted[10]) in his characteristic histrionic way. "I have been shattered by the revelations," the novelist wrote in one ominous message, demanding that Oppenheimer respond.[11] A few weeks later, he wrote that "I have loved you as I have loved no other man," adding that Oppenheimer's words have "hounded me, plagued and blocked me and played untold havoc with my career and my life."[12] Oppenheimer replied that "I have never done anything or said anything or taken any step with the intent to hurt you or to make things difficult for you," and expressed skepticism that "my cock and bull story" had really cast a shadow over Chevalier, saying that "I had supposed that for a long time it had been recognized for the fabrication that it was."[13] A few months later Chevalier wrote again still more operatically, referring to how "incalculably disastrous," and "monstrous and calamitous" Oppenheimer's words had been: "[Y]ou and I are linked together in a cloudy legend, which nothing, no fact, no explanation, no truth will ever unmake or unravel . . . you are so close to me that despite the immensities that separate us, I somehow regard you as almost a part of myself."[14]

That October, more judgments about the Oppenheimer affair were ignited by two publications which saw it from opposite poles. One was *The Hydrogen Bomb*, a book by Time-Life writers James Shepley and Clay Blair, Jr., which portrayed Teller and Strauss as heros in the quest to make the hydrogen bomb, and Oppenheimer as an obstructionist. The book stirred more reexaminations of the hydrogen bomb episode. The other controversial publication was "We Accuse," a lengthy cover story in *Harper's* by columnists Joseph and Stewart Alsop, likewise a good-versus-evil polemic that cast the same characters in opposite roles.

The Alsops had known Oppenheimer for years, had covered nuclear issues for the *Saturday Evening Post*, were strongly anti-Soviet, and were concerned about McCarthy's rise and influence at the time the hearing began. "The Oppenheimer affair represented the kind of issue the Alsop brothers liked best," writes their biographer, "a powerfully symbolic and nationally significant controversy given to interpretation in terms of good and evil."[15] After learning of the PSB's recommendation, in fact, the voluble Joseph dashed off an angry letter to Gray, condemning his "foolish and ignoble act." The letter triggered an equally angry reply from Gray, and the episode made the Washington gossip rounds.[16] The Alsops devoted many columns to the Oppenheimer affair, but felt that the matter was so complex as to demand a longer venue. When the Strauss-friendly *Post* turned them down, the Alsops approached *Harper's*, submitting a lengthy, 21–page polemic that they had to battle to get past the magazine's lawyers. "We accuse the Atomic Energy Commission and the American government of a shocking miscarriage of justice in the case of Dr. J. Robert Oppenheimer," the Alsops wrote, "We accuse the security system itself as inherently repugnant to high traditions of the American past." "The AEC, by its decision in the Oppenheimer case, has dishonored and disgraced the high traditions of American freedom."

The polemical title invoked the Dreyfus affair, adapting Emile Zola's of his famous book thereabout, and was one of the earliest sustained attempts to interpret the Oppenheimer case by drawing a historical analogue. The article, and the book which sprang of it, sparked its own controversy and new reexaminations of the hearing. One of the AEC's lawyers at the hearing,

C. A. Rolander, Jr., drew up an extensive rebuttal sent to hundreds of editors and reporters in what the *New York Times* noted was a rare example of a government agency actively seeking to influence a book's reception. *U.S. News & World Report* allowed the Alsops a reply. And so the judgments multiplied.

Post-Mortems

The discrepancy between Oppenheimer's immense charisma and power prior to the hearing, and his pallid and crumbling performance at it, seemed to demand explanation and to make post-mortems irresistible.

Well before the hearings had opened, Rabi had urged Oppenheimer to write an autobiographical article for the *Saturday Evening Post*, sensing that a "tell-all" piece would serve to innoculate him from any suspicions that the growing Cold War intolerance would cast on his past leftist associations. Oppenheimer would come across as a "common man," and thenceforth be untouchable. But Oppenheimer's was not the "common man" style; he was not a confessional speaker and had little appreciation for the value and impact of American popular opinion. "[H]e didn't have the political understanding of the nature of [the good that] an article in the *Saturday Evening Post* . . . would push him in the stream of American values." Once the hearing was set in motion, "Oppenheimer's big mistake was to consent to a secret panel. He should have wanted this out in the open, public . . . open hearings."[17] He would then have been playing to a different audience, one more sympathetic to him, and—at the time of the Army-McCarthy hearings—would have forced Robb to do the same, and play to a less sympathetic audience.

Oppenheimer's friend Charles Wyzanski had a similar thought after he learned of the impending hearing:

> [M]y proposal is that you forthwith publish in a medium of wide circulation (say the *New York Times*, or perhaps *Life*, or *The Atlantic*) a more than candid, a philosophical autobiographical account of your intellectual curiosity, your detailed conduct, your personal and family relations, your and their experiences, your record of patriotic contribution, and your understanding loyalty. This would be more than a psychoanalytic performance. Its literary equivalent might be Montaigne's Essays. But it would be something far greater because it would be an unprecedented contribution to the political education of this country. The true "witness" this nation needs is not a recusant Communist but an independent citizen who can explain what it was like in the '30's and '40's to be a man of character and adventurousness seeking to learn the truth about one of the undeniably major forces of our time, and simultaneously to advance the welfare of mankind.

But Wyzanski added a curious caveat. He remembered having encouraged Alger Hiss, whom Wyzanski originally believed to be innocent of espionage charges, to bring a libel suit—and when Hiss did so, it led to the disclosure of the "pumpkin papers" used to establish Hiss's guilt and precipitate his downfall. Thus Wyzanski concluded cautiously, "[D]o not follow my advice unless there is no corner of your or your wife's lives which you are unwilling to expose."[18] This struck at the matter more deeply than he knew. Oppenheimer had things to hide but did not know exactly what Robb knew of them. One has to fight cautiously in the dark.

Oppenheimer's secretary at the Institute, Verna Hobson, once made a remark critical of Robert's approach during the hearings. "I fight as hard as I can in the best way I know," he replied, sharply.[19] We have every reason to think this a true remark.

Cultural Judgments

Long after the hearing, Oppenheimer remained a lightning-rod for controversies, political and moral. In spring 1955, he was invited to the University of Washington by a former student who was head of its physics department—but the university's president, Henry Schmitz, refused, calling Oppenheimer's presence not "in the best interests of the university." The action sparked protests and Schmitz was hanged in effigy. The following year, when Oppenheimer appeared on campus at a conference, reporters asked if he had any "special feelings" given Schmitz's action the previous year. Oppenheimer, as usual, was conspicuously silent. "I am very glad to be at this conference at this place. Period."[20] In the fall of 1955, when Harvard University announced that Oppenheimer would be its William James lecturer on ethics and philosophy for 1957, the action prompted castigating letters to Harvard's board of overseers.

Meanwhile, in a protest poem entitled, "Thou Shalt Not Kill" (1955), Kenneth Rexroth included "Oppenheimer the Million-Killer" among the leading scientists and writers who, the poet alleged, had created a brutal and murderous culture responsible for the death of Dylan Thomas. But also in 1955, Oppenheimer received a more enthusiastic valuation from William Gaddis, a young, polymathic writer whose books are based around absurd, spiraling, cataclysmic events. Gaddis included with the letter a copy of his recent novel *The Recognitions*, at 956 pages nearly as long as the transcript of Oppenheimer's hearing, which was about the loss and recovery of personal integrity, and the meaning of fraudulence from all angles. You must get fan mail and crank letters of all kinds, Gaddis wrote Oppenheimer, but few half a million words long.[21]

Outside the United States, judgments on Oppenheimer tended to be more uniformly favorable. In 1957, the French Government made Oppenheimer a Chevalier of the Legion of Honor. The official ceremony was held at the French Embassy on September 25. On conferring the honor, Cultural Counselor Edouard Morot-Sir noted "a certain spiritual kinship" between Oppenheimer and "French scientists and philosophers of the eighteenth and nineteenth centuries who placed their confidence and their hopes in science," and pointedly spoke of his thinking as "one of the most generous and loyal of our time."[22] As usual, Oppenheimer was tight-lipped and refused comment when contacted by reporters: "A number of my colleagues have received such honors and I've heard about it only when I read their obituaries."[23]

The following week the Soviet Union launched Sputnik, the world's first artificial satellite. Sputnik's regular winking overhead in the nighttime skies was taken as a stunning indication of the loss of U.S. superiority in missile technology and defense preparedness. In the ensuing soul-searching, part of the blame was laid to the declining influence of U.S. scientists in government circles. Oppenheimer's absence from governmental circles was noted; editorials and petitions urged his reinstatement. Even former AEC Commissioner Murray, who had found Oppenheimer both a security risk and possibly disloyal, said that "I would not be at all displeased if he were reinstated."[24] The groundswell alarmed Strauss, causing him to reconsider his intention to leave the AEC and retire to his farm, saying that he might not do so "if it would mean that the scientists would get their way as far as Oppenheimer is concerned."[25]

Yet the time was not yet ripe for a rehabilitation, and Oppenheimer remained an emotionally charged symbol. In 1958, when a school board in the famed planned community of Levittown, Pennsylvania, voted to name its new $3,000,000 school after Oppenheimer, protests erupted among PTA committees, veterans organizations, and political groups. Hundreds of people attended the next school board meeting and argued about the decision until 3 AM. The state and national American Legion protested the decision, and a local Republican organization called for an investigation of the (Democratic) school board. Why not name it after someone whose name evokes "unquestioned admiration" and who represents "loyalty and inspiring leadership," such as "Christopher Columbus, Washington, Abraham Lincoln, James Monroe, Patrick Henry, or Nathan Hale"? "If a person of scientific achievement were sought, why didn't they consider Admiral Lewis L. Strauss"?[26] Under heavy fire, the school board backed down and named it after Woodrow Wilson. When a reporter asked him how he felt, Oppenheimer said he had "no comment, no comment at all."[27]

In 1959, Chevalier published a thinly disguised roman à clef, *The Man Who Would Be God*. On the eve of the Second World War, physicist Sebastian Bloch belongs to a secret communist unit, though he carefully avoids the trappings of formal commitment. One of his best friends is Mark Ampter. But when Bloch begins work on a top-secret military project involving a nuclear bomb ("the Monster") at a remote location ("Valhalla"), he dumps Ampter because only he, Bloch, sees deeply enough into things to play . . . God.[28] The novel is poorly written and melodramatic. Nevertheless, a few of the fictional passages are uncanny in the way that, almost inadvertently, they ring truer than any nonfiction that anyone has yet produced about the episode, Chevalier himself included. Witness the following:

> In any case, if he had regarded himself as a communist—which was rather in the perspective of history than in the context of a specific time and place—he had not been a communist in the commonly accepted sense, and technically had in fact not been a communist at all. Only the other members of his unit supposed him to be an actual member like themselves (a cheap deception, it seemed to him now), and he knew that he could count on each and every one of them to keep that presumed knowledge absolutely secret. His position was, besides, a little special in that he had never paid any real dues, as had the others. The sums that he had handed over . . . sums too large, in any case, to be considered dues—had been by way of special contributions, and there was, he believed, no record of them of any kind. So far as his actual involvement with the party was concerned, therefore, he could consider himself reasonably safe.[29]

And in the following decade, German playwright Heinar Kipphardt wrote a play "freely adapted" from the transcript, which opened in Munich and Berlin in 1964. When Oppenheimer received a copy of the text he objected to Kipphardt's portrayal of Bohr as opposed to the bomb project, and to a final speech in which Oppenheimer expressed regret: "We have spent years of our lives in developing ever sweeter means of destruction," the Oppenheimer character says, "we have been doing the work of the military, and I feel it in my very bones that this was wrong."[30] As Oppenheimer angrily wrote Kipphardt: "Even this September in Geneva, during a conference of the Rencontres de Genève, I was asked by the Canon Van Kamp whether now, knowing the results, I would again do what I did during the war: participate in a responsible way in the making of atomic weapons. To this I answered yes. When a voice in the audience angrily asked "Even after

Hiroshima?" I repeated my yes. . . . It seems to me that you may well have forgotten Guernica, Dachau, Coventry, Belsen, Warsaw, Dresden, Tokyo. I have not. I think that if you find it necessary so to misread and misrepresent your principal character, you should perhaps write about someone else."[31]

Oppenheimer publicly condemned the play, and for a while considered suing Kipphardt.[32] "The whole damn thing was a farce," he told the *Washington Post*, "and these people are trying to make a tragedy out of it."[33]

One French producer, Jean Villars, stopped rehearsals on learning of Oppenheimer's opposition to the play, contacted him, and worked with Oppenheimer on a version that was advertised as "cleaner and purer" than Kipphardt's. It would open in Paris on January 1965. Now it was Kipphardt's turn to be horrified; he claimed that it "pulls all the teeth out of my play" and turned it into the theatrical equivalent of a popular magazine article.[34] Many reviewers agreed; *Variety* called it "more tract than play," and cited the "generally pedestrian quality of the material."[35]

By 1966, Kipphardt's play had been performed in two dozen countries. Attempts were made to produce it in the United States—by David Merrick and Herbert Blau, among others—but abandoned after threats from Garrison's law firm: "Mr. Oppenheimer does not want this play performed here under any circumstances."[36] Kipphardt's play was performed in the United States only after Oppenheimer's death. Gordon Davidson directed its American premiere in Los Angeles in May 1968.[37]

The Sense of Tragedy

The attempt to make a bona fide drama of the Oppenheimer story was inevitable. His remark that the hearing was more farce than tragedy was yet more dissembling; his life seemed to provoke comparisons with tragic protagonists. Years before the hearing, in 1946, Lilienthal had called Oppenheimer a "tragic figure." Historian Richard Polenberg, who recently reedited and abridged the transcript of the hearing, noted that, aside from the numerous historical information it provided, "like a latter-day Greek tragedy, the transcript also offered insight into such timeless traits of human character as honor, fortitude, and humility, and, sadly enough, their less admirable counterparts: treachery, timidity, and pride."[38] Years after the hearing, at Oppenheimer's memorial service, George Kennan noted "that strong element of tragedy" which all who knew Oppenheimer sensed in his situation.

Historical figures to whom Oppenheimer has been compared include Xerxes, the Persian king who audaciously built a bridge of ships across the

Hellespont; Galileo, the scientist who was tried and convicted by the church; Alfred Dreyfus, the French officer whose court-martial was incited by anti-Semitism; Warren Hastings, who was impeached while serving as the first Governor-General of India; and T. E. Lawrence, another man with a scholarly background who turned revolutionary leader before meeting a political downfall.

Literary figures to whom Oppenheimer has been compared include Thomas Becket, in *Murder in the Cathedral,* whose well-intentioned actions were undermined by arrogance and pride; Faust, who made a pact with the devil; Lear, who became more human in the end; and the Sorcerer's Apprentice, who unleashed forces he could not control.

Some writers, such as the Alsops, merely invoked a historical analogy, while others sought to elaborate these analogies in depth. These include Giorgio De Santillana, who compared Oppenheimer's trial with that of the subversive and articulate Galileo. One similarity is that each scientist went into his hearing convinced that he would prevail over his less intelligent, more politically minded accusers, and was utterly shocked when he did not. Another similarity was that an important trigger in each case was the fear on the part of the accusers of the charisma of the accused. Santillana quotes the Fiorentine ambassador: "He reminded me that Galileo wrote exquisitely, and had a marvelous capacity for persuading people of whatever he wanted to, and there was a danger that through his influence some fantastic opinion might take hold among those Fiorentine wits, which are too subtle and curious."[39]

In the Washington, D.C., of 1954, the "fantastic opinion" of which Oppenheimer's enemies were afraid was "that one does not immediately have to rush ahead to make any weapon that can conceivably be made."[40]

Another intriguing analogy was explored by Freeman Dyson, between Oppenheimer and M.F., the protagonist of Auden and Isherwood's *F6,* "a Hamlet-like figure compounded of arrogance, ambiguity and human tenderness . . . an intellectual polymath, expert in European Literature and Eastern philosophy" who, because of his gifts, is offered the chance to lead a politically imperative expedition up a difficult mountain peak, initially balks, eventually accepts, and dies at the summit.[41]

How illuminating are such analogies? Much about the Oppenheimer hearing indeed suggests the classic Greek formulation of tragedy in which a well-intentioned leader "of great reputation and good fortune," as Aristotle says, is brought down by mistakes due to character—usually pride or aggressiveness—in a story involving reversal and recognition. While enemies assist in the downfall, the fault ultimately lies in the protagonists themselves—they trip themselves up by their own virtues, their personalities so powerful that only they are powerful enough to do themselves in. The Oppenheimer hearing even seems to reveal the deepest truth that we can learn from the tragic, what philosopher Dennis Schmidt refers to as the mutability of human praxis: "We learn that things may well, without warning, convert into their opposite. We learn that what was once divine can, in a flash, become monstrous. . . . What becomes visible here is the expanse of the human condition—the possibilities belonging to praxis—an expanse so great that it is capable, at any given moment, of converting its situation into its other."[42] The tragic figure, in the words of philosophers Jean-Vernant and Pierre Vidal-Naquet, "discovers himself to be enigmatic, without consistency, without any domain of his own or any fixed point of attachment, with no defined essence, oscillating between being the equal of the gods and the equal of nothing at all. His real greatness consists in the very thing that expresses his enigmatic nature: his questioning."[43]

While the tragic denouement of the Oppenheimer hearing does not involve the usual fate of tragic heroes—death—the reversal (conversion into the opposite) was surely thorough, complete, and extreme enough to qualify. The wildly successful and indispensable leader of the most advanced military project ever excluded from military service. The passionate architect of a scheme for world community banished from government circles. The man who loved his country labeled its scapegoat.

The sheer variety of tragic heros to whom Oppenheimer is compared, however, suggests he does not fully resemble any. In his reaction to the hearing he seemed to lack that dimension of the tragic Aristotle called recognition. The tragic protagonist is never mere victim, buffeted by events beyond his control, but fully embraces the world and takes personal responsibility. Even while struggling against the world he acknowledges his own participation in it, and that he has no choice but to embrace that world. But Oppenheimer appeared unworldly, detached from events around him. Writer John Leonard noted this exasperating quality—"We pursue him, and he eludes us"—in a review of a collection of Oppenheimer's letters and recollections. "Even the jacket photograph of this handsome book from Harvard raises more questions than it answers. A dreamy Oppenheimer, as if doped or deliquescent, stares back at us, sad that we don't know what he is tired of thinking about. His expression combines condescension and misadventure; we would never understand. We ask of him a few notations on sin. He replies with a machine that is noiseless, when it isn't speaking Sanskrit. I am sure, after reading so many books on Oppenheimer, that we were stupid to deny him a security clearance, but I wonder whether he ever belonged to our world at all."[44]

We are used to more worldly engagement from our tragic heros. Oppenheimer's description of the hearing as a "train wreck" implies that he saw himself merely as a passenger who had nothing to do with building the rails or running the train. His remark that the tragic element of the hearing came not from his being a protagonist but from the "chorus," or those around him, likewise repudiated his agency in the affair. His comment to a reporter of the existence of a story behind the story was surely true—but he himself was a key player in that story behind the story. Oppenheimer's strength was his weakness—he spontaneously and instinctively reached out to seize hold of and dissect external problems, but without pausing to introspect. Stern remarks that, at the hearing, Oppenheimer revealed that "he had never come to a full understanding of his own behavior."[45] What's untragic is that he seems to lack curiosity about that behavior, as if it were not part of who he was. The Oppenheimer story evokes tragedy without fulfillment because it involves reversal without recognition.

Almost a decade after the hearing, when Oppenheimer went to the White House to receive the Enrico Fermi Award, given out by the Atomic Energy Commission according to the terms of the Atomic Energy Act of 1954, the *New York Times* stated that the honor "served to write finis" on the Oppenheimer controversy.[46] Hardly. The judgments have only multiplied and diversified. No end is in sight.

CHAPTER 26

INSIDER IN EXILE

Shortly after the hearing, Oppenheimer told a reporter that he was looking forward to returning to the "cloistered life of abstract slants."[1] Said by an ambitious man of expansive interests yearning to change—or at least impress—the world, who had been enjoying a life as a government insider and an internationally recognized celebrity, this was surely posturing.

But a dextrous posture. Oppenheimer flourished as an insider—when handed a clearly defined mission with institutional support. This created a magnetic field, in Holton's perceptive words, which served to line up the various fragments of his complex personality.[2] The Institute now provided him with the sole opportunity—however modest—that he had. Briefly, it appeared possible that Strauss, on the Board of Trustees, would seek to remove Oppenheimer. The threat never materialized—Strauss eventually would push through Oppenheimer's reconfirmation to be on record as a magnanimous figure[3]—but Oppenheimer was henceforth careful to keep to himself thoughts on controversial matters of government policy, and on his exile from government service. When Pais interviewed Garrison, the latter reported that at the first trustee meeting after the hearing, when Oppenheimer and Strauss next met, Garrison was impressed with the correctness with which Oppenheimer treated Strauss.[4] Pais adds in his notes, "I am myself also impressed with the fact that RO kept his physics interests going without reference to his problems, now that I look back."[5]

Indeed, Oppenheimer now played the role of the good Institute soldier. "[H]e was a better director after his public humiliation than he had been before," writes Dyson.[6] Oppenheimer appeared in seminars more frequently. He continued to brutalize guest speakers. He generated new vigor in the physics program by expanding the number of faculty and bringing in youthful members on a temporary basis. He followed their work, digested what they were saying, and pushed them in productive directions. He thereby transformed the Institute into a leading center for physics.

Pais:

> To be sure, we had our seminars. They were lively—sometimes very lively. And Oppenheimer's sharp insights played a major part in making them so. Yet Oppenheimer's main contribution to the work and the style of the institute was not merely the conducting of a seminar. His influence was far more important, more subtle perhaps but no less enspiriting. He could convey to young men a sense of extraordinary relevance of the physics of their day and give them a sense of their participation in a great adventure, as for example in the Richtmyer lecture: "There are rich days ahead for physics; we may hope, I think, to be living in one of the heroic ages of physical science, whereas, in the past, a vast new field of experience has taught us its new lessons and its new order." He could define and thereby enhance their dedication, by words such as these: "People who practice science, who try to learn, believe that knowledge is good. They have a sense of guilt when they do not try to acquire it. This keeps them busy.... It seems hard to live any other way than thinking that it was better to know something than not to know it; and that the more you know the better, provided you know it honestly." To an unusual degree, Oppenheimer possessed the ability to instill such attitudes in the young physicists around him to urge them not to let up. He could be critical, sharply critical at times, of their efforts. But there was no greater satisfaction for him than to see such efforts bear fruit and then to tell others of the good work that someone had done.[7]

But as Pais knew from years of close proximity to the man, Oppenheimer also experienced dissatisfactions—both professional and personal, and some extremely painful—during his years as Institute director.

Institute Director

Oppenheimer had performed brilliantly as head of Berkeley's theoretical physics group and as director of the Los Alamos laboratory. But these were unique leadership opportunities, for Oppenheimer had built up both communities virtually from scratch. Moreover, these communities had tightly focused missions: the excitement of prewar theoretical physics, and the urgency of the bomb project in an all-out war, provided the magnetic field strong enough to orient Oppenheimer's leadership skills. At the Institute, the magnetic field was considerably weaker. Now he inherited a community with preexisting tensions and a less focused goal. He would be deeply disappointed by his failure to bring disciplines together, at his inability to even get the mathematicians and historians to join each other's tables for lunch.

Robert and Kitty lived at Olden Manor, the director's mansion at the Institute. Even long-standing acquaintances were impressed and awed by the decor and atmosphere of the Oppenheimer household. A van Gogh painting of a sunset hung in the living room, and a Renoir portrait of a woman with a veil; a Dürer etching graced the study. Said Bethe: "A visit to the Oppenheimer's was like a visit to the Royal Court."[8]

The Oppenheimers had only a few close personal friends at Princeton even among frequent physics associates such as Dyson, Pais, and Yang. This was unfortunate. Oppenheimer's father figures Conant and Bohr were gone, and he might have benefited from intimate friends who feared not to point out his vulnerabilities. Rabi counted as a kindred spirit—"I was perhaps the only person in the world who spoke to him with complete honesty, to criticize him, and this was important to him"[9]—but he and Oppenheimer were not in regular enough contact. Another intimate was his brother Frank, whom Robert loved dearly and would have seen more of, but the mutual hostility of their respective wives—Jackie acted the role of the working class girl, Kitty that of an aristocrat—helped to keep them apart more than Robert would have wished. After the war, the two brothers did not correspond regularly until Robert's very last years.[10]

Instead of friendships, Oppenheimer now often forged associations with princes of the cultural domain, latter-day versions of Haakon Chevalier. An example was composer Nicholas Nabokov, the Russian-born cousin of novelist Vladimir. Nabokov, whose ability as a composer was modest, was nevertheless well-connected, and as the first secretary-general of the Congress of Cultural Freedom—a bastion of liberal anti-communism—he organized a series of cultural festivals designed to match and overpower a similar set sponsored by the Soviets. The sometimes impressionable Oppenheimer was dazzled by Nabokov's flamboyance and his ability to introduce Oppenheimer to glamorous people in the arts, such as George Balanchine, and Oppenheimer once used the Director's Fund to have Nabokov invited as a visitor to the Institute.

As director, Oppenheimer leaned heavily on Verna Hobson, who became his secretary in the fall of 1953 and would stay on until nearly the end of his life. She found him remarkable: when she took dictation, "he would speak for about half an hour in fully constructed sentences, then say, 'Let's break for five minutes—I have to think,' then go on."[11] But getting used to his strange behavior took adjusting. She was often puzzled as to whether he was being complimentary or nasty—as when once, upon seeing her broken down in tears, he said, "Somebody must have been kind to you."[12] Hobson organized his calendar and was instructed to open all his correspondence, with the exception of letters from Ruth Tolman, Oppenheimer's occasional clandestine lover. "RO nearly always carried a few of her letters in his pocket."[13]

Hobson also had to help Robert navigate his often troubled relationship with Kitty. Robert and Kitty treated each other as equals and gave each other mutual criticism and support—and to that extent were good for each other—but were "always competing" in destructive ways, a friend remarked.[14] She was protective of his privacy, provided the much-needed buffer between himself and the world, and was short and sharp with those who wanted to pry into their lives. "KO tended to isolate RO," Frank Oppenheimer told Pais. "FO thinks that RO may actually have liked that in view of too much pressure on him by outsiders."[15] In the often stiflingly formal Princeton environment, moreover, Kitty often acted in spontaneous and genuinely thoughtful ways to help neighbors such as the Dysons. But Kitty, like Robert, not only had a sharp wit but could also be vicious; one acquaintance remarked that she had two personalities.[16] It did not help that, about 1950, she suffered severe abdominal pains in what was diagnosed in 1958 as chronic pancreatitis, leading her to turn more heavily to alcohol and pills.[17] Kitty over-indulged in the former and at least once had to be hospitalized for overdosing on the latter, and these habits sometimes made her careless; Hobson told Pais that on at least two occasions fire broke out at home because of Kitty's negligence.[18] On another occasion, Kitty passed out as a limousine was waiting to take Robert and her to New York, where he was to give an address. Robert left by himself, but when Kitty came to she called the state police, who stopped Robert en route.[19] On many occasions Hobson had to intercede on Robert or Kitty's behalf. She fielded the telephone call, which came during an IAS Board meeting, bringing the news of Kitty's mother Mutti's apparent suicide when she evidently jumped off a cruise ship. And as Kitty's father Franz lay dying at his home in Pennsylvania, Kitty, unable to face him, sent Hobson and another friend to visit—but by the time they arrived, Franz was in a coma.[20]

Robert and Kitty, like Robert and Jean Tatlock, enjoyed being "miserable together"; today, we would call them co-dependents. But while Robert's relationship with Tatlock had been all but private, his with Kitty was high profile. Sometimes he had to control an impulse to lash out against her in public.[21] Robert sometimes spoke "in frankness and in privacy" to Hobson about his difficulties, but then always returned to Kitty and told her about the conversation.[22] To some acquaintances, Robert's strategy for coping with Kitty was to try to spoil her and make her comfortable: "That did not work well."[23] Robert tried to keep the worst of Kitty's behavior quiet with the collaboration of Hobson, a few other friends, and certain maids and grounds people of the Institute. "We lived in conspiratorial ways," Hobson told Pais.[24]

Directing the Institute might seem to be a dream job for the polymathic physicist. It was small and required little administration. The principal duty of the director was to raise money and make appointments. But Oppenheimer had made it clear at the time he was hired that he would not engage in fund-raising, and his early appointments were excellent. They included mathematicians Armand Borel, Deane Montgomery, Atle Selberg, and Andre Weil; physicists Pais, Dyson, Lee, and C. N. Yang.

Oppenheimer, though, soon found the Institute directorship more frustrating than anticipated. He did push through a new library at the Institute, designed by Wallace K. Harrison, whose other buildings included the U.N. building. But conflicts mounted with the mathematicians, who opposed in particular his attempts to expand the scope of the Institute in the social sciences and—in their view—to marginalize their role. While the physicists charitably coped with Oppenheimer's autocratic behavior, fierce remarks and elliptical utterances, the mathematicians were less tolerant, some suspecting that he trafficked in ambiguity to suggest a nonexistent depth. The most vociferous opponents were Montgomery and Weil, two leading mathematicians. Weil in particular was a formidable antagonist—of European Jewish origin, classically trained, familiar with Sanskrit, as brutal and sharp-tongued as Oppenheimer himself, and unafraid to direct that tongue against Oppenheimer. "Oppenheimer was a wholly frustrated personality," Weil once remarked, adding that he would provoke faculty members into quarreling for his own amusement. "He was frustrated essentially because he wanted to be Niels Bohr or Albert Einstein, and he knew he wasn't."[25] By 1960, faculty meetings grew so acrimonious that even physicists found the atmosphere of the Institute poisoned.

The fiercest battles arose over the director's two chief duties: money and permanent appointments. While in the 1940s and early 1950s the Institute was well-endowed enough for large salaries, that began to change. When Jürgen Moser, an important mathematician, turned down the Institute, the grousing mounted. After one heated meeting on salaries at which a mathematician had attacked Oppenheimer, Yang challenged him to state the reason for his hostility. The mathematician mentioned Oppenheimer's failure to raise more money. Yang reminded him of the agreement under which Oppenheimer had become director. The mathematician sighed, and said it recalled the story about the young man seeking to marry a beautiful young woman. "But I don't cook!" the woman protested. "That doesn't matter," answered the young man, "I love you!" Ten years later, the mathematician said, it *does* matter.

More hostility surrounded an attempt by the mathematicians to appoint John Milnor a permanent member. Milnor was then at Princeton, which created a problem for Oppenheimer. In the recollection of Leidesdorf and other Institute trustees, a "gentleman's agreement" forbade the Institute from raiding members of the Princeton faculty, which could disrupt cordial relations between the two institutions.[26] Several of the mathematicians doubted the existence of a non-raiding agreement—there are no "bloodstained letters," Oppenheimer had to admit—challenged in any case its wisdom, and demanded the freedom to appoint the finest scholars they could find. Oppenheimer argued vehemently against Milnor's appointment, while the mathematicians replied in kind. "[H]e is a big boy," Weil said of Milnor at one meeting, "he should be allowed to make his own decision."[27] The physicists rallied as best they could behind Oppenheimer. But, recalled Yang, "The faculty meetings became so acrimonious, I was afraid to go unless I had to."[28]

Oppenheimer prevailed. Milnor eventually would become a permanent member of the Institute, but only after leaving Princeton for a few years. Demoralized by failing to hire Milnor, several of the mathematicians thought about retreating into their own work or resigning entirely, even en masse. They then blindsided Oppenheimer by presenting two nominations rather than the expected one, and the action incited another controversy, this time about procedures for handling appointments. At a trustees meeting in April 1963, Oppenheimer proposed postponing the appointments, but the trustees accepted the mathematicians' request.

Some of Oppenheimer's allies who had stood loyally behind him now began to entertain thoughts of leaving. "I have decided to resign from my present position at the Institute," Pais wrote in May 1963, explaining that he had long wanted to blend research with teaching. "The detailed timing of this move has been determined to a considerable extent by my desire not to leave until the recent faculty developments at the Institute would take a hopeful turn, as I now believe they have."[29] Oppenheimer himself soon began to think about stepping down as director.

"The greatest tragedy of Oppenheimer's life," wrote Silvan Schweber, "was not the ordeal he went through over the issue of his loyalty, but his failure to make the Institute for Advanced Study a true intellectual community."[30] George Kennan said of Oppenheimer: "His fondest dream had been, I think, one of a certain rich and harmonious fellowship of the mind. He had hoped to create this at the Institute for Advanced Study; and it did come into being, to a certain extent, within the individual disciplines. But very little of it could be created from discipline to discipline; and the fact that this was so—the fact that mathematicians and historians continued to seek their own tables at the cafeteria, and that he himself remained so largely alone in his ability to bridge in a single inner world these wholly disparate workings of the human intellect—this was for him, I am sure, a source of profound bewilderment and disappointment."[31]

Science Impresario

Once in the 1950s, during the oral part of the physics qualifying exam at the University of Wisconsin, a student was asked what J. Robert Oppenheimer had contributed to physics. "I don't know," the student answered—and was informed that was the correct answer.[32]

The remark was caustic and flip. Any physics student should have been able to cite at least the Born-Oppenheimer approximation, the Oppenheimer-Phillips effect, and black holes. Nevertheless, the remark was true in spirit to Oppenheimer's ambiguous legacy during the 1950s.

The war had made Oppenheimer renowned as *the* physicist, not only among the public but also the physics community. The first issue of *Physics Today*, the flagship publication of the American Physical Society, was adorned with a cover of Oppenheimer's trademark pork pie hat. Many physicists viewed him in effect as a statesman, able to present their case effectively in government circles and to the public, and viewed his exile from government circles as a serious blow. Late in 1954, when the first Atoms for Peace conference was being planned, Lewis Strauss asked Rabi who should be chairman. Rabi replied, "You killed Cock Robin."[33]

Oppenheimer had a unique kind of persona for a scientist in the public eye. He was no Feynman—that lusty and conspicuously crude Far Rockaway enfant terrible Jew who played the bongo drums and affixed his name to zany tell-all books. Oppenheimer was more elitist, an upper-class Manhattanite who knew Sanskrit, owned van Goghs, sailed yachts, and quoted the likes of Baudelaire, Rousseau, John Donne, and Pindar (in the original Greek) in his popular addresses. Oppenheimer was hotly sought-after as a keynote speaker or conference raconteur of sessions presenting other people's work, for he delivered brilliant summaries in which he mastered and explained complex situations, turned unforgettable phrases, and attracted reporters and idolaters. He was half-legendary, though also loathed and feared for the brutal way he treated people. One often heard barbs directed against him; he was "highly respected and cordially disliked," a physicist once told me.

Oppenheimer attempted to keep abreast of physics at the Institute seminars. Dyson provides a portrait of his behavior at these gatherings:

> I have been observing rather carefully his behavior during seminars. If one is saying, for the benefit of the rest of the audience, things that he knows already, he cannot resist hurrying one on to something else; then when one says things that he doesn't know or immediately agrees with, he breaks in before the point is fully explained with acute and sometimes devastating criticisms, to which it is impossible to reply adequately even when he is wrong. If one watches him one can see that he is moving around nervously all the time, never stops smoking, and I believe that his impatience is largely beyond his control. On Tuesday we had our fiercest public battle so far, when I criticized some unwarrantably pessimistic remarks he had made about the Schwinger theory. He came down on me like a ton of bricks, and conclusively won the argument so far as the public was concerned. However, afterwards he was very friendly and even apologized to me[34]

But physics was difficult to keep on top of—especially for someone who, as Serber once remarked, "spread his intellectual energy too broadly."[35] Every Tuesday, Oppenheimer hosted a working lunch in his office attended by a half-dozen or so regular physicists, including Dyson, Goldberger, Lee, Pais, Treiman, Yang, and sometimes a visitor. But his participation in the discussion grew less decisive. Gradually, the field was walking away from this erstwhile universalist. The Tuesday lunch meetings grew less technical. Recalls Treiman, "We starved on those sparse tuna salad sandwiches, overdrank the sherry, and just rambled on about current developments in physics as seen by us, the University contingent. I was never clear why established [sic] these lunches or why we weren't joined by one or two IAS members. The purpose was certainly not to gossip about the IAS people or assess their work. I guess Oppie just wanted to hear about the wider scene from some outsiders. He attached great importance to the lunches, often calling me a day in advance to remind. The conversation was never highly technical. It had more to do with who's in, who's out, what are the best bet, etc."[36]

Another difficulty was generated by Oppenheimer's gut instincts about how physics progressed. In Göttingen, he had been nurtured by an atmosphere of exciting and revolutionary physics in which Nature was experienced as something profoundly mysterious, and if you made bold guesses most times you failed but possibly you would discover something revolutionary. Oppenheimer had arrived at the tail end of this time of intense intellectual foment, led by the likes of Dirac, Pauli, and Heisenberg, and felt he had just missed out on his chance to participate—on his chance for immortality. He desired, so strongly as to beget a belief in the imminence in, another scientific revolution whose crest he could ride.

This belief emerged, for instance, in his skepticism toward quantum electrodynamics. Oppenheimer had remained convinced through the 1930s that QED was not good enough, not deep enough, to penetrate the secrets of space, matter, and light—that there were indeed grounds for another revolution. He was "on the lookout for the breakdown" of QED, Serber said,[37] expecting it at mc^2, then 137 mc^2, then at some higher energy. Although after the war Oppenheimer was interested in renormalization theory—as evidenced by 1948d, his contributions to the Shelter Island conferences, and his recruitment of Dyson to the Institute—he remained skeptical. When Dyson presented his seminal work on renormalization theory[38]—work all but universally recognized as tremendously important, which put the capstone on the renormalization program, and which vastly extended confidence in QED—Oppenheimer was severely critical and it took Bethe to open his eyes to the significance of Dyson's achievement.

With the renormalization program all but finished and continued mainly by specialists, the attention of nuclear physicists shifted to elementary particles. And here, for a moment in the 1950s, it seemed as though the hoped-for revolution might be at hand—at least to Oppenheimer and the members of the older generation including Heisenberg, Pauli, and Dirac—thanks to a peculiar and unexpected property of so-called K or "strange" particles. As more and more such particles were discovered and studied in the 1950s, thanks to the operation of accelerators like Brookhaven's Cosmostron and Berkeley's Bevatron, they appeared to exhibit "degeneracies," to be associated in groups whose members had similar masses and lifetimes, as if they "belonged" together but some characteristics were preventing them from identity.[39] Which were the right groups, and what was the meaning of the groupings?

Oppenheimer's participation in these developments illustrates much about his role in the physics community at the time: as a skillful synopsizer, as an inventor of vivid phrases, as a sometimes frustrating fashioner of enigmatic utterances, as a would-be revolutionary—and in general as an insider among insiders. At the fifth Rochester Conference (January 31–February 2, 1955), for instance, Oppenheimer presided over a session which he began by writing down a table of 11 particles in various decay products, over half of them K particles, and said that the main focus of the session would be to examine how to classify the puzzling array. "This year I think there is a new point which will come out, and that is, in addition to the charge degeneracy, there appear to be other degeneracies, or quasi-degeneracies which do have a connection with the theory of the stability of these particles."[40] Oppenheimer clearly had an intuition of the simplifying classifications to come.

But by the next, sixth, Rochester conference (April 3–7, 1956), the puzzle had grown. On its second day, Oppenheimer gave a public address to an overflow audience, in the course of which he referred to the proliferation of the new particles as a "sub-nuclear zoo." The phrase was enthusiastically picked up by reporters and repeated by conference participants throughout the conference. The zoo's biggest problem involved two creatures called the tau and the theta. These two K particles exhibited a puzzling degeneracy in that they seemed to be identical in all properties except parity, a fundamental conservation principle. Oppenheimer presided over the penultimate session, and in his opening remarks pointed to one of the main puzzles in particle theory. "There are the five objects $K_{\pi 3} K_{\pi 2} K_{\mu 2} K_{\mu 3} K_{e3}$. They have equal, or nearly equal, masses, and identical, or apparently identical lifetimes. One tries to discover whether in fact one is dealing with five, four, three, two or one particle. Difficult problems arise no matter what assumption is made. It is to this problem of the identity of the K particles that larger part of the present section is devoted." Yang followed with a talk in which he noted that he would like to be able to say what we have learned about the subnuclear zoo, but that unfortunately "a clear picture does not exist." More talks followed on the tau-theta puzzle. Oppenheimer then made one of his famous Delphic remarks: "The τ meson will have either domestic or foreign complications. It will not be simple on both fronts."

The conference participants liked this remark as well, and without knowing quite what to make of it repeated it in informal discussions. It, too, was classic Oppenheimer, who when addressing difficult problems often crafted enigmatic utterances that sounded insightful not because they added anything new, but because they allowed each listener to interpret them in the way he or she wanted to. His contrast between the domestic and foreign front, for instance, might refer to the contrast between the properties, such as mass, of the τ particle and those of other particles; between strange and nonstrange particles; between field theoretic and non field theoretic approaches; between normal and revolutionary science. No doubt Oppenheimer did not intend any one of these meanings, but rather the ambiguity itself. And a few minutes later in the discussion he produced yet another cryptic remark: "Perhaps some oscillation between learning from the past and being surprised by the future of this [τ-θ dilemma] is the only way to mediate the battle." Again, the sentence hinted at a rising wave of possibly revolutionary physics without advancing the problem.

A great physics puzzle tends to invite bold initiatives in different directions—and in the aftermath all but the final one appear silly and misguided. The willingness of practitioners to appear silly and misguided is part and parcel of a vital and exciting field, and Yang and Lee took one of these routes. In June, Yang sent Oppenheimer the draft of a paper he and Lee had written, and were submitting to *Physical Review*, entitled "Is Parity Violated in Weak Interactions?" It pointed out that physicists did not, after all, know for sure whether parity was conserved in weak interactions. The great achievement of this paper was not that Yang and Lee had the courage to question a sacred cow—sacred cows are obvious and tempting targets for theoretical physicists—but rather that they recognized that it could be questioned in the first place. Samuel Goudsmit, the editor of *Physical Review*, had only a stylistic objection, removing the question mark and rephrasing the title to maintain the dignity of his flagship journal. Oppenheimer's comment on the draft had to do with content. He thought possibly that the mirror properties of space itself "could conceivably vary cosmologically." He wanted to leave open the possibility, in short, that solving the puzzle would require altering fundamental conceptions of space and time.[41]

A team of physicists from Columbia and the National Bureau of Standards, co-led by Columbia's Chien-Shiung Wu, took up the challenge offered by the paper, and began a test for parity violation that involved measuring the relation between two numbers G and G′ which, if nonequal as expected, would mean that neutrinos had four components and could spin—or "screw," in the terminology—either right or left; while if they were equal, neutrinos had only two components and spun or screwed only one way. (Goudsmit, again protecting his journal from contamination by popular language, insisted on changing the terminology from "screw" to "handedness," and delegated to the unflappable Serber the job of alerting the Chinese physicists to the special nuances of the former term in English, though usage persisted for a time out of habit.)

In January 1957, when the results came in, Yang cabled Oppenheimer, who was vacationing at the Club Comanche in St. Croix: WU'S EXPERIMENT YIELDING LARGE ASYMMETRY SHOWING G EQUAL TO G PRIME STOP. THEREFORE NEUTRINO IS A TWO COMPONENT WAVE FUNCTION STOP. IT IS A PURE SCREW. GREETINGS. FRANK

Oppenheimer cabled back: WALKED THROUGH DOOR. GREETINGS.

The discovery of parity nonconservation thrilled many members of the older generation of physicists, who thought that it provided a glimpse of a new crack in the mystery of nature, hinting at the ultimate untenability of field theory and traditional assumptions about space and time—at another wave of revolutionary physics like that of the 1920s. Heisenberg wrote of Pauli, "Never before or afterward have I seen him so excited about physics."[42] Oppenheimer shared their excitement. "No one today knows where this discovery will lead . . . something has been found whose meaning only the future will reveal."[43]

But parity nonconservation was soon shown to be easily incorporated into QED, once again extending its reach. In one discussion at the time, Yang remarked that physicists were like a group of people in a darkened room, who know there is a way out but do not know what it is. Oppenheimer and other old-timers were hoping that when the light came back on, it would reveal them in an entirely different building. Instead, it turned out to reveal only the door. Once again, Oppenheimer was disappointed. The progress of particle physics had not taken the form of a revolutionary break with the existing theory but rather an extension of its depth and versatility.[44]

Oppenheimer exerted his greatest impact on physics during this time as an impresario—in the way he stayed on top of developments, spotting opportunities in sometimes surprising directions, and initiating work on them by pushing the right people on them. This had been his forte since the 1930s—as evidenced, for instance, by the Oppenheimer-Phillips process and his work on what would become known as black holes.

One example: Oppenheimer's role in fostering the application of neutron activation to art and archaeological materials. By the mid-1950s, a few attempts had been made to use neutron activation as a noninvasive way to analyze the composition and origin of artifacts. Some Institute archeologists, including Homer A. Thompson, discussed with Oppenheimer whether there was a possibility of developing neutron activation into a systematic tool. Oppenheimer thought it was possible that reactors could be used as a tool to carry out a detailed analysis of pottery, allowing the fingerprinting of trace elements in a way that would pinpoint the source of the clay. In fall 1954, Oppenheimer telephoned Richard Dodson, an old friend who had worked at Los Alamos and was now chairman of the chemistry department at Brookhaven National Laboratory. The Brookhaven Graphite Research Reactor (BGRR) was the first built explicitly for peacetime research, and had excellent facilities for irradiating samples such as potsherds as well as much bigger objects, and Oppenheimer suggested that Brookhaven develop a program in archaeology. Oppenheimer invited Dodson and his wife to Olden Manor for the night, and during the stay presented Dodson with a bag of archaeological samples that Thompson and others had provided him. Dodson gave the samples to Brookhaven scientist Ed Sayre to irradiate and analyze for sodium and magnesium content. "The results, which were expressed as ratios of ^{56}Mn:^{24}Na, showed distinct differences between sherds from different sources, but similarities between sherds from the same region. These were reported by Sayre and Dodson to a group made up of archaeologists, chemists, and Professor Oppenheimer at the Institute in March, 1956, and eventually published."[45] The work was so successful that the program blossomed, and Brookhaven became internationally known for its work on neutron activation and collaborated on important art preservation projects involving frescos by Giotto and oil paintings by many artists, and involving research collaborations with institutions such as the Isabelle Gardiner museum in Boston and the Institute of Fine Arts at New York University. All the Rembrandts in the collection of the Metropolitan Museum of Art (except for those painted on wooden panels) eventually went to Brookhaven and were autoradiographed there to help determine their authenticity.

Rabi liked to tell Oppenheimer that he read too much Indian philosophy and too little of the Talmud. This remark can be interpreted in several ways. One is that it refers to the way Indian philosophy is apocalyptic—things end in a great crash before beginning anew—while the Talmud's message is different; that things were messy in the past, are messy now, and will continue to be messy in the future, even for those who are chosen. The prudent person therefore heeds the Talmud's lessons on how to navigate wisely within one's community.

The remark points to a suggestive difference between Rabi's career and Oppenheimer's. While Rabi made great strides based on his conviction that quantum mechanics was fundamentally correct, and therefore he looked to elaborate and extend it, Oppenheimer was constrained by his conviction that the theory was fundamentally flawed, which encouraged him to look far ahead, perhaps too far.

This may be one reason for Oppenheimer's dissatisfaction with his signal achievements. It may be a reason why, given his formidable reputation and talents, neither the University of Wisconsin student mentioned above nor his examiner thought that the Born-Oppenheimer approximation, or the Oppenheimer-Phillips process, or black holes sounded correct, making "I don't know" the right response.

Speaker and Author

After the hearing, Oppenheimer remained widely sought-after as a speaker and author on issues concerning science and society. He reveals high ambitions in these talks and addresses, many of the seeds of which can be found in his farewell speech to Los Alamos in 1945. There, he had remarked that "what has happened to us" is so major as to beg comparison in some ways with the discovery of relativity and the development of quantum mechanics in that they "forced us to reconsider the relations between science and common sense." The development of the atomic bomb even invited comparison to a much earlier time, "the days of the renaissance . . . when the threat that science offered was felt so deeply throughout the Christian world" that the existence and value of science were threatened. Oppenheimer's hope clearly was that just as this threat ultimately had not undermined society and culture but improved it once properly integrated, so would the atomic bomb. Atomic weapons offered not only "a great peril, but a great hope," in being so terrible that they might frighten human beings into establishing "a community of interest" which might grow into "a pilot plant for a new type of international collaboration."

While Oppenheimer's optimism about international collaboration faded after the failure of the 1946 Achenson-Lilienthal report, and about revised relations between science and common sense after the 1954 hearing, many themes involving the interaction between science and society persist in his later writings, several collections of which have been published. In his eulogy to Oppenheimer, Pais noted that the talks and writings after the hearing focus "more and more on the fact that the relations between the modern sciences and the general culture of our time are not as intimate and fruitful today as they could be." Pais continued: "What really preoccupied him was that the span of things the intelligent man can cope with is dangerously narrowing; that the relationships between common sense and specialized knowledge are in greater difficulty now than ever, because the rate of increase of that which is known is now greater than ever. Even to the scientist is it often difficult to appreciate the essentials of a neighboring discipline, not completely foreign but not quite his own, 'even in physics we do not entirely succeed in spite of a passion for unity which is quite strong.' Was it then his intent to explain isotopic spin to philosophers? No harm in trying, he thought, but 'as for particle physics, what we are sure of today may not yet be ready to make its contribution to the common culture.'"

Pais found that Oppenheimer's essays broached three main themes.

> First, he addressed himself to what is loosely called the intellectual community. He wished to foster a common understanding primarily within this community. Second, as an example of what in his opinion could profitably be shared, he mentions the lesson of quantum theory which we call complementarity. He wished and in fact tried to explain this lesson to the biologist, the statesman and the artist because he believed that what to the physicist is a technique represents at the same time a general way of thinking that could be liberating to all. Third, he saw a two-fold duty for our educational system. In the face of increasing demands on education we should continue to stress that the cultural life of science lies almost entirely in the intimate view of the professional. At the same time, "no man should escape our universities without . . . some sense of the fact that not through his fault, but in the nature of things, he is going to be an ignorant man, and so is everyone else." Of the great effort needed to achieve these aims he said the following: "I think [. . .] that, with the growing wealth of the world, and the possibility that it will not all be used to make new committees, there may indeed be genuine leisure, and that a high commitment on this leisure is that we reknit the discourse and the understanding between the members of our community. [. . .] As a start, we must learn again, without contempt and with great patience, to talk to one another; and we must hear."[46]

But Pais was also aware of a strange property of Oppenheimer's addresses: while evocative and impressive in style and delivery, they are also often prosaic in content. To be sure, most were delivered at public occasions for general audiences, occasions that call for wisdom, reflection, or edification without tears or sweat. At this, Oppenheimer succeeded brilliantly, and forged his own genre of public talk; if we find his contributions to this genre dissatisfying, it is only because we expected so much more from *him*. The talks tend to promise more depth and insight than they contain. They are both rhetorically evocative and conceptually stagnant.[47]

Pais had experienced this already in his first encounter with Oppenheimer at the 1946 meeting of the American Physical Society in New York, when Pais described himself as "moved by [Oppenheimer's] words" yet was afterward "unable to reconstruct anything of substance"—which, Pais said he later realized "was not just a matter of stupidity from my side." Pais jotted down on one page of his notes that "Bohr's dictum never to express yourself more clearly than you think was to Robert an upper bound." And on another, "O's talent: to withhold a piece of information which then makes a statement elevated & mysterious while in fact there is not that much to it."[48] Nor was Pais by any means the only contemporary to have trouble with the essays. "I could follow the words but not the argument," confided Ruth Tolman—perhaps Oppenheimer's most sympathetic intimate audience—apropos of his Reith Lectures.[49]

Oppenheimer's strengths in these essays give rise to their weaknesses. As in his physics, one of his strengths was the ability to take stock of a situation, to grasp it in all its complexity and articulate it in a way that preserves the intricacy. The correlative weakness—again as in his physics—was that he did this so well that it left him unable to propose a way forward, for to do so would involve a crass simplification, which would do an injustice to the intricacy of the situation that he so well mastered. His voice is simultaneously oracular—fascinated by the meaning of a situation, the potential for novelty, and the possibility of revolution—and cautious and humble—impressed by what's known, the obstacles in the way to progress, and the weight of tradition. Oppenheimer appears to characterize his voice, in one essay, as an attempt to have a style: style, he writes, is the means by which we do "justice to the implicit, the imponderable, and the unknown. . . . It is style which complements affirmation with limitation and humility."[50] But the voice can be characterized, less charitably, as schizophrenic, and one FBI agent described it as Oppenheimer's "typical 'egotistically modest' manner."[51] As a result, the essays end up being both stirring and insubstantial, dangling before us the prospect of a coming breakthrough and future harmony but ultimately leaving us empty-handed. Some typical examples of conclusions:

- "In the discouragements of the day, good example must come to be our firmest ground for hope."[52]
- "For all this it will clearly not be enough that we preserve the integrity of our communication and comprehension, either among us, or with our fellows, but it is the least that we can do."[53]
- "We, like all men, are among those who bring a little light to the vast unending darkness of man's life and world. For us as for all men, change and eternity, specialization and unity, instrument and final purpose, community and individual man alone, complementary each to the other, both require and define our bonds and our freedom."[54]

Oppenheimer's knack for crafting messages that left listeners free to interpret in their own ways poses the serious danger of us reading into his essays more than is present.

A second strength of these essays is that they forcefully articulate the insider perspective, of the professional scientist, in which progress consists of the gradual absorption and integration of science and its methods into society, with tensions merely temporary or clouding a deeper harmony. Science is a prime example of community and of inquiry for society at large; a "special interest," as he once put it, that was also in the general interest. "Science in being, research," Oppenheimer writes in 1949, citing such virtues as openness, the absence of authority, and the willingness to doubt, "may be to the liberal education, not an accident, not an ancillary or secondary or convenient thing to be held in balance—it may be the scripture itself."[55]

Consider one of his most striking images, the "house of science," from his 1953 essay "An Open House."

> It is a vast house indeed. It does not appear to have been built upon any plan but to have grown as a great city grows. There is no central chamber, no one corridor from which all others debouch. All about the periphery men are at work studying the vast reaches of space and the state of affairs billions of years ago; studying the intricate and subtle but wonderfully meet mechanisms by which life proliferates, alters, and endures; studying the reach of the mind and its ways of learning; digging deep into the atoms and the atoms within atoms and their unfathomed order. It is a house so vast that none of us know it, and even the most fortunate have seen most rooms only from the outside or by a fleeting passage, as in a king's palace open to visitors. It is a house so vast that there is not and need not be complete concurrence on where its chambers stop and those of the neighboring mansions begin. . . . And even those who live here live elsewhere also, live in houses where the rooms are not labeled atomic theory or genetics or the internal constitution of the stars, but quite different names like power and production and evil and beauty and history and children and the word of God. We go in and out; even the most assiduous of us is not bound to this vast structure. One thing we find throughout the house: there are no locks; there are no shut doors; wherever we go there are the signs and usually the words of welcome. It is an open house, open to all comers.[56]

Oppenheimer, in short, was a Comtean, who held science and its methods to be exemplary for society at large. The activity in the house can and should guide the rest of life. But Oppenheimer was a modern-day Comtean with soul and sophistication; he never believed that one science could be reduced to another, nor sought to underestimate the complexity of the human world. Indeed, in an influential address to the American Psychological Association, he argued that psychology should not be based on the model of the natural sciences, as many practitioners during those years were attempting to do.[57] After the 1954 hearing, some of Oppenheimer's optimism dimmed. He came to recognize the gaps and fissures that separate the community of the scientist from wider society, and to compare to that extent the loneliness of the scientist to that of the artist. He even speaks of incompatibilities: the diversity of life, he said in 1954, is such that "there have always been modes of feeling that could not move the same heart; there have always been deeply held beliefs that could not be composed into a synthetic union." Nevertheless, the underlying Comteanism persists. Oppenheimer frequently and skillfully wielded the metaphor of complementarity to downplay these incompatibilities, and to suggest a more profound harmony. It is a good and evocative metaphor, though not a deep one. A conceptual patch, it expresses a faith that different experiences or situations that appear to be independent, mutually exclusive, and even conflicting, ultimately belong together—without providing any hints of a blueprint to indicate how so.

But the weakness is that he does not call this insider perspective into question: "The discoveries of science, the new rooms in this great house, have changed the way men think of things outside its walls." Not even scientists, however, are born inside the "open house," and though one may work there one does not live there. Oppenheimer does not inquire into how people travel from the inside back to the outside of the house, and whether any difficulties attend that trip. While in the later years he seems discouraged about the "community of interest and understanding" needed to meet the upcoming cultural and political challenges, he still assumes an underlying complementarity and does not explore or inquire into the discontents and tensions that have arisen. What would have been truly profound would have been to seek to articulate our discontent, rather than merely point to it. And Oppenheimer's own experiences leading up to the hearing would have been an excellent starting point, because the hearing was a paradigmatic experience of the kind of disruption in the relation between science and society he was alluding to. A curious, distressing, even ominous aspect of the later essays is his absence of reflection about an event that was not only the deepest thing to shake his soul, but one of the deepest things to shake up the relations between science and society. It was impersonal; it was still always "what has happened to us" not "what has happened to me." Oppenheimer almost acts as though he were not a part of the world in which *that* event took place, in *that* part of the house. This is what gives his later essays such an unsettling serenity.

Nevertheless, colleagues were inspired by Oppenheimer's ability to express the perspective of an insider of what he often called "the community of science" or "the intellectual community," and knew how to make use of Oppenheimer's special talent for giving voice to it. In November 1963, for instance, Brookhaven scientist Luke Yuan began worrying about the ability of politicians and the public to support the rapidly rising cost of new accelerators, and conceived the idea of publishing a book of essays by physicists on the goals and values of high-energy physics. The essays he secured comprise a fascinating picture of the views and values of high-energy physicists of the day. Some excerpts follow. Julian Schwinger: "The world view of the physicist sets the style of the technology and the culture of the society and gives direction to future progress." Bethe: "I believe that particle physics deserves the greatest support among all branches of our science because it gives the most fundamental insights. . . . [T]his is indeed the most basic field of knowledge in the physical world." Gerald Feinberg: "If we cut back on [high energy physics] for reasons of budgetary limitations or political squabbling, I think we will have seriously damaged the best single element we have contributed to human culture." Pais: "A great society is ultimately known for the monuments it leaves for later generations. . . . [S]uch a machine, which is on the scale of a national effort, will without question be a source of inspiration for new science and a monument to our days." Steven Weinberg: "[I]t would be fitting for scientists to think of themselves as members of an expedition sent to explore an unfamiliar but civilized commonwealth whose laws and customs are dimly understood. However exciting and profitable it may be to establish themselves in the rich coastal cities of biochemistry and solid state physics, it would be tragic to cut off support to the parties already working their way up river, past the portages of particle physics and cosmology, toward the mysterious inland capital where the laws are made."

Yuan then asked Oppenheimer to compose "a general introduction setting forth the basic objectives of high energy physics and its implications."[58] Telling Oppenheimer that the project was "of extreme importance and urgency," Yuan wrote, "At present there seems to be tremendous lack of understanding of the objectives of high energy physics, not only among the general populace and Government officials, but also among the scientific community as a whole."

Oppenheimer obliged, superbly. "We do not understand the nature of matter, the laws that govern it, the language in which it should be described," Oppenheimer wrote. Nor, he continued, are we likely to find enough clues within the energy range accessible to us; we need a much larger accelerator. One might well ask, therefore, what makes the search for a theory of matter "important enough to warrant the effort, the expense, the public support needed to enter the domain of much higher energy physics." The answer, Oppenheimer said, is not only that the techniques of physics create spin-offs that benefit all science and technology, nor that they generally give rise to unanticipated but useful discoveries.

It is also this: the last centuries of science have been marked by an unabating struggle to describe and comprehend the nature of matter, its regularities, its laws, and the language that makes it intelligible. The successes in this struggle, from the Sixteenth Century until our own day, have inspired the whole scientific enterprise, and lightened the world of technology, and the whole of man's life. They have informed the education and the devotion of young people. They have played an ineluctable part in the growth, the health, the spirit, and the nature of science. We are now, despite tempting and brilliant topical successes, deep in the agony of this struggle. This volume attests the conviction of those who are in it that, without further penetration into the realm of the very small, the agony may this time not end in a triumph of human reason. That is what is at stake; that is why this book is written.

Whatever their shortcomings as excursions into philosophy, political science, or human culture, Oppenheimer's talks were excellent in context, as general addresses by the head of a research institute, a situation in which style is more important than content. Even those who listened carefully enough to note their flaws, and to disagree with the occasionally dark tone, found them inspiring. One of the darkest notes is struck in *Prospects in the Arts and Sciences*, which was recorded in November 1954, and broadcast by the Columbia Broadcasting System on December 26, 1954. In it, Oppenheimer considers what the world of the arts and sciences looks like.

> There are two ways of looking at it: One is the view of the traveler, going by horse or foot, from village to village to town, staying in each to talk with those who live there and to gather something of the quality of its life. This is the intimate view, partial, somewhat accidental, limited by the limited life and strength and curiosity of the traveler, but intimate and human, in a human compass. The other is the vast view, showing the earth with its fields and towns and valleys as they appear to a camera carried in a high-altitude rocket. In one sense this prospect will be more complete; one will see all branches of knowledge, one will see all the arts, one will see them as part of the vastness and complication of the whole of human life on earth. But one will miss a great deal; the beauty and warmth of human life will largely be gone from that prospect.

But Oppenheimer seems almost overwhelmed by the view. "Yet never before today have the diversity, the complexity, the richness so clearly defied hierarchical order and simplification; never before have we had to understand the complementary, mutually not compatible ways of life and recognize choice between them as the only course of freedom. Never before today has the integrity of the intimate, the detailed, the true art, the integrity of craftsmanship and the preservation of the familiar, of the humorous and the beautiful stood in more massive contrast to the vastness of life, the greatness of the globe, the otherness of people, the otherness of ways, and the all-encompassing dark. . . . This cannot be an easy life. We shall have a rugged time of it. . . ."[59]

After reading this, Pais wrote to Oppenheimer applauding his conviction: "you leave no doubt about your view that one should be in the village and that too much bird's eye viewing is dispiriting." But Pais found too much of a tone of despair, and cited back to Oppenheimer the two following passages from Charles Morgan's essay, "On Singleness of Mind," which the playwright added as a preface to his play, *The Flashing Stream*:

> This singleness of mind, called by Jesus purity of heart, the genius of love, of science and of faith, resembles, in the confused landscape of experience, a flashing stream, "fierce and unswerving as the zeal of saints," to which the few who see it commit themselves absolutely. They are called "fanatics," and indeed they are not easily patient of those who would turn them aside; but, amid the confusions of policy, the adventure of being man and woman is continued in them.
>
> [A] single minded man, however simple his life or unspectacular his behaviour, slowly produces upon his associates an impression that he is inspired—or, to avoid a word that begets controversy—that his subconscious mind is continuously nourished and impregnated from sources not at once apparent to them or to him. Finding this to be so, he may say, simply, that God provides for him, or he may use another form of words with which to describe the renewals within himself: the effect is the same—that he is renewed, and, in his face, the youth of another world looks out from the age of this.[60]

Pais then told Oppenheimer, "And this is what I hope you will weave into your own writing. That single mindedness is the ultimate of strength we can reach, that it is totally different from the spirit of specialism while superficially its techniques seem not dissimilar and that the flying over the landscape is a good excursion every once in a while, as long as there is a full knowing of a necessarily limited number of makers. I know I say nothing you do not know. But I want it said, hard and with hope. You must use your talents to do this. As to myself, I have now other battles, but I hope that also for this my time may come."[61]

St. John

During the 1950s, the Oppenheimers began to take regular vacations at a remote island retreat, on St. John, in the U.S. Virgin Islands. The island had no telephone service nor paved roads, only narrow dirt trails that threaded up and down the steep hills, navigated by jeep, horseback, and foot. It was a spectacularly beautiful island, but to get there required island-hopping: fly to San Juan in Puerto Rico, take a smaller plane to Charlotte Amalie in St. Thomas, then take a car to the end of that island where a ferry—in the early days, only one a day—takes you to Cruz Bay on St. John. Everyone had the same address: Cruz Bay Post Office, St. John, U.S. Virgin Islands. The mail was sorted about 10:30 every morning, and standing in the line that began to form half an hour earlier was an important social occasion.

The island population then was about 800. Of these, about a tenth were "Continentals," the pleasant euphemism for white-skinned island inhabitants, while "natives," the now politically incorrect term for black islanders, comprised the rest. "Locals" referred to people of either color who stayed around a long time. Continental society was small and fairly segregated, and depended heavily on jeeps and alcohol; "Jeep Society" was the working title of one never-completed book about it. The Continentals hung out together, partied frequently, and dropped by each others' houses on holidays. For them, life was like one long reunion of distant cousins, not all of whom got along. Nobody cared who you were or what you did, as long as they felt free to talk about it.

In the mid-1950s, the Oppenheimers took several vacation excursions to the Caribbean, shunning the popular resorts for informal guest houses run by families—such as the Club Comanche in Christiansted on St. Croix, run by the Dale family, where Oppenheimer had received Yang's telegram about parity violation. On St. John, the Oppenheimers' favorite guest house was the Trunk Bay Estate, run by Paul Boulon and his mother Erva (short for Minerva) on the north shore of the island, about three miles east of Cruz Bay. "They have the finest beach in the Caribbean, and a small place, informal, with wide views and plenty of wind," Oppenheimer wrote an acquaintance. "[T]he food is remarkable for the Caribbean and is good, because Mrs. Boulon has learned what to do with the native fauna and flora."[62]

Trunk Bay was a wooden house with seven guest rooms, built about halfway up the hill. There was no electricity, just lantern light and a kerosene-powered refrigerator. Robert and Kitty normally stayed in "Chicago," the most comfortable room which had a private terrace and bathroom and the most breeze, whence its name. Toni would stay in the long and narrow room next door nicknamed "Pullman." Everyone ate breakfast and dinner together, and behaved like family.

The intimacy of the environment made it next to impossible for the FBI to keep Oppenheimer discreetly under surveillance. In 1955, when AEC chairman Daniel Lilienthal stayed at Trunk Bay a month after Oppenheimer, he ran into people who complained about the FBI agents who showed up to ask him whom Oppenheimer had talked with, what he saw, and so forth. "They will hound that fellow as long as they can," Lilienthal wrote in his journals.[63] Eventually, the FBI gave up.

Attracted by the remoteness, the Oppenheimers grew interested in purchasing property in the Virgin Islands, and made inquiries about possible properties. But land, especially beach property, is scarce and precious on small islands, often a source of conflict, and at least one deal fell through. Finally, in 1957, the Oppenheimers sold a Van Gogh to purchase two small packets of beachfront property on St. John. The previous owners had been Robert and Nancy Gibney, eccentrics in their own way, known for occasionally chasing people off their property with shotguns. The Gibneys were inspired to part with a strip of their otherwise private beach by the new owner's fame, but they lost more privacy than they bargained for. The Oppenheimers asked Wallace K. Harrison to design a cottage, and while it was under construction, in summer 1958, they camped out at the Gibneys'. It did not take long for the latter to regret their sale, as is clear from a humorous but mean-spirited profile of Kitty that Nancy later wrote, full of obviously inflated stories. The cottage consisted of one large open space and bedroom behind which was a tiny bathroom. It had running water thanks to a pump in a cistern and a pressure tank, and was electrified; that part of the island had just been wired via a power line had been brought across from St. Thomas. But the cottage had been built too close to the beach. The din made by a ground sea—the name for a type of swell in which the waves do not roll in but pick themselves up and drop themselves on the beach—was so loud as to make it virtually impossible to hear anything inside.

The Oppenheimers now came to St. John more frequently: for much of the summer, and from Christmastime to New Year's. It was the one chance that Robert and Kitty took to relax, and be comfortable, happy, and have a truly private life for an extended period of time. Robert rarely wore anything besides shorts and sandals, while Kitty took to the bold Marimakko dresses then popular. Her health seemed to improve at St. John, though she still had attacks and cynics still said she was sick when she wanted to be.

The Oppenheimers quickly became a fixture of Continental life—insiders in a society of outsiders. They got along well with the island's children, and Robert taught at least one local youth to play darts on a makeshift board he drew himself. Rarely was there anyone at their home who was not a close friend. They were particularly close to the Denham family—Paul and Erva Boulon's daughter, Erva, and her husband John Denham—with whom they were in nearly daily contact. Toni befriended Erva Denham's daughter—*also* named Erva—and the two loved to ride horseback up and down the steep trails of the island. Erva Denham dropped in nearly every morning—often before the late-rising Robert and Kitty were up—to leave fresh papaya and other fruit. This was fortunate—and surely one reason why Kitty's pancreatic attacks declined—for she and Robert rarely kept food at home. The Denhams and other regular visitors learned to bring their own food even when invited for meals, out of concern for what, or even whether, food would be found. As at Princeton, parties at the Oppenheimers tended to be long on drinks and low on food.

Even on St. John, though, the Oppenheimers stood out by an elegance that extended to the smallest possessions, from Kitty's clothes to their jeep. While all the other Continentals had jeeps with steel bodies that eventually rusted, for instance, the Oppenheimers had a Land Rover, with an aluminum body, the only one on St John. Years after Robert's death, Kitty had a terrible accident coming back from a visit to a member of the Boulon family, losing control while coming down a steep hill on a dirt road that is still treacherous, fully paved, today. The Oppenheimers also had one of the best views on the island, for at the mouth of the bay a magnificent pillar of granite called Carvel Rock protruded above the water.

Rehabilitation and Retirement

In 1961, John F. Kennedy succeeded Eisenhower as president. During Kennedy's administration, scientists and government officials alike—with national security adviser McGeorge Bundy, a longtime Oppenheimer admirer, quietly campaigning—began to try to rehabilitate Oppenheimer. In 1962, Kennedy invited Oppenheimer to the White House as a special guest in a dinner for Nobel Laureates. That same year, he received several nominations for the prestigious Enrico Fermi Award, given out by the Atomic Energy Commission according to the terms of the Atomic Energy Act of 1954. One of several letters of nomination came from four Institute members: Dyson, Lee, Pais, and Yang.[64] In April 1963, Kennedy announced that Oppenheimer would indeed be that year's Fermi award winner. Dean Acheson expressed the feelings of many physicists when he called it "the A.E.C.'s recantation."[65] *Life* called it an "unofficial rehabilitation."[66] Teller sent Oppenheimer a note of congratulation: "I had been often tempted to say something to you. This is the first time I can do so with full conviction and knowing that I am doing the right thing." Typically, the congenital one-upper could not help adding, "I enjoyed getting the Fermi prize last year."[67] Some speculated that this was a first step toward restoration of Oppenheimer's security clearance.

On November 22, the White House announced that Kennedy would hand Oppenheimer the award himself in a ceremony to take place on December 2, the anniversary of the first self-sustained chain reaction. Later that November afternoon, President John F. Kennedy was assassinated.

Oppenheimer and Kennan were standing in the director's office as the news, fragmentary at first, came over the radio of Kennedy's death. Both he and Oppenheimer, Kennan recalled, felt that it meant that "the world we cared about had been grievously diminished, together with our own ability to be in any way useful to it." Kennan continued, "For Oppenheimer, with his great imaginative insight, it was a dreadful blow; and I wonder if I am wrong when I ascribe to that moment, as I instinctively tend to do, the beginning of his own death."[68]

A week and a half later, Oppenheimer received the award at the White House. It was signed by Kennedy but handed to Oppenheimer by Johnson. At the White House ceremony, accompanied by Kitty and their two children, Oppenheimer said to Johnson, "I think it just possible, Mr. President, that it has taken some charity and some courage for you to make this award today."

Afterward, Oppenheimer and his wife met the late president's widow, who was still at the White House, packing her belongings. He told her that when he first wrote out his note of acceptance two weeks previously he had intended to say "some charity, some humor and some courage," but that after Kennedy's assassination Kitty had insisted that the reference to humor should be omitted. The president's widow reportedly replied, "Yes, you were right to put it in, and Kitty was right to take it out."[69]

The following April, in 1964, Robert Oppenheimer turned 60. To commemorate the occasion, four Institute colleagues—Dyson, Pais, Strömgren, and Yang—sought to surprise him with a special issue of *Reviews of Modern Physics* dedicated to him.[70] Dyson wrote about 40 eminent physicists, but had difficulty persuading contributors.[71] It was not simply that Oppenheimer lacked close friends who might be expected to leap at the occasion; he had also stepped on the toes of those who might have been expected to contribute to such an issue. Max Born, for instance, Oppenheimer's former teacher, who felt overlooked in history to begin with, had particularly smarted when Oppenheimer had failed to mention him in the Reith lectures, and was still aggrieved.[72] But Dyson ultimately persuaded the latter to write a short letter "of reminiscences and congratulations."

On April 24, Oppenheimer went to a party in his honor at the Strömgrens, where the surprise was to be the presentation of the special issue. Dyson wrote, in one of his weekly letters to his mother (The "Dyson Weekly"): "The first copy was rushed down from New York hot from the press the same day. Oppenheimer seemed to be genuinely surprised and greatly moved. It was the first time I have ever seen him at a loss for a suitable speech. He just said 'Thank you' rather incoherently and sat down."[73]

By early the next year, Oppenheimer had been thinking about retiring as director of the Institute. According to the Institute bylaws, which mandated that the director retire at the end of the fiscal year in which that person reached 65, he still had several more years. But he had several reasons in mind, which he ran past a few colleagues. The Institute "needs to expand into new fields and do new things," he told Dyson, saying that this needed to be the work of a younger director; also, he added, Kitty was growing weary of entertaining.[74] Oppenheimer told Cherniss that he had held off retiring lest people think the mathematicians had driven him out, but that he wanted to retire before the current IAS chairman—Leidesdorf, who had one more year to go—did, for an aggressive faction on the board of trustees wanted Lewis Strauss as the next director and Leidesdorf would prevent that.[75] Oppenheimer told Yang that he wanted to propose Yang as his successor, but Yang declined. Yang was supportive about the decision to resign, however, telling him that the timing was right, given Oppenheimer's recent distinction in receiving the Fermi Award, coupled with the fact that his difficulties with the Institute mathematicians had quieted down. On April 15, 1965, Oppenheimer informed Leidesdorf that he intended to resign as IAS director—but still remain on the faculty—as of the end of June 1966.[76]

Oppenheimer wanted to keep the decision secret until the April 24 trustees meeting, not wanting to give the impression that the mathematicians had forced him out. He told Hobson that even if the day before the board meeting the mathematicians somehow heard about it and claimed credit for ousting him he would stay on. While the meeting was in progress, however, the phone rang: the *New York Times*, which was checking a story they were running about Robert's resignation.[77] A trustee to whom Robert had confidentially mentioned his retirement, General Greenbaum, had leaked the news to a *Times* reporter.

Oppenheimer told the *Times*: "There are some things that I have wanted to do: physics, of course, which is in a most dramatic and hopeful stage, and to seek and understanding, both historical and philosophical of what the human sciences have brought to human life. After 18 years as director of the Institute I hope to turn to those questions, unencumbered by important problems of institute policy and administration."[78]

Meanwhile, Yang had also decided to leave, to become the Einstein Professor at the new State University of New York being built in Stony Brook, Long Island. The double blow worried several people at the Institute, including Dyson, about the future of the physics group at the Institute.[79] But Oppenheimer moved decisively to counter these fears, hiring two young (under-30) and able physicists. "The danger that the place would simply evaporate seems to be removed," Dyson wrote. "I am impressed with Oppenheimer's ability to do things fast."[80]

In Paris, Oppenheimer gave a talk on Einstein at a UNESCO celebration on December 13, 1965. The speech is honest and thoughtful, but also one of the few talks Oppenheimer gave where the words did not suit the occasion and deeply upset the Einstein family, among others. The occasion called for polite words about an icon. Oppenheimer did so, but also pointed out that in his later years Einstein had been working all by himself on what many considered to be a fruitless quest—something many people in the field had been saying for years, but never at a public occasion. Also unusually, Oppenheimer felt the criticism keenly. When Oppenheimer was then asked to speak when the first Einstein stamp was issued in Princeton, he declined, saying he did not feel well, and asked Yang to speak for him instead.

In Paris, too, Oppenheimer learned that the French government-owned Administration des Monnaies et Medailles de Paris was striking a medal in his honor. The medal was to contain his portrait, with some meaningful symbol, to be chosen by Oppenheimer himself, on the reverse. Initially Oppenheimer suggested the word "Caritas." It was revealing choice. Caritas represents the Greek agape, and comes into English as "charity," as in St. Paul's triad of fundamental Christian virtues: faith, hope, and charity. The word had also been mentioned by Kennan at the hearing as the kind of virtue exercised by those, like Oppenheimer, who exercised compassion towards misguided friends.

But two weeks later, Oppenheimer wrote back insisting on using a formula instead:

$$C\,(\psi) \,=\, \pm\psi^*.$$

This, too, was an intriguing choice. Many scientists, including Archimedes, Bernoulli, Boltzmann, and Fermat, requested that equations or discoveries be engraved on their tombstones, This equation expresses a basic relativistic field theoretic symmetry: the properties of a system composed of a number of "elementary" particles and anti-particles can be related to that obtained by replacing each of the particles by their anti-particles, and each anti-particle by its corresponding particle. The equation would not normally be identified with Oppenheimer, though it is related to Oppenheimer's 1930s work on Dirac's theory. It entails that both electrons and positrons are an intimate part of the unified theory; that these polar opposites cannot be separated without breaking the symmetry. It is tempting to read it as partly a psychological choice—a symbol, proposed by a man with a complex and divided personality, of a unity which depends on the presence of polar opposites.

The artist at the Monnaie added the formula but hesitated to remove the word and left the medal unstruck, hoping that on Oppenheimer's next visit to Paris she could persuade him to let it stay.[81]

Shortly after his return from Paris, in December 1965, Robert and Kitty left for St. John.

CHAPTER 27

CLOAKED MOUNTAIN PEAK

By the beginning of 1966, Robert Oppenheimer was looking thin and frail. Official records often pegged him at 6 feet tall and 100 lbs, though in later years he was shortened by an increasing stoop and the three figure weight had always been an upper bound. His face looked, one journalist wrote, like "that of a moon-man, with eyes that were like craters," photographs of which were haunting and made one "pause and wince."[1] Once, friends and colleagues had described Oppenheimer as attractive, beautiful—even angelic. Now he was haggard. After having compared pictures of him in 1945 and the present, a correspondent wrote, "Somebody has given you a terrible beating!"[2]

Still, when the Oppenheimers returned from St. John on January 8, Robert promptly resumed his usual demanding schedule. He attended the week's physics lunch, and left the following week for a conference at the Center for Theoretical Physics at the University of Miami in Coral Gables. Colleagues there found him still mentally bright and acerbic, still seeking to spot and punish weaknesses in others. At one cocktail party, a brash young theorist noticed Oppenheimer sitting uncharacteristically off by himself, seemingly worn out. "You see the old man—he's dying," the theorist said to his conversational partners. "But I wouldn't cross him!"[3]

Over the holidays, Robert had developed a pronounced cough. At the beginning of February, Kitty insisted he see a doctor. A lump was discovered in his throat. The biopsy revealed cancer.

The next "Dyson weekly" was full of unfortunate news, including some politics surrounding the selection of the Institute's new director, Carl Kaysen, whose appointment had been announced on February 14. Then: "Yesterday [Feb. 16] came the worst bomb-shell of all. Oppenheimer has a throat cancer and is in New York having radiation treatment. The doctors say it is a very superficial thing, discovered early and with a very good chance of being cured. I do not know how much of this to believe...."[4] A week later: "Last Sunday Kitty O. telephoned me very distraught, saying she did not believe the doctors were telling her the truth and asking me whether I could find her somebody who would."

Dyson put her in touch with Gertrud Szilard, a medical doctor whose husband, the physicist Leo Szilard, had been cured of bladder cancer thanks to radiation therapy (when Szilard died in 1964 it was of a heart attack). Gertrud calmed Kitty down by phone, and dropped in to visit a few days later. That helped prepare Kitty for Robert's three-week hospitalization in March. During the stay in New York Hospital, which he grimly referred to as "Round 1," he was able to talk on the phone and receive visitors. Afterward, he made frequent, sometimes daily, trips from Princeton by limousine to New York City for cobalt treatments.

Dyson again:

> I am now finding out how lonely the Oppenheimers really are in spite of their huge numbers of "friends." I feel oddly more sad in leaving them for these two weeks than in leaving Imme [Dyson's wife] and the children. These are the last two weeks of Robert's radiation treatment, and in this time he must know whether it is life or death.
>
> I have been over three times to talk with Robert and Kitty. Kitty believes, perhaps rightly, that I can help Robert to keep alive by keeping alive his interest in physics. She feels desperately that he needs to be convinced that he is still needed in the community of physicists. On the other hand, I find that Robert is just so physically tired from the radiation that my instinct is to hold his hand in silence rather than burden him with particles and equations.[5]

The radiation therapy ended early in April. Doctors told Oppenheimer that the tumor had shrunk dramatically and was barely visible, and predicted that it would either disappear entirely or could be removed with a minor operation. But his throat remained tender and dry.[6] He spent a few weeks recovering from the effects of the treatment, then began working half-days in his office and resuming his routines.

By June, assisted by a cane, he was back traveling: on June 10–12 to a meeting of intellectuals he had helped organize in Mt. Kisco, New York, then flying on June 13 to Ohio for Toni's graduation from Oberlin, then on June 14 back to Princeton for commencement exercises, at which he received an honorary degree.

Robert Oppenheimer
Doctor of Science, *honoris causa*

Honored by three presidents of our country, he holds the nation's supreme award for the advancement of the peaceful application of that awesome power in whose unleashing he was so instrumental. Combined with the austerity of mind of one of the foremost theoretical physicists of his generation is great sensitivity of spirit and a personal magnetism that has attracted to him many of the outstanding intelligences of the world. Physicist and sailor, philosopher and horseman, linguist and cook, lover of fine wine and better poetry, he has added distinction to an already great institute and strengthened the Princeton community of learning.[7]

The next day, he was interviewed about his life and the current state of physics by Gerald Piel for *Newsweek*. Oppenheimer still believed in a coming revolution, saying there was "something cooking" in the way of a breakthrough, though "I do not know how far off it is. . . ." ("It seems to me that we are in for a far greater novelty than the discovery of 'more fundamental' particles," he would write a few months later in *Physics Today*.)[8] He also mentioned that he was working on a manuscript about the history of recent physics. In putting off the hordes of thrilled publishers who then contacted him he wrote back, "I have a long time and much work ahead."

At the end of June, Oppenheimer stepped down officially as director. The Oppenheimers moved out of Olden Manor into the house just vacated by the Yangs. The small, art deco home had been built for mathematician Hermann Weyl on Institute grounds in the 1930s, bought by the Institute after Weyl's death in 1955, and used to house temporary members until Yang had moved in. Robert moved out of the director's office, and lost Hobson's assistance as his secretary. She had served with Robert as the director's secretary since 1954, decided to leave the Institute, but was persuaded by Kaysen to stay on for a few months until he could hire a replacement.

In July, doctors were optimistic and told Oppenheimer that his cancer seemed to have disappeared. But his throat hurt, and his normally quiet but clear tenor-to-baritone voice had turned raspy and hoarse. "Recovery from radiation is very very slow."[9] Later that month, the Oppenheimers went on their usual summer excursion to St. John. At one evening amongst continentals, he complained grimly about his diet of protein powder and milk and stared enviously at the lamb chops. Still complaining of "an impossible throat, which lends itself neither to eating or speaking," Robert visited the doctors the day after his return at the end of August.[10] The doctors said they saw no trace of cancer, though the lab test results would take a few days, and attributed his discomfort to the lingering aftereffects of radiation.

Robert then took off for the annual APS meeting, held that year in Berkeley. There he was reunited—for what would turn out to be the last time—with many of his former students from the 1930s, including Robert Serber. One evening Edward McMillan had arranged a party for Serber. Oppenheimer failed to appear, but called while the party was in full swing. "He asked [Serber recalled] if I could join him and Kitty for dinner in San Francisco. I told him it would be difficult to get away, because the party was more or less in my honor. But he was rather insistent. I made my apologies . . . and drove over the bridge to meet Oppie and Kitty at Jack's. Meeting him there brought back memories of the 1930s. The food was excellent; I still remember that Oppie told me to order a mutton chop. But the mood seemed a little subdued. When we left, I walked the Oppenheimers to their car. As I was leaning in the window to say goodnight, Oppie told me that he had just heard from the hospital that his throat cancer had recurred."[11]

In October the cancer was found to have spread from his throat to his palate, tongue, and eustachian tube. It was considered inoperable, and he was returned to radiation therapy, though this time not with cobalt but with a betatron, which produces fast and precisely tunable electrons. "What the doctors say is that cancers have responded favorably to this treatment, but everybody knows that reradiation with a still ulcerated throat is no great joy. It is not got bad yet, but I cannot be very sure of the future."[12] One doctor counseled him that it was time to think "in terms of being the exception to collective statistics."[13] By November he was telling friends that he has "no confidence at all of enjoying good health in the future."[14]

Reluctantly, and at the doctor's orders, Oppenheimer began to cancel long-planned and warmly anticipated trips: to Providence, Rhode Island, in November, where he was supposed to chair a session of a theoretical physics conference; to Lisbon, Trieste, and Paris in December—even the winter St. John's trip. "We are tied to Memorial Hospital and the betatron," he wrote a friend.[15] One day Yang dropped in. "I had planned to urge him to consider writing something, a kind of last testimonial, about the atomic bomb and mankind," Yang wrote later. "But I found him so frail physically that I did not bring up the subject."[16]

For the first time in ten years, the Oppenheimers spent Christmas and New Year's in Princeton. Kitty asked Hobson to secure a gun for her "so that Robert could put an end to it himself if the brain were affected."[17] Early in the new year, just before embarking on a cruise to London on vacation, Hobson paid a final visit to the Oppenheimers. She found Kitty unbearable, trying to "force over-expensive presents" on her and "intoxicated, as usual." Shepherding Hobson to the door for the final time, Robert said to her, "I hope that one day you will see this, too, as a joke."[18]

Robert told colleagues that he still hoped to see them at the Coral Gables conference, to be held toward the end of January 1967. On January 12 he sent a letter to the conference organizer: "I cannot now with any candor pretend that I can come, or even if I come, be of any use to anyone or any comfort. You should make your plans knowing that I cannot be there."[19] The word "now" revealed that Oppenheimer had become convinced that his days were numbered. He began to drop hints to this effect to friends and colleagues. At his last Tuesday lunch he made two parting remarks to Sam Treiman: "(1) he'd been looking at post doc applications and thought he might not be around when the selectees arrived on the scene; (2) 'Sam, don't smoke.'"[20] Oppenheimer started to make arrangements for his memorial service, contacting the Juilliard String Quartet, a group much beloved by physicists. Prior to the group's formation, several of its members had played during the war for Manhattan Project physicists in Chicago, and after its formation it had visited the Institute, and on one occasion, at Einstein's home, even recruited Einstein himself to join them on violin.

On January 27, T. D. Lee went to the Institute to give a colloquium on "Neutral Vector Mesons and the Hadronic Electromagnetic Current."[21] In an almost unprecedented departure from routine, Oppenheimer failed to appear at Lee's talk and stayed home. He told Lee that he was not feeling well, but wanted to discuss the paper and invited him over to his house. Lee found Oppenheimer at his desk, reading through the preprint—which was lengthy and highly technical—and the two launched into a discussion of it. After half an hour Lee had to leave for a dinner engagement, and Oppenheimer stood up and escorted him to the door. "He seemed frail but not ill," Lee recalled, "though when you talk physics you tend to forget." Then, just before parting, he asked Lee a personal favor—to look after Toni in the future—in a way that implied Oppenheimer knew his death was imminent.[22]

Two weeks later, Oppenheimer attended a faculty meeting at which a new (nonpermanent) Institute member was hired. Dyson: "Poor Oppenheimer is coming close to his end. He insisted on coming to this faculty meeting but he can barely speak any more. We were all very polite and told him how glad we were that he came; but really it is a torture for everybody to watch him sit there speechless and suffering. His doctors have now given him up and we can only hope for a quick end."[23]

The last faculty meeting he attended was on February 15, 1967: "After making the supreme effort to come to our faculty meeting on Wednesday, he went home to bed so exhausted that he slept almost continuously until Saturday. On Saturday his sleep became gradually deeper and nobody could tell just when he died. After hearing this, one must admire the extraordinary will-power and courage that kept him going until Wednesday. He not only came to the meeting on Wednesday but he also had done the home-work for it, which meant reading and remembering a big box-full of papers."[24]

His death was announced in the papers on Sunday morning, as having taken place the previous day, February 18.

A memorial service was quickly arranged for the following Saturday, February 25. The event began with lunch for invited guests at Olden Manor, Oppenheimer's home for almost 20 years. The presence of so many figures from Oppenheimer's career, including former AEC chairman David Lilienthal, lawyer Lloyd Garrison, political colleague Arthur Schlesinger, Jr., and others, made the event, Pais recorded in his diary, seem "in the style of the epilogue."

After lunch, the group moved to Alexander Hall on the Princeton campus for the memorial service. A bitter cold spared the expected crowd from overflowing the space. Several inelegant details revealed the event's hasty organization—such as the way a big set of speakers, a podium, and setup for a string quartet were awkwardly crammed in a room for academic lectures. Pais's diary: "The Stravinsky piece was played from a tape. It was *extremely* eerie—an empty stage but with the chairs and music stands for a quartet—who were to play Beethoven later on—a lectern without speaker—and the new sounds of a Dies Irae coming from a big loudspeaker."

"J. Robert Oppenheimer did more than any other man to make American theoretical physics great," Hans Bethe began, the first of the three speakers, and Bethe continued with an overview of Oppenheimer's career in science and as a government adviser. Henry DeWolf Smyth (who never warmed to Oppenheimer), spoke of casting the sole vote among the five AEC commissioners in favor of reinstating Oppenheimer's security clearance, during the height of the McCarthy epoch. "It was a horrible period in American history, and we paid horribly for it."

Concluding speaker George Kennan was the most eloquent, and in short remarks tried to characterize Oppenheimer's ambitions and his acute disappointment when these were frustrated. While passionately desiring "to be useful in averting the catastrophes to which the development of the weapons of mass destruction threatened to lead," Kennan said, Oppenheimer knew that it was "as an American, and through the medium of this national community to which he belonged, that he saw his greatest possibilities for pursuing these ambitions." Shortly after the 1954 hearing, Kennan had asked Oppenheimer why he hadn't left the country, noting that he would be welcomed in "a hundred academic centers" around the globe. "Damn it, I happen to love this country," Oppenheimer had replied, tears in his eyes. Kennan continued,

> The truth is that the U.S. Government never had a servant more devoted at heart than this one, in the sense of wishing to make a constructive contribution; and I know of nothing more tragic than the series of mistakes (in part, no doubt, his own, but in what small part!) that made it impossible for him to render this contribution—that obliged him to spend the last decade and a half of his life eating out his heart in frustration over the consciousness that the talents he knew himself to possess, once welcomed and used by the official establishment of his country to develop the destructive possibilities of nuclear science, were rejected when it came to the development of the great positive ones he believed that science to possess. There was, I suspect, no conviction he held more dearly— none that meant more to him—than the belief that the science of nuclear physics harboured possibilities for communication and understanding among men as exciting in their way as its destructive possibilities were terrifying. It was one of the great disappointments of his life that he was permitted at the official level to contribute so greatly to the one, not at all to the other.

Kennan also tried, briefly and hesitatingly, to shed light on Oppenheimer's personality. "[H]e was also a man who had a deep yearning for friendship, for companionship, for the warmth and richness of human communication. The arrogance which to many appeared to be a part of his personality masked in reality an overpowering desire to bestow and receive affection. Neither circumstances nor at times the asperities of his own temperament permitted the gratification of this need in a measure remotely approaching its intensity; and in this too lay a portion of that strong element of tragedy which all who knew him sensed, I think, in his situation."[25]

Not long after the service, Kitty took Robert's ashes to St. John. She and Toni, accompanied by Erva and John Denham, went out on the Denham's boat and scattered the ashes by Carvel Rock, the dramatic up-cropping of granite blocks that the Oppenheimers had seen every day from their hut, past the mouth of Hawksnest Bay.[26] Years later, Kitty's ashes would be scattered there.

Meanwhile, the Monnaie de Paris struck the Oppenheimer medal with both the word "Caritas"—his initial, and then rejected, choice—and the equation $C(\psi) = \pm\psi^*$, his final choice, expressing a unity that depends on the presence of polar opposites.[27]

The American Physical Society held a memorial service at their April meeting in Washington, D.C. Speakers addressed different aspects of Oppenheimer's career: Serber "The Early Years," Weisskopf "The Los Alamos Years," Pais "The Princeton Period," Glenn Seaborg "Public Service and Human Contributions."[28]

Only Rabi ventured to step back to make direct comments (already quoted above by Pais) on the connections, good and bad, between Oppenheimer's life and his work.

In an unpublished review of the book made from these speeches,[29] Dyson wrote that "the real personality of Oppenheimer remains hidden." Indeed, Dyson continued, portions of the book "remind me uncomfortably of the testimony of the defense witnesses who failed to convince the judges in 1954;" that is, testimonials by eminences about Oppenheimer's greatness and virtue, which were rather simplistic and put "Oppenheimer upon so high a pedestal that it was easy for the prosecution in the end to knock him down." Dyson mentioned a comment Oppenheimer himself had made about Einstein in his controversial talk about Einstein: "I thought that it might be useful . . . to start to dispel the clouds of myth and to see the great mountain peak that these clouds hide. As always the myth has its charms; but the truth is far more beautiful."[30] Mt. Oppenheimer, Dyson was suggesting, remains similarly cloaked, and the effort to chart its peaks was threatened not only by mists but also by unwary surveyors.

This was not all their fault. Oppenheimer himself did little to dispel the clouds of myth. Despite his seemingly candid remark in Geneva in 1964 regarding his life being an open book, he did not act, either to himself or others, as though this were the case. He left no personal diary, no autobiography. He repeatedly—and clearly deliberately—frustrated efforts by interviewers to elicit personal feelings and reflections about what he'd been through. He sought successfully to prevent performance in the United States of a play based on his life. He would only speak, as in the words of the 1945 farewell speech at Los Alamos, of "what has happened to us" rather than "what has happened to me."

Kennan's reference, at Oppenheimer's memorial service, to "that strong element of tragedy . . . in his situation" refers to more than the hearing, when he was abruptly, traumatically, and publicly removed from the realm in which he was flourishing. It also refers to his failure to achieve in physics what his capacity seemed to promise. In his introduction, Pais called this, rather than the hearing, Oppenheimer's real tragedy. And in another note, Pais wrote of Oppenheimer, "His tragedy is that he was almost a genius."[31] Yet a final tragic element of Oppenheimer's life is the way he evoked the promise of more than he delivered. He gave the appearance, as Weisskopf once put it, of representing "the spirit and the philosophy of all that for which we are living," but also gave the appearance of, to some extent, having let us, and himself, down. Something about J. Robert Oppenheimer indeed made us want mermaids.

Oppenheimer provided a few tantalizing remarks in which he may have referred to what he felt about what he had been though, but he puts them, of course, into the mouths of others while keeping a safe distance. The following remark about Galileo made in 1964, for instance, surely invites allegory: "The later days, when he lived in some fear and suffered the great indignity of his abjuration, and alienation from many of his friends, were certainly sad years." But despite all that, Oppenheimer continued, Galileo continued to display to the end "a quality which I believe to be true of science in the making: a great sunniness in the act of finding out new things, things that he had not quite expected, things that reflected deeply on beliefs long held, and that pointed both in hope and in mystery to the future."[32]

The remark is classic Oppenheimer, and not only for the way it suggests an implausible complementarity between suffering and joy, past and present; nor for its manufactured grandeur and simulated sincerity; nor for the expectations it creates of personal revelation without satisfaction. It is also the way its note of depth sounds just a little hollow, and again a note of optimism that rings just a little false, so that it seems less a personal expression than a statement issued by a public custody. But Oppenheimer was acute enough to have heard these notes himself.

When thinking of a literary analogue for Oppenheimer's life, Pais thought not of tragedy, but of Henry James's sentimental novel *The Beast in the Jungle*. Its protagonist, John Marcher, lives his life keeping a distance from those around him, in the belief that he has been selected for some prodigious event—in his dreams it takes the form of an encounter with a beast lying in wait—only to find, in the end, that the event in question has already taken place, which thanks to his aloofness has passed him by. This aspect may also be why, when Pais interviewed Melba Phillips, she suggested that he read J. P. Marquand's book *The Late George Apley*, whose eponymous hero, born into wealth and privilege, takes himself far too seriously and never quite lives up to his own expectations. Both of these books resonate with important aspects of Oppenheimer's life, but neither are tragedies.

In multiple ways, then, Oppenheimer's life both attracts and yet repels the characterization "tragic." It's a tragedy without a tragic hero; or, to put it another way that paraphrases Pais, the tragedy of J. Robert Oppenheimer was that he was *almost* a tragic figure.

In a photocopy of a few pages on which he had written "For Epilog," Pais marked the following lines from Sanskrit, that Oppenheimer translated himself and recited to Vannevar Bush two nights before Alamogordo:

In battle, in the forest, at the precipice in the mountains
On the dark great sea, in the midst of javelins and arrows,
In sleep, in confusion, in the depths of shame,
The good deeds a man has done before defend him.[33]

And at the eulogy which Pais delivered for Oppenheimer, Pais said, "Any single one of the following contributions would have marked Oppenheimer out as a pre-eminent scientist: his own research work in physics; his influence as a teacher; his leadership at Los Alamos; the growth of the Institute for Advanced Study as a leading center of theoretical physics under his directorship; and his efforts to promote a more common understanding of science. When all is combined we honor Oppenheimer as a great leader of science. When all is interwoven with the dramatic events that centered around him we remember Oppenheimer as one of the most remarkable personalities of this century."[34]

NOTES

FREQUENTLY USED ABBREVIATIONS

AEC	Atomic Energy Commission
Am. J. Phys.	*American Journal of Physics*
Am. Scientist	*American Scientist*
Am. Scholar	*American Scholar*
Ann. d. Phys.	Annalen der Physik
AP	Abraham Pais
Astrophys. J.	*Astrophysical Journal*
Biogr. Mem. F. R. S.	*Biographical Memoirs of Fellows of the Royal Society*
Bull. At. Scientists	*Bulletin of the Atomic Scientists*
CUOHO	Columbia University Oral History Office
Deutsch. Phys. Ges.	*Deutsche Physikalische Gesellschaft*
IAS	Institute for Advanced Study, Princeton University
IMJRO	*In the Matter of J. Robert Oppenheimer: Transcript of Hearing Before Personnel Security Board, United States Atomic Energy Commission*
J. Appl. Phys.	*Journal of Applied Physics*
J. Chem. Phys.	*Journal of Chemical Physics*
JCAE	Joint Committee on Atomic Energy
J. Gen. Physiology	*Journal of General Physiology*
JRO	J. Robert Oppenheimer
LC	Library of Congress
Nature	*Nature*
Naturw.	*Naturwissenschaften*
NBA	Neils Bohr Archive, Copenhagen
O.	Oppenheimer
O. FBI	Oppenheimer FBI File

Phys. Rev.	*Physical Review*
Phys. Today	*Physics Today*
Political Sci. Quarterly	*Political Science Quarterly*
Proc. Cambr. Phil. Soc.	*Proceedings of the Cambridge Philosophical Society*
Proc. Nat. Ac. Sci.	*Proceedings of the National Academy of Sciences of the United States of America*
Proc. Phys.-Math. Soc. Japan	*Proceedings of the Physics-Mathematical Society of Japan*
Proc. Roy. Soc.	*Proceedings of the Royal Society*
Progr. Theor. Phys.	*Progress of Theoretical Physics*
Quart. Appl. Math.	*Quarterly of Applied Mathematics*
Rev. Mod. Phys.	*Review of Modern Physics*
SAC	Strategic Air Command
Sci. Am.	*Scientific American*
UNAEC	United Nations Atomic Energy Commission
Zeitschr. f. Phys.	*Zeitschrift für Physik*

Abraham Pais employed a unique system of citation. When citing works that have been referred to in an earlier note, his notes will cite the number of that note rather than the title or author of the work. Thus Note 7 refers the reader to Note 5, which cites *Robert Oppenheimer, Letters and Recollections*. Cross-references in the text use the same method. Pais left the manuscript incomplete at the time of his death; in preparing the book for publication Ida Nicolaisen and Robert P. Crease made the decision to preserve the notes as Pais had left them, emended as necessary, because of the risk of introducing errors by attempting to revise and renumber every note. The reader will find that the notes are not always numbered consecutively and that there are occasions in which a numbered note appears with a letter (e.g., note 26a). These characteristics reflect the deletion or interpolation of notes as the text was prepared for publication.

1. K. Darrow, Phys. Rev. *70*, 784, 1946.
2. A. Pais, Phys. Rev. *70*, 796, 1946.
3. O., Phys. Rev. *71*, 460, 1947.
4. T. S. Kuhn, interview with O., November 18, 1963, NBA.
5. *Robert Oppenheimer, Letters and Recollections*, p. 2, where Frank Oppenheimer is quoted, A. K. Smith and C. Weiner, eds., Harvard University Press, Cambridge 1980. Reprinted by Stanford University Press, 1995.
6. P. Michelmore, *The Swift Years*, p. 142, Dodd, Mead and Co., New York 1949.
7. Ref. 5, p. 5.
8. P. Goodchild, *J. Robert Oppenheimer: Shatterer of Worlds*, p. 11, Ariel Books, London 1980. Reprinted by BBC Books, 1980.
9. Ref. 5, p. 6.
10. See H. Bethe, Biogr. Mem. F. R. S., *14*, 391, 1968.
11. I. Rabi, in *Oppenheimer*, p. 4, Scribner's, New York 1969.
12. Ref. 5, pp. 6–8.
13. *Ibid.*, p. 9.
14. Ref. 8, p. 13.
15. *Ibid.*
18. O., Proc. Cambr. Phil. Soc. *23*, 327, 422, 1926.

20. M. Born and O., Ann. d. Phys. *43*, 27, 1927.
21. O., Nature, 118, 711, 1926. *See also* O., Naturw. *14*, 1282, 1926; O., Zeitschr. f. Phys. *41*, 268, 1927.
22. T. S. Kuhn, interview with O., November 20, 1963, NBA.
23. O., letter to F. Fergusson, November 14, 1926, Ref. 5, p. 101.
24. T. S. Kuhn, interview with P. A. M. Dirac, May 14, 1963, NBA.
25. M. Born, *My Life*, p. 229, Taylor & Francis, London 1978.
26. *Ibid.*, p. 233.
27. Ref. 5, p. 86.
28. *Ibid.*, p. 91.
29. *Ibid.*, p. 94.
30. Ref. 8, p. 18.
31. Ref. 5, p. 110.
32. O., Proc. Nat. Ac. Sci. *13*, 800, 1927.
33. O., Phys. Rev. *31*, 66, 1927.
34. *Ibid.*, 349.
35. O., Proc. Nat. Ac. Sci., *14*, 261, 363, 1928 (the quotation in the text is from the second of these). *See also* O., Phys. Rev. *31*, 914; *32*, 361, 1928.
36. T. Kuhn, interview with G. E. Uhlenbeck, March 30, 1962.
36a. O., letter to H. Casimir, November 29, 1946, copy in my personal files.
37. P. Ehrenfest, letter to W. Pauli, November 26, 1928, *Wolfgang Pauli, Scientific Correspondence*, Vol. 1, p. 477, Springer, New York 1979.
38. P. Ehrenfest and O., Phys. Rev. *37*, 333, 1931.
39. W. Pauli, letter to P. Ehrenfest, February 15, 1929, ref. 37, p. 486.
40. O., Zeitschr. f. Phys. *55*, 725, 1929.
41. W. Pauli, letter to A. Sommerfeld, May 16, 1929, ref. 37, p. 500.
42. W. Heisenberg and W. Pauli, Zeitschr. f. Phys. *56*, 1, 1929.
43. W. Heisenberg and W. Pauli, Zeitschr. f. Phys. *59*, 168, 1930.
44. W. Pauli, letter to N. Bohr, July 17, 1929, ref. 37, p. 512.
45. W. Heisenberg, letter to W. Pauli, July 20, 1929, ref. 37, p. 514.
46. O., Phys. Rev. *35*, 461, 1930.
47. R. Serber, ref. 11, p. 11.
48. R. Serber with R. Crease, *Peace and War*, p. 42, Columbia University Press, New York 1998.
49. W. Lamb, in *The Birth of Particle Physics*, p. 311, L. Brown and L. Hoddeson, eds., Cambridge University Press 1985.
50. R. Serber in ref. 47, p. 16.
52. O., Phys. Rev. *35*, 562, 1930.
53. P. A. M. Dirac, in *History of Twentieth-Century Physics*, p. 144, C. Weiner, ed., Academic Press, New York 1977.
54. O., Phys. Rev. *35*, 939, 1930.
55. O. and H. Hall, Phys. Rev. *38*, 57, 71, 589, 1931.
56. O., Phys. Rev. *30*, 725, 1931.
57. O. and F. Carlson, Phys. Rev. *39*, 864, 1932.
58. O. and F. Carlson, Phys. Rev. *41*, 763, 1932.
59. See e.g. A. Pais, *Inward Bound*, Chapter 14, section (b), Oxford University Press, New York 1986.
60. See ref. 59, section (d).
61. J. Chadwick, Nature *129*, 312, 1932.
62. J. Carlson and O., Phys. Rev. *41*, 763, 1932.

63. C. D. Anderson, in Science News Letter of December 19, 1931. *See also* Science *76*, 238, 1932; Phys. Rev. *43*, 491, 1933.
64. O. and M. S. Plessett, Phys. Rev. *44*, 53, 1933.
65. W. Heitler and F. Sauter, Nature *132*, 892, 1933. *See also* E. Fermi and G. E. Uhlenbeck, Phys. Rev. *44*, 510, 1933; H. Bethe and W. Heitler, Proc. Roy. Soc. *A146*, 83, 1934, footnote on p. 108.
66. L. Nedelsky and O., Phys. Rev. *44*, 948, 1933. *See also* L. Nedelsky and O., Phys. Rev. *45*, 136, 1934.
67. L. Nedelsky and O., Phys. Rev. *45*, 283, 1934.
68. W. L. Severinghaus, Phys. Rev. *45*, 284, 1934.
69. W. Furry and O., Phys. Rev. *45*, 343, 903, 1934.
70. P. A. M. Dirac, Proc. Cambr. Phil. Soc. *30*, 150, 1934.
71. R. Serber, Phys. Rev. *48*, 49, 1935.
72. E. Uehling, Phys. Rev. *48*, 55, 1935.
73. A. Wightman and S. Schweber, Phys. Rev. *98*, 812, 1955.
74. C. Lauritsen and O., Phys. Rev. *46*, 80, 1934.
75. O., Phys. Rev. *47*, 144, 1935.
76. *Ibid.*, 146.
77. *Ibid.*, 44.
78. O., Phys. Rev. *43*, 380, 1933.
79. O., Phys. Rev. *47*, 845, 1935. *See also* O. and M. Phillips, Phys. Rev. *48*, 500, 1935.
80. O. and R. Serber, Phys. Rev. *50*, 391, 1936.
81. G. and L. Nordheim, O. and R. Serber, Phys. Rev. *51*, 1037, 1937.
82. F. Kalckar, O. and R. Serber, Phys. Rev. *52*, 273, 1937.
83. *Ibid.*, 279.
84. O. and R. Serber, Phys. Rev. 53, 636, 1938.
85. O., Phys. Rev. *50*, 389, 1936. *See also* ref. 48, p. 47.
86. F. Carlson and O., Phys. Rev. *51*, 220, 1937.
87. H. Snyder, Phys. Rev. *53*, 960, 1938.
88. R. Serber, Phys. Rev. *54*, 317, 1938.
89. W. Heisenberg, Zeitschr. f. Phys. *101*, 533, 1936.
90. W. Heisenberg, Verl. Deutsch. Phys. Ges. *18*, 50, 1937.
91. S. Neddermeyer and C. D. Anderson, Phys. Rev. *51*, 884, 1937. *See also* J. Street and E. Stevenson, Phys. Rev. *51*, 1005, 1937.
92. O. and R. Serber, Phys. Rev. *51*, 1113, 1937.
93. H. Yukawa, Proc. Phys.-Math. Soc. Japan *17*, 48, 1935.
94. Ref. 48, p. 44.
95. C. F. Powell, et al. Nature *159*, 694, 1947.
96. O., H. Snyder, and R. Serber, Phys. Rev. *57*, 75, 1940.
97. R. Christy and S. Kusaka, Phys. Rev. *59*, 405, 414, 1941.
98. O., Phys. Rev. *59*, 462, 1941.
99. R. Christy and O., Phys. Rev. *60*, 159, 1941; *See also* O. and E. Nelson, Phys. Rev. *60*, 159, 1941; *61*, 202, 1942.
100. O., H. Lewis and S. Wouthuysen, Phys. Rev. *73*, 127, 1948.
101. O., Phys. Rev. *59*, 908, 1941.
102. O. and J. Schwinger, Phys. Rev. *60*, 150, 1941.
103. O. and J. Schwinger, Phys. Rev. *56*, 1066, 1959; *See also* O., Phys. Rev. *60*, 164, 1941.
104. O. and R. Serber, Phys. Rev. *54*, 540, 1938.

105. L. D. Landau, Nature *141*, 333, 1938.
106. R. Tolman, Phys. Rev. *55*, 364, 1939.
107. O. and G. Volkoff, Phys. Rev. *55*, 374, 1939.
108. For further details see C. Misner, K. Thorne, and J. Wheeler, *Gravitation*, p. 627, Freeman, San Francisco 1973.
109. O. and H. Snyder, Phys. Rev. *56*, 455, 1939.
110. J. Wheeler, Am. Scholar *37*, 248, 1968. *See also* J. Wheeler, Am. Scientist *56*, 1, 1968.
111. S. Weinberg, *Gravitation and Cosmology*, Chapter 14, section 5, Wiley, New York 1972.
112. Ref. 5, p. 144.
113. *Ibid.*, p. 145.
114. *Ibid.*, p. 146.
115. *In the Matter of J. Robert Oppenheimer*, p. 8, U.S. Government printing office, Washington, D.C. 1954. Reprinted by MIT Press 1971.
116. Ref. 48, p. 27.
117. Ref. 5, p. 138.
118. *Ibid.*, p. 149.
119. *Ibid.*, p. 183.
120. Ref. 8, p. 35.
120a. Ref. 48, p. 86.
121. Ref. 115, pp. 8–10.
124. Ref. 48, pp. 59–60.
125. Ref. 8, pp. 39–40.
126. Ref. 115, p. 11.
127. O. Hahn and F. Strassmann, Naturw. *27*, 11, 1939. *See also* Engl. transl. by H. Graetner, Am. J. Phys. *32*, 9, 1964.
128. G. Seaborg, ref. 11, p. 47.
129. O., letter to W. Fowler, January 28, 1939, ref. 5, p. 207.
130. O., ref. 115, p. 11.
132. L. R. Groves, *Now It Can Be Told*, p. 62, Harper and Row, New York 1962.
133. N. P. Davis, *Lawrence and Oppenheimer*, p. 144, Simon and Schuster, New York 1968.
134. Ref. 132, p. 63.
135. O., ref. 115, p. 12.
136. D. Hawkins, *Toward Trinity*, Chapter 1, Tomash, San Francisco 1983.
137. Ref. 5, p. 261.
138. V. Weisskopf, ref. 11, p. 23.
139. H. Bethe, Science *155*, 1082, 1967.
140. R. Rhodes, *The Making of the Atomic Bomb*, Simon and Schuster, New York 1986.
141. Ref. 133 pp. 233–240.
142. O. Frisch, quoted in ref. 8, p. 161.
143. Ref. 8, p. 162.
144. Ref. 133, p. 241.
145. O., ref. 115, p. 14.
146. Ref. 133, p. 242.
147. Ref. 140, p. 613.
148. "Notes on the Interim Committee meeting of May 31, 1945." Reprinted in M. Sherwin, *A World Destroyed*, p. 295, A. Knopf, New York 1975.
149. Ref. 148, p. 304–5.

149a. Ref. 115, p. 34.
150. Ref. 8, p. 167.
151. The letter is reproduced in full in ref. 5, p. 293.
152. Quoted in ref. 8, p. 173.
153. Quoted in ref. 133, p. 254.
153a. Ref. 5, pp. 310–11.
153b. *Ibid.*, pp. 315–25.
154. Ref. 115, p. 15.
155. *New York Times*, January 21, 1923. See also *New York Times*, March 13, 1924.
156. A. Flexner, *An Autobiography*, Simon and Schuster, New York 1960.
157. A. Flexner, *The American College*, Century, New York 1908.
158. A. Flexner, *Medical Education in the United States and Canada: A Report to the Carnegie Foundation for the Advancement of Teaching*, Arno Press, New York 1972.
159. *New York Times*, May 28, 1928.
160. A. Flexner, *Universities: American, English, German*, Oxford University Press 1930.
161. *New York Times*, June 8, 1930.
162. *Ibid.*, October 12, 1930.
163. *Ibid.*, April 19, 1955.
164. IAS, minutes of October 10, 1932.
165. P. Frank, *Einstein, His Life and Times*, pp. 178, 266, A. Knopf, New York 1947.
166. Minutes, Trustees' meeting, October 11, 1937.
167. The Rockefeller Foundation Annual Report for 1936, pp. 46, 290, 351, 379.
168. Most of my information on the Gest Library comes from Hu Shih, Princeton University Library Chronicle *15*, Spring 1954. Reprinted in 1967.
169. A. Flexner, letter to L. Bamberger, July 1, 1933.
170. Minutes, Trustees' meeting, January 27, 1936.
171. W. Riefler and O. Veblen, letter to A. Flexner, March 14, 1936.
172. A. Flexner, *Harper's Magazine*, October 1939.
173. Chairman, letter to Flexner, February 22, 1939.
174. A. Flexner, letter to Professor Riefler, May 10, 1939.
175. Minutes, Trustees' meeting, May 22, 1939.
176. A. Flexner, letter to Trustee Leidesdorf, June 29, 1939.
177. Earle, letter to Flexner, June 9, 1939.
178. Earle, letter to W. O. Aydelotte, June 28, 1939.
179. Minutes, Trustees' meeting, October 9, 1939.
180. Aydelotte, cable to Flexner, October 18, 1939.
181. Flexner, letter to Aydelotte, October 17, 1939.
182. Minutes, Trustees' meeting, January 22, 1940.
183. A. Flexner, *I Remember*, p. 397, Simon and Schuster, New York 1940.
184. *Newark Evening News*, March 13, 1944.
185. *Newark Sunday Call*, March 12, 1944.
186. *New York Herald Tribune*, July 27, 1944.
187. IAS Bulletin No. 11, March 1945.
188. A. Einstein, letter to W. O. Aydelotte, December 24, 1941.
189. O. Veblen, letter to Aydelotte, January 1, 1940.
190. Veblen, memorandum to Policy Committee, November 8, 1944.
191. Aydelotte, penciled note of meeting with Trustee Douglas, November 20, 1944.
192. Minutes, Trustees' meeting, January 19, 1945.
193. IAS Bulletin No. 12, 1945–1946, October 1946.

194. For the history of this computer see my essay on von Neumann in A. Pais, *The Genius of Science*, Oxford University Press, New York 2000.

195. For obituaries of Flexner see *New York Times* and *Washington Post*, both on September 22, 1959.

196. Trustee Moe to Faculty, October 26, 1945.

197. Alexander, Earle, and Panofsky to Faculty, February 4, 1946.

198. Minutes, School of Mathematics, September 25, 1945.

199. Ref. 115, p. 15.

200. *New York Times*, October 18, 1945.

201. *Ibid.*, October 14, 1945.

202. Ref. 8, pp. 177–78.

203. R. Hewlett and O. Anderson, *The New World, 1939–1946*, p. 647, Pennsylvania State University Press, University Press 1969.

204. Private communication from Roger Meade, Los Alamos archivist.

205. The text of the McMahon bill is reproduced in ref. 372a, p. 714.

206. *New York Times*, August 2, 1946.

207. *Ibid.*, October 29, 1946. *See also* L. Strauss, *Men and Decisions*, pp. 210–13, Doubleday, New York 1962.

208. *New York Times*, December 13, 1946.

209. *Ibid.*, December 23, 1946.

210. Aydelotte, letter to Pais, December 6, 1946.

211. Veblen, letter to Strauss, April 12, 1946.

212. Earle, letter to Strauss, November 4, 1946.

213. Strauss has recalled that he did so during a meeting with Oppenheimer at San Francisco Airport, ref. 207, pp. 270, 271.

214. Minutes, Trustees' special meeting, April 1, 1947.

215. Memorandum by Einstein and Weyl to the School of Mathematics, meetings February 2, 1945; March 5, 1945.

216. Ref. 115, pp. 26, 27.

217. Aydelotte, letter to O., April 5, 1947.

218. John F. Fulton Papers, Manuscript and Archives Division, Yale Library, New Haven; Diary entry, March 15, 1947.

219. Lloyd Garrison, summation, ref. 115, p. 971.

220. Patterson, letter to Lilienthal, March 25, 1947, ref. 115, p. 377.

221. Groves, letter to Patterson, March 24, 1947, ref. 115, p. 179.

222. Conant, letter to Lilienthal, March 27, 1947, ref. 115, p. 378.

223. Ref. 115, p. 425.

224. Minutes, Faculty Standing Committee, September 29, 1947.

225. Minutes, Trustees' meeting, December 16, 1947.

226. G. Kennan, in *Foreign Affairs*, July 1947.

227. *New York Times Magazine*, April 18, 1948.

228. *Time Magazine*, November 8, 1948.

229. Minutes, Faculty Meeting, March 8, 1949.

230. O., letter to A. Pais, April 20, 1949.

231. "Director's Report for 1948–1953," published by the Institute, 1954.

232. O., letter to H. Marshall Chadwell, September 26, 1949.

233. P. Morrison, J. Appl. Phys. *18*, 133, 1947.

234. A. Pais, *Inward Bound*, Chapters 18, 19, Oxford Universitiy Press, New York 1986.

235. O., in *Science in the University: by the Members of the Faculties of the University of California*, p. 23, University of California Press, Berkeley 1944.

236. O., with H. Bethe, Phys. Rev. *70*, 451, 1946.
237. O., with S. Epstein and R. J. Finkelstein, Phys. Rev. *73*, 1140, 1948.
238. O., Rev. Mod. Phys. *21*, 34, 1949.
239. O., with W. Arnold, J. Gen. Physiology *33*, 423, 1950.
240. O., Rev. Mod. Phys. *28*, 1, 1956.
241. O., Science *89*, 335, 1939.
242. O., Sci. Am., September 1950, p. 21.
243. They were S. Epstein, R. Finkelstein, L. Foldy, H. Lewis, and S. Wouthnizen. All these were to become full professors at various universities.
244. O., *Knowledge and the Structure of Culture*, The Helen Kenyon Lecture [no. 16], Vassar College, Poughkeepsie, New York 1958.
245. F. J. Dyson, Phys. Rev. *73*, 1272, 1948.
246. D. Weeks and J. James, *Eccentrics*, Orion Books, London 1966.
247. F. J. Dyson, *Disturbing the Universe*, Harper and Row, New York 1979.
248. F. J. Dyson, Phys. Today *42*, February 1989, p. 32.
249. F. J. Dyson, Phys. Rev. *75*, 486, 1736, 1949.
250. F. J. Dyson, *Values at War: Selected Tanner Lectures on the Nuclear Crisis*, University of Utah Press, Salt Lake City 1983.
251. F. J. Dyson, *Weapons and Hope*, Harper and Row, New York 1984.
252. F. J. Dyson, *Origins of Life*, Cambridge University Press, Cambridge 1986.
253. F. J. Dyson, *Infinite in All Directions*, Harper and Row, New York 1988.
254. F. J. Dyson, *From Eros to Gaia*, Pantheon Books, New York 1992.
255. F. J. Dyson, *Foreign Affairs*, April 1960, p. 457.
256. C. N. Yang, *Selected Papers*, pp. 3, 4, Freeman, San Francisco 1983.
257. C. N. Yang, J. Chem. Phys. *13*, 66, 1945.
258. Ref. 256, p. 305.
259. C. N. Yang, Phys. Rev. *74*, 764, 1948.
260. C. N. Yang, Phys. Rev. *77*, 242, 722, 1950.
261. C. N. Yang and J. Tiomno, Phys. Rev. *79*, 495, 1950.
262. Minutes, Executive Committee, February 21, 1950.
263. Minutes, School of Mathematics, April 2, 1952.
264. C. N. Yang, Phys. Rev. *85*, 808, 1952.
264a. [Pais refers to the Ising model, a model of ordering of atoms in magnets— first in one dimension, then extended to two—developed by Ernst Ising, that has frequently captured the attention of theorists—RPC]
265. T. D. Lee, Astrophys. J. *111*, 625, 1950.
266. T. D. Lee, Phys. Rev. *77*, 842, 1950. *See also* T. D. Lee, Astrophys. J. *112*, 561, 1950; T. D. Lee, J. Appl. Phys. *22*, 524, 1952; T. D. Lee, Quart. Appl. Math. *10*, 69, 1952.
267. T. D. Lee, M. Rosenbluth, and C. N. Yang, Phys. Rev. *75*, 905, 1949.
268. T. D. Lee and R. Christian, Phys. Rev. *94*, 1760, 1954. *See also* T. D. Lee, R. Christian, and R. Friedman, Phys. Rev. *100*, 1494, 1955.
269. E. Henley and T. D. Lee, Phys. Rev. *101*, 1536, 1956.
270. T. D. Lee, F. Low, and D. Pines, Phys. Rev. *90*, 297, 1953. *See also* T. D. Lee and D. Pines, Phys. Rev. *92*, 883, 1953.
271. T. D. Lee, Phys. Rev. *95*, 1329, 1954.
272. T. D. Lee and C. N. Yang, Phys. Rev. *104*, 254, 1956.
273. S. Tomonaga in *Les Prix Nobel en 1965*, p. 151, Norstedt, Stockholm 1966.
274. For more details about Bohm's career, see H. J. Hiley, Biogr. Mem. F. R. S. *43*, 107, 1997, which has also been of help in my own sketch of parts of Bohm's life.

275. Ref. 115, p. 150.
276. Minutes, Trustees' Meeting, April 15, 1948.
277. E. Corson, Phys. Rev. *70*, 728, 1946.
278. This information is part of a write-up distributed by the local press to participants of "Shelter Island II," a conference held June 1–4, 1988 to commemorate the conference I am about to describe.
279. They were Hans Bethe, David Bohm, Gregory Breit, Darrow, Herman Feshbach, Feynman, Kramers, Willis Lamb, Robert Marshak, von Neumann, Arnold Nordsieck, Oppenheimer, Pais, Linus Pauling, Rabi, Bruno Rossi, Julian Schwinger, Robert Serber, Edward Teller, Uhlenbeck, Van Vleck, Weisskopf, and Wheeler.
280. *New York Herald Tribune*, June 3, 1947. *See also* the September 29, 1947 issues of both *Newsweek* and *Time*.
281. K. K. Darrow, diary entry for June 3, 1947. Diaries deposited in Niels Bohr Library, New York.
282. V. Weisskopf, interview by S. Schweber, February 14, 1981.
283. A. Pais, *Inward Bound*, Chapter 18, Oxford University Press, New York 1986. The best historical accounts of the conference are by S. Schweber, in *Relativistic Groups and Topology*, p. 40, B. de Witt and S. Stora, eds., Elsevier, New York 1984; and in *Shelter Island II*, p. 301, N. Khuri et al., eds., MIT Press, Cambridge, Mass. 1985.
284. W. Lamb and R. Retherford, Phys. Rev. *72*, 241, 1947. *See also* J. Nafe, E. Nelson, and I. Rabi, Phys. Rev. *71*, 914, 1947.
285. R. Marshak and H. Bethe, Phys. Rev. *72*, 506, 1947.
286. O., letter to F. B. Jewett, June 4, 1947, copy in Rockefeller University Archives.
287. C. F. Powell et al., Nature *159*, 694, 1947.
288. H. Bethe, letter to O., June 9, 1947.
289. H. Bethe, Phys. Rev. *72*, 339, 1947.
290. J. Schwinger, Phys. Rev. *73*, 416, 1948.
291. For an excellent review of the history of the subject up to 1950, see S. S. Schweber, *QED*, Princeton University Press, Princeton 1994.
292. Ref. 281, entry for June 4, 1947.
293. S. Tomonaga, Progr. Theor. Phys. *1*, 27, 1946; *2*, 101, 1947.
294. Z. Koba and S. Tomonaga, Progr. Theor. Phys. *2*, 218, 1947.
295. T. Tati and S. Tomonaga, Progr. Theor. Phys. *3*, 391, 1948.
296. S. Tomonaga, Phys. Rev. *74*, 224, 1948.
297. O., in *Les particules élémentaires*, p. 269, R. Stoops, ed., Coudenberg, Brussels 1950.
298. A. Pais, *Developments in the Theory of the Electron*, Princeton University Press, Princeton 1948.
299. Ref. 297, pp. 117–28, discussion following the communication by C. F. Powell.
300. R. P. Feynman, Phys. Rev. *76*, 749, 1949; *See also* Feynman, Phys. Rev. *76*, 769, 1949; Feynman, Phys. Rev. *80*, 440, 1950.
301. J. Steinberger, W. K. H. Panofsky, and J. Steller, Phys. Rev. *78*, 802, 1956.
302. J. Polkinghorne, *Rochester Roundabout*, Freeman, San Francisco 1989.
303. L. Brown and L. Hoddeson, *The Birth of Particle Physics*, Cambridge University Press, Cambridge 1983; contribution by R. Marshak, p. 376.
304. Ref. 302, p. 29.

305. *Ibid.*, p. 32; for details, see ref. 283, chapter 20.
306. *Ibid.*, p. 35.
307. Address by Dr. J. Robert Oppenheimer, Tuesday, April 7, 1953, published by IBM.
308. O., *New York Times Book Review*, October 18, 1953.
309. G. Dean, *Report on the Atom*, Knopf, New York 1953.
310. For more details of this conference, see A. Pais, *A Tale of Two Continents*, Chapter 22, Princeton University Press, Princeton 1997.
311. L. V. Berkner, Phys. Today, January 1954, p. 14.
312. Proc. 4th Rochester Conference (mimeographed), p. 28.
313. R. Wilson, in *All in Our Time*, p. 142, ed. J. Wilson, Educational Foundation Med. Sci., Chicago 1975.
314. *Critical Assembly: A Technical History of Los Alamos During the Oppenheimer Years, 1943–1945*, p. 104, L. Hoddeson et al., eds., Cambridge University Press, Cambridge 1993.
315. H. Bethe, *The Road from Los Alamos*, p. 224, Simon & Schuster, New York 1991.
316. Ref. 140, p. 570.
317. *Ibid.*, p. 444.
318. J. Bernstein, *Hans Bethe: Prophet of Energy*, p. 72, Basic Books, New York 1980.
319. Ref. 140, p. 417.
320. R. Coughlin, *Life Magazine*, December 13, 1963.
321. S. Blumberg and G. Owens, *Energy and Conflict*, p. 77, Putnam, New York 1976.
322. O., letter to E. Teller, September 11, 1942, ref. 5, p. 228.
323. N. P. Davis, *Lawrence and Oppenheimer*, pp. 178, 180, DaCapo Press, New York 1986.
324. E. Teller and A. Brown, *The Legacy of Hiroshima*, pp. 39, 40, Doubleday, New York 1962.
325. O. papers, July 21, 1943, box 20, LC.
326. E. Teller in *Los Alamos Science*, winter 1983 issue.
327. Ref. 140, p. 565.
328. *Ibid.*, p. 444.
329. *Ibid.*, p. 468.
330. *Reminiscences of Los Alamos 1943–1945*, p. 107, L. Badasl, J. O. Hirschfelder, and H. P. Broida, eds., Reidel, Boston 1980.
331. L. Alvarez, *Adventures of a Physicist*, p. 78, Basic Books, New York 1987.
332. Ref. 330, p. 128.
333. R. Serber, with R. Crease, *Peace and War*, p. 85–86, Columbia University Press, New York 1998.
334. Ref. 333, p. 89.
335. Bohr's war experiences are described in detail in A. Pais, *Niels Bohr's Times*, Chapter 21, Oxford University Press 1991.
338. O., letter to Gen. Groves, January 1, 1944, copy in NBA.
339. H. Bethe and E. Teller, memorandum to Gen. Groves, January 1, 1944, copy in NBA.
340. Ref. 318, p. 77.
341. Letter reproduced in ref. 5, p. 270.
342. W. Akers, letter to Michael Perrin, British officials, January 27, 1944, copy in NBA.

343. J. Rud Nielsen, Phys. Today, October 1963, p. 22.
344. N. Bohr, letter to Gen. Groves, March 22, 1944, copy in NBA.
345. N. Bohr, letter to O., June 19, 19144, copy in NBA.
346. O., *New York Review of Books*, December 17, 1964.
347. Ref. 330, p. 41.
349. O. papers, box 66, LC.
350. O., FBI file doc. 65.
351. Letter by Gen. Groves to O., July 29, 1943. Reprinted in ref. 5, p. 262.
352. Ref. 5, p. 265.
353. President Roosevelt, letter to O., June 29, 1943, O. papers, box 62, LC.
354. O., letter to President Roosevelt, July 9, 1943. Reprinted in ref. 5, p. 260.
355. A. Einstein, letter to O., September 29, 1945. Reprinted in O. Nathan and H. Norden, *Einstein on Peace*, p. 338, Methuen, London 1963.
356. O., letter to A. Einstein, October 10, 1945. Reprinted in ref. 5, p. 309.
357. O., Sci. Am. *183*, September 1950, p. 20.
358. Ref. 302, pp. 90, 91.
364. G. Seaborg, ref. 11, p. 51.
365. O., in *One World or None*, p. 22, McGraw Hill, New York 1946.
366. For other contemporaneous estimates of the costs of atomic explosives and of their delivery see the article by Henry "Hap" Arnold, head of the U.S. Air Forces from 1943–1946, ref. 365, p. 26.
367. O., letter to N. Bohr, December 14, 1945, NBA.
368. N. Bohr, letter to O., stamped SECRET, June 19, 1944, NBA.
369. O., Bull. At. Scientists *7*, 7, January 1951.
370. D. Acheson, *Present at the Creation*, p. 151, Norton, New York 1969.
371. Ref. 8, pp. 178–79.
372. D. Lilienthal, *Journals*, Vol. II, p. 13, Harper and Row, New York 1964.
372a. Richard G. Hewlett and Oscar E. Anderson, Jr., *The New World, 1939–1946. A History of the Atomic Energy Commission, Volume I*, p. 535, University of California Press, Berkeley, 1990.
373. Ref. 372, p. 16.
374. Lilienthal, letter to H. Marks, January 14, 1948, O. papers, box 46, LC.
374a. Ref. 372a, p. 536.
375. O., Bull. At. Scientists *1*, 2, December 1946.
376. Ref. 372, p. 25.
377. *Ibid.*, p. 27.
378. *Ibid.*, p. 28.
379. Ref. 372a, p. 501.
380. For much more detail about the Nunn May affair see R. Rhodes, *Dark Sun*, p. 150ff, Simon and Schuster, New York 1995.
381. O., letter to N. Bohr, March 30, 1946, copy in NBA.
382. N. Bohr, letter to O., April 17, 1946, copy in NBA.
383. R. Jungk, *Brighter than a Thousand Suns*, p. 241, Harcourt Brace, New York 1986.
384. Ref. 370, p. 154.
385. Ref. 372, p. 30.
386. Ref. 323, p. 260.
388. Ref. 379, p. 559.
389. Ref. 323, p. 258, 260.
390. Reprinted in O., *The Open Mind*, p. 3, Simon and Schuster, New York 1955.

391. Ref. 379, p. 577.
392. UNAEC, official record, June 14, 1946.
393. Ref. 372, p. 69.
394. For more on the tests, see ref. 379, p. 580.
395. O., letter to President Truman, May 3, 1946, O. papers, box 73, LC.
396. Ref. 11, p. 52.
397. Quoted in G. Alperovitz, *The Decision to Use the Atomic Bomb*, p. 429, Harper Collins, New York 1995.
398. McG. Bundy, *Danger and Survival*, p. 166, Random House, New York 1988.
399. Ref. 115, p. 38.
400. Ref. 398, p. 173.
401. O., letter to N. Bohr, November 17, 1948, copy in NBA.
402. Ref. 372, p. 186.
403. O., ref. 390, p. 21.
404. O., in *Uncommon Sense*, p. 1, Birkhäuser, Boston 1984.
405. O., *Foreign Affairs*, January 1948. (Original title: International Control of Atomic Energy.)
406. Ref. 390, p. 17.
407. R. Lapp, *The New Priesthood*, p. 62, Harper and Row, New York 1965.
408. Harry S. Truman papers, Harry S. Truman Library and Museum, Independence, Mo., box 1533.
409. H. S. Truman, *Memoirs*, Vol. 1, p. 418, Doubleday, New York 1955.
410. H. Chevalier, *Oppenheimer, the Story of a Friendship*, pp. ix, xii, George Brasiller, New York 1965.
411. D. Lilienthal, Journals, Vol. 3, p. 173, Harper and Row, New York 1966.
412. As was already noted in Chapter 17, Section (d), ref. 402.
413. R. Hewlett and F. Duncan, *Atomic Shield*, p. 81 ff. U.S. Dept. of Commerce 1972.
413a. Ref. 8, p. 191.
416. U.S. Congress, JCAE hearings, Part 6, June 9, 1949, p. 233.
417. U.S. Congress, JCAE hearings, Part 7, p. 30.
418. U.S. Congress, JCAE hearings, Part 6, June 9, 1949, pp. 278–309.
419. Lilienthal and Dean quoted in ref. 411, pp. 522, 391.
420. O. papers, box 70, LC.
421. The Ph.D. thesis by S. Newman, "The Oppenheimer Case," New York University 1977, has been helpful in the search for references to this section.
422. Quoted in R. Rhodes, *Dark Sun*, p. 310, Simon and Schuster, New York 1995.
423. J. Alsop and R. Lapp, *Saturday Evening Post*, June 31, 1954.
424. *Life Magazine*, December 29, 1947.
426. Ref. 115, p. 467.
427. *Ibid.*, pp. 615, 801, 910–11.
430. Ref. 324, pp. 231–32.
431. For a few more details see A. Pais, Phys. Today, *43*, 13, 1990.
432. Quoted in ref. 398, p. 177.
433. O., quoted in M. Rouzé, *Robert Oppenheimer*, p. 78, Eriksson, New York 1965.
434. Ref. 390, pp. 40–41, 47–48.
435. R. Gilpin, *American Scientists and Nuclear Weapons Policy*, p. 71, Princeton University Press, Princeton 1962.
436. Ref. 390, pp. 62, 122.

437. O., quoted in H. S. Truman, *Memoirs*, Vol. 2, p. 300, Doubleday, New York 1956.

438. O., letter to Admiral C. H. McMorris, April 14, 1948, O. papers, box 47, LC.

439. Ref. 324, p. 23.

440. Los Alamos report LA-575, 1971.

441. H. York, *The Advisors*, p. 24, Freeman and Cy., San Francisco 1976.

442. R. Rhodes, *The Making of the Atomic Bomb*, p. 568, Simon and Schuster, New York 1986. More biographical details on Fuchs are found in H. M. Montgomery Hyde, *The Atom Bomb Spies*, Ballantine, New York 1980.

444. Ref. 380, p. 298.

445. Forrestal papers, box 112, Princeton University Library.

446. *The Forrestal Diaries*, p. 378, W. Mills, ed., Viking, New York 1951.

447. *Ibid.*, p. 476.

448. *Ibid.*, p. 466.

449. Ref. 445, box 81, February 14, 1948.

450. P. Hammond, *Organizing for Defense*, p. 387, Princeton University Press, Princeton 1961.

451. Ref. 133, p. 288.

452. J. Shapley and C. Blair, *The Hydrogen Bomb*, pp. 171, 177, Greenwood, New York 1971.

453. Ref. 442, p. 769.

454. Ref. 452, p. 178.

455. R. Gilpin, *American Scientists and Nuclear Weapons Policy*, p. 116, Princeton University Press, Princeton 1962.

456. T. Coffin, *Passion of the Hawks*, pp. 63–64, McMillan, New York 1964.

457. D. McCullough, *Truman*, p. 749, Simon and Schuster, New York 1992.

459. O., letter to J. Conant, October 21, 1949. Reprinted in full in ref. 115, pp. 242–43.

460. Report of the Scientific Panel to the Interim Committee by H. Smyth, AEC, ca. June 1954, p. 109.

461. O. papers, box 175, LC.

462. Ref. 452, p. 101.

463. W. Schilling, Political Sci. Quarterly *76*, 32, 1961.

464. Ref. 115, p. 785.

465. Ref. 8, pp. 188–89.

466. O., Bull. At. Scientists *4*, 66, 1948.

467. Ref. 8, p. 185.

469. The report is reproduced in full—apart from small deletions demanded by security—in ref. 441, pp. 150–59.

471. Ref. 411, Vol. 2, pp. 587, 613.

472. Ref. 207, p. 219.

473. Ref. 115, p. 87.

474. *New York Times*, February 1, 1950, p. 1.

474a. Ref. 8, p. 204.

476. R. Hewlett and J. Holl, *Atoms for Peace and War, 1953–1961*, p. 31, University of California Press, Berkeley 1989.

477. P. Stern, *The Oppenheimer Case*, p. 150, Harper and Row, New York 1969.

478. Ref. 411, Vol. 2, pp. 634–35.

479. Ref. 422, p. 411.
480. Ref. 422, p. 412.   •
481. R. Williams, *Klaus Fuchs*, p. 116, Harvard University Press, Cambridge 1987.
482. JCAE, *Soviet Atomic Espionage*, pp. 5–6, Government Printing Office, April 1951.
483. For many more details see refs. 422 and 443.
484. Ref. 481, p. 183.
485. R. Peierls, *Bird of Passage*, p. 163, Princeton University Press, Princeton 1985.
486. Ref. 481, p. 184.
487. R. Lamphere and T. Shachtman, *The FBI-KGB War*, Random House, New York 1986.
488. Ref. 133, p. 324.
489. Quoted in ref. 133, p. 189.
490. S. Ulam, *Adventures of a Mathematician*, p. 463, University of California Press, Berkeley 1991.
491. H. Bethe, Los Alamos Science, p. 49, Autumn 1982.
492. J. C. Mark, Los Alamos Report LA 5647.
493. Ref. 422, p. 466.
494. More details of the structure of the Super are found in ref. 422, Chapter 23, and ref. 442, Epilogue.
495. Quoted in ref. 442, p. 773.
498. Ref. 413, p. 537.
499. E. Teller, Science *121*, 267, 1955.
500. Ref. 441, p. 77.
503. For more on the Russian hydrogen bomb projects, see H. York *The Advisors*, Freeman, San Francisco 1976.
504. O., letter to R. Tolman, September 20, 1944. Reprinted in ref. 115, p. 954.
505. O., ref. 115, p. 20.
506. Ref. 115, p. 720.
507. *Ibid.*, p. 251.
508. *Ibid.*, p. 250.
509. *Ibid.*, p. 229.
510. Ref. 441, pp. 441, ff.
511. Ref. 413, p. 518.
512. Memorandum, April 12, 1952, O. papers, box 186, LC.
513. O., Bull. At. Scientists 7, 43, 1951.
514. J. Gavin, *War and Peace in the Space Age*, p. 115, Harper, New York 1958.
515. O., "Project Vista draft report," O. papers, box 218, LC.
516. J. McCormack, letter to O., O. papers, box 47, LC.
517. L. Garrison, on January 19, 1954, O. papers, box 202, LC.
518. Ref. 441, p. 139.
519. "Notes of Conference," January 19, 1954, O. papers, box 202, LC.
520. O. papers, box 187, LC.
521. Griggs testimony, ref. 115, p. 764.
522. S. Huntington, *The Common Defense*, p. 334, Columbia University Press, New York 1961.
523. See e.g. the Alsop columns in *New York Herald Tribune*, June 18, 1952. See also *Saturday Evening Post*, October 25, 1952.
524. Ref. 115, p. 751.
525. O. papers, box 4, LC.

526. Reprinted in ref. 133, p. 333.

526a. O., letter of F. Oppenheimer, July 12, 1952. ●

527. See e.g., T. Finletter, *Power and Policy*, Harcourt Brace, New York 1954.

528. *New York Times*, April 20, 1954.

529. Nixon quoted in T. Finletter, *Power and Policy*, p. 146, Harcourt Brace, New York 1954.

530. Nathan Twining, quoted in *New York Times*, January 27, 1954.

531. *Fortune Magazine*, January and November 1953.

532. Acheson and Stevenson quoted by C. Murphy, *Fortune Magazine*, June 1954.

533. D. Eisenhower, letter to J. F. Dulles, April 15, 1952, Dulles Papers, Box 2, Princeton University Library.

534. O., letter to J. Volpe, December 19, 1954, O. papers, box 77, LC.

535. S. Huntington, *The Common Defense*, p. 336, Columbia University Press, New York 1961.

536. O. papers, box 4, LC.

537. C. D. Jackson, memorandum to H. Luce, October 12, 1954, Jackson papers, box 66, Eisenhower Library.

538. O., Bull. At. Scientists *9*, 202, 1953.

539. O., interviewed by Gertrude Samuels, *New York Times Magazine*, June 21, 1953.

540. O.'s speech was later reproduced in O., *Uncommon Sense*, p. 17, Birkhäuser, Boston 1984.

541. L. Berkner, Bull. At. Scientists *9*, 154, June 1953.

542. O., *Foreign Affairs*, July 1953.

543. J. Dupré and S. Lakoff, *Science and the Nation*, p. 123, Prentice Hall, Englewood Cliffs, N.J. 1962.

544. O. papers, box 180, LC.

545. R. Lapps, Bull. At. Scientists *10*, 314, 1954.

546. Truman, in *New York Post*, April 13, 1954.

547. *New York Times*, April 28, 1953.

548. *Fortune Magazine*, Vol. 47, May 1953.

549. D. Lilienthal, ref. 411, p. 370.

550. D. Parsons, letter to O., September 25, 1953, O. papers, box 56, LC.

551. Ref. 476, p. 53.

552. Ref. 207, p. 275.

553. Ref. 115, p. 502.

554. Quoted in *New York Times*, April 14, 1954.

555. C. Murphy, *Fortune Magazine*, *48*, pp. 97, 202, August 1953.

556. P. Stern, *The Oppenheimer Case*, p. 113, Harper and Row, New York 1969.

557. Ref. 556, p. 178.

558. See ref. 115, p. 837 for this and subsequent quotations from the Borden letter.

559. Ref. 556, p. 2.

560. Ref. 115, p. 442.

561. J. Kunetka, *Oppenheimer*, p. 197, Prentice Hall, Englewood Cliffs, N.J. 1983.

562. The letter is reproduced in full in ref. 115, p. 3.

563. O. quoted in *New York Journal American*, April 29, 1954.

564. *Life Magazine*, December 13, 1963.

565. Ref. 476, p. 79.

566. Ref. 115, p. 3.

567. Ref. 476, p. 80.

568. Ref. 207, Chapter 14.
569. Ref. 476, p. 78.
570. Quoted in ref. 561, p. 207. *See also* J. M. Brown, *Through These Men*, p. 230, Harper, New York 1956.
571. *New York Times*, January 8, 1954.
572. On this subject, including the contents of the FBI summary report, I rely exclusively on Dr. Newman's account, ref. 421.
573. Ref. 207, p. 267.
574. C. P. Anderson, *Outsider in the Senate*, p. 186, World, New York 1970.
575. Jackson, memorandum to Luce, October 12, 1954, Eisenhower Library, Abilene, Kansas.
576. Ref. 207, p. 365.
577. Edwin, interview with Eisenhower, July 20, 1967, Eisenhower Library.
578. Jackson, memorandum to Luce, October 12, 1954, Eisenhower Library.
579. *Washington Post*, April 14, 1954.
580. The letter is found in full in ref. 115, p. 22.
581. Ref. 8, p. 224.
582. Ref. 476, p. 81.
583. Ref. 8, p. 227.
584. *Ibid.*, p. 230.
585. *Ibid.*, p. 228.
586. For these and more questions regarding the Q-clearances, see ref. 477, p. 245–58.
587. Ref. 115, p. 527.
588. *New York Times*, April 14, 1952.
589. This letter is quoted in full in ref. 207, p. 281.
590. Ref. 115, p. 7.
591. *Ibid.*, p. 20.
592. Robert Coughlan in *Life Magazine*, December 13, 1963.
593. Ref. 477, p. 197.
594. Ref. 476, p. 48.
595. Brown, ref. 570, p. 242.
596. *New York Times*, April 7, 1954.
597. Ref. 574, pp. 185, 186.
598. Unfortunately I lost the text of Einstein's statement.
599. A. Einstein, Bull. At. Scientists *10 no. 5*, 190, 1954.
600. Quoted in O. Nathan and H. Norden, *Einstein on Peace*, p. 607, Simon and Schuster, New York 1960.
601. O., in *Einstein, a Centenary Volume*, p. 44, A. P. French, ed., Harvard University Press, Cambridge 1979.
602. Ref. 411, p. 467, entry on January 31, 1954.
603. Ref. 477, p. 264, footnote.

SUPPLEMENTAL MATERIAL

CHAPTER 24

1. Bart Bernstein, "The Oppenheimer Loyalty-Security Case Reconsidered," *Stanford Law Review* 42 (1990) 1386–88.
2. W. A. Branigan to A. H. Belmont, 31 March 1954, O. FBI Sect. 31, 1279.
3. B. F. LaPlante to file, 3 December 1953. O. FBI .

4. V. F. Weisskopf to JRO, O. papers, 5 April 1954, box 202, LC.
5. AEC "Security Clearance Procedures," *Federal Register*, 19 September 1950, 6244.
6. G. Herken, *Brotherhood of the Bomb* (New York: Henry Holt and Co., 2002).
7. J. Zacharias to JRO, O. papers, 6 April 1954, box 202, LC.
8. W. A. Branigan to A. H. Belmont, 9 April 1954, O. FBI Sect. 25, 1057. *See also* SAC Newark to Director, FBI, 16 April 1954, O. FBI Sect. 25, 1108.
9. Harold Green, "The Oppenheimer Case: A Study in the Abuse of Law," *Bulletin of the Atomic Scientists* (September 1977), 14–15. *See also* Bernstein, 1990, 1465.
10. AEC "Security Clearance Procedures," *Federal Register*, 19 September 1950, 6243.
11. A. H. Belmont to L. V. Boardman, 24 May 1954, O. FBI Sect. 36, 1540.
12. W. A. Branigan to A. H. Belmont, 31 March 1954, O. FBI Sect. 31, 1279.
13. P. Goodchild, *J. Robert Oppenheimer: Shatterer of Worlds* (New York: Fromm, 1985), p. 231.
14. "Reminiscences of I. I. Rabi," 11 January 1983, CUOHO, p. 409.
15. Administrative Procedure Act, Statutes at Large 60, sect. 10, 766–67, 1947.
16. P. Stern, *The Oppenheimer Case* (New York: Harper & Row, 1969), pp. 276–77.
17. *Ibid.*, 313.
18. *IMJRO* (Cambridge: The MIT Press, 1971), p. 154.
19. Herken, 2002.
20. AP notes, "Interviews" folder, "Talks with Verna Hobson," 12–14 October 1979.
21. *Ibid.*
22. *IMJRO*, p. 137.
23. Stern, 1969, p. 283.
24. Rabi, CUOHO, p. 809.
25. *IMJRO*, pp. 280–81.
26. *Ibid.*, pp. 271–72.
27. AP notes, "Interviews" folder, "Talk with Lloyd K. Garrison," 25 June 1979.
28. *Ibid.*, McGeorge Bundy told Pais, "Garrison will go to heaven but not for his brains." AP notes, "Interviews" folder, "Talk with McGeorge Bundy," 13 April 1982.
29. A. H. Belmont to L. V. Bordmann, 17 April 1954, O. FBI Sect. 26, 1139.
30. *IMJRO*, p. 385.
31. Rabi, CUOHO, p. 801.
32. *Ibid.*, p. 245.
33. *IMJRO*, pp. 649–50.
34. *Ibid.*, p. 746.
35. G. Herken, "A Martian's Chronicles," *Science* (2001) 294, 1657.
36. AP notes, "Interviews" folder, "Discussions with Hans Bethe," 24 October 1981.
37. When Lord Charwell visited Los Alamos, Oppenheimer showed him around and hosted a party. Through a secretarial error, Rudolf Peierls never received his invitation. Oppenheimer was profusely apologetic, and told Peierls, "There is one consolation. It would have been much worse if it had happened to Teller." AP notes, "Interviews" folder, "Peierls," 3 December 1981.
38. E. Teller, *Memoirs* (Cambridge, Mass.: Perseus, 2001), p. 163.
39. *Ibid.*, p. 374.

40. "J. R. Oppenheimer," O. FBI, 15 March 1954.
41. AP notes, "Interviews" folder, "With C. N. Yang," 3 August 1979.
42. Stern, 1969, p. 357.
43. "Findings and Recommendations of the Personnel Security Board in the case of Dr. J. Robert Oppenheimer."
44. The order of these two paragraphs is reversed from how they stand in Smyth's opinion; this follows Pais's ordering as indicated in the margins of his copy of Smyth's opinion. When Pais interviewed Smyth in 1979, the latter said that it angered him to hear people say he had based his decision on the fact that JRO was a friend and colleague. "Bram, I didn't like him," Smyth emphasized, for he found JRO "vain and arrogant." Smyth told Pais that he did not know how to interpret JRO's performance at the hearings, except that JRO's "vanity may have received such an enormous blow that he turned defeatist" (AP notes, "Smyth" folder).
45. Bernstein, 1990, p. 1388.
46. W. A. Branigan to A. H. Belmont, 19 April 1954, O. FBI Sect. 31, 1296.
47. C. A. Rolander to G. W. Bates, 14 May 1954, O. FBI Sect. 37, 1581.
48. *New York Times*, 13 June 1954.
49. A. Pais to F. J. Dyson, 22 June 1954.
50. A. H. Belmont to R. R. Roach, 9 July 1954, O. FBI Sect. 46, 1866.
51. *Ibid.*
52. L. V. Boardman to A. H. Belmont, 24 May 1954, O. FBI Sect. 36, 1540.
53. F. J. Dyson, *Disturbing the Universe* (New York: Harper and Row, 1979), p. 77.
54. Stern, 1969, p. 435.
55. JRO, *Uncommon Sense* (Cambridge, Mass.: Birkhäuser Boston, 1984), p. 165.
56. AP notes, "Interviews" folder, "Talks with Verna Hobson," 12–14 October 1979.
57. "KO to Betty, Ted and Guy," 5 July 1954, O. papers, Ra-Re file, box 59, LC.
58. JRO to J. Edgar Hoover, 17 July 1954, O. FBI Sect. 46, 1876.
59. SAC Newark to Director, FBI, 14 July 1954, O. FBI Sect. 46, 1887.

CHAPTER 25
1. *Minneapolis Tribune*, 16 June 1957. Cited in Stern, 1969, p. 459.
2. AP interview with Kay Russell, 10 January 1980.
3. O. papers, box 202, LC.
4. Stern, 1969, p. 391.
5. *Time*, 28 June 1954.
6. A. Pais to JRO, Telegram 2 June 1954, O. papers, box 202, LC.
7. Stern, 1969, pp. 397–98.
8. "Drama Packs Amazing Oppenheimer Transcript," Alfred Friendly, Section II, p. 1.
9. Stern, 1969, p. 435.
10. Rabi, CUOHO, p. 811.
11. Chevalier to JRO, 7 July 1954, O. papers, box 26, LC.
12. Chevalier to JRO, 27 July 1954, O. papers, box 26, LC.
13. JRO to H. Chevalier, 3 September 1954, O. papers, box 26, LC.
14. Chevalier to JRO, 13 December 1954, O. papers, box 26, LC.
15. Robert W. Merry, *Taking on the World: Joseph and Stewart Alsop* (New York: Viking, 1996), p. 269.
16. *Ibid.*, pp. 260–61.

17. Rabi, CUOHO, pp. 712, 762.

18. Charles Wyzanski to JRO, 17 January 1954, O. papers, box 202, LC.

19. AP notes, "Interviews" folder, "Talks with Verna Hobson," 12–14 October 1979.

20. *Seattle Times*, 17 September 1956, "Noted Physicists, Including Oppenheimer, Meet Here."

21. William Gaddis to JRO, O. papers, box 158, LC.

22. E. Morot-Sir to JRO, 30 September 1957, O. papers, box 227, LC.

23. *New York Times*, 5 November 1957. "French Decorate Dr. Oppenheimer," O. papers, box 210, LC.

24. *Herald Tribune*, 19 November 1957, O. papers, box 210, LC.

25. R. R. Roach to A. H. Belmont, 13 December 1957. O. FBI.

26. *Levittown Times*, 7 March 1958, "School Name Probe Urged."

27. *Levittown Times*, 13 March 1959, p. 1. "Oppenheimer School Name Changed to Woodrow Wilson by Twp. Board," by Gordon Parker.

28. See *Time* review, 2 November 1959.

29. H. Chevalier, *The Man Who Would Be God* (New York: G. P. Putnam's Sons, 1959), p. 234.

30. Heinar Kipphardt, *In the Matter of J. Robert Oppenheimer*, trans. R. Speirs (New York: Hill and Wang, 1969), p. 127.

31. JRO to H. Kipphardt, 12 October 1964, O. papers, box 42, LC.

32. AP notes, "Interviews" folder, "Talks with Verna Hobson," 12–14 October 1979.

33. *Washington Post*, 13 November 1964, p. A18; not intended for publication, JRO to V. Weisskopf, 30 November 1964, O. papers, box 77, LC.

34. *New York Times*, 27 December 1964, p. 52.

35. *Variety*, 13 January 1965, p. 76.

36. Robert H. Montgomery, Jr. to Robert Whitehead, 28 November 1966, O. papers, box 207, LC.

37. Alan Mandell, one of the producers of a later production at the Vivian Beaumont Theatre in New York City, recalled: "Oppenheimer's wife Kitty attended a performance and I later took her backstage where she met and was quite taken with Joe Wiseman [who played JRO]. She gave him one of Oppenheimer's pipes which Joe still has. She kept calling him Robert. Her behavior during the performance was somewhat odd in that she kept banging her purse against her lap making a very audible sound. The actors were aware that something was going on and so I went back and explained that Kitty Oppenheimer was in the house and would come back stage." (Personal communication, thanks to Herbert Blau.) Pais photocopied an advertisement ("Last 3 Weeks!") for that performance, taken from the *New York Times* of 30 March 1969, juxtaposing an ad for the ("complete & uncut") porn film "I am Curious (Yellow)," also playing at the same time. An example of Pais's quirky imagination at work.

38. R. Polenberg, ed.: *In the Matter of J. Robert Oppenheimer: The Security Clearance Hearing* (Ithaca: Cornell University Press, 2002), p. xxviii.

39. Cited by Gerald Holton, *New York Times Book Review*, 4 January 1970, p. 3.

40. *Ibid.*, p. 16.

41. Dyson, 1979, ch. 7.

42. Dennis Schmidt, "Tragedy and Metaphor," in *American Continental Philosophy: A Reader* (Bloomington: Indiana University Press, 2000), p. 77.

43. Quoted in *ibid.*
44. John Leonard, review of JRO. *Letters and Recollections*, ed. Alice Kimball Smith and Charles Weiner, *New York Times*, 12 May 1980, p. C16.
45. Stern, 1969, p. 360.
46. *New York Times*, 3 December 1963; Cited in Stern, 1969, p. 465.

CHAPTER 26

1. *Trenton Evening Times*, 6 July 1954, AP dispatch.
2. G. Holton, *Advancement of Science* (Cambridge, Mass.: Cambridge University Press, 1986), p. 155.
3. AP notes, "Interviews" folder, "Talks with Verna Hobson," 12–14 October 1979.
4. AP notes, "Interviews" folder, "Talk with Lloyd K. Garrison," 25 June 1979.
5. *Ibid.*
6. Dyson, 1979, p. 76.
7. A. Pais, *Physics Today* (October 1967) 43–44.
8. AP notes, "Interviews" folder, "Discussions with Hans Bethe," 24 October 1981.
9. Rabi, CUOHO, p. 822.
10. AP notes, "Interviews" folder, "Talks with Verna Hobson," 12–14 October 1979.
11. *Ibid.*
12. *Ibid.*
13. *Ibid.*
14. AP notes, "Interviews" folder, "Harold Cherniss," 5 September 1979.
15. AP notes, "Interviews" folder, "Frank Oppenheimer," 12 January 1980.
16. AP notes, "Interviews" folder, "Francis Fergusson," 27 November 1981.
17. JRO to S. D. Leidesdorf, 2 November 1960, O. papers, box 45, LC.
18. AP notes, "Interviews" folder, "Talks with Verna Hobson," 12–14 October 1979.
19. *Ibid.*
20. *Ibid.*
21. AP notes, "Interviews" folder, "Talk with McGeorge Bundy," 13 April 1982.
22. AP notes, "Interviews" folder, "Talks with Verna Hobson," 12–14 October 1979.
23. AP notes, "Interviews" folder, "Francis Fergusson," 27 November 1981.
24. AP notes, "Interviews" folder, "Talks with Verna Hobson," 12–14 October 1979.
25. Quoted in E. Regis, *Who Got Einstein's Office?* (New York: Addison-Wesley, 1987), p. 152.
26. Samuel D. Leidesdorf to JRO, 14 February 1962, O. papers, box 45, LC.
27. Minutes, IAS Faculty Meeting, 7 February 1962.
28. Yang, personal communication.
29. A. Pais to JRO, May 15, 1963.
30. S. S. Schweber, *In the Shadow of the Bomb: Bethe, Oppenheimer, and the Moral Responsibility of the Scientist.* (Princeton: Princeton University Press, 2000), p. 40.
31. George F. Kennan, *Memoirs 1950–1963*, Vol. II (Boston: Little, Brown, 1972), p. 19.
32. Robert Adair, personal communication.
33. AP notes, "Interviews" folder, "Rabi," 14 May 1982.

34. Dyson, 1979, p. 73.
35. AP notes, "Interviews" folder, "Discussion with Robert Serber," 21 May 1979.
36. S. Treiman to A. Pais, 19 August 1999, AP "End" folder.
37. AP notes, "Interviews" folder, "Discussion with Robert Serber," 21 May 1979.
38. F. J. Dyson, *Physical Review* 75 (1949) 486, 1736.
39. The word degeneracy had been used in the 1920s about atomic spectra to refer to different states that had the same essential energy but were yet different.
40. Rochester Conference Proceedings, 1955.
41. JRO to C. N. Yang, 11 June 1956, O. papers, box 79, LC.
42. W. Heisenberg, *Physics and Beyond* (London: G. Allen & Unwin, 1971), p. 233.
43. JRO to D. S. Fahrney, 28 May 1957, O. papers, box 79, LC.
44. As Pais wrote in his diary in April 1966, not long after the discovery of CP violation, "The present situation is the opposite of atomic physics pre-1925. Then: with known particles find the rules of unknown laws. Now: with unknown particles find the rules within a totally conventional dynamics." A. Pais, diary 1964–1983, p. 28.
45. G. Harbottle, "Activation Analysis in Archaeology," *Radiochemistry* 3 (1976) 33.
46. Pais, *Physics Today* (October 1967) 47. The final quotations are from *Uncommon Sense*, p. 138.
47. If one were in the least intimidated by JRO's reputation or enthralled by his friendship, it was difficult not to feel touched by grandeur in his evocative words and images, even to think them oracular. Wyzanski wrote JRO that he wrote "as profoundly as Lincoln did, and for the same reasons . . . a noble, sensitive man, charged with an awful responsibility, misunderstood and maligned, has been forced by the circumstances to wrestle with ultimate problems." O. papers, box 79, LC.
48. AP notes, handwritten note, miscellaneous notes file.
49. Ruth Tolman to JRO, 3 April 1954, O. papers, box 72, LC.
50. O., *Uncommon Sense*, p. 23.
51. W. A. Branigan to A. H. Belmont, 5 January 1955, O. FBI Sect. 54.
52. O., *Uncommon Sense*, p. 189.
53. *Ibid.*, p. 154.
54. *Ibid.*, p. 77.
55. *Ibid.*, p. 38.
56. *Ibid.*, pp. 67–68.
57. O., "Analogy in Science," *The American Psychologist* 11 (March 1956).
58. L. Yuan to JRO, 25 September 1964.
59. O., *Uncommon Sense*, p. 86.
60. From "On Singleness of Mind," in *The Flashing Stream*, by Charles Morgan (London: Macmillan, 1938), pp. 7, 28.
61. A. Pais to JRO, May 18 (no year), O. papers, box 55, LC.
62. JRO to B. Becker, 29 August 1957, O. papers, box 17, LC.
63. Lilienthal, *Journals* 3 (March 1955) 615.
64. F. J. Dyson, T. D. Lee, A. Pais, and C. N. Yang to AEC Chairman Glenn T. Seaborg, 1 March 1962.
65. D. Acheson to JRO, 29 April 1963, O. papers, box 14, LC.
66. Robert Coughlan, *Life Magazine*, 13 December 1963.

67. E. Teller to JRO, undated note, O. papers, box 71, LC.
68. Kennan, *Memoirs*, V. 2, p. 21.
69. F. Dyson, "Dyson Weekly," 12 December 1963.
70. *Rev. Mod. Phys.* 36:1 (April 1964).
71. F. Dyson to Colleagues, 7 May 1963.
72. M. Born to JRO, 12 November 1953, Born folder, O. papers, box 22, LC.
73. F. Dyson, "Dyson Weekly," 25 April 1964.
74. F. Dyson, "Dyson Weekly," 30 June 1965.
75. AP notes, "Interviews" folder, "Harold Cherniss," 5 September 1979.
76. JRO to S. D. Leidesdorf, 15 April 1965, O. papers, box 45, LC.
77. "Oppenheimer to Retire as Head of Institute for Advanced Study," *New York Times*, Sunday, 25 April 1965, p. 1.
78. "Oppenheimer to Retire as Head of Institute for Advanced Study," *New York Times*, no author, 25 April 1965, p. 1.
79. F. Dyson, "Dyson Weekly," 30 April 1965.
80. F. Dyson, "Dyson Weekly," 28 October 1965.
81. V. Von Hagen to A. Pais, 29 August 1979; JRO to C. Engels, 15 December 1965, O. papers, box 227, LC.

CHAPTER 27

1. John Leonard, *New York Times*, 12 May 1980, p. C16.
2. B. Alonzo to JRO, 6 January 1965, O. papers, box 14, LC.
3. Nicholas P. Samios, personal communication.
4. F. Dyson, "Dyson Weekly," 17 February 1966.
5. F. Dyson, "Dyson Weekly," 30 March 1966.
6. H. Burnett to JRO, 18 April 1966, O. papers, box 18, LC.
7. Princeton University, Citation by the University Orator, 14 June 1966, O. papers, box 228, LC.
8. JRO, "Thirty Years of Mesons," *Physics Today* (November 1966) 58.
9. Telegram, JRO to N. Nabokov, 11 July 1966, O. papers, box 52, LC.
10. JRO to N. Nabokov, 20 September 1966, O. papers, box 52, LC.
11. R. Serber with R. Crease, *Peace and War* (New York: Columbia University Press, 1998), p. 202.
12. JRO to N. Nabokov, 28 October 1966, O. papers, box 52, LC.
13. H. Burnett to JRO, 28 October 1966, O. papers, folder Bu, LC.
14. J. D. B. O'Toole to JRO, 21 November 1966, O. papers, box 17, LC.
15. JRO to N. Nabokov, 16 December 1966, O. papers, box 52, LC.
16. C. N. Yang, *Selected Papers 1945–1980, with Commentary* (San Francisco: W. H. Freeman, 1983), p. 66.
17. AP notes, "Interviews" folder, "Talks with Verna Hobson," 12–14 October 1979.
18. *Ibid.*
19. JRO to B. Kursunoglu, 12 January 1967, O. papers, LC.
20. AP notes, "End" folder, S. Treiman to A. Pais, 19 August 1999.
21. "Neutral Vector Mesons and the Hadronic Electromagnetic Current," by Norman M. Kroll, T. D. Lee, and Bruno Zumino," *Physical Review* 157 (1967) 1376–1339.
22. AP notes, "Interviews" folder, "Talk with T. D. Lee," 16 August 1979; personal communication, T. D. Lee.
23. F. Dyson, "Dyson Weekly," 16 February 1967.

24. F. Dyson, "Dyson Weekly," 24 February 1967.

25. Hans A. Bethe, Henry DeWolf Smyth, and George Kennan, "Three Tributes to J. Robert Oppenheimer," a pamphlet issued by the Institute for Advanced Study.

26. When Kitty died, on a round-the-world sailing trip with Robert Serber, the cottage passed to Toni. When Toni died—she committed suicide in the cottage—she willed the property to the "people of St. John," probably in part to keep it out of the hands of the Gibneys, who might otherwise have had some claim on it. The cottage was impractical to keep up, and has been torn down and replaced by a small building used as a community center.

27. V. Von Hagen to A. Pais, 29 August 1979; JRO to C. Engels, 15 December 1965, O. papers, box 227, LC.

28. Pais noted that, in years to come, JRO's life and career will fascinate not only physicists but historians, psychologists, playwrights, and poets. Still, he added, "it would take the singular combination of talents of this extraordinary man himself to characterize his life in brief," and concluded his talk by wondering whether JRO himself had come as close as humanly possible in the following lines: "The wealth and variety of physics itself, the greater wealth of the natural sciences taken as a whole, the more familiar, yet still strange and far wider wealth of the life of the human spirit, enriched by complementarity, not at once compatible ways, irreducible one to the other, have a greater harmony. They are the elements of man's sorrow and his splendour, his frailty and his power, his death and his passing, and his undying deeds."

It was a perceptive choice: a passage that is classic JRO in the way it aims at the whole, notes that the divisions within this whole are incompatible, yet despite that promises more simplicity than is credible—cloaking the not credible by the articulateness and ambition with which it is spoken. Pais surely aware that JRO was darker than that.

29. Robert Serber, Victor F. Weisskopf, Abraham Pais, and Glenn T. Seaborg, *Oppenheimer*, Introduction by I. I. Rabi (New York: Scribner's, 1969).

30. Personal communication, F. Dyson, in Dyson's files. I am grateful to Freeman Dyson for allowing me to quote from this.

31. AP notes, "Interviews" folder, "undated, untitled note."

32. O., *Uncommon Sense*, p. 170.

33. The photocopy is of pages from Vannevar Bush, *Pieces of the Action* (New York: William Morrow, 1970); the poem is cited on p. 148.

34. *Oppenheimer* (New York: Scribner's, 1969), pp. 42–43.

PRINCIPAL SOURCES USED

D. Acheson, *Present at the Creation*. Norton, New York, 1969.

McGeorge Bundy, *Danger and Survival*. Random House, New York, 1988.

N. P. Davis, *Lawrence and Oppenheimer*. Da Capo, New York, 1986.

P. Goodchild, *Oppenheimer*. BBC Corp., 1983.

L. Groves, *Now It Can Be Told*. Harper, New York, 1962.

R. Hewlett and O. Anderson, *The New World, 1939–1946*. Pennsylvania State University Press, 1962.

R. Hewlett and F. Duncan, *Atomic Shield, 1947–1952*. University of California Press, 1990.

R. Hewlett and J. Holl, *Atoms for Peace and War, 1953–1961*. University of California Press, 1989.

D. Lilienthal, *Journals, Vol. II*. Harper and Row, New York, 1964.

S. Newman, "The Oppenheimer Case." Ph.D. Thesis, New York University, 1977.

J. R. Oppenheimer, papers in the Library of Congress.

J. R. Oppenheimer, *The Open Mind*. Simon and Schuster, New York, 1955.

J. R. Oppenheimer, *Science and the Common Understanding*. Oxford University Press, Oxford, 1954.

J. R. Oppenheimer, *Uncommon Sense*. Birkhauser, Boston, 1984.

J. R. Oppenheimer, *Atom and Void*. Princeton University Press, 1989.

A. Pais, *Subtle is the Lord*. Oxford University Press, 1982.

A. Pais, *Inward Bound*. Oxford University Press, 1986.

A. Pais, *Niels Bohr's Times*. Oxford University Press, 1991.

R. Rhodes, *The Making of the Atomic Bomb*. Simon and Schuster, New York, 1986.

R. Rhodes, *Dark Sun*. Simon and Schuster, New York, 1995.

A. K. Smith, *A Peril and a Hope*. University of Chicago Press, 1965.

A. K. Smith and C. Weiner, *Robert Oppenheimer: Letters and Recollections*. Harvard University Press, 1980.

P. Stern, *The Oppenheimer Case*. Harper and Row, New York, 1969.

E. Teller, *The Legacy of Hiroshima*. Doubleday, New York, 1962.

S. Weart, *Nuclear Fear*. Harvard University Press, 1988.

I. Wimmler, "Technically Sweet—Politically Sweet?" Ph.D. Thesis, Graz University, 1999.

INDEX

Note: The abbreviation JRO denotes J. Robert Oppenheimer. The term "Institute" refers to the Institute for Advanced Study.